GRACE
IN THE
NEW TESTAMENT

BY

JAMES MOFFATT

D.D.. D.LITT., LL.D.,

WASHBURN PROFESSOR OF CHURCH HISTORY IN UNION
THEOLOGICAL SEMINARY, NEW YORK

Ray Long & Richard R. Smith, Inc.

New York · · · · 1932

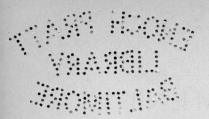
First Published . . . January, 1932

ERRATA

P. xxvi—17 lines from foot. "Valentine" should read *Valentinus.*

P. 10—10 lines from foot. "varity" should read *variety.*

P. 27—10 lines and 17 lines from foot. θελήμα should read θέλημα

P. 59—6 lines from foot. "pasada" should read *prasada.*

P. 93—11 lines from foot. "unreluctant" should read *reluctant.*

P. 182—14 lines from foot. "for later, from which" should read *latter; from law*

P. 242—footnote. "VI" should read *Vol.*

P. 270—8 lines from top. "past position of" should read *past, for*

P. 362—7 lines from top. ὑπεβάλετο should read συνεβάλετο

P. 394—12 lines from top. "and" should read *amid.*

Index—"condescencion" should read *condescension.*

TO

C. C. H.
F. B.
A. C. M.
H. S. C.

—'*unus quisque, sicut accepit gratiam, illam administrantes,
sicut boni dispensatores multiformis gratiae Dei.*'

" He who seeks to live the life which is life indeed is bidden first of all to know Him ' whom no man knoweth save the Son and he to whomsoever the Son reveals Him ' ; next after Him, he must understand the greatness of the Saviour and the newness of His grace, inasmuch as, according to the apostle, ' the law was given through Moses, grace and truth through Jesus Christ,' and gifts given through a faithful servant are not equal to those bestowed by a true Son."—Clement of Alexandria : *Quis dives salvetur*, viii. (second century).

" We who acknowledge and honour new prophecies and visions new, as alike promised by God . . . cannot but set them forth and celebrate them openly by reciting them, lest a weak or a despairing faith imagine that divine grace, in its glories of martyrdom and revelation, was to be found only among the men of old ; whereas God is ever performing what He promised."— *Passio SS. Felicitatis et Perpetuae*, i. (third century).

" You believe in grace, Porphyry. . . . You frankly use the very word in declaring your conviction that whilst a man is unable to reach perfect wisdom in this life, nevertheless after this life those who live here according to the mind of God may have all their defects supplied by His providence and grace. Oh, had you but recognized the grace of God in Jesus Christ our Lord, you might have seen the supreme proof of grace in this incarnation of His, whereby He took to Himself man's soul and body."—Augustine : *De Civitate Dei*, x. 29 (fifth century).

" Tua nos, Domine, quaesumus, gratia semper et praeveniat et sequatur, ac bonis operibus jugiter praestet esse intentos."—*The Georgian Sacramentary* (eighth century).

" In monte coram Petro et Jacobo et Joanne transfiguratur, insinuans nobis quod si tanquam Petrus (qui *agnoscens* interpretatur) nostram infirmitatem humiliter agnoscere, si vitiorum *supplantores* (quod Jacobus sonat) fieri, si *Dei gratia* (quae per Joannis nomen innuitur) fideliter nos submittere studuerimus, ad Jesu gloriam contemplandam illum coelestem montem, eodem rege nostro duce, feliciter conscendemus."—Anselm : *Meditationes*, i. 8 (eleventh century).

" Caeterum quid agat anima tua, scire cupio, utrumne tandem suam pertaesa propriam justitiam discat in justitia Christi respirare atque confidere. Fervet enim nostra aetate tentatio praesumptionis in multis, et iis praecipue, qui justi et boni esse omnibus viribus student, ignorantes justitiam Dei, quae in Christo est nobis effusissime et gratis donata, quaerunt in se ipsis tam diu operari bene,

vii

donec habeant fiduciam standi coram Deo, veluti virtutibus et meritis ornati, quod est impossibile fieri. Fuisti tu apud nos in hac opinione, imo errore ; fui et ego, sed et nunc quoque pugno contra istum errorem sed nondum expugnavi."—Luther to a fellow Augustinian (April 8th, 1516).

" Le neud qui devroit attacher nostre jugement et nostre volonté, qui devroit estreindre nostre ame et joindre à nostre createur, ce devroit estre un neud prenant ses replis et ses forces, non pas de noz considerations, de noz raisons et passions, mais d'une estreinte divine et supernaturelle, n'ayant qu' une forme, un visage et un lustre, qui est l'auctorité de Dieu et sa grace."—Montaigne : *Essais*, ii. 12 (sixteenth century).

" To say, we are saved for the worthiness of any thing which is ours, is to deny we are saved by grace. Grace bestoweth freely, and therefore justly requireth the glory of that which is bestowed. We deny the grace of our Lord Jesus Christ, we imbase, disannul, annihilate the benefit of his bitter passion, if we rest in those proud imaginations that life everlasting is deservedly ours, that we merit it, and that we are worthy of it."—Hooker : *Sermons*, ii. (sixteenth century).

" When the day that he was to be gone was come, he addressed himself to go over the River. Now the River at that time overflowed its banks in some places ; but Mr. Honest in his life-time had spoken to one Good-conscience to meet him there, the which he also did, and lent him his hand, so helped him over. The last words of Mr. Honest were, ' Grace reigns.' So he left the world."—Bunyan : *The Pilgrim's Progress*, The Second Part (seventeenth century).

" Man shall find grace ;
And shall Grace not find means, that finds her way,
The speediest of Thy winged messengers,
To visit all Thy creatures, and to all
Comes unprevented, unimplored, unsought ?
Happy for man so coming !"—
Milton : *Paradise Lost*, iii. 227 f. (seventeenth century).

" Les jansénistes font de la grâce une espéce de quatrième personne de la sainte Trinité. Saint Paul et saint Augustine, trop étudiés, ou étudiés uniquement, ont tous perdus, si on ose le dire. Au lieu de grâce, dites aide, secours, ou mieux influence divine, céleste rosée ; on s'entend alors. Ce mot est comme un talisman dont on peut briser le prestige et le maléfice, en le traduisant ; on en dissout le danger par l'analyse. Personnifier les mots est un mal funeste en théologie."—Joubert : *Pensées Titre*, iv. (eighteenth century).

" Men of elevated minds are not their own historians and panegyrists. So is it with faith and other Christian graces. Bystanders may see our minds; but our minds, if healthy, see but the objects which possess them. As God's grace elicits our faith, so His holiness stirs our fear, and His glory kindles our love. Others may say of us, ' here is faith,' and ' there is conscientiousness,' and ' there is love '; but we can only say, ' this is God's grace,' and ' that is His holiness,' and ' that is His glory.' "—Newman : *Lectures on Justification*, xiii. (nineteenth century).

" Let us think of Christ as the Son who reveals the Father, that we may know the Father's heart against which we have sinned, that we may see how sin in making us godless has made us orphans, and understand that the grace of God, which is at once the remission of past sin and the gift of eternal life, restores to our orphan spirits their Father and to the Father of spirits His lost children."—McLeod Campbell : *The Nature of the Atonement*, vii. (nineteenth century).

" Grace is grace precisely because, though wholly concerned with moral goodness, it does not at all depend on how moral we are . . . God's gracious relation to us can have no meaning for us without moral sincerity. But, as it is while we are yet sinners, and to deliver us from sin, to make our moral goodness its condition would be to defeat its purpose. The condition of faith in it is penitence, and not any form of self-approbation, however well-founded." —Oman : *Grace and Personality*,[3] pp. 194, 195 (twentieth century).

" Gott selbst gibt sich uns, nicht mehr bedingt, durch das Gesetz, sondern unbedingt, aus freer Gnade. Das ist die Liebe Gottes : der unbedingte Gemein-schaftswille Gottes. Das ist der neue Lebenstand ; das der Mensch sein Leben nicht mehr im Sollen hat, sondern im Sein, nämlich in dem gottgeschenkten Sein. Das Wort der Gnade ist kein Imperativ wie das des Gesetzes, sondern ein Indikativ. Nicht ; der Mensch soll sein, sondern du bist bei Gott, durch Gott. Das ist die grosse Umkehrung der Existenz—und sie ist es, durch die sich das Evangelium von aller Religion, Philosophie und Moral unterscheidet." —Brunner : *Gott und Mensch*, pp. 32, 33 (twentieth century).

PREFACE

THIS was drafted as a course of lectures at Oxford as far back as 1912. But lectures are lectures and a book is or ought to be a book. I have therefore recast the manuscript entirely. Besides, the original draft had to be revised in the light of work done upon the subject during the interval, for the interpretation of a fundamental conception like that of grace is affected directly and indirectly by nearly every movement of New Testament criticism, literary and historical. In the course of the past eighteen years there have been notably three such movements : investigations into the sources and motives of the synoptic gospels, fresh appreciations of the apostle Paul as an interpreter of Christianity, and researches into the organic connexion between primitive Christianity and the syncretism of the period. These three frequently run into one another. Thus the interests of what Germans call the 'Formgeschichte' school are not confined to the genesis of the synoptic gospels ; they touch the problem of Paul's theology as well. If some Hellenistic cult within the church of Antioch had the importance which is sometimes claimed for it by members of that school, then not simply are the gospels spontaneously generated by such a cult, with little more significance historically than as they mirror contemporary interests in the situation of the community, but the apostle's conception of Christianity is resolved into a brilliant product of the same tense transition, without very much basis either in the faith of the primitive church or in any traditions about the historical Jesus. Such lines of enquiry, which are still being pursued, have advanced our knowledge of the complex environment in which the Christian faith arose, and of the various factors, devotional, social,

political, and philosophical, which went to the formation of
it as a religion for the world. So far as the question of
grace is concerned, the first and the third have been specially
challenging and suggestive. But after a double and drastic
rehandling of my first draft, I am relieved to find that the
outline drawn in 1912 remains substantially the same. Whatever has had to be modified or altered, the main thesis has
been upon the whole corroborated, namely, that the mission
of the Lord Jesus was a mission of grace, that the apostle
Paul's message or what he called his ' gospel ' presupposes
this more seriously than some have been prepared to admit,
and that a fair appreciation of the affinities and indebtedness
of Christianity to its environment leaves the historical student
impressed with the creative energy of the new faith both
mentally and morally. I always believe it wise to test general
conceptions or reconstructions in the history of religion by
applying them to some specific aspect or element of the faith
under discussion. A religion is known at its centre rather
than on its circumference. Now, belief in grace, as we
encounter it in the pages of the New Testament, has a distinctive accent. I find myself in agreement with a growing
group of scholars who recognize in such a belief one clue
to the identity of early Christianity, a clue which is dim but
definite.

Some special work has been done upon the subject. The
new approach is illustrated by Dr. G. P. Wetter's *Charis*
(1913) ; the Scandinavian scholar brings out among other
things the dynamic associations of grace both within and
outside Christianity. In the third edition of Dr. A. Rade-
macher's *Gnade und Natur* (1925) or in Dr. Joseph Pohle's
manual, which is now accessible in an English edition, *Grace
Actual and Habitual* (revised edition, 1917), the dogmatic
scheme of the Roman Church may be found. The catholic
doctrine of the Greek Church is excellently stated by Professor
Gavin in *Greek Orthodox Thought* (1923, pp. 218 f.). As for

the historical variations, Dr. Jauncey's *Doctrine of Grace up to the end of the Pelagian Controversy historically and dogmatically considered* (1925), and the *De Gratia* (1929) of the Jesuit scholar Hermann Lange, cover the early and mediaeval period. The short monograph by Dr. N. P. Williams on *The Grace of God* (1930) is more comprehensive and constructive. On the positive content of the idea there is no better book in English or indeed, so far as I am aware, in any language, than Dr. John Oman's difficult and rewarding *Grace and Personality* (third edition, 1925).

This book is intended to be a companion to my *Love in the New Testament* (third edition, 1930). As far as possible, it has been written on the same lines. The different disposition of the material has involved some change of method, but I have again endeavoured to remember readers who may have more grace than Greek. Not that it is feasible to handle a subject like this without dipping into technical or linguistic details now and then. It is only by reading continuous passages from the literature of the New Testament and especially from the letters of the apostle Paul that the sweep of a new conception such as grace can be appreciated, and the reading must be exact. It is with Paul as with any great classic, to read him is more important than to read about him, unless reading about him sends us back to read with more intelligence what he has written. In order to understand what he meant by certain words such as righteousness or grace or Spirit, one does require information about his ' milieu ' in the world of Jewish and Hellenistic religion, for he repeatedly uses terms and ideas which have a history behind them. This information does not explain his vision of God but it goes to explain how he came to write of it. I make no apology for paragraphs that attempt to reach a more accurate understanding of grace and its cognate terms in Paul or in any other of the New Testament writers. It is a line along which patient continuance is rewarded before very long. True, one must never forget that Pascal's saying in the second Provincial, " le monde se paye de paroles, peu approfondissent les choses," was elicited by the seventeenth-century debates over grace itself. Perhaps no subject in Christian thought has led men more often to rest on words and definitions. The controversy over grace may indeed be said to have more life-blood in it than any other. Here men have vaguely felt that all was at stake. They have rightly, if not always intelligently, perceived that to ask, 'Is our religious hope and trust to be based on ourselves or upon God?' was too supreme a question to be answered merely in the schools. Nevertheless the disputes over its answer have been needlessly verbal. From Augustine, indeed from Tertullian onwards, men have been inclined to use the term 'grace' in senses which had changed insensibly, until confusion arose, largely because later generations were unconsciously modernizing the word, using New Testament language about its truth because this meant so much to them, and yet attaching meanings of their own to it. The truth which 'grace' conveys is certainly larger than the term. It is not a mere question of words and names. Nevertheless, it becomes imperative to ascertain the exact range of the word and indeed of the group of words to which it belongs in the vocabulary of the primitive Church. This is why some attention has been paid in the following pages to items of Hellenistic Greek, the mine from which the term was dug in the first two centuries. At the same time I recognize that the truth and power of the belief can come through an English rendering, and so the bulk of the evidence has been presented, I hope, in such a way that the essential argument may be followed by the Greekless.

Even a preliminary enquiry like the present throws some light upon later developments of the belief in the history and dogma of the Church, but the enquiry is limited to first-century experience and reflection. I have endeavoured to make it as objective as possible. Without raising such a question as, ' How far can statements of the New Testament be regarded as the norm of Christian thinking on grace ? ' I am concerned here to outline their meaning. The conclusion upon which the various lines of such an enquiry seem to converge is as follows : the religion which underlies the New Testament writings is a religion of grace, or it is nothing. This is by no means a novel view, but it has received confirmation and support recently in circles of historical criticism which are far from reactionary. Much depends, no doubt, upon the precise meaning attached to grace in such a connexion, and that is not so simple a question to answer or even to ask, as it sounds upon the surface. Still, upon the whole, one is not indisposed to claim, a critical examination of the truths conveyed by ' grace ' to those who first employed it will run up into no other conclusion than this, that here we are in touch with a characteristic of primitive Christian faith which is so vital and distinctive that apart from it the historian finds it difficult to discover any satisfactory explanation of how the gospel ever managed to rise or to hold its own.

Let me put it thus. In music there are grace-notes, ' les agréments,' as the French say, trills, slides, and variations, with which a melody may be graced. They brighten a musical theme, but they are not absolutely necessary to it. These cadenzas merely touch it up ; they may be left out, if the player so desires, for the fundamental theme of the composition is there, no matter what may happen to the grace-notes. In Christianity there are grace-notes but not grace-notes of this kind. No grace, no gospel ; that is what it comes to, when you study the classical documents of the primitive Church. The literature of the New Testament has many words about grace ; some of these notes make up chords which may sound more like discords than anything else to a modern ear, and some require to be transposed into other keys by a later generation. But the point is, that the grace-notes here belong to the central theme ; they are essential to the symphony, not ornamental.   If they are omitted at the whim of an interpreter, something may be left indeed, but it is not music which is worth calling Christian.

JAMES MOFFATT.

CONTENTS

CONTENTS   xix

PART B
JESUS AND GRACE

PART C
THE NEW TESTAMENT LANGUAGE OF GRACE

PART D
PAUL ON GRACE

CONCLUSION

INTRODUCTION

I

IN one of his dialogues Berkeley brings forward a candid free-thinking philosopher who is utterly puzzled by the Christian word 'grace.' Alciphron confesses that to him the term is meaningless ; he does not think that it calls up any real idea before the thinking mind, at least as religious people are in the habit of using it. " I can easily understand grace," he admits, in the popular sense of beauty or favour, but how unintelligible it is on the pages or upon the lips of theologians ! " At the request of a philosophical friend I did cast an eye on the writings he showed me of some divines, and talked with others on the subject, but after all I had read or heard could make nothing of it, having always found, whenever I laid aside the word ' grace ' and looked into my mind, a perfect vacuity or privation of ideas. And, as I am apt to think men's minds and faculties are made much alike, I suspect that other men, if they examined what they call grace with the same exactness and indifference, would agree with me that there was nothing in it but an empty name." By " indifference " Berkeley meant impartiality. That word has altered since the eighteenth century. But otherwise might not this frank confession have been written to-day ? Inside the Church as well as outside, some, after two centuries, would still agree with Berkeley's friend that when they read or hear the word ' grace ' in connexion with religion, it fails to suggest anything real to their minds. They might further be justified in claiming that this is not wholly their own fault, if indeed it is their fault at all. No doubt, what some people are pleased to call their mind may be incapable of under-

1

standing 'grace' or, for the matter of that, any deeper term of our human experience in the religious sphere. Even Berkeley's Alciphron is one of those persons who are inclined impatiently to brush aside not only the words but the very ideas of religion as irrelevant to the serious business of thought or action. Nevertheless, like Joubert later in the same century, he does appear to have recognized that a Christian term such as 'grace' required fresh definition, in view of the fact that it had recently become conventional or technical and therefore unreal, thanks to the treatment it had received in the course of religious controversy. Evidently Berkeley knew, as we know to-day, contemporaries who may be honestly perplexed by some religious phrases and who deserve serious attention when they plead that it is difficult or even impossible for them to understand how this particular term can mean anything definite to intelligent persons. In the past, religion may have found 'grace' valuable, but in the present it sounds vague. Once the word may have been significant ; nowadays what is it but an empty name ?

By the seventeenth century, the English word 'grace' had come to be a term for the Christian religion. There is an apt illustration of this in George Herbert's poem, " The Church Militant." He wrote,

> Religion stands on tip-toe in our land,
> Ready to pass to the American strand.

The Vice-Chancellor of Cambridge hesitated to allow the poem to be printed, on account of this unpatriotic sentiment, and only agreed after some pressure, remarking sardonically that he hoped the world would not take the poet " to be an inspired prophet." What Herbert meant was that the shortcomings of the English Church might induce God to transfer His favour to a settlement like the Virginia colony across the Atlantic. He played seriously with the possibility that whereas up till now Europe had drained America of its

gold, it might have to yield the gospel as a better treasure
to the West.

> When height of malice and prodigious lusts,
> Impudent sinning, witchcrafts, and distrusts—
> The marks of future bane—shall fill our cup
> Unto the brim and make our measure up . . .
> Then shall religion to America flee ;
> They have their times of gospel ev'n as we.
> My God, thou dost prepare for them a way,
> By carrying first their gold from them away ;
> For gold and grace did never yet agree,
> Religion always sides with poverty.
> We think we rob them, but we think amiss ;
> We are more poor and they more rich by this.
> Thou wilt revenge their quarrel ; making grace
> To pay our debts, and leave our ancient place
> To go to them.

The poet not only identifies grace with Christianity, but also
implies that God is free to enlarge one nation and straiten
another, as religious privilege is abused.   This is a character-
istically Pauline conception of grace, which combines freedom
and favour on the part of God.   The more general sense
of the term prevailed, however.   Although the more technical
meaning of the word in theological controversy of the eighteenth century is well-marked (so much so that, as we have
seen, it tended to discredit the use of ' grace ' altogether
in certain circles of culture), nevertheless the larger usage
survived, and the paradox is that whilst in some semi-Christian
circles ' grace ' has been almost tabooed, it has passed into
common speech at the present day as a favourite and telling
term.   This is not a mere trick of style.   It witnesses to a
sound instinct, in many cases.   Yet there is a danger that
this accepted use of the word may be misleading.   Just as
the Latin Church soon began in all good faith to read back
' gratia ' as a term of its new theology into the NT without
realizing that it was using the word in a different connotation,
so the English word may be taken to cover NT sayings for

which it is not adequate.   Our modern Alciphron may find
that the word does suggest something tangible to his mind,
and yet that something may not be precisely the value that
the early Christians who stamped the term intended it to
bear.   Hence the need of examining the word in the light
of the special truth or truths which it was originally designed
to convey to the religious consciousness.   The specific and
distinctive meaning may be lost sight of in the wider applications of a later day.

For example, when Mr. Kipling bids us strive and pray

> That in our time Thy grace may give
> The truth by which the nations live,

we need no commentary on his deep words.   We know in a vague
but definite way what grace means here.   We also know that it is not
precisely what the NT means by the word.   Or again, when a modern
philosopher [1] invites us to conceive of " Grace as a spiritual environment of the soul, consisting in social and personal influences to which
it responds by conscious acts, and making for good," we recognize an
acute estimate of the independent moral sphere covered by religion,
while at the same time we realize as historical critics that this definition
of the term is outwith the apostolic consciousness.   When Wordsworth
taught his age that instead of over-educating themselves they should
lay their lives open to truths that steal into the mind from God through
the visible universe, since

> A gracious Spirit o'er this earth presides,
> And o'er the heart of man—invisibly
> It comes—to works of unreproved delight
> And tendency benign,

he too was using 'gracious' in a sense foreign to the NT.   It is not
that such applications of the noun or of the adjective are illegitimate ;
the ideas are implicit in the many-sided synthesis of the Christian religion.
But in such extensions of the term the original sense may be forgotten
or flattened.   Only a pedant would claim that the usage even of writers
in the classical age of Christianity should determine for all time the

[1] Mr. C. C. J. Webb in *Problems in the Relations of God and Man*, p. 121.

applications of a word like ' grace.'   But the Christian religion stamped
' grace ' with a sense of its own at the very start, and the rich, looser
usage has not been enjoyed without introducing a certain confusion into
the ordinary mind.   Anyone who is familiar with the range of a term
like ' grace ' in modern literature must realize how deeply the word
has appealed to thoughtful people as they have sought to interpret religion
sympathetically and vividly ; it is remarkable how this term comes to
the lips of many who are anything but theologically minded, as a telling
and adequate term for the spirit of the relations which exist between
God and man.   Still, much as one appreciates this, it is fair to insist
that later extensions of its usage must not be taken to represent the
authentic core of that truth which in the dawn of Christianity man
often found they could not otherwise express than by calling it ' grace,'
namely, the love of God in power and beauty, shining against the dark
background of human demerit.

2

If religion is the consciousness of man's relation to God
within the world, ' grace ' implies that this relationship is
due to His initiative and eternal goodness, especially in view
of mortal sin and weakness.   (i) When Christianity is regarded
as a religion of grace, it may be said as a rule to imply a
humble and grateful recognition of God in worship and fellowship.   The fibre of this means a consciousness (a) that men
owe the boons and blessings of their lot to God as good and
generous ; (b) especially as He enters human life to be
forgiving ; (c) that this attitude of kindness, in which He
bestows His favours, is one of authority or majesty, since
it is as His creatures and subjects that men enjoy His free
goodwill ; (d) and that, so far from being aloof and austere,
this relationship of God to men is gracious in the sense of
being morally attractive.   For Christians, however, all this
turns upon the revelation of God through Jesus Christ His Son,
as the royal Father who is to be served as He is to be trusted
by men with all their heart.   The confidence and awe which
mark the Christian religion are elicited by dependence upon

I

this gracious God, who has dealt with sin as He imparted new powers and hopes of life to men. This is what is distinctive and central in the Christian message of grace. When sin or moral evil is omitted from the view of the world, the content of ' grace ' as presented in the gospel is missed, no matter how belief in a friendly Spirit or causal Reality within the universe may be stated in terms of grace. Also, although no religion thrives by dissevering the moral impulse from the love of beauty any more than from the love of truth, Christianity understands grace primarily in its religious and ethical connotation. Like the Greek word which it translates, ' grace ' means both attractiveness of form or character and also divine favour. This double meaning has been a drawback as well as an advantage on the whole ; it has been responsible for misconceptions in the popular mind. In fact, we may say that to these two misinterpretations, the disinclination to connect grace with sin (which is an inclination to interpret the divine Reality apart from the reality of moral evil), and the tendency to think of grace as beauty or charm, most of the reactions against it have been due.

For reactions there have been. Despite the wide use of the word, it has not escaped disfavour, sometimes because it had acquired theological associations which seemed irrational, as in the eighteenth century, when some felt that the controversies in and outside the Roman Church had made ' grace ' a meaningless term, which ought to be replaced by some intelligible equivalent. But this dislike in France as well as in England was due to a deeper cause ; there was an antipathy if not to Christianity as a whole, at any rate to evangelical interpretations of it, which employed the Pauline language. Any message about grace and mercy was resented as an outrage upon equality and the self-respect of men. Such a reaction is still felt in many quarters, where the word ' grace ' has practically disappeared from religious circles, partly owing to dubiety about any view of the atonement which would naturally employ it, and partly because it seems to be associated with a doctrine of election which is distasteful to democratic sensibilities. ' Love ' is preferred as a rule. ' Grace ' is regarded as less flexible ; it is held to belong too exclusively to the credenda of the faith, whereas ' love ' can be spread over the agenda, as they are interpreted by almost any school, however little the credenda are esteemed. Furthermore, ' grace ' suggests that one is under an obligation to God, whereas the unwritten creed of many is that God is under some obligation to them, or at any rate that He (or, what ' God ' stands for in their pseudo-humanism) is to be used rather than adored. Again, belief in grace withers within circles where Jesus is viewed as only a leader of the human enterprise or as an incentive to moral aspiration. It is irrelevant and indeed obnoxious to such impressionism. If the term be retained at all, it is in an æsthetic rather than in a dynamic sense, very much as Leibniz proposed when he distinguished the kingdom of nature from the kingdom of grace by arguing that in the former, i.e. in the physical realm, God ruled as architect, seeking order, whereas in the latter, the moral realm of grace, He ruled as the monarch who sought above all things the happiness of spirits. Many theists would not go so far as Leibniz, however ; they would prefer to speak of ' gracious,' when they speak of it at all, as equivalent to benignant or pleasing, as the opposite of unfriendly or ugly, and little more. Under the influence of the romantic spirit, in fact, ' grace ' has been sentimentalized as ' love ' has been, and this was the more easy since the use of the word in æsthetics had invested it with associations of attractiveness rather than of majesty and power.

It is not that Christianity as a religion of grace has no place for the conception of moral beauty. As we shall see, almost from the outset this element in grace was recognized, even as the redeeming significance of the term was uppermost. The twofold meaning of ' grace ' commended itself to Christians in the early Church. They found them-

selves able to use both freely, very much as Donne could praise George
Herbert's mother by writing,

> No spring nor summer beauty hath such grace
> As I have seen in an autumnal face,

and also could ask, " Will God infuse his first grace and not reward
it with more, without which we can no more use his first grace
when we have it than we could dispose ourselves by nature to have
it ? " It is true that the two meanings of the term did fall apart
in many circles, for reasons into which we need not now enter.
Indeed they could be employed as opposites rather than as complementary terms, as by Lord Morley at the opening of his *Voltaire*,
speaking of Calvinists with their " forces of grace, election and predestination " and then of the Renaissance " ideas of grace and beauty."
But these two associations of the word were not originally so far apart,
and a closer study of grace as redeeming love reveals the fact that it
did not necessarily exclude some recognition of attractiveness and charm
in God or in man. This is to anticipate, however. The point here is
that all depends upon the emphasis. Christianity is primarily a religion
which lives upon grace as the royal saving power of God manifested
through His Son Jesus Christ. It is as an element in this truth, and as
an element alone, that the so-called ' æsthetic ' side of grace can be
reckoned fairly. All interpretations of Christianity which make this
primary, in whatever degree, throw the religion out of focus, just as, on
the other hand, interpretations which taboo the idea of beauty in religion
prove inadequate. The thought of Christianity as grace involves
ultimately truth, goodness, and beauty, although, as we shall see, the
third element was the last to move the Christian consciousness.

(ii) In the New Testament, read even casually, it becomes
clear that ' grace ' is almost absent from the gospels and never
absent for very long from the pages of the apostle Paul.

Paul came into Christianity as the Faith or the Truth or
the Way opened up by Jesus the Lord. His powerful statement of it as a religion of grace, or rather as the religion
of grace, was due to his dominant conception of God bestowing undeserved favour and fellowship upon men. In this
divine Action the grace of God or of His Son deals with

men in their mortal weakness and estrangement, reconciling them to Himself. All is of grace, in the religious life. Paul sees grace here and nowhere else. When he speaks of it, he is thinking of its core in this redeeming Action ; he confines his attention to grace as originally manifested in Jesus the Lord and as verified in the experience of Christians who yield to God's gracious love and serve Him in the fellowship of the Church. In this vital relationship he is absorbed. The faith which God's grace elicits is for him incompatible with anything like merit, and it is also beyond any racial distinctions ; these are the two foci of his ellipse, ' all is of grace ' and this ' grace is for all.' God's love is free to make its own terms, and they are terms of trust in His gracious offer of life. Man is also free to accept the offer ; there are no barriers of nationalism in the Faith, and no favourites of God by birth or caste or privilege. It was on these aspects of the revelation of God in Jesus His Son that the apostle fixed his mind when he spoke of ' grace.' It fell to him to maintain these as primary. In the circumstances nothing was more needful than to single out man's dependence upon God as the essential truth of the revelation in Jesus Christ. For Paul indeed a man's religious experience was his experience of the grace or mercy of God. That, above all things. His grace-teaching went on to describe the joy and certainty produced by this experience, the new life and power which it brought to human beings who were disillusioned or in despair of themselves. But it was enough for him as a rule with unflinching seriousness to urge that the source and spring of all this lay in the redeeming sacrifice of Christ, and therefore to discourage anything in the shape of human effort that threatened to infringe the supreme value of this divine Action which he taught men to comprehend as grace. The coming of Grace had changed the world for him and his. Why it had come, why it had to come, if men were to have any hope for life, and how it had come—this was what Paul

set himself to explain and express.   In the Action of grace
he was supremely conscious of two elements.   It produced
the humility and the confidence that belong together in the
great moments of life as it encounters love.   Hence Paul
sees grace as at once a release and a challenge, a gift and
a demand, a free pardon that strips men of self-esteem and
also a summons that brings them to their feet with the glow
of expectation.   " Arise, shine ; for thy light is come, and
the glory of the Lord is risen upon thee."   The tension in
Paul's thought is due to the fact that he held both of these
truths together and grasped their unity in Jesus Christ.

" Shine " in Isaiah lx. 1 means *be glad*, or, as Rosenmueller puts it,
" sereno sis animo."   It corresponds to Paul's " joy and peace in believing " that through Jesus the Christ of God grace has dawned upon
a dark, inert world.

The general faith of the Church during the apostolic age
adjusted itself to this interpretation by broadening the conception of ' grace ' till it touched the End, till it was related
to the preceding revelation in the OT, and till it began to
enter into the interpretation of the sacraments.   More
definitely than in Paul ' grace ' now became a term for the
Christian religion as a whole.   Other categories than those
chosen by him to explain the significance of grace in the
crucifixion were sought out.   Furthermore, later writers
devised a varity of expressions for the truth of ' grace,' and
even when it was retained it was often modified or re-cast.
All these extensions, adaptations, and alternatives are exhibited
by the NT literature which follows in the wake of Paul.

However versatile the terms were, the NT writers presupposed a
faith which, they knew, was ' grace ' as no previous religion had been
and as no contemporary cult could be.   They have transmitted the
religious essence of Christianity as man's faith answering to God's own
grace.   It is a mistake to make a fetish of the term.   The word does
not occur in the Apostles' Creed nor in the Te Deum, for example.

Both are charged with the truth, yet neither avails itself of the actual term. This has to be borne in mind, especially as we try to estimate the Pauline statement in relation to what went before and what came after it. Historically Paul's grace-teaching was an original attempt to express the original Reality of God which in Jesus the Lord had already called the Church into being. It was no mere bundle of idiosyncrasies more or less irrelevant to the Faith, and the early Church, in its most independent conceptions of grace, never thought so. Nevertheless, a larger synthesis was often felt to be needful, partly because Paul's very intensity led him to ignore what seemed to be legitimate considerations of religion, partly because new issues arose which called for other presentations of the truth, and partly because some of his categories of thought no longer made the same appeal to Christian intelligence.

" Man's faith answering to God's own grace," for example, is a valuable statement of the objective truth in Christianity, for which Paul like all the NT writers stood, but some of his phrases about the sheer goodwill of God are couched in terms that suggest a regal authority which imposes its purpose on human beings. It is true that in his teaching on grace we feel indications of the religious centre from which somehow the two rays flash, that of the transcendent Will of God which meets man with gracious favour in his utter need, and that of a Lord whose character and spirit in this approach are to be reproduced in measure by those who owe all to Him. In this twofold conception of the divine nature Paul carries on the gospel of Jesus. But it was not always easy to grasp the harmony of the two ideas, and, as we are well aware, later interpreters who were sincerely anxious to uphold the free initiative of God in grace sometimes isolated it until it bore no real reference to any condition or quality in man, and even seemed like the over-riding of personality by a supernatural force or the summons of a celestial Lord to rebels who were asked for submission to His terms and no more. This at once involved unreality, as it always does, for when the saving grace of God is represented as an unconditioned boon or offer, the logical deduction is a salvation for all, irrespective of their personal acceptance, or else a redeeming purpose for some which is little more than the arbitrary fiat of the Lord, or finally an objective salvation without any subjective element corresponding to it.   Even in Melanchthon's *Loci Communes*, for all its fine spirit, the reader is sometimes sensible of this tendency to interpret Paul's language.   It was the more easy to slip into such a view since the apostle himself occasionally argues about the unmerited goodness of God in ways that do suggest the misinterpretation.   His categories of eschatology and apocalyptic were not always adequate to the message of grace which he sought to convey through them to his age.   Neither was it easy for after-ages to appreciate their influence upon the original presentation of that message.

Once again, the grateful recognition of God's grace breaking into his life did not incline him to allow for any previous preparation in experience.   In holding that all was of grace, he was so anxious to disclaim anything like merit on the part of the recipient, that later Christians, without desiring to infringe the truth of man's indebtedness to love divine, made more room for the fact of human aspirations and efforts than, as it seemed to them, the great apostle had done.   When this was healthy, it abjured the notion that human needs were to be taken as the ultimate reason for God's grace, or that any human efforts draw down that grace.   But it is deplorably easy to become unhealthy in religion.   The merit-theology of Latin mediaevalism was one result of this tendency, and at an opposite angle the undue reliance upon feelings proved a weakness.   Dr. Chalmers [1] told a correspondent, " the truth is that your great error lies in making your comfort lie upon the question, Do I believe ? when you should

---

[1] *Life of Dr. Chalmers*, ii. 450. " I do God great injustice," he writes elsewhere (ii. 42), " for I feel that I do not rise to an adequate conception of his loving kindness and tender mercy."

make it turn upon the question, Is God willing to receive me into fellowship for Christ's sake ? " It was a wise diagnosis. He was putting his finger on a weak introspectiveness due to an ultra-individualism which had been fostered by some misinterpretations of what Paul taught, and he was also stating the real essence of the apostle's position upon grace. So far as we know, it was not a temptation which beset the primitive Christians. Paul's counsels to his churches, ' before whose eyes Jesus Christ was evidently set forth,' would prevent any such error. But as soon as the faith which responded to this presentation of grace began to be analysed, even when in all sincerity it was examined by the devout consciousness, a misunderstanding of the apostle's teaching was inevitable, a misunderstanding which was due to misplaced conscientiousness.

The fact is that although in his grace-teaching Paul touches the vital heart of the Christian religion—this is the very nerve of his gospel, and in the evangelical consciousness of the Church there has been a constant response to it—the appreciation has not always been intelligent, even when it has been sympathetic. Thus it is not accurate to read Paul's words on grace through Luther's agony of soul, for much as Luther was indebted to the apostle, and much as he has made us indebted to him for insight into some of the deepest factors in Paul's message of grace, his interpretation is not always true to the original bearing of the apostle's argument. It is a fair question for instance, whether Luther's " Simul peccator simul justus " is genuinely Pauline. Unconsciously many read Paul through Luther as they read Genesis in the light of Milton, with more profit than accuracy. On the other hand, it was a whiff of anti-Lutheran bias which once deflected Newman [1] as he interpreted Paul's words about justification. ' A man is not justified by the works of the Law,' wrote the apostle, ' but (ἐὰν μή) by faith in Jesus Christ.'

[1] *Lectures on Justification*, pp. 278 f.

Perhaps Newman was misled by the literal Vulgate with its
nisi per fidem, as though Paul had meant, 'a man is not
justified by the Law unless he believes in Jesus Christ';
that is, if a man has faith, moral actions and obedience do
justify him. "It does not follow that works done in faith
do not justify, because works done without faith do not
justify." So Newman explains Galatians ii. 16. But it does
follow. Newman is really making Paul sponsor the very
idea against which he was protesting with such vigour that
the Greek shakes in his hand.

Apart from such possible deflections, there is another obstacle to the
modern appreciation of Paul's witness to the grace of God. It is sometimes conveyed in terms which are alien to our age. Coleridge, in
demanding thought and attention from those who were to read his
essays in *The Friend*, explains that by 'thought' in this connexion he
means " the voluntary production in our minds of those states of consciousness to which, as to his fundamental facts, the writer has referred
us." But the states of consciousness to which Paul's argument of grace
refers us, often are expressed in categories that do not rise in our minds.
The fundamental needs of the religious life are the same. The essential
truth of grace is not affected by the change of the centuries. Yet our
minds do not produce exactly what Paul meant by ' Spirit,' ' flesh,' or
' Law.' These imply a metaphysic and a view of the world into which
we have to think ourselves back, before their inner truth reaches us.
In the following pages it will be our task to estimate such expressions
and also the many-sided truth of religion which they were designed to
carry to the Christian consciousness.

3

If our modern Alciphron opens his English Bible, he
encounters 'grace' at the very threshold of the book, in
the Epistle Dedicatorie to the English Version of 1611:
" To the most high and mightie Prince, James by the grace
of God King of Great Britaine, France and Ireland, Defender
of the Faith, etc., the translators of the Bible wish Grace,
Mercie, and Peace, through Jesus Christ our Lord." If he

happens to be a student of history, he notes in the first mention of the word here a sign of the ethical current which was so strong in human nature that it turned even ' grace ' into an alien channel. Pride apes humility on the throne as well as in the Church, and this comes out in the very use of the phrase ' by the grace of God.' Originally applied in the mediaeval vocabulary to ecclesiastics, the words ' gratia Dei ' came to be used of monarchs from the ninth century onwards. Thus Charles the Great was hailed as " Carlomagnus gratia Dei Rex Francorum " ; the title then passed into the court-language of France as a humble recognition that the supreme power was due to God's favour, not to any personal merit. In form at any rate the phrase was a confession that high rank and authority were bestowed by God's grace. This was or might be sincerely held by the monarch. Religious feeling was at first strong enough to make the phrase more than a merely conventional renunciation of pretension or merit. But eventually the words came to denote an antithesis to the will of the people. They were turned into the expression of an attitude which looked down upon the lower orders rather than to God above. As Fustel de Coulanges observes, in his *Histoire des Institutions politiques de l'ancienne France* (vi. 221), "aujourd'hui et depuis trois ou quatre siècles, les mots 'roi par la grace de Dieu' signifient que l'autorité ne vient pas du peuple . . . C'est bien ainsi que les peuples, sinon les rois, comprennent cette formule." How far King James understood the phrase as a recognition of responsibilities rather than as an assertion of privileges, we cannot say. But the Translators took it in its original and religious sense. Furthermore, towards the close of the dedication they hope that if they are " traduced by Popish persons at home or abroad " or " maligned by self-conceited brethren " among the English sectaries, they may be " sustained by the powerful protection of your Majestie's grace and favour." Here are sufficiently varied uses of ' grace.'

When one passes on to the NT as the direct literature of Christianity at its origin, the impression of grace as a primary term deepens. The New Testament is the smallest sacred book in the world. Anyone coming to it for the first time might reasonably expect to find without much difficulty what were the characteristic terms of the religion which it represents. Even in the vast Koran, as sura after sura echoes ' The Most Merciful ' as a title of Allah, one infers that such a phrase must be characteristic of Islam. Are there any such in the New Testament ? Well, our Alciphron might be struck by such recurring words as these : ' Grace and peace,' ' The grace of God,' ' The God of all grace,' ' The grace of the Lord Jesus Christ,' ' The Spirit of grace,' and so forth. He would notice that the last word of the sacred book was, ' The grace of the Lord Jesus Christ be with you all.' It would not be unnatural for an enquirer of any penetration to deduce from this that the religion of the New Testament was a religion of grace, whatever that might mean.

He would be confirmed in such an opinion if he went below the surface and discovered that there are grace-words that do not contain the word grace. ' Ye have not chosen me, but I have chosen you,' ' It is not of him that willeth nor of him that runneth but of God that showeth mercy,' ' Come unto me, all ye that labour and are heavy laden, and I will give you rest,' ' Christ Jesus came into the world to save sinners,' ' God having raised up his Son Jesus sent him to bless you in turning everyone of you from his iniquities,' ' The Father sent the Son to be the Saviour of the world,' ' The Bread of God is he which cometh down from heaven and giveth life to the world,' ' The Son of God is come and hath given us an understanding, that we may know him that is true,' ' The Son of man is come to seek and save that which is lost,' ' The Son of man came not to be ministered unto but to minister and to give his life a ransom for many,' ' I will give to him that is athirst of the fountain of the water of life,' ' Whosoever will let him take the water of life freely,' ' Fear not, it is your Father's good pleasure to give you the kingdom,' ' His divine power hath given unto us all things that pertain unto life and godliness,' ' Every good gift and every perfect gift is from above and cometh down from the Father of lights,' ' What hast thou that thou didst not receive ? '—when we read such sentences we are in touch with the truth of grace, even although the actual word is absent.

Even when the term is employed, however, it is not invariably in the same sense. The writings which compose the New Testament represent different standpoints. Some are less important for our purpose than others ; there are diversities of interpretation and real differences of emphasis. Yet the common element here is more important than the varying attitudes. While there are distinctive features in the Pauline letters, for example, which mark them off as unique in the presentation of grace, the unity which pervades the letters of the apostle and the other NT writings and which differentiates them from all contemporary religious and philosophical treatises, is still more noticeable. One real advantage of studying grace in the NT is that you get an impression of the coherence of primitive Christianity. It is far more than a verbal coherence. Yet the verbal data reveal the vital self-consciousness of the new faith. The Greek spoken by educated persons in the Empire, whether Jews or Gentiles, put at the command of the NT writers material for conveying their new message. No word in that material was more useful than ' charis ' or grace ; it had acquired a range of content in Hellenistic Greek which was singularly acceptable to the primitive Christians. As they felt themselves carried forward by a tide of new life which swept them beyond Hellenistic religion and Hebrew faith, they borrowed and transformed this term till it became characteristic of their belief alone.

PART A
THE ANTECEDENTS OF GRACE

I

THE GREEK AND JEWISH VOCABULARY

' CHARIS ' had been long upon the lips of men, and always, in all ways, it had been one of the shining words that serve the world. Beauty, kindness, gratitude ; charm, favour, thankfulness :—these were the main facets of the Greek word, whether it was Greeks or barbarians, inside or outside Hellas, who made use of it. Joy, thanks, a favour or a gift: ' charis ' carried all these meanings, and on the fringe of it the clinging associations of charm and attractiveness. What rejoiced men was called ' charis.' Χαρά was the emotion roused by χάρις. Nothing thrilled life like beauty, and there was no beauty like kindness. A boon or benefit conferred graciously was a true source of pleasure. It was delightful to help or to be helped. Such were the ideas attaching to ' charis ' in ancient life, which formed a ' praeparatio evangelica ' for the faith that was to use this term in order to express the deep things of God and man. The mind that borrows and employs such terms and ideas is more important than what it thus presses into its service. Paul, we are told, stayed in ' hired lodgings ' at Rome as he preached the kingdom of God and taught about the Lord Jesus Christ. His mind occupied furnished lodgings also as it developed its own original message ; but, although the latter is not to be explained out of its environment, there is significance in the apostle's discriminating use of a current word like ' grace.'

I

The scope of the word may be seen from two sayings which are almost side by side in the Jewish Greek of Sirach (xl. 17, 22). First, there is ' charis ' as kindness or bounty :

Bountifulness (χάρις) is like an Eden of blessings,

so rich and rare it is. Then,

> Your eye may long for gracefulness and beauty (χάριν καὶ κάλλος)
> But better than both is the green blade of corn,

where the author praises the fresh corn above the attractiveness of physical beauty in a human being. And with it went always the breath of pleasure. ' Charis ' echoed to ' chairein ' or ' chara.' When the hero of Euripides' play *Ion* (645 f.) asserts that it is equally delightful for him to enjoy much and to delight in small pleasures, the Greek runs :

> ἴση γὰρ ἡ χάρις
> μεγάλοισι χαίρειν σμικρά θ' ἡδέως ἔχειν.

The sensation of pleasure or delight conveyed by ' charis ' might range from inward to outward qualities. It was roused by taste or hearing as well as by sight. Words and wine afford ' charis,' for example. A pleasant way of speech, delicacy, tact, consideration, a Greek would call that ' charis.' Plutarch contrasts it with roughness or bad temper in intercourse, for example (εὐνοίας καὶ χάριτος οὐ μέμψεως οὐδ' ὀργῆς Quomodo adulator 34), and the author of Second Maccabees closes his book by remarking that " as wine mixed with water proves at once wholesome and delightful (τὴν χάριν ἀποτελεῖ), so the skill with which a book is composed is a delight to the taste of readers," meaning that the combination of piquant style and sound history is most attractive.

But the word went deeper and further. Sometimes it meant simply affection or loving-kindness in later Greek, as in Theocritus, the Alexandrian poet of the third century B.C. (Idyll, xxviii. 24, 25, μεγάλα χάρις δώρῳ σὺν ὀλίγῳ, there may be great affection. shown by one who can only make a little gift). And earlier than this, Greeks had turned it to such a nobler end. The most attractive trait of human character, the Greek felt, was kindness or generosity. Hence ' charis ' naturally came to mean favour or benefit, just as in English we can speak not only of a person being well-favoured in appearance but of the favours he does to others. There were many other terms for beneficence or help or kindly service, but ' charis ' was a favourite word in this connexion. By a further turn it came to mean the pleasure or gratitude evoked by kindness ; a good action is a delight to witness or to experience, and the resultant emotion of thankfulness was conveyed by ' charis ' also.

In one of Plutarch's moral essays, On Talkativeness (*De Garrulitate* iv.–v.), it denotes charm of character in action, charm of language, and the pleasure afforded by good literature, all within a few lines of prose. In describing the talkative person, he remarks that " his unseasonable chatter destroys all the charm (χάριν) of his deeds." Whereas, " look at the persuasiveness and charm (χάριν) of Lysias " the Attic orator, and think how " Homer, alone of the poets, is ever new and excelling in charm " (πρὸς χάριν ἀκμάζων), ever able to afford supreme pleasure to his readers. Another example of the flexibility of the term is afforded by Clement of Alexandria in the Stromateis (vii. 6. 34) ; as he speaks of the real sacrifices to be offered by spiritually-minded men, he clinches his argument by a quotation, κατὰ τὴν ποιητικὴν χάριν, i.e. " by way of adding the charm of poetry to a prose statement.

> " For who is such a fool, so credulous
> Past all bounds, as to think that bones and gall,
> At which even hungry hounds would sniff, if burnt
> Would make all gods rejoice and take such food
> As their due meed,

yes, and make them grateful (χάριν) to the sacrificers ! " Here literary charm and thanks are alike expressed by ' charis.' But more often it is the double meaning of ' charis ' as boon and gratitude which occurs.

Thus Aristotle uses ' charis ' almost in our modern sense of a charitable gift or favour, in the Nikomachean Ethics (v. 8). After arguing that it is the interchange of services which holds the social order together, he continues, " Hence it is that men erect a public temple of the Graces (Χαρίτων), as a reminder of repayment (ἀνταπόδοσις, i.e. to remind people that they should repay what they have received as citizens), for this is characteristic of χάρις." What he means by ' charis ' here is explained in his next sentence : " For one ought to make a return (ἀνθυπηρετῆσαι) to anyone who has been gracious to oneself (χαρισαμένῳ), and then again to take the initiative in being gracious to him." The philosopher is for once playing on the double meaning of ' charis '; the Graces were the goddesses of charm and beauty, but Aristotle suggests pleasantly that they have an ethical significance. He could do this, just as Seneca could in the *De Beneficiis* (i. 3), because ' charis ' like the Latin ' gratia ' denoted not only loveliness but gratitude or kindness.

Theocritus plays on the double sense of χάρις as favour and thanks in his sixteenth idyll on The Graces. The similar range of ' gratia ' may be illustrated from Augustine's *Confessions* (ii. 7): " I will love thee, O Lord, and thank thee (gratias agam). To thy grace (gratia) and mercy I ascribe it that thou hast melted away my sins like ice. To thy grace I ascribe the evils I have not committed ; for what might not I have done, I who actually loved sin for its own sake (or, for nothing : gratuitum) ? "

The fact that ' charis ' could mean both favour or benefit and at the same time either delight or gratitude for the gift, enabled a Greek to play upon the word, as the tragedians do often. Thus Sophocles speaks of occasions in life when a favour is no longer a delight (ὅτ᾽ οὐδὲν ἡ χάρις χάριν φέροι, Œdipus Colon. 779), and of kindness ever begetting some grateful return (χάρις χάριν γάρ ἐστιν ἡ τίκτουσ᾽ ἀεί, Ajax 522). This turn of language does not occur in the NT. Paul concludes a long passage (2 Cor. viii.–ix.), in which he has been speaking of human bounty and of God's gracious favour alike as ' charis,' by exclaiming, " Thanks be to God for his unspeakable gift ! " The Greek is, χάρις τῷ θεῷ ἐπὶ τῇ ἀνεκδιηγήτῳ αὐτοῦ δωρεᾷ. What he means by δωρεά is the divine bounty or χάρις. But he chooses the equivalent term δωρεά for ' gift.' Also, when he wishes to speak of the inner delight stirred by the divine χάρις he says ' rejoicing ' or ' joy '; χάρις is not employed in that special sense, although it may mean, as it does here, man's thankfulness for God's grace. Indeed the two notes of grace as experienced by man are for the apostle an utter, glad sense of indebtedness to God and an equally vital sense of obligation. Joy and duty are the proofs of grace in human life. The free gift of God's favour stirs man to wonder and praise; also it inspires life with the desire and power to put this gift to use in the service of the Lord. It was partly because ' charis ' already possessed the former significance even on lower levels that Paul appropriated it for the Christian revelation.

2

What made χάρις so attractive to Paul was its connotation of active favour, however. In its central sense, as he employs the term, ' grace ' signifies more than God's favour. It is a quality of His character but a quality which is a motive ; to call it an attitude is to suggest something too passive for the apostle's meaning. Grace is rather God giving to men, acting upon men, moving in the life of His People. " Il designe l'amour de Dieu en action, intervenant directement et positivement dans les destinées de l'humanité pour la relever." [1] We may speak, if we choose, of grace being God's disposition, but only as ' disposition ' is taken to mean more than a mental or moral attitude ; it is God disposing the human lot, God with a mind for action. To his readers such suggestions of divine goodwill acting on behalf of men were already present in the Greek word. Apart altogether from the usage in the Greek Bible, they had gathered round the term in the vernacular language on the lips of pagans.

' Charis ' from the first, in the sense of kindness had carried with it a suggestion of free generosity. When Aristotle defined it as " helpfulness towards some one in need, not in return for anything (μὴ ἀντὶ τινός), nor that the helper may get anything, but for the sake of the person who is helped " (Rhetor. ii. 7), he meant that for a Greek grace

[1] Sabatier's definition in his L'Apôtre Paul, p. 348.

was essentially unselfish, an active expression of unmerited aid or succour.   Also, he adds, " it is particularly great if the helper be the only one or the first or the chief person to help " (ἢ μόνος ἢ πρῶτος ἢ μάλιστα).   From this idea of uncalculating unique kindness, which was never quite lost from ' charis ' in its ethical usage, it was not a far step to the further thought of kindness as aid undeserved or unexpected.   The language of the imperial inscriptions (see below) shows that the use of ' charis ' as a boon or favour, in Hellenistic writers of Judaism like Philo and Josephus, corresponds to the political usage of the period.   The lordly favour bestowed on a nation by Egyptian or Roman emperors was a ' grace ' in our modern sense of the term, the benefaction of one in power who grants some relief or practical benefit to his subordinates.   " Faire de grâces, repandre des grâces, est le plus bel apanage de le souverainté, c'est faire du bien, c'est plus que justice."   This remark of Voltaire is true to the vogue of the term ' grace ' in such circles of early life and thought.

When Paul taught the saving will and generous power of God in Jesus Christ, he had therefore some language ready for his message.   The truth of grace in his gospel vibrates with such thoughts of power.   This authoritative character of grace, no less than the vital union between God the Father and the Lord Jesus Christ in the transaction, emerges in the end of the opening words of Galatians, for example.   There, after wishing *grace and peace* to his readers *from God our Father and the Lord Jesus Christ who gave himself for our sins to rescue us from the present evil world*, the apostle adds—summing up the entire movement of grace—*by the will* (θελήμα) *of our God and Father*.   The phrase recalls the teaching of Jesus about the royal Father.   It signifies that the divine will is a will of love, and that the grace of love comes with authority into life.   This meaning of God's θελήμα is developed in the later letters ; in the letters to Thessalonica the divine will is only set forth as determining the clean, moral life which the ' saints ' are expected to reproduce as the result of their call, but this deeper truth answers to the idea of the gracious call and choice being itself determined by God's love in power.

In Clement's Cohortatio (xii.) there is an illustration of the same truth. " The prophet makes no secret of this gracious boon ($\chi\acute{\alpha}\varrho\iota\varsigma$), when he writes, ' I said, Ye are gods, and all sons of the Most High ' (Psalm lxxxii. 6). 'Tis we, 'tis we whom He has adopted, 'tis of us, not of the disobedient, that He wills to be called the Father." What makes the grace of adoption all the more sure and wonderful is that it comes from God's supreme will. This thought probably underlies the almost synonymous $\gamma\nu\acute{\omega}\mu\eta$ which Ignatius is fond of using as an equivalent for the mind or ruling purpose of God. It is common in Philo, but in the NT is only employed of human purposes, good or evil, whereas Barnabas can speak of the Father's purpose of kindness ($\tau\grave{\eta}\nu$ $\gamma\nu\acute{\omega}\mu\eta\nu$ $\tau\tilde{\eta}\varsigma$ $\dot{\alpha}\gamma\alpha\theta\omega\sigma\acute{\nu}\nu\eta\varsigma$, II. 9). Another expression for the same truth is $\varkappa\acute{\epsilon}\lambda\epsilon\upsilon\sigma\iota\varsigma$ as employed, for example, in the *Acta Justini*, where the arrested Christians reply to the Roman magistrate, " I am a Christian," adding either " by God's free favour ($\delta\omega\varrho\epsilon\tilde{\alpha}$) " or " by God's command ($\varkappa\epsilon\lambda\epsilon\acute{\upsilon}\sigma\epsilon\iota$) " or " freed by Christ and sharing the same hope by the grace of Christ." Unlike $\theta\epsilon\lambda\eta\mu\alpha$, which is purely biblical, $\varkappa\acute{\epsilon}\lambda\epsilon\upsilon\sigma\iota\varsigma$ is an ethnic word which is thus taken over for the gracious summons that explains the Christian life. In the new creation, " Let there be light " was the first commanding word with promise. " For God who commanded the light to shine out of darkness hath shined in our hearts, to give the light of the knowledge of the glory of God in the face of Jesus Christ." Philo only uses $\theta\epsilon\lambda\eta\mu\alpha$ once, and then of God ; it is late in the LXX, but occasionally there it does connote gracious favour, as in Psalm xxx. 5.

This connotation of the word may be illustrated further from the use of $\chi\acute{\alpha}\varrho\iota\varsigma$, e.g. in Euripides' *Heracles* 134, where it denotes not the personal charm of Heracles but his vocation or function of doing good to men, and also the right of such a hero-god to be thanked for his services. ' Charis ' in such connexions is linked to the activity of a divine hero. Or again, there is the remark of Plutarch in his life of Lucullus (xviii) where he tells how during the Mithridatic wars that general captured a city in which a number of Greeks had been imprisoned. Their release from captivity was utterly unexpected.[1] " They had long been supposed to be dead, so that it was not a rescue (σωτηρίαν) but a resurrection (ἀναβίωσιν) and a sort of second birth which the gracious help (χάρις) of Lucullus provided them with." The language shows how in Hellenistic Greek the term ' charis ' could be employed naturally of an active service rendered by some one in power, even apart from religion, and also how easily ' charis ' called up terms for rescue and re-birth which might be filled with religious significance in other quarters.

Furthermore (a), ' charis ' had been associated with supernatural power or aid. Partly this was derived from the sense of ' spell,' which occurs as early as the Attic dramatists. This meaning of mystical or magical influence was derived from the sense of ' charis ' as power in the religious or semireligious sphere. In the older Greek literature of poetry the word was almost personified in order to represent the effective spell of Song or of Love, for example. Pindar's ' Charis ' has often the connotation of Spell ; he attached a semi-supernatural significance to Song, and expresses this by ' Charis ' (as in Olymp. i. 49). Euripides again uses the word for the binding authority of oaths (Medea 439) and for the overpowering spell of Love " instilling into the soul its own sweet grace " (χάριν, Hippolytus 527). For the Greeks there was a ' grace ' or shining quality pouring from jewels or robes which affected human life with its potent supernatural influence. The controlling appreciation of beauty developed this sense of beauty's power as a dæmonic force, which passed into the lower strata of popular religion as seen in magical papyri, for instance, till we have actually the cry of a headless dæmon, " I am the Truth . . . I am he who sends lightning and thunder. . . . I am the Charis of the world " (ἡ χάρις τοῦ αἰῶνος), χάρις here meaning Spell or Binding Power.[2]

[1] See Von Wilamowitz-Moellendorff, *Euripides' Heracles* (1889), p. 36.
[2] *Greek Papyri in the British Museum*, i. 69 f. (a fourth-century papyrus).

(b) But there was another channel along which the dynamic sense of ' charis ' was already operating in pre-Christian days. It was believed that there was a supernatural grace issuing from the other world, in some circles of Greek religion. The powers of the underworld were supposed to convey from a dead hero some χάρις to the living who tended his tomb and venerated him on earth. Such chthonian grace [1] emanates from the departed, bringing good to his group or followers above ground. It is this idea which underlies references like Æschylus's *Septem* 702, Sophocles' *Œd. Col.* 1751 f., and Euripides' *Heracles* 1026 f. To this there is not any parallel in primitive Christianity, but it indicates how χάρις was capable of acquiring a religious meaning which varied from spell to power ; favour arising from a supernatural source and conveying protection to living people was already covered by this flexible Greek word.

This extension of ' charis ' was not confined to poetry. Philosophers used it in their own way, as we may judge from the traditional saying of Empedocles' Χάρις δύστλητον 'Ανάγκην στυγέει (Diels, *Fragmente d. Vorsokratiker*, i. 268), and from the allegorizing of Χάρις and Δίκη by Cornutus the Stoic. In the second-century Vercelli Acts of Peter (ii), the apostle Paul prays at Rome, " O God eternal, God of the heavens, God of unspeakable majesty who hast established all things by Thy word, who hast bound upon all the world the chain of Thy grace." Here the metaphor plainly recalls the binding power of the spell in Greek religion, as well as the majesty of the God of ' grace.' Thanks to the mediaeval use of ' gratia ' almost as an equivalent for ' virtus,' grace sometimes became the term for an impersonal force or influence emanating from things as a power or spell of good.

> O mickle is the powerful grace that lies
> In herbs, plants, stones, and their true qualities !

---

[1] Cp. T. Zielinski, in *The Classical Quarterly* (1924), pp. 160 f. In a sepulchral inscription of the second century from Euboea, those who attend to the tomb are commended to the kindly care of Charis and Health ἐπισκοποίη δὲ χάρις καὶ 'Υγεία, Dittenberger's *Sylloge* [2] 891).

3

' Charis' was thus common in Hellenistic Greek as a term for active favour or gracious goodwill, particularly as shown by some individual or group in power towards another for whom affection was entertained. This dominant meaning of a benefit or gift freely bestowed by God or man upon the undeserving was not obscured by the less honourable uses to which the word was also being put. For in three directions the vogue of ' grace' was not wholly favourable to the new Christian message. The term was not entirely free from associations which might have unfitted it for Paul.

(*a*) One of these was the suggestion of caprice on the part of Authority, and even of merit on the part of the recipient. It is to avoid any such suggestion that the apostle drops all mention of " finding grace or favour in the sight of God." The absence of this phrase from the NT is significant. It was by far the most common use of ' charis' as rendering the Hebrew word ' chên' in the LXX. Men were fortunate or blessed as they found the Lord in a good mood or as they could induce Him to favour them by some meritorious action, by prayer and entreaty, or by some silent appeal to His gracious consideration of their plight. The idea varied ; it had its higher as well as its lower levels. But in Semitic usage " to find favour in the sight of the Lord " tended to convey the notion, not only that His favour could be secured by means of a sacrifice or service rendered, but that the deity was like a chief or monarch, of whom one could never be quite sure. To the nobler side of religion this latter idea did express a deep sense of awe and reverence ; it excluded anything like presumption on the part of the worshipper, and certainly it ruled out the feeling that one could take the Lord's favour as a matter of course. But it was capable of misconception. As time went on and religious feeling altered, the phrase suggested a fitfulness on the part of God which was felt to be incongruous with His character, and it was probably this consciousness of its inadequacy which led to Paul and the NT writers dropping the phrase altogether. ' Grace ' was retained and filled with a higher meaning, in the light of Jesus Christ's revelation of the divine purpose. Paul was convinced indeed that no other word was so suitable for the essence of the gospel ; he felt that he could use it without fear of being misunderstood by his hearers and readers in the Greek-speaking world. The chief precaution he took was to leave out the classical sentence of his Greek Bible about men finding grace in the sight of God. For him grace was provided in the gospel by a God who had no moods or caprices ; grace meant His characteristic, unvarying attitude towards men in need of help, it was favour to be accepted rather than sought out, favour that was offered freely to faith. Nor did it depend upon anything that man could offer ; it was not to be secured in virtue of any consideration. The apostle's desire to discourage the slightest notion of merit on the part of man also entered into his unwillingness to employ the biblical phrase.

To this there are three or four partial exceptions. Luke in the archaic style of his early chapters in the gospel speaks of the Virgin Mary as having found grace or favour with God (i. 30), and quotes similar phrases from the OT in Acts vii. 46 (see 2 Tim. i. 18) and 10. The author of Hebrews also encourages his readers to *approach the throne of grace* that they may receive mercy and *find grace to help* them *in the hour of need* (iv. 16), but this is only a verbal parallel, as the context shows. The avoidance of the phrase, from Paul onwards, was due to the fact that ' grace ' denoted for the primitive Christians the standing relationship of God towards men, not any mood of His which needed to be aroused. Men did not appeal to His grace ; His grace appealed to them. The initiative was with Him. Men might refuse grace, or desert it, or fail to use it when it was offered ; but it did not occur to the primitive Church to speak of finding grace as the OT faithful had done. Grace had found them.

It is most significant how Philo interpreted this phrase. He too seems to have been sensible of a difficulty when he first met it in Genesis vi. 8 : " Noah found favour in the eyes of the Lord God." It means, he thinks, that the good man who practises religious speculation " finds this supreme truth, that all existence, earth, water, air, fire, sun, stones, heaven, all animals and plants, are God's gracious gift " (χάριν ὄντα θεοῦ τὰ πάντα). Indeed, " if anyone were to ask me what was the cause of the creation of the world, I would answer, It is the goodness of Being (τοῦ Ὄντος), which is the eldest of the graces (πρεσβυτάτη τῶν χαρίτων, Quod Deus Sit Immut. 23)." In the Leg. Alleg. iii. 24 he returns to this verse, explaining that the good Noah, reposing on justice, found grace before God, and " to find grace is not, as some suppose, merely to be well-pleasing (εὐαρεστῆσαι) ; it means that the just man in search of the nature of things makes the supreme discovery that all things are God's gracious favour (χάριν), not any gift (χάρισμα) of being or nature, that nothing is one's own possession but that all is God's possession, so that grace (χάριν) belongs to Him alone. Those who ask, what is the principle of being ? may be answered thus : it is the goodness and grace (χάρις) of God, which He presents to those who come after Him, for all that is in the world, yea and the world itself, is a benefaction, a gift, a gracious favour (χάρισμα) of God." So Philo evaded the suggestion of a casual mood in God, which Paul avoided by omitting the phrase altogether from his vocabulary of religion.

Another (b) drawback was the phrase about God granting favour or grace in an outward sense, for in Jewish Greek the connexion of beauty with religion was conserved on a line of its own.

When Josephus has to speak of the traditional charm of Moses in his childhood, he describes the divinely fair boy as invested with ἡ χάρις ἡ παιδική (Ant. ii. 231). ' Charis ' thus is an equivalent for the classical μορφή or κάλλος. Luke prefers the LXX phrase ἀστεῖος τῷ θεῷ (Acts vii. 20), which the Vulgate renders by ' gratus Deo,' i.e. ' grateful ' in our sense of ' pleasing.'

The Greek associations of χάρις with beauty or delight had persisted, till comeliness or charm of person or of speech is a frequent meaning of the word in the Wisdom literature. Yet a religious element in the former application appears curiously in two passages. Tobit tells how at Nineveh he would eat nothing but kosher food, and how in reward for his strict religious scruples " the Most High granted me χάριν καὶ μορφήν (i.e. favour and attractiveness) " in the sight of the pagan monarch (Tobit i. 11–13). The two words might be a mere periphrasis for ' favour,' as in contemporary Greek (cf. e.g. Witkowski's *Epist. Priv. Graecae*, p. 89), but notice how Joseph in Potiphar's household also remarks that " those who fast for God's sake receive favour (χάριν) of face " (Test. Jos. iii. 4). The idea is that outward good looks and the bloom of health are the outcome of strict religion ; either alone or with a complementary term ' charis ' is used to express this. God's favour is manifested somehow in such a form.

A similar notion occurs in Daniel (i. 9), where Daniel and his three companions at the Babylonian court do as Tobit did ; " the Lord granted Daniel favour and pity," according to the Hebrew text ; that is, the governor kindly agreed to let them observe their food taboos. But here there is a difference. The LXX rendered the words by τιμὴν καὶ χάριν, i.e. honour (or, respect) and grace simply from the authorities' favour ; nothing is said of χάρις in the outward sense of healthy bloom, even when the author comes to describe that (in verses 15, 16). The Jewish reviser Theodotion altered χάριν here to the more literal οἰκτειρμόν.

Furthermore, ' charis,' on this level of favour or charm, was sometimes linked with δόξα in the sense of mere popularity or fame. Prayers for favour and fame of this kind did not rise high, but they are common, especially in Egypt. There is, for example, the inscription found by Professor Sayce (*Academy* ; 1893, p. 41) at the entrance to the quarries opposite Kusae :

Ἑρμῆς, Ὧρος, Ἀφροδίτη
διδῶσι δόξαν καὶ χάριν :·

and a magical formula in the fourth-century erotic papyrus edited by Dr. Eitrem (*Papyri Osloenses*, i. 45, 202) invokes the deities for ' victory, favour (χάριν), fame (δόξαν), and success with all men and with all women,' one votary praying, ' grant me the favour of all, Adonai.' Within Jewish Hellenism it is noticeable that when χάρις is linked to words like δόξα or τιμή, it means little more than honour or reputation, i.e. what wins favour in the world, even when this is attributed to the power of God, as in Epist. Arist. 272 and 249 ('God grants you this, that all are pleased with you,' θεοῦ διδόντος σοι πρὸς πάντας χάριν). When Luke with Hellenistic aptitude uses ' charis ' thus (see below), it is invariably in the good sense.

In Sirach xxiv. 16 f. where Wisdom proclaims, " My branches are branches of glorious beauty (δόξης καὶ χάριτος), I am like a Vine producing what is delightful (χάριν, v. l. εὐωδίαν)," the Christian Latin translator added carefully, " in me is all the grace of the Way and the Truth," in order to fill out the sense of ' charis.'

(*c*) A third drawback to ' grace ' was that in non-Jewish circles it had acquired evil associations as it denoted favour, for favour might be and was taken in social and political life to mean favouritism. The Greek citizen swore an oath that he would act μήτε χάριτος ἕνεκα μήτ᾽ ἔχθρας, i.e. without any prejudice in favour of or against a fellow-citizen (e.g. Demosth. lvii. 63, *Orientis Graeci Inscript. Sel.* 789, Aristotle, Nik. Ethics v. 9, 12). In an Athenian court of justice ' charis ' was as irregular as vindictiveness (τιμωρία) ; it was the Greek equivalent for what a Hebrew termed ' respect of persons.' The good citizen pledged himself in public life to act without bias, and bias in favour of a friend or political ally, bias in favour of one who had bribed you or put unfair pressure upon you in any way, was ' charis.'

The only use of ' charis ' in the LXX of Ezekiel is in the similar, sinister sense of flattery or wheedling, when the prophet bursts out, *No more vain visions and smooth* (τὰ πρὸς χάριν) *oracles in Israel* (xii. 24) ! In rendering the lines of Proverbs xxviii. 23 :

> *He who will reprove*
> *gets more thanks than a flatterer,*

the LXX translators actually coined a verb from ' charis ' for ' flatter ' (γλωσσοχαριτοῦν), substituting this for the normal Greek verb χαριτο-γλωσσεῖν.

Josephus actually uses χάρις in contrast to the will of God, when he is arguing (Ant. iv. 29) that Moses did not elect his brother to be highpriest ; Aaron, the lawgiver protests, was not made priest by my influence (οὐ μὴν ἐξ ἐμῆς χάριτος). The associations of the term with partiality were evidently familiar. Had not Aristotle long ago used it for the under-hand influence which breeds political corruption ? " In a democracy small bodies are more liable than larger bodies to be corrupted either by bribes or by undue influence " (καὶ κέρδει καὶ χάρισιν, Athen. Polit. xli). But the ancient Hebrew normally dubbed this vice ' respect of persons,' and ruled it out of judicial precedure by warning judges that the Lord was absolutely impartial. *Let awe for the Lord control you ; be careful to act in that spirit* (of impartiality), *for the Lord our God knows nothing of injustice nor of favouritism* (θαυμάσαι πρόσωπον) *nor of bribing* (2 Chron. xix. 7). This Semitic conception (see Deut. x. 17, Jubil. v. 15) was shared by the NT writers in their own way, applied not to judges but to individual Christians in the social life of the Church. They are warned against the sin of προσωπολημψία (Col. iii. 25, James ii. 1), and reminded that as God judges human beings impartially (1 Peter i. 17, Rom. ii. 11) and has no favourites, i.e. as His grace or favour is not racial or national (Acts x. 34), He will not tolerate partiality or injustice in His people. Neither will He treat them on such lines. It is the spirit

of Woolman's protest in his Journal, when saddened by
reports of legal injustice to some slaves he writes (ch. v.)
to his American friends : " Many slaves on this continent
are oppressed, and their cries have reached the ears of the
Most High. Such are the purity and certainty of His
judgments that He cannot be partial in our favour." In
the only NT warning against bias (1 Tim. v. 21), however,
church officials are bidden beware of πρόκριμα and πρόσκλισις,
not against χάρις in this sense. Plainly the word was not
compromised as a religious term by its sinister associations
in democratic and imperial quarters. Like the Latin equivalent ' gratia,' it retained the higher meaning. Just as Cornelius Nepos could describe the popularity of Pomponius
Atticus at Athens by saying that " besides the influence
(gratiam) he exercised, he often aided the State in its poverty
by financial help from his own resources " (Vita Attici ii.),
so, in writers who adhered to the theocratic view of the
world, ' charis ' was by no means discredited as a term for
the divine favour to men.

It certainly is strange to a reader of the NT familiar with ἐν χάριτι
in its deep sense, to come across it as an equivalent for partiality, as in
Theocritus v. 39 where one character is told not to judge out of favouritism (κρίνειν ἐν χάριτι). The ethnic sense of χάρις on this lower
level occurs indeed in Acts. When Luke narrates how Roman gover-
nors deflected the course of judicial procedure in the case of Paul because
they wished to curry favour with the Jews, he uses the common phrase
χάριν καταθέσθαι (xxiv. 27, xxv. 9). Both Felix and Festus desired
to *ingratiate* themselves, as we say, with the Jewish authorities, who
actually begged Festus as a special favour (χάριν, xxv. 3) to arrange
matters so that they could have the apostle murdered.

II

GRACE IN THE OLD TESTAMENT

THUS χάρις commended itself to the apostle. It was familiar to his churches as a religious term in their Greek Bible, and also it had acquired or was acquiring some vogue in Egyptian circles of Jewish Hellenism as well as, perhaps, of ethnic syncretism. In these two quarters some antecedents of χάρις as a religious word may be traced; such a usage was limited in certain directions, but the limitations only serve to bring out the new content which Paul put into the term.

I

The truth of God's grace in the OT is rarely expressed in terms of ' grace.' God's free choice of Israel, embodied in the covenant with Abraham, is fundamental; the existence of the People is due to His goodwill, selecting them from the nations around. In the sacrificial system He had provided for the maintenance of fellowship with Himself, even when human failure threatened to interrupt it. The Law and the prophets glorify His patience and forbearance, His repeated acts of help, His vindication of the righteous cause. The hope of Israel lies in His generous, loyal aid, and nowhere else. Such fundamental truths, however, are commonly linked to the word ' hesed ' and its derivatives, and in the Greek Bible ' hesed ' was not rendered by χάρις but by ἔλεος, whereas χάρις was almost invariably used to translate the word ' chên ' in phrases like " to find favour with the Lord." What Paul does is to use χάρις in preference to ἔλεος when he speaks of the grace of God in Jesus Christ, and (as we have seen) to omit the phrase " find favour " altogether.

When the poet writes (in Job. x. 12),

Thou didst bestow upon me life and love,
my spirit was in thy charge and care,

he is using ' hesed ' for the divine love or favour, a thought which is
missed by the LXX ἔλεος and the Vulgate ' misericordiam,' though
the phrase ἡ δὲ ἐπισκοπή σου for the divine care in the second line
throws light upon a passage like 1 Peter ii. 25.

The passing of ' hesed ' into ἔλεος with its associations of compassion
is paralleled by the transition from the mediaeval Latin ' pietas ' or
religion to the Old French ' pieté ' and the English ' pity '; the latter
word was etymologically a form of ' piety,' so that Wyclif could render
the words of 2 Peter iii. 11 thus, " what maner men bihoveth you to
be in holy livings and pitees." The drawback, so far as ἔλεος is
concerned, was that the rich content of ' hesed ' was apt to be unduly
narrowed to commiseration, especially for sinful men. One most unfortunate example is in the twenty-third Psalm. The poet reflected
thankfully that ' Goodness and Kindness (hesed) ' would attend him
as the Lord's guest. The LXX not only reduced the two Angels of
life to one, but made that one ἔλεος, and the Vulgate followed suit
with ' misericordia.' But even if this compassionate regard was in the
poet's mind, it was by no means all that he intended. His outlook upon
life with its expectations of God's handling included much more than
' mercy.'

As for ' chên,' with its verb and adjective (always used of
God), like χάρις it denoted in later Hebrew beauty of speech
or of human form, the delight and charm of life, but χάρις
is never used for it in these connexions by the LXX (in
Eccles. x. 12 the word means ' favour,' not beauty), though
some periphrasis of χάρις is employed like εὐχάριστος or
χαρίτων. Even when ' chên ' denotes a kindly favourable
disposition, shown usually by a superior, it is not invariably
grace or pardon extended to sinners ; the range of the idea
is much wider.

The few wider uses of χάρις as rendering ' chên ' are in Zechariah
iv. 7, vi. 14, and xii. 10. On the last of these three phrases see below

(p. 355). The meaning in vi. 14 (εἰς χάριτα) is ' in honour of.' As for the enigmatic phrase in the LXX of iv. 7, there is equally little religious meaning attached to the term. One of Doddridge's hymns closes by declaring that grace, after working in the present life,

> Lays in heaven the topmost stone,
> And well deserves the praise.

This is an echo of the prophet's words which predict the successful building of the second temple in Jerusalem, when the leader of the community, according to the English Bible, ' shall bring forth the headstone with shoutings, crying, Grace, grace unto it ' (Zech. iv. 7). Such is not exactly the sense of the Hebrew, though it is a better rendering than that of the LXX which (ἰσότητα χάριτος χάριτα) went wrong upon a Hebrew word that puzzled the translators. The error, perpetuated by which was followed by the Vulgate (exacquabit gratiam gratiae), led Luther, for example, to remark that the text might be taken by some as a subtle allusion to the scholastic ideas of grace. In commenting on Psalm lxxiii. 2–3 (Weimar Edition iii. 478) he explains, ' Hanc differentiam gracie Zecharias exprimit dicens ; Exacquabit gratiam gratiae eius.' Et nostri usitatissimo verbo dicunt ' gratia gratis data ' et ' gratia gratificans.' But this scholastic distinction has no basis in the prophet's words. The Hebrew simply means a triumphant shout of ' Splendid ! Splendid ! ' from the beholders. Even if it is a prayer, ' Favour to it ! ' (from God and men), there is no thought of ' grace ' in the deeper sense of the term.

From the Greek Bible, therefore, Paul could derive little or no material for his message of grace, so far as language went. Knowing the broader sense of ἔλεος he could use it, with its verb and adjective occasionally, but he never quotes a single phrase about ' grace ' from the OT. For early Christians, to whom the Greek OT was a Christian book, the truth of the divine favour and active goodwill was as plain in its pages as was the absence of ' grace '-language.

2

One remarkable instance of this may be seen in the book of Psalms. There you find a gracious God, who gives and forgives, a God of loving-kindness and generous favour to His people, a God of goodness and mercy, in whose favour the upright find life. The Psalms at their deepest speak of His character and purpose in a way so moving that it does not seem possible for more to be said about His free and full blessing bestowed on human faith. Read the Psalms and you find practically everything about ' grace,' except the word itself.

It occurs twice and twice only, both times in a secondary sense. In xlv. 2 (ἐξεχύθη ἡ χάρις ἐν χείλεσίν σου) it is charm of words ; *charm is playing on your lips.* Even in lxxxiv. 11, where again it renders the Hebrew term ' chên,' the meaning is that the Lord bestows *favour and honour* upon the loyal and upright ; ' the Lord will give grace and glory ' calls up ideas which were not present to the mind of the psalmist, who was thinking of the devout being rewarded by God with the blessing of outward honour in the world. The collocation of χάριν καὶ δόξαν indicates that human goodness is not to be left dishonoured on earth ; it rests on the thought which opposes dishonour to favour or *grace* in Judith viii. 23, etc. Similarly, the sage in Ecclesiasticus (iv. 20.) can say that, even apart from any outward mark of God's favour, a good conscience is not a thing to be ashamed of but the reverse. *Be not ashamed concerning thy soul . . . for there is a shame that is δόξα καὶ χάρις,* i.e. *an honour and a credit;* the man who is not ashamed to speak the truth and to eschew evil is thereby honoured. Even in this passage on true and false shame the Greek term ' charis ' does not bear its full religious weight as yet ; as in the eighty-fourth Psalm the horizon is the present world, just as in the later Testament of Simeon (iv. 5), where men are bidden to live ἐν ἁπλότητι καρδίας, that God may bestow upon them χάριν καὶ δόξαν, i.e. favour and honour among their fellows. It is a long step from this to the range of the phrase in Justin Martyr (Dial. xlii.), when he speaks of the twelve apostles through whose voices ' the whole world has been filled with the glory and grace (i.e. the glorious grace) of God and his Christ,' or in Barnabas's close to his epistle, ' The Lord of glory and of all grace be with your spirit.' In his lines on ' The World ' George Herbert describes how the stately house of Life was almost demolished by Fortune, Pleasure, and Sin ; whereupon Grace intervened.

> Then Sin combin'd with Death in a firm band
> To raze the building to the very floor ;
> Which they effected, none could them withstand ;
> But Love and Grace took Glory by the hand
> And built a braver palace than before.

This collocation of grace and glory was outwith the range of the Psalter.

So deeply was this felt that later Christians often read back ' grace ' into the Psalms as they rendered them into other tongues. Thus the early Scots version of the eighty-third Psalm (a special favourite during the first half of the sixteenth century, when the reformed faith was struggling for existence) began,

> God, for thy grace, thou keep no more silence ;

and the ninety-first Psalm opened,

> O God, my hope and all my grace.

When Milton puts psalms into English verse he cannot help slipping in the term ' grace '; three times in the eightieth Psalm he expands ' Turn us again, O God ' into

> Turn us again ; thy grace divine
> To us, O God, vouchsafe.

In the eighty-sixth Psalm he not only puts the adjective in the first line (' Thy gracious ear ') but later on expands ' gracious ' into ' Readiest thy grace to show.' Similarly, Herbert feels that ' loving-kindness ' in the seventh verse of the fifth Psalm is the same as grace, as indeed it is, for the Greek ἔλεος here no more represents the original than the Latin ' misericordia '; he agrees with the metrical version,

> But in th' abundance of Thy grace
> Will I to Thee draw near.

In the fourth Psalm he is still more explicit :

> The Lord will hearken unto me
> When I His grace implore ;
> O learn to stand in awe of Him,
> and sin not any more.

Within your chamber try your hearts ;
offer to God on high
The sacrifice of righteousness,
and on His grace rely.

Again, when Thomas à Kempis meditates on Psalm xxx. 6f., it is terms of grace (*Imitatione Christi*, ii. 9). " One said, when grace was present, ' I said, in my prosperity I shall never be moved.' But he goes on to tell what his experience was when grace was absent : ' Thou didst hide thy face and I was troubled.' Never have I found any religious person who had not sometimes a withdrawing of grace, or an experience of zeal decreasing." He also comments thus on the eighth Psalm: " What is man, that thou art mindful of him, and the son of man, that thou visitest him ? What hath man deserved that Thou shouldest grant him thy grace ? "

3

In the OT as in the NT, however, not all the great grace-words contain the word ' grace.' A classical example is to be found in the opening lines of the hundred and fifteenth Psalm. ' Not unto us, O Lord, not unto us, but unto thy name give glory, for thy mercy and for thy truth's sake.' Or, as the Vulgate rendered it, ' Non nobis, domine, non nobis.' In common usage this has become a grace-word; it has been on the lips of men who disclaimed humbly any credit for their successes, and ascribed them gratefully to God. It is the psalm which Shakespeare's Englishmen, led by King Henry the Fifth, sung after the victory of Agincourt:

O God, Thy arm was here ;
And not to us but to Thy arm alone
Ascribe we all . . .
Be it death proclaimed through our host
To boast of this or take that praise from God
Which is his only . . .
Do we all holy rites ;
Let there be sung ' Non nobis ' and ' Te Deum.'

Originally the psalm was an appeal to God to act, lest His honour should be affected by the defeat or disgrace of His People. The singer implores Him to vindicate His name by vindicating those for whom He is responsible in the sight of the pagans; he asks this favour, not for the sake of any merit in the people, but simply from regard to God's reputation, as it were.

> *Not for us, O Lord, not for us,*
> *but for thyself, win praise,*
> *to prove that thou art kind and true.*

God's credit rather than the People's is the plea. The nuance of the verse is therefore not precisely what the popular interpretation of it has been, and yet the instinct which turned it into a grace-word is not alien to the original spirit of the hymn.

So, in the teaching of the Deuteronomist, any notion of self-righteousness is banned as incompatible with the Lord's free grace. Like his predecessor the prophet Hosea, he glories in the free, ungrudging affection of the Lord as the sole hope for an undeserving People. The Lord, as it were, has fallen in love with Israel; like a father He cares for the nation. But it is not on account of any merit, for the record of the People is broken and bad. *It was not because you were larger than any other nation that the Lord set his heart upon you and chose you. . . . Never say to yourselves, ' It is for my goodness that the Lord has brought me in to possess this country.' For no goodness of yours, for no integrity of mind, are you entering upon possession of the country . . . for you are an obstinate race* (Deut. vii. 7, ix. 4–6). The sheer love of God to undeserving men could not be put more stringently. It was the spirit of such high teaching that corresponded to the grace-gospel of the Christian Church, though the actual terms of grace were absent from the Deuteronomist's message.

Sometimes one might have expected that Paul would have availed himself of an OT word on the gracious favour of the

Lord, notably of the lines in the opening stanza of the sixty-fifth Psalm,

> *Though our sins be too much for us,*
> *'tis thine to cancel our transgressions ;*
> *Happy is he whom thus thou choosest—*

i.e. to draw near to Thy presence.   The LXX for ' choosest ' has ἐξελέξω καὶ προσελάβου, and the latter term is Paul's word for the divine welcome in Romans xiv. 3, xv. 7.   But ' cancel ' renders the LXX ἱλάσῃ, a verb which, as we shall see, the apostle avoids.   It is the spirit, not the letter of this divine welcome (indeed of the divine choice and forgiving call), which is echoed in the NT.

On the other hand, in echoing an OT phrase, the NT writers may turn it to bring out the gracious initiative of God more definitely. Thus in citing words from some current paraphrase of the sixty-eighth Psalm Paul makes God the giver of gifts, not the receiver (see below, on Ephes. iv. 8 f.) ; he preferred the traditional interpretation which represented man as in debt to God, since this accorded with his conception of grace divine.   *He granted gifts to men* in the Church.   Again, in recalling some scripture words from another psalm about man's confidence in God being justified by experience, Peter makes a slight but significant alteration for a similar reason.   The original made God's help the result of faith, but Peter makes it the reason for faith (1 Peter v. 7).   Instead of repeating the LXX version, ' Cast your anxious care upon the Lord, and he will sustain thee,' the apostle writes, Let all your anxieties fall upon him, for his interest is in you (ὅτι αὐτῷ μέλει περὶ ὑμῶν).   It is a very loose reminiscence of the last words in the fifty-fifth Psalm, but it proves how deeply the NT writer realized the gracious initiative of God in religion.   ' He will sustain thee ' is a deep truth, but it is a deeper re-assurance to know that God's character already elicits human faith and justifies it.   That God's eternal concern is for the faithful is even more than the fact that He will reward them for trusting in Him under the strain of life.   This is the supreme revelation to which faith, here as elsewhere, is always an answer.

III

GRACE IN THE WRITINGS OF PHILO

JUST at the time when Christians in the East were recognizing in the incarnation of their Lord the fulfilment of the word,

'Unto us a Child is born,
Unto us a Son is given,'

a wise man from the West was confessing that he could not conceive of God as given. The devout Philo believed in God the giver. No one in his day urged this religious conviction with more power and moving passion. But that God could be in any intelligible sense a gift to men, was beyond what he could understand. 'I know God as giving and granting favours (χαριζόμενον), but I am unable to conceive of Him as given' (Quod Deterius 44). The reason he offers is that what is given must be passive, whereas God as real Being must of necessity be active. For Philo nature and human nature were full of God's grace or 'gracious favours'; he saw God upholding the moral order by means of Powers or semi-personal forces working together for good, but these he never conceived as 'grace.' In other words, the religious philosophy of Philo had no place for a dynamic conception of 'grace.' When he thought and spoke of God at work, it was not in terms of 'grace,' which he confined to the inner disposition of God as Good or to specific favours bestowed upon mankind in creation and providence. Philo's transcendentalism prevented him from realizing that God could give Himself to men; He showers benefits and blessings on the godly, which ought to draw them to Himself in gratitude and service, Philo gladly declares, but He does not enter into human life in such a manner that His presence could be described as the gift of Himself to man's heart.

Such, however, was the belief of Christian faith, and one of its most characteristic and central expressions was ' grace ' divine, the imparting of God's own life to men as the supreme boon of existence, an endowment which was itself an active power.   This interpretation in terms of grace was a service rendered by the apostle Paul, who first taught the Church to believe not only in God as giving but in God as given through Jesus Christ His Son, and to recognize the active power of the grace or gift thus bestowed on men.

I

At most other angles, however, Philo's language reveals a wide use of ' grace ' in the interpretation of religion, for which we are unprepared as we come to it from the earlier Wisdom literature.   A new note is struck when a writer can express his faith thus, commenting on the words of Genesis xvii. 4 κἀγώ, ἰδοὺ ἡ διαθήκη μου μετὰ σοῦ (literally, "And I, behold my covenant is with thee ").   It is God saying, " There are many forms of covenant, conferring favours and gifts (χάριτας καὶ δωρεάς) on the deserving, but I myself am the highest kind of covenant. . . .   The source and spring of all favours (χαρίτων) is I myself " (Mutat. Nomin. viii.). A similarly mystical warmth is felt in the comment on Genesis xv. 2.   Literally " What wilt thou give me ? " is a wistful appeal of Abraham to the Lord for a son and heir, but Philo ingeniously reads it as the ecstatic cry of one who feels that God can have no more to give, after what He has so richly bestowed.   It is " the cry of one who is grateful (εὐχαριστοῦντος) for the fulness and greatness of the boons he has received," so satisfied that he has no more to expect or desire.   " O Lover of giving (φιλόδωρος), lavish are thy favours (χάριτες), limitless, unending ! " (Quis Rerum Divin. vii.).   This is preaching which sits loose to the text in order to rise into a rare height of religious emotion.   So is it in the comment upon Exodus ii. 23 (in De Legum Alleg. iii. 76), " The cry of the Israelites came up unto God," from their bondage in Egypt. The very fact that their prayer reached the Lord is a proof of His grace (μαρτυρῶν τῇ τοῦ ὄντος χάριτι), for only He could have inspired the prayer with power to rise to Him above the low level of the material universe ; such prayer could not have reached Him had not He been not only kind but generous in anticipating the need of men. Philo then adds the saying of Exod. xx. 24 to prove how great is the grace of the First Cause (τοῦ Αἰτίου ἡ χάρις), the words being, " I will come to thee and bless thee."

Like Paul, Philo never views the end in terms of grace, but this is because he lacks interest in eschatology altogether ; his sole prospect is the success of the Law as a natural, not as a national principle, which may be expected by God's grace to make a cosmopolitan appeal. What absorbs him is the effectiveness of this revelation here and now, and it is in discussing its conditions and processes within experience that he develops the vital truth of grace. To any divine purpose in the future of history he is indifferent ; the messianic hope fades from his horizon. But apart from this, Philo's teaching on religion might be not unfairly summed up, like Paul's, in 'All is of grace, and Grace is for all.'

Nothing is more characteristic of Philo than this emphasis upon the grace of God. He loves to use the word, often in a deep meaning. Thus he insists that the very activities and endeavours of the soul are due to God ; instead of attributing to itself any credit for moral achievements, the soul must acknowledge humbly that " moral attainments are due not to any power or strength in itself but to him who bestowed (χαρισάμενος) the very love of goodness " (Leg. Allegor. iii. 46). From the religious life he excludes anything like self-satisfaction. " See what grace (χάρις) belongs to the First Cause, in that he anticipates our hesitation and comes to meet us with all manner of benefits to the soul " (Allegor. Leg. iii. 76, a comment on Exodus xx. 24). " Often," he confesses, " when I get rid of a foul suggestion in my mind by a rush of good thoughts, it is God flooding my soul with his grace " (τῇ

ἑαυτοῦ χάριτι, Leg. Allegor. ii. 9).   One could compile a catena of
grace-passages from Philo, to illustrate his belief in the Creator raining
favours upon undeserving man, lavishing his graces (Philo is fond of
the plural) on life outward and inward.   This true philosopher, who
was at the same time genuinely religious, not an amateur like Cicero
writing about religion as a subject—this Alexandrian sage and saint
is never tired of speaking about God, and he never speaks very long
about any aspect of God without introducing grace, whether or not he
happens to meet the word in the OT section round which he is weaving
his religious philosophy.

2

In some sections, as he allegorizes the Graces, of whom
God is the Father, he is obviously indebted to Stoics like
Cornutus.   But in the less speculative passages it is a twofold aspect of grace that engages him, the universal range
of grace divine, not restricted to one race but bestowed on
man as man, and also, as a corollary from this, the utter
indebtedness of man to God.   The former flows from his
view of creation directly, as indeed the latter does also,
although it is specially stressed in reference to the moral
development of the race.

Thus, in describing the creation of the world (Opific. vi.)
he finds the gracious purpose of God at the very start, for
" God Himself, without help from any counsellor (παρακλήτος)
whatsoever, decided that it was needful to benefit (εὐεργετεῖν),
with favours (χάρισι) unmeasured and rich, that nature which
apart from the divine bounty (δωρεᾶς) could not of itself obtain
aught good."   Still more emphatic is the healthy protest
against merit in his description of the three failures of the
religious life (Sacrif. Abelis xiii.).   " Some, by forgetting
their blessings, lose that great treasure, thankfulness (εὐχαριστία).
Others by excessive pride think they have themselves made
the good that has befallen them instead of ascribing this to
Him who is really the Cause.   Others again . . . acknowledge
the Ruling Mind as the Cause of good (καλόν), but claim good

as their proper possession, holding that, as they are prudent, brave, self-controlled, and just, they are on that account worthy of God's favours (χαρίτων)." Philo was in touch with some ' philosophes ' in circles of culture at Alexandria who attributed the aims and attainments of life to human power, excluding anything like revelation or inspiration from above ; he also knew people who in less speculative ways took credit to themselves for moral purpose or relied on innate goodness for the pursuit of culture. His true consciousness of what religion meant is shown in passing protests, as, for example, when he tells how " God, who loves to give (φιλόδωρος) bestows (χαρίζεται) good things on all, even on the imperfect, encouraging them to a zeal for morality and a share in it " (Leg. Alleg. i., xiii.), or when he observes that " it belongs to God alone to sow and generate (γεννᾶν) the good in man " (Mutat. Nomin. xxiv.). In his own way Philo believed in the truth put by Pascal's Pensée, out of a Christian experience: " Pour faire d'un homme un saint, il faut bien que ce soit la grâce ; et qui en doute, ne sait ce que c'est que saint et qu' homme." The fact is, Philo is not unlike Pascal in his strong conviction that man is nothing apart from God. It is this belief which throbs in his allusions to grace. Like Paul himself, the Alexandrian sage raises, without solving, the problem of grace and merit, as Bréhier points out.[1] Grace comes freely to any man, not for the sake of merit on his part, and yet somehow the reception of it does depend upon a certain capacity. How these two truths are to be reconciled, we are not told. It is one of the ultimate mysteries for religion, and the importance of Philo lies in this, that for the first time the consciousness of this antinomy begins to be felt in his pages, felt perhaps more by his readers than by himself.

[1] *Les Idées de Philon*, p. 278.

3

Three differences between Philo and the early Christians on grace may be noted, however. (*a*) "O taste and see how gracious the Lord is," the psalmist wrote—ὅτι χρηστὸς ὁ κύριος, as the LXX rendered Psalm xxxiv. 8. Paul spoke freely of "the grace of the Lord Jesus Christ." But Philo could not talk thus. He distinguished the gracious name of ' God ' (θεός, χαριστικῆς δυνάμεως) from Κύριος or ' Lord,' which seemed to him royal or ruling in the sense of punitive (κολαστική : Somniis i. 162, Quis Rerum Divin. 166). In commenting on Genesis xxi. 33 (De Plant. 20) he explains that θεὸς αἰώνιος or ' Eternal God ' means not " One who is gracious (χαριζόμενος) at one time and ungracious at another, but invariably gracious . . . providing an uninterrupted succession of linked favours (χάριτας), never letting slip a single opportunity of benefiting men, though He is Lord (ὁ κύριος ὤν, ὡς καὶ βλάπτειν δύνασθαι)." [1] (*b*) Paul does not hypostatize Grace, as Philo hypostatizes the Graces, Wisdom, or the Logos. (*c*) Furthermore, as we shall have occasion to observe later on, the NT does not relate nature to grace. One of Philo's characteristics is that the constitution of the universe as well as the nature of man is the outcome of grace divine (compare Josephus, Apion. ii. 190 God, ἔργοις μὲν καὶ χάρισιν ἐναργής). It is the Stoic idea which recurs in Epictetus, where (i. 16. 15, ii. 23. 2) it is employed for the same practical end, to urge the duty of thankfulness for such benefits of creation. But in primitive Christianity the rational being of man and the origin of the cosmos are not referred to grace.

On the other hand, his remark on Genesis xv. 9 λάβε μοι (in God's word to Abraham) is important not simply for its own sake but because it is one of the Philonic passages which throw light on the meaning of

[1] In his *Kyrios als Gottesname* (iii. 701 f.) Baudissin shows how this term is primarily for Greek-speaking Jews a designation of the gracious God, not so much as above time as ever the same in helpfulness to His own.

John i. 14 (see below). These words, our author explains, mean (i) " that you have no good possession of your own ; what you think you possess, Another has provided." (ii) Also, " whatever you take, be sure to hold it as a trust or loan from the God who makes a newer grace replace an older one " (πρεσβυτέραν χάριν χάριτι νεωτέρᾳ ἀμειψάμενος : Quis Rerum Divin. 21).

Such data about grace in Philo are sufficient to show that he is interested in grace because he is interested in salvation, in the salvation of the soul as it finds its way into the invisible, inward world of realities, thanks to the gracious inspiration of God. For Philo, God is to be worshipped ; He is not simply an explanation of the cosmos, though He is conceived philosophically. The thinker's predilection is for the moral rather than for the metaphysical issues of life. Yet like the Stoics he does tend to regard salvation as the preservation of human beings by the gracious providence of God in the cosmos, and on the whole interprets God the Father as the Creator, when he speaks of the grace or graces with which human beings are endowed. As in the Timaeus of Plato, which influenced this type of religious thought in all directions, it is the cosmological aspect of the Deity which tends to be uppermost ; He is πατὴρ καὶ ποιήτης for Philo, if not Being or the First Cause (τὸ ὄν, ὁ ὤν, τὸ αἴτιον), and such a predominantly creative relationship prevails in allied movements like those represented by the Hermetic tracts.

IV

GRACE IN THE HERMETICA

POSSIBLY another source of grace-teaching may be found in the Hermetic theosophy. The term ' grace ' was used by some circles of the semi-Egyptian mysticism reflected in the corpus of writings called Hermetica or Poimandres, a labyrinth of cosmic revelations where a mystical doctrine of release from material conditions by means of re-birth is taught, the process being inspired by divine favour to helpless mortals. Unfortunately the literature is late, in its present form, and the efforts of Reitzenstein and Bousset to bring back part of it to the first century A.D. are more ingenious than convincing. But some elementary and characteristic form of the theosophy itself may well have been current in Egyptian circles during the first century, although we possess no reliable data on the exact date or provenance of the passages in which ' grace ' happens to occur. Some of these indeed may be tinged with Jewish, if not with Christian infiltrations, as they appear in their extant form. The type of gnosticism which the Hermetica breathe is generally nearer to Valentinianism than to anything else. Yet, considering the vogue of ' charis ' in the speculations of Philo, we may provisionally assume a certain likelihood that the term and the idea had already passed into this or that circle of contemporary syncretism. There is no proof that any NT writer was indebted to the conglomerate of the Hermetic tracts, but the latter represent a current of really pious belief in the initiative and revealing favour of the deity, which now and then throws up remarkable parallels in more than language to Philonism and primitive Christianity.

For example, we come across the Platonic belief in a divine communication of truth to the world, rousing, as it does in the devout mind of Philo, hopes which assume the form of a religious metaphysic. In the cosmos the soul is not left to itself, but visited and endowed with supernatural aid, till the mind or ' nous ' wins relief from matter.

In Hermetic theosophy the supreme reality is not spirit (which is semi-material) but mind (νοῦς) ; man is redeemed from ignorance by a sort of repentance, which is often of an ascetic character, but the so-called ' regeneration ' in this philosophy of religion means the substitution of the higher reason for sense-perception, i.e. a mental change in personality. The semi-divine Son of God or second deity creates in man a new form of being, and he who is possessed of this fresh ego acquires new modes of insight into the mystery of things. Whether Paul was unfamiliar with such categories of thought, or whether he deliberately ignored them, it is significant that he does not speak of regeneration ; it is baptism into Christ that he prefers as a symbol. One definite reason for preferring this to the notion of regeneration may have been that in the Hermetic theosophy the regenerate who rose to an upper level of being was relieved by ecstatic vision from the need for moral endeavour, whereas Paul's ethical passion required a conception which was devoid of such associations.

The divine initiative is stated in the first tract of the corpus. That Hermetic treatises were in existence by the second century may be inferred from the references in Tertullian and Clement of Alexandria, though what they were and how far they corresponded to any of the extant tracts, it is seldom possible to say. This first tract, however, betrays the atmosphere of the second century, and in it is the following revelation, made to a man who believed that he had received inspiration which fitted him for transmitting the higher ' gnosis ' to a darkened world. The Mind Divine commissions the worshipper to be a prophet of the truth. " I, Mind (Nous), come to the holy and good and pure and merciful, to pious folk, and to them my advent (παρουσία) proves a help ; straightway they know all and win the Father's grace (ἱλάσκονται) lovingly, giving thanks to Him in praise

4

and hymns " (*Poimandres*, i. 22). This is the Hermetist's way of saying, in Platonic speech, that the Creator-Father not only is accessible to men, but visits them with gracious revelations. Later on the worshipper prays, " Strengthen me, that having obtained this favour (χάρις)," of persevering in the knowledge of God, " I may enlighten my brothers, sons of thine, who are in ignorance."

Towards the close another characteristic specimen of this expectation of personal religion is found in the epilogue to the Poimandres, where the Hermetic worshipper is taught to address the deity thus. ' Thanks (χάριν) do we render to thee, O Most High . . . for by thy grace alone (χάριτι) have we received this light of knowledge (γνῶσις). O Name unutterable, thou whom we honour by addressing thee as ' god ' and bless by invoking thee as ' father '—for to all hast thou displayed fatherly goodwill and affection and loving-kindness . . . bestowing (χαρισάμενος) on us mind (νοῦς), reason (λόγος), and knowledge, mind that we may understand thee, reason that we may comprehend thee, knowledge that we may rejoice (χαίρωμεν) in the knowledge of thee our light and salvation. We rejoice that thou hast shown thyself to us fully. We rejoice that thou hast deigned to deify us when still we are in the body. The only thanks (χάρις) man can offer thee is to know thy goodness.' There are several features in a touching prayer like this which are relevant to our purpose, e.g. the variety of cognate terms, the association of grace and thanks and joy, and also the belief that a mystical ' knowledge ' of God is everything. But most significant is the belief in the divine initiative ; all that man enjoys is God's free gift. Or, as it is put elsewhere in the same corpus (i. 31), ' Holy is God, who willeth to be known and is known by his own,' the aim of this knowledge being to redeem the soul from the tyranny of Fate and Matter.

The Greek and the Latin texts are sometimes obscure, but details of uncertainty do not affect the essential meaning of the prayer. See

Walter Scott's *Hermetica*, i. 374 f., iii. 284 f., for a critical discussion. Bousset's review of Kroll's book in the *Gött. Gelehrt. Anzeigen* (1914, 697–755) seeks to prove that Cornelius Labeo, the authority of Arnobius for Hermetism, was prior to Suetonius, and therefore that the movement is at least contemporary with primitive Christianity.

The affinities between Philo's teaching and contemporary gnosticism of this kind are easily recognized. Thus his mystical piety turns upon a moral purification of the soul which results in transformation into the divine being ; repentance or conversion becomes an initiation, a change from ignorance to the ' knowledge ' by means of which the soul becomes fully conscious of God within, and this saving process is attributed to what Philo loves to call the grace of the Deity, just as we find religion stated in the Hermetica or in the cult-piety reflected by Plutarch's treatise on Isis.[1] The teaching of Philo on grace is unique, but it is not to be isolated from its environment ; it forms the chief but not the only element in a contemporary movement towards an emphasis upon the initiative of God in mystical religion before the rise of Christianity.

[1] See Bréhier, op. cit., pp. 245 f.

V

GRACE IN THE MYSTERY-RELIGIONS

MATTHEW ARNOLD pleads for appreciation of any form of religion, however quaint and limited, since all forms have been of some service to the race.

> Which has not fall'n on the dry heart like rain ?
> Which has not cried to sunk, self-weary man,
> Thou must be born again ?

The student of comparative religion would answer the poet by saying " Many." But in the second century, as Christianity began to move out upon its mission around the Mediterranean basin, it did find so-called mystery-cults making this demand or rather making this offer to the age. There was a widespread yearning for personal religion on the part of those who no longer found satisfaction in philosophical representations of the divine nature as the Absolute or in the older Olympian deities. The latter might have their gracious and genial moods ; some could be generous to their votaries. But the pressure of fatalism in the shape of astrology was heavy. Men wanted deities who could be touched with a feeling for their infirmities. When Prometheus in his agony cried, "Alas !" (ὤμοι, Agamemnon 980), Hermes coolly reminded him that " Zeus does not understand that word " ; it was not a word that the Olympian Father had ever learned ! But the soul now sought deities who were better acquainted with the human lot from within, and who were interested in man's wanderings, perplexities, and mortality. Gods were desired who might draw closer to actual life than the shining majestic Powers of traditional mythology, closer as they shared human existence and in sharing it ensured to their worshippers a triumph over evil and death. This yearning had created mystery-cults of a nature-kind. Into the processes of nature, with its annual rebirth, there was woven a mystical identification of the soul with some 'sympathetic' deity, as in the Isis cult pre-eminently. "Alle Schwärmerei ist und wird nothwendig Naturphilosophie," says Fichte. The cults, some of them Greek, like the Orphic and the Eleusinian, but the majority Oriental, illustrate the truth of this verdict; their highly wrought ritual, with its revivalist, emotional appeal, went back to the reproductive powers of nature, which were invested with a semi-mystical significance for the soul. Despite the sensual associations which, as in Hinduism, often assumed phallic symbolism, these cults ministered to the craving for a religion which was both individualistic and universal. A corybantic cult like that of the Magna Mater, for example, which penetrated the world from Asia Minor, represented the Great Mother as "full of tenderness and grace, and giving peace through her cleansing rites." [1] Figures like Isis and Serapis, as they passed out into the Hellenism of the Roman world during the first century, had acquired a rich humanism; their native rudeness was softened in the syncretism of the age, until they embodied large needs of the soul, promising to impart divine attributes to the individual, and especially holding out the satisfaction of a new birth for the soul, which meant that the ordinary man could be assured of divine support and satisfaction here and hereafter, not because he belonged to a nation or a city but to the god.

One deity of the cults, Dionysus, actually bear a name which suggests grace, but the suggestion is merely superficial. This Hellenistic deity was worshipped at Ephesus, where he was enthusiastically hailed by the crowd as Χαριδότης (see Plutarch, Demetr. ii. Anton. xxiv.), i.e. as the Giver of Joy and sweetly kind (μειλίχιος). In reality this title implies that while Dionysus was a militant power, he showed himself mild and delightful after war was done, providing χάρις or delight to

[1] Dill, *Roman Society from Nero to Marcus Aurelius*, p. 559.

his votaries. It is far-fetched to connect this conception with the allusions to ' grace ' in the Ephesian Fourth Gospel, as Grill attempts to do (*Untersuchungen über die Entstehung des Vierten Evglm.* ii. 104 f.).

Our direct evidence for the inside data of such cults is both scanty and late ; also, there is no evidence at all that ' grace ' was a characteristic term in any of them, with the exception of Hermetism, and Hermetism was not really a cult. Nevertheless, one or two of the ideas that gather round ' grace ' were operative in the piety of the mystery-religions. In some there was undoubtedly the recognition that any deity, to be of service to the hapless soul of man, must be gracious, and gracious not simply by showing favour but by entering into the sufferings of his votaries. The most popular cults were salvationist. Release by means of divine action was the core of their ritual ; by purification and a form of sacramental initiation a dramatic impression was made upon the votary, till he believed that he shared the death and resurrection of the god, and thereby was assured of life eternal. Thus, in the Orphic cult, the hope lay not in any endeavour of man but in the gracious favour of the θεοὶ λύσιοι or emancipating deities. In Orphism the release from an intolerable recurrence of things or deliverance from the wheel of being, which resembled the pitiless cycle of the Hindu *samsâra*, was certainly regarded as a boon bestowed by Dionysus upon his devout worshippers, if they were vegetarians and strict in observing the rites and regulations of the cult. " The self-reliance of older Greece is breaking down ; in humility of heart the pious look elsewhere for help." [1]   In the Isis-cult, particularly, there was a distinct recognition of some divine initiative ; man's craving for salvation was not only met but anticipated by the deity, if we may trust the sympathetic interpretation of Plutarch (De Iside xlii.), who hails Osiris

---

[1] Rohde's *Psyche* (Eng. Tr.), p. 342. See further on this point Kurt Latte's remarks in his fruitful essay on " Schuld and Sünde in der griechischen Religion " (*Archiv fur Religionswissenschaft*, 1921, pp. 278, 295, 296).

as the Giver of Good (ἀγαθοποιός), a name which also means, he declares, beneficent power (κράτος ἐνεργοῦν).

A century and a half later there is a partial parallel to NT language in the promise which Apuleius puts into the lips of Isis (Metam. xi. 5) as she encourages her votary to become initiated ; ' adsum favens et propitia . . . iam providentia mea illucescit dies salutaris.' One would fain believe that this grace-language was available for seekers in that cult. But it would be precarious to infer this from a poseur like Apuleius, a literary artist who picks up phrases from any quarter to suit his purpose. The historical student will always be chary of assuming without further evidence that such terms were used by Isis worshippers during the first half of the first century. And there is a further need for caution. It is one of the recurring difficulties in estimating the significance of these mystery-cults and especially their relation to contemporary Christianity, that certain terms are common to both ; the modern reader is prone to value them alike, whereas when they are employed by Christianity they possess a specific quality. A common instinct led to such terms being honoured in the mystery-religions and in Christianity. But experts are quick to offer warnings, apparently in vain as a rule, against the misleading practice of translating some Greek phrases of the cults or of Hellenistic piety by words like ' grace,' ' regeneration,' ' salvation,' ' purification,' and so on, or at any rate against reading into them a full Christian significance, as though ἁμαρτία, for example, meant for the average Greek what ' sin ' does. The same risk is run in translating what seem to be equivalents used by the Indian bhakti cult. The Sanskrit ' pasāda ' may correspond either to ' grace ' or to ' peace,' and yet it moves on another level of meaning : ' klesa ' is no more sin than ἁμαρτία, for it denotes the woe suffered by the soul under the grip of samsāra. The misinterpretation of such specious analogies is not a modern error. It is older than to-day. Thus there is no

historical evidence that the Eleusinian votaries understood
their rite to mean what Tertullian thought was ' regeneration.'
Nor was baptism in Mithraism the final sacrament that it
seems to mean to Christians. Nevertheless, there is sufficient
evidence to prove that these mystery-cults did evoke genuine
religious feeling in their better worshippers ; the rites represented a conviction that somehow the deity took an active
interest in the purification, the illumination, and the attainment of immortality by those who submitted to the ritual
and moral discipline of the group.

In these cults the idea of a gracious initiative on the part
of the deity is much more prominent than in contemporary
Judaism, at least in Palestinian Judaism. This was particularly marked in mystery-cults which produced a hero-
deity, who satisfied the craving for a god of rescue from the
material and mortal coils of existence, or from the grip of
fatalism, which in those days burdened life as the thought
of karma burdened the Indian soul. A typical representative
of this cult was the mythical man-god Asclepius, who was
hailed at his shrines as ' saviour ' from the pains of life.
Asclepius was a considerate, unselfish deity, the divine
Physician, who visited men on errands of healing. The
significance of his worship has been idealized, but it did
embody the longing for divine interposition of a sympathetic
kind, which was not satisfied with a deity of nature-life.

In Jewish Hellenism, as represented by the ' Wisdom of Solomon,'
the Spirit of God or Wisdom does pervade the world, as Stoicism taught ;
nay more, for the writer is a Jew, it amounts to God revealing and
imparting Himself to those who may be willing to receive Him. But
we do not feel here the urgency of personal religion which is so pathetic
and appealing in the cults and in bhakti.

What carried Christianity beyond the restrictions of a
national theism such as Judaism implied, and enabled it to
survive the competition of the various international cults, was
its distinctive interpretation of grace. The rich antecedents

only serve to bring out the originality of the gospel in this connexion. Thus, in repeating words of grace such as, ' This man receiveth sinners ' or ' by grace you are saved, and that by the gift of God,' the primitive Church was affirming the unity of two truths, of God over all and of God graciously entering human life. The cult-heroes of salvation, on the other hand, were not supreme. Above these deities there was Someone or Something higher ; the ' saving ' god might be commissioned to carry out his good work, but between him and the Supreme Power there was not the vital union that Christians saw in their God and Father with the Lord Jesus Christ His Son. *' Grace to you from God our Father and the Lord Jesus Christ* ' : ' God was in Christ reconciling the world to himself ' : such confessions of faith implied a relation of the Lord Jesus to God the Father which was different from any relation between the rescuer or friend of men and the higher Powers in the cult-worship. With this went the knowledge that Jesus had lived and died deliberately for the sake of men ; salvation was not a boon which was somehow connected with his experiences, it was the purpose of his life. And, as Paul also knew, the character of his Saviour or Lord was gracious. The unstinted, active love of God which met Christians in the order of grace or of the Spirit had been manifested in Jesus on earth with a reality which all could verify. It was as he was sure of what Jesus had been and was, that Paul could speak about grace and peace. The character and mission of the Lord explained all this and justified belief in it as no cult-worship ever succeeded in doing.

In cults like those of Isis and Orphism particularly, belief in the soul as saveable, in the divine initiative, and in a sacramental embodiment of faith in this divine initiative, is adumbrated. At the latter point, the symbolism of the cults may have furnished Paul with suggestions, in his restatement of baptism as a mystical process of dying and rising again in or with Christ. Otherwise there is little or no evidence that the sacramentalism of the cults entered into his theology with any direct influence.   In point of fact, the NT shows practically no sign of the primitive Christians having been sensible of the cults as serious rivals of their faith.   Now and then we may surmise that this or that item in mystery-religions lies in the background, but apparently the vogue of the cults was not felt by Christians until the second century.   Some of the early converts from paganism must have been familiar with their beliefs and practices, but the NT writers never warn their readers against the contemporary cults as if the latter formed a serious factor in the situation.   Probably, like Plato confronted with Orphism or Philo with Egyptian cults, they instinctively disliked what they knew of them, whilst at the same time they availed themselves occasionally of ideas and words current in the movement generally.

VI

GRACE IN THE RELIGIOUS PHILOSOPHY OF THE AGE

WHEN Faust is borne to heaven, the angels exult that to one who has put forth all his powers the help of heaven is given for his salvation.

> Wer immer strebend sich bemüht,
> Den können wir erlösen.

Man's activity, said Goethe to Eckermann in explanation of the chorus, " becomes ever more high and pure, and there is eternal love ever coming to his aid. This corresponds to our religious belief that we cannot attain blessedness by our own exertions but only by the help of heavenly grace." It is not so much the Pauline as the general thought of grace, however. And in the first century this belief was widely diffused. A more or less vague consciousness of divine power somehow drawing near to men reappears in preachers of philosophy as well as among votaries of the mysteries. Thus a really profound sense of man's dependence upon God is overheard in some of the most moving passages in Epictetus, when his warmth of tone becomes theistic in form. As e.g. in his remonstrance with the discontented rebellious spirit (iv. 1. 101 f.) which will not learn to say (if we may put into his lips the equivalent Bible phrase), ' The Lord hath given, the Lord hath taken away. Blessed be the name of the Lord.' You mutter, says Epictetus, that God is hard on you. ' He who has given takes away.' Well, but ' after receiving everything, even your very personality, from Another, are you going to chafe and grumble at Him the Giver, if He removes something from you ? . . . Was it not He who brought you here ? Did not He show you the light ? ' And so on. This is not far from the spirit of the words,

'what hast thou that thou hast not received ?' The truth
is that we have here another 'praeparatio evangelica,' in the
warmer current of religious and even theistic feeling which
is traced back to Poseidonius, the recognition that the soul
of man as part of the world-spirit needed aid from above
in its struggle to be brave and good, a recognition voiced by
Seneca (e.g. Epist. xli. 2–5, 'no one can be good apart from
God,' good, that is, in facing adversity), and in the famous
lines of Manilius which begin

> Quis caelum possit nisi caeli munere nosse,
> Et reperire deum, nisi qui pars ipse deorum est.

Yet all this leaves the difference between the Christian faith
and the religious philosophy of Stoicism the more distinct.
As Liechtenhan sums up, after his sympathetic and critical
study of the Stoic mission,[1] even in this movement of Poseidonius and his school we do not find rationalism being replaced
by a real belief in revelation. " The element of affinity with
the divine is praised indeed by Poseidonius as a divine gift,
but at bottom it is an original factor of nature, whereas in
Paul it is a marvel of grace, it is redemption. . . . The Stoic
says to his god, ' I have come to thee ' ; Paul says, ' Thou
hast drawn me to Thyself by pure gracious favour.' No
doubt this requires something in man which responds to the
call, answers it, and acts upon it. But with Paul the initiative
lies always with God ; in Stoicism it lies with man " (p. 117).

I

The sense of dependence on God in these contemporary
circles is notable. Saint-Cyran was moved by the ethical
fervour of treatises like Cicero's De Officiis to exclaim, " Dieu
a voulu que la raison fît ses plus grands efforts avant la loi
de Grâce, et il ne se trouvera plus de Ciceron ni de Virgile ! "

[1] *Die göttliche Vorherbestimmung bei Paulus und in der Poseidonianischen
Philosophie* (Göttingen, 1922).

One might remark that writers like Epictetus, Plutarch, and Marcus Aurelius, who lived after Christianity, show even more of the religious spirit which acknowledges the need of higher help than man. Still, so far as ' grace ' means this confession that man's faculties are of themselves insufficient for the satisfaction of his requirements and moral aspirations, the religious side of Stoicism did furnish an atmosphere in which this truth throve. There were indeed writers like Musonius Rufus who refused to share such a view.[1] A humanistic eddy is perceptible in their protests against the Poseidonius-teaching, as though they feared the moral energy of man was compromised. Yet on the whole there was a recognition that man could not face the universe without some support from sources other than his own capacities. In a man like Epictetus this is all the more impressive, as it is incongruous with the monism of his metaphysic. Yet, whether due to some personal temperament or to an infusion of the general Oriental religious emotion which worked in Poseidonius from his Syrian background, it is significant that there is a widespread refusal to regard God finally as an indifferent principle of existence or as an abstraction. God does provide for the world, say such Stoics, and He provides man with reason and conscience as well as with a standard of religious imitation. Some belief in revelation even under- lies the popular passion for divination ; it was dimly felt that the deity could not have left man without direct instruc- tions at times about how the world went. All this was part of a general current which is to be traced in Orphism and Neo-Pythagoreanism. It is not quite isolated from the cults, and yet it has its distinctive features, so far as ' grace ' is con- cerned, for the Stoic presentation did more justice than the cult-worship did to the religious need for an objective element in the idea of God ; the emotionalism of the cults tended

---

[1] E.g. in the Pelagian assertion, πάντες φύσει πεφύκαμεν οὕτως ὥστε ζῆν ἀναμαρτήτως καὶ καλῶς, οὐχ ὁ μὲν ἡμῶν ὁ δ' οὔ (Stobaeus ii. 183.1).

to emphasize the experience of the individual, whereas the philosophic statement allowed for the objective aspect of religion, without which religious feeling, however warm, is in the long run inadequate.

2

Here again Christianity as a religion of grace embraced both ideas, by its revelation of grace entering human life in a historical person who was vitally part of the divine nature, and by its conception of grace as the revelation of a divine purpose, not of occasional truths about the future. Most definitely the two may be compared in regard to the desire for redemption from fate. It is not clear to what extent Paul was indebted to Stoicism for any part of his interpretation of the gospel to the Greek world. Possibly behind his argument (in Gal. iv. 1-10) about deliverance from the Law as part of a fatalistic system of the Elemental Powers, there may be some idea of the latter as inferior deities contributing to the reign of Law—a notion traced by Reitzenstein to the pre-Christian Mandean cult.[1]   In the argument of Romans viii. 14 f., the apostle seems to be conscious of the prevalent need for escape from Destiny or Fate, but for him redemption is primarily relief from the power of moral weakness and guilt rather than, as in Hellenistic religion, from cosmic tyranny of the stars.   Thus in Romans v.-vi. he does not condescend to notice the superstition of astrology, according to which the planets were really responsible, as circumstances were, in some Stoic circles, for human error.   Not that the astral mysticism stripped life entirely of moral responsibility, any more than did the fatalistic monism of the Stoics.   Yet neither was conducive to a sense of personal responsibility, and on the latter the apostle builds his message of grace. Grace, in short, for Paul denoted much more than the emanci-

[1] *Das Mandäische Buch des Herrn*, 36 f.

pating power of the divine favour as presented either in Hermeticism or in other circles, where deliverance came to mean release from the material heritage of the body which culminated in the restoration of the soul to metaphysical re-union with its source in the deity.[1]

[1] See Latte in *Archiv für Religions Wissenschaft*, 1921, pp. 290 f.

VII

AFFINITIES WITH CONTEMPORARY MOVEMENTS

IT is in the gnostic movement that the two characteristics
of all this piety are really taken up, viz. that (*a*) salvation
is the preservation of the soul-stuff in the individual (which
is the tenet of astral Hellenism), and (*b*) that redemption is
enlightenment or ' knowledge.' These notions are outside
the development of primitive Christianity as it is reflected
in the NT. The term ' salvation ' must not mislead us
here. Deliverance from danger, from illness, from political
oppression, and even from errors of the mind—all this and
much else was covered by the word ; above all, it could
serve the purpose of a cosmic mysticism. This latter possibility made it welcome to the later gnostics. As for knowledge
' the gnosis of God ' becomes in the Hermetic writings almost
a personified Power of God, acting on life. It does open
into a conviction of the divine Providence which selected
chosen souls for escape into a personal union with the Deity.
But the sequel to this is the gnostic theosophies, not the
NT writings. At the same time, familiarity with the piety
of the cults, particularly with mystery-religion such as that
of the Isiac groups,[1] must have helped to popularize the
purer faith of the Church. Already there were increasing
numbers of people who were depressed and anxious, needing
to be lifted into some higher world, and assured of a hope
beyond the grave, even of a fellowship with gods in this life
which would bring relief from the strain or stain of existence
in the flesh. And this relief, they were taught by the cults
to believe, came not from their efforts alone ; it was not
their doing, but revealed and imparted to them by the deity.
The preaching of the gospel drew upon such materials in its

[1] See Clemen's paper in *Neutestamentliche Studien für G. Heinrici*, 28–39.

environment. They were anticipations of some truths in Christianity as a religion of grace, whether grace was viewed in terms of revelation or of redemption. Round the primitive church was a world in which, so far as interest in the gods went, the situation was favourable to a propaganda of religion as grace. The very Greeks who sought for ' wisdom ' were not seeking it in the old sense of the term, but as a religious concept. Both the religious philosophy of the Stoics and the Hellenistic piety of the cults felt for a God who was not what a modern describes as

> " Some unit of cold thought,
> Such as Greek sages gave to Christian saints,
> A primal number, lone, creationless."

There was a widespread emotion of the supernatural, which took the form of belief in the divine nature as somehow interested in the personal life of men, with an interest which identified the god with his worshipper, and which implied an action of heavenly providence upon mortal existence. All this made for the reception of Christianity as a message of divine initiative.

In this general period, roughly speaking, between 150 B.C. and A.D. 150, there is a stirring within religion, which we may describe by thinking of it as four concentric circles. (i) The first and most inclusive is belief that the universe is neither malign nor indifferent to the human spirit, but that, however handicapped the soul may be, it possesses allies and resources within the moral order : (ii) It is an advance upon this semi-theistic attitude when God is conceived as making known His saving purpose and taking steps to realize it, so that man may be aware of it and co-operate with it. This is, in a high form, the level of grace within the OT religion; God is gracious as He befriends those who carry out His revealed will : (iii) A further step was taken when the divine initiative was stressed by those who sought and found religious satisfaction in an epiphany or incarnation, which brought the deity nearer to human life. It is this feature, common to all grace-religions, which carries faith beyond (i) and (ii). What forms the quest of the soul is no longer intercourse with God or dutiful obedience to Him, but the union of man with Him as the result of some personal movement upon His part. (iv) Finally, this intuition is expressed by Christianity in the form of belief in the divine Son entering life to die and suffer and triumph over death, thus fulfilling the hopes and satisfying the needs of mortal, sinful men. Historically, the interest of this period, from about 150 B.C. to A.D. 150, is that under a breath of God there was a simultaneous and varied rise of such ' grace-movements ' throughout the world. From some inner springs they bubble to the surface of the dry earth. These two centuries witness the vogue of apocalyptic piety in the later Judaism, of Jewish Hellenism, of which the chief representative known to us is Philo of Alexandria (though in Egypt he had contemporaries and predecessors who were θειοὶ ἄνθρωποι), of the semi-gnostic Egyptian theosophy represented in the later Hermetica, of the mystery-cults, particularly the Egyptian Isis-cult, of the current of religious philosophy which is attributed to Poseidonius, and in India of the attractive bhakti-pietism which underlies the contemporary Bhagavad-Gita. The last is only a parallel. But the others entered into the religious situation of primitive Christianity.

Of all these growths on the rich soil of the grace-interest between 150 B.C. and A.D. 150 only two survived, Christianity and Hindu bhaktism. Both had a severe struggle for existence. Both started religious problems, for the famous Cat or Monkey controversy in India corresponds to the Pelagian dispute in Christianity. Both encountered opposition. The bhakti faith of the Bhagavad-Gita, a remarkable effort to graft personal religion of a grace-type on the stem of the caste-system, was like a white flower nearly choked by weeds in late days. Its hero Krishna became degraded by rank growths of sensualism in the Puranas. Nevertheless,

it enjoyed a mediaeval revival, like grace-Christianity in Europe during
the sixteenth century.

In Jewish Hellenism, especially as it is voiced by Philo,
(ii) is carried to a remarkable length. The religious philosophy of the period developed (i) with a vague but significant
intensity, until it was as near to (ii) as any movement could
reach which lacked the Hebrew sense of sin. The mystery-
religions in their elementary forms represent (iii) with a new
accent and appeal ; but the universe, now viewed under the
sombre light of fatalism, is practically unfriendly, and the
worshipper has to be rescued from it by means of identification with some deity, just as in the higher forms of bhakti
the Indian sought to draw breath under the fatalistic samsāra
of monism. The apocalyptic piety also had its despair of
the present world, but it had more hope than despair, and the
hope did not look to a severance of the worshipper from history
and the world, as the Hermetic and the bhakti faiths did.
In apocalyptic religion the decisive factor was not simply
the divine intervention in the struggle but an intervention
in and through history, which neither reduced the soul to
nothingness before the Infinite nor held out as its best hope
the prospect of individual incorporation with the divine
outside the moral order of the world. The Bhagavadgita
or ' Lord's Song ' with its idea of incarnation repeatedly on
the part of the deity is nearer to Christianity than the mystery-
cults, though in using the literary form of a dialogue it corresponds to the Hermetica. But the cults did preach a god
who suffered, as the Indian classic could not. It is true that
their deities were mutilated or murdered hero-gods as a rule,
yet they were superior in this aspect to the Bhagavadgita,
which, for its mystical philosophy of a gracious relationship
between the soul and the Divine, had to posit an apotheosis
of Krishna.

One blessing of nearly all these grace-movements was
supposed to be the redemption of man from what the apostle

Paul called 'the beggarly Elements' of the world, i.e. from the paralysing grip of a cosmic necessity.   Relief from this was promised in the shape of fellowship with a deity whose favour meant 'salvation.'   It was at this point that Christianity at once approached and drew away from all these movements.   In its truth of grace there was a distinctive quality which came to light as it developed among the forces of its period.   Self-sacrifice in the heart of God and a deep consciousness of sin in the human soul, these are implicit in Christianity as it emerges.   But where else ?

For the bhakti cult see *Love in the New Testament*, pp. 11 f.   Dr. Otto's book on *India's Religion of Grace* (1930) gives a sympathetic account, and there is a special monograph by K. Hutten on *Die Bhakti-Religion in Indien und der christliche Glaube im Neuen Testament* (Stuttgart, 1930).   But for soundness of estimate there is no book like Dr. Sydney Cave's *Redemption, Hindu and Christian* (1919), especially pages 98 f., 179 f., and 219 f.

PART B
JESUS AND GRACE

JESUS AND GRACE

I

THE TRUTH OF 'GRACE' IN THE SYNOPTIC GOSPELS

JESUS never speaks of grace, and none of his disciples ever applied the word to him. Like hope and freedom, grace does not occur in his teaching as preserved by the gospels. Yet the ideas of all three religious words are there. While the writers of the gospels never put 'grace' on the lips of the Lord, they preserved traditions which show how the truth of grace was implicit in his mission.

(*a*) He was in the world to further and fulfil the Father's will and purpose for his own. This conviction underlies his preaching of the kingdom. 'Last of all he sent to them his son'; 'it is your Father's good pleasure to give you the kingdom'; 'the Son of man is come to seek and to save the lost.' Whether he was viewed as the messianic Son of David or as the second Moses, his authority rested on the divine will; the course of service on which he entered was undertaken by him as a commission from God, and all his help by word or deed was inspired from above. In other words, the initiative lay with God.

As the synoptic tradition deepened, this was brought out more precisely. Thus Mark relates how he said ' I came out here ' (from Capernaum, to preach far and wide throughout the country), but Luke alters it to ' I was sent ' (from heaven for this purpose). That is, a local reference (Mark i. 38) is changed into an allusion to the divine mission (Luke iv. 43). Jesus is 'sent' by God in the primitive tradition (Mark ix. 37, xii. 5, Matt. xv. 24), but this is emphasized in the Fourth Gospel, where the priority of God's love is axiomatic, and the vocation of Jesus is interpreted less in terms of a messianic commission than as the fulfilment of the divine aim of loving care for men.

(*b*) The new note of spontaneous interest is sounded in his search for men, that is, in his direct appeal to the sinful

75

and degraded. Instead of leaving them severely to themselves or being content to promise them forgiveness if they
repented, he sought them out with his message from God.
He encouraged them and led them to God by his intercourse
with them.   This direct approach, as Mr. Montefiore admits
(*The Synoptic Gospels*, second edition, ii. 520), is more than
any rabbinic piety practised.   " The virtues of repentance
are gloriously praised in the rabbinical literature, but this
direct search for, and appeal to, the sinner, are new and
moving notes of high import and significance.   The good
shepherd who searches for the lost sheep, and reclaims it,
and rejoices over it, is a new figure."

Thus, after showing that God opened His realm to those
who on the current Jewish view had the least right to expect
it (Matt. v. 1 f.), Matthew describes how Jesus made this
the determining note of his mission (viii. 1 f.) by dealing
with lepers and pagans, who belonged to classes outside the
pale and were conventionally ranked as ' sinners.'   He cared
nothing for ceremonial defilement or caste taboos if he could
come into touch with those who needed God, though they
might be ostracized by the Pharisees.   The latter were
genuinely anxious at their best " to make the return of the
sinner easy."   Judaism did proclaim " God's readiness to
take the first step," but " it was inclined to leave the initiative
to the sinner." [1]   Whereas Jesus showed God taking the
first step.   The distinctive feature of his mission, in practice
as well as in preaching, was this deliberate initiative.   " I
have come," he said repeatedly, come to heal and help.   Twice
Luke alters the $\mathring{\eta}\lambda\theta o\nu$ of Mark and Matthew to $\mathring{\epsilon}\lambda\mathring{\eta}\lambda\upsilon\theta a$ (v. 32,
vii. 33, 34), but the sense is the same ; what Jesus means is
not simply " I am here, on the spot," but " I have come for
this purpose."

(*c*) The section upon rank and reward in the Realm of
God, which is preserved in Mark x. 13–48, shows further

---

[1] Abrahams, *Studies in Pharisaism*, i. pp. 58 f.

the opposition of Jesus to the popular merit-religion of his day. Thus his answer to the rich young ruler implies that to gain a foothold in the Life or New Age was not an achievement of obedience to the Torah. But more definitely still his reply to the disciples afterwards is decisive on this point. Naïvely they ask, " Then who can be saved ? " If salvation is so difficult, if even a rich man finds the way of life so hard, who can attain it ? The answer, " With men it is impossible but not with God ; anything is possible for God," states the religious truth which Paul afterwards enunciated.

Indeed several critical editors have to use the very term ' grace ' at this point, in order to explain the heart of the saying. No other term answers so adequately to the truth and principle of these words. Professor Bacon (*Studies in Matthew*, p. 240) describes this story as one of " the forms of contrast between the religion of Law and the religion of Grace " ; Lagrange observes that " cette parole très authentique de Jésus contient en germe la doctrine de Paul " (i.e. of God's grace being needed for salvation) ; Wellhausen's comment is, " Die höchste Anstrengung wird gefordert, aber sie ist Gnade Gottes " ; Loisy explains, " Les hommes, par leurs propres lumières et leurs propres forces, ne sont pas capables du sacrifice qui est exigé d'eux, mais la grâce de Dieu peut suppléer à leur infirmité."

It is the same with the answer to the equally naïve remark of Peter, when the rich young ruler had gone away and thus failed to meet the test. " Lo (ἰδού, well, but look at us), we (ἡμεῖς) have left all and followed thee ! " He calls attention to the sacrifices made by the twelve, implying, as Matthew actually adds, " And what are we to get (by way of reward for our devotion) ? " Jesus in his reply fully recognizes that self-sacrifice will have its due reward, though not exactly the reward which Peter perhaps expected ; but he closes with the warning, ' Many who are first will be last, and many who are last will be first ' (when the final reckoning is made). That is, even the fact of the twelve being among the first to believe is not a title to supreme rank in the Realm ;

that does not *ipso facto* entitle them to any prerogative. God judges not by such claims to pre-eminence or merit.

How natural it was for an Oriental to assume that priority in service entitled a man to special claims, may be seen in the history of Islam, as Wellhausen points out. " Auch im Islam werden die früheren Genossen des Propheten von der späteren unterschieden, beide von den erst nach seinem Tode hinzugekommen, und auch unter diesen wiederum die älteren von den jüngeren. Während aber im Islam der Vorgang der zeitlichen Priörität durchaus anerkannt wird, wird er in unsere Parabel " (he is referring to Matthew xx. 1–16) " geleugnet, wenigstens was den Lohn anbetrifft."

The word to the sons of Zebedee, *it is not for me to grant seats at my right or my left hand—these belong to the men for whom they have been destined* (Mark x. 40, Matthew adding *by my Father*) again stresses the sovereign will of God and at the same time discourages any thought of prerogative. But more vital is the teaching of the parable which Matthew has preserved at this point, the story of the workers in the vineyard (xx. 1–16). It is an answer to Peter's query, *What are we to get?* The point of the parable is that men must not try to bargain with God, and that the final principle of His dealings with men is generosity. What the tale teaches is not that men can earn heaven or that God is arbitrary or that there are no differences of position in the next life, but simply that there must be no complacent or calculating attitude towards Him. Jesus brushes aside any such estimate of religion, and especially the idea that those who became His disciples first could plume themselves upon getting a richer reward than those who came into the kingdom later. Just as, in the parable of the prodigal son, the criticism of the older brother serves to bring out the generosity of the father, so here the petulant criticism offered by the disappointed workers leads to the full climax at the end. All notions of self-esteem in the religious life are ruled out. In such parables, as in the story of the Pharisee and the Publican, the essence of what Paul meant by opposing grace to works is contained, nowhere perhaps so trenchantly as in the parable of the servant and the farm (Luke xvii. 7–10), where *We have only done our duty* is set forth against any thirsty claim for thanks or reward. Jesus never bribes men nor bargains with them, and men, he teaches, must never think to bargain with God. Whilst God will take account of human life, He does not keep account-books against man ; nor is He to be regarded as One with whom we can hold reckoning upon the score of this and that item of credit.

This danger of religion was not unmarked by the more spiritual rabbis. One traditional protest was : " Be not like servants who minister to their lord on condition of receiving a gift (or, reward), but be like servants who minister to their lord without expecting to receive a gift ; and let the fear of Heaven be on you " (*Pirke Aboth*, i 3) The last clause corresponds to the " fear and trembling " of Philippians ii. 12 ; it means the deeply conscientious spirit which is afraid of failing in the service, an overpowering sense of reverent responsibility which is the very opposite of an easy-going temper of obedience. As for the saying itself, it is a warning against the Pharisaic pride which Jesus disliked. But so long as the Law was conceived as a code with one duty and another of various degrees of difficulty, the temptation to self-esteem was always present. When the will of God was conceived as love, not as a detailed code of quantitative morals, the temptation was removed ; then the servant could never think he had done enough, and he could not dream of claiming credit for what he had done. According to Jesus the divine will for life was a unity, determined by the inward spirit or motive ; it was no longer so many manifold precepts obeyed as parts of a code. The moral personality was confronted with the will of the royal heavenly Father as a will of love. This ultimately differentiated his teaching from that of scribism, and eliminated the notion that one could do extra service and thereby accumulate credit. The type of Pharisee denounced by Jesus was the unworthy type afterwards exposed by the rabbis as the ' What-is-my-obligation-and-I-will-do-it ? ' Pharisee.[1] But more than Pharisees shared this complacent

[1] See Klausner's *Jesus of Nazareth*, pp. 213 f.

spirit which imagined it was capable of doing even extras in the way of obedience, and on that ground could afford to feel superior to those who were less devout and strict in the community. Such a temper of the Precisians led to a wrong attitude towards God and man. It was a widespread source of self-righteousness as well as of censoriousness, and for both reasons it was alien to the teaching of Jesus upon love. Paul's interest in denouncing false καύχησις is precisely this interest of Jesus, as voiced in sayings like those of Matthew xviii. 21 f., xx. 14 f., and Luke xvii. 7 f., none of which, by the way, is anti-Pharisaic.

(d) The Realm or order in which this divine will would be finally realized, depended upon his mission. What inspired him was the conviction that he was sent on a vocation shared by no one else, not even by the great prophet John, and this vocation came to involve the sacrifice of himself in the interests of those who were called to the Realm. There is evidence that he faced death not simply as a prophet of old who had to suffer for loyalty to spiritual ideals, but as one whose death was to be decisive for the inauguration of a better Era than the present. This consciousness is occasionally expressed, as for example in the saying of Mark x. 45 :

> *The Son of man has not come to be served but to serve,*
> *and to give his life as a ransom for many,*

and definitely in the interpretation of the cup at the Last Supper :

> *This means my covenant-blood which is shed for many.*

In the latter passage—one of the best authenticated in all history—the employment of the gracious term ' covenant ' (already associated with ' ransom ' in the LXX of Psalm cxi. 9) throws light upon the former. It indicates that the institution of the Supper, with this redeeming significance, was " not the improvisation of an instant, but the ripe fruit of all his life and indissolubly connected with the great object of his work on earth." [1]   His death was not to be unavailing,

---

[1] Resch, *Paulinismus*, p. 342.

a silent protest against human misconception and hatred, but the inauguration of the new Era promised and prepared by God the Father. Behind a saying like the former lies the consciousness of a mission like that of the Suffering Servant ; service, death, and redemption, are knit together.

That this was present to his mind is more than probable.   In what sense he called himself Son of Man, we cannot say, but the only critical question nowadays is how often he used the title and how he understood it.   The apocalyptic connotation in Judaism may have been affected by some Iranian speculation [1] about a figure called Man, who was supposed to appear in the world on a mission from his Father, suffering on earth and finally saved by God, so that he became " the agent and means and example of humanity's redemption, re-appearing at the end of time as the head and pledge of the redeemed."   But this is a remote and doubtful reconstruction, which in any case corresponds to Marcionitism and gnosticism rather than to primitive Christianity.   ' Son of man ' had acquired other significance by the time that Jesus used it.   Like the Suffering Servant, it was a form of thought inherited from the faith of Judaism ; the reality was his consciousness that his death no less than his life was needed by God for the kingdom to come.   When discussion turns upon the ' messianic ' nature of his vocation, the underlying thought is that his life of obedience led to a death for the redeemed, which realized the divine purpose.   As Jesus anticipated, it was to be followed by a resurrection.

[1] Reitzenstein, *Das Iranische Erlösungsmysterium*, p. 117.

II

RECOGNITION OF JESUS' 'GRACE' BY THE PRIMITIVE CHURCH

FROM the first this was believed by the Church. Had not Jesus lived and taught and died and revealed himself after death as the Lord, there would never have been any word of grace in Paul's teaching. That his life led to a death in which the new 'Covenant' was inaugurated by his blood and ratified by his resurrection, was the assured faith of the primitive Church. Jesus who had sacrificed his life 'for many' was alive in power as Christ. Without such a gospel, as Professor Bacon pertinently asks,[1] how could the faith of Peter and the Galilean disciples have rallied from the shock of Calvary? But this was not all. Jesus was not merely believed to have done this ; he intended to do it, and he did it. The authentic tradition underneath the synoptic gospels attests this : at some period and in some way Jesus became aware that his death no less than his life was needed by God for the kingdom to come. This is not a post factum explanation of what had occurred. " In the beginning was the preaching or kerugma," we are sometimes told ; the preaching of Jesus as Lord is the first stage in the Christian movement. Behind that, we are in a mist of vague uncertainty. But one who had the advantage, for all his limitations, of knowing the kerugma at first hand, gave a different account of it, which may well be deeper. *How are men to believe in One of whom they have never heard? And how are they ever to hear, without a preacher? And how can men preach unless they are sent—as it is written, 'How pleasant is the coming of men with glad, good news'?* In the beginning it was the content of this good news that counted. Wherever the kerugma may be held to have started, at Jerusalem or Dam-

[1] *Harvard Theological Review*, 1915, p. 512.

ascus or Antioch, it was the task of men who were conscious
of being sent by a Lord whose life on earth had made the
message and the experience of such grace possible. The
content of ' Lord ' on the lips of Christians depended on
what Jesus had been.   It was not the enthusiastic proclamation of some cult rejoicing in a ' Lord ' who is, irrespective
of what He once had been ; rather it was due to the impact
of a movement of the Spirit which went back to the original
and originating life of Jesus on earth and to his triumph over
death.   Those who hailed Jesus as the risen and living Lord
did so because of the life which led up to the resurrection.
In that they saw what may be called a real gospel of reconciliation; all that they called καταλλαγή was in essence the atoning
self-devotion of Jesus to the cause of God's People.   What
we have in the gospels is one product of faith in this revelation, but they are also a reflection of the actual life that produced such a faith within the primitive Church.

The announcement of the kingdom as near signified for Jesus a
consciousness that he was not simply the herald of the realm and its
approach but committed to the reconciling enterprise of God.   It was
in this consciousness of vocation that the consciousness of himself as
the Son of God expressed itself.   Son and Servant were cognate terms
or titles.   The synoptic tradition reflects this truth, and so far from
being a mere deduction drawn by the Church's faith from its inner
logic of religion, it is the source of that faith ; the gracious initiative
of God was the movement to which Jesus devoted himself freely, and,
in the light of the resurrection which formed the climax and attestation
of the movement, the Church began to realize what the ministry of
Jesus had thus meant for the world.   This realization is expressed in
various ways.   But when Luke, for example, tells how Jesus took the
responsibility of identifying himself with the prediction of the divine
Year of favour, the evangelist is only portraying vividly a truth which
had come down to the common resurrection-experience of the Church
from the actual career of the Lord on earth.

The nucleus of historical tradition which yields evidence

for this ' grace '-attitude on the part of Jesus was shaped and
coloured as the preaching-stories which enshrined it passed
on within the Church.   At one time some circles of the
Formgeschichte school, in an agnostic despair of history, even
imagined that the anti-Pharisaic teaching of the gospels was
no more than the dramatic expression of anti-Semitic feeling
on the part of some Hellenistic group of Christians at Antioch,
who wove round Jesus their propaganda of a grace-gospel
with which he could never have had any sympathy.   Sayings
such as those which have been quoted from the gospels were
referred to this salvation-cult ; its creative genius was supposed to explain all that in the gospels would represent Jesus
as other than a good amiable rabbi who, so far as we know
anything about him, cannot have had any quarrel with the
Pharisees.   Neither on literary nor on historical grounds
does this require to be taken very seriously.   It fails to account
for the tension at Antioch, which must have been an effect
as well as a cause.   Catechetical and apologetic tendencies
have affected the tradition undoubtedly, and even created
some expressions of faith, but the incisive criticism of Pharisaic
praxis and principles, in the sayings and actions of Jesus,
is not the spontaneous generation of a later crisis at Antioch,
when gentile Christians set themselves to impose a cult-
interest upon casual reminiscences of a Jesus which were
devoid of such aims, or to concoct tales about him in order
to convey their private beliefs in a purely Midrashic style.
Long before the Antioch tension there was a belief in Jesus
Christ which started the Gentile mission ; not only did it
originate this movement but it originated in what Jesus
himself had been and done and said.   How this belief took
shape during the first two or three decades, is another problem.
But, if guess-work is set aside, it becomes fairly clear that
when Paul described his preaching as telling *the story of the
Cross* (1 Cor. i. 18), he was not embroidering the primitive
faith with some private notion of his own ; he was true to

the original ethos of the Christian religion as it had been founded by the Lord Jesus. The bare fact of Jesus having been executed at Jerusalem, even when it is supplied with a few sayings which for some reason are rescued from the deluge of sceptical research, would never explain the real nature of the Christian religion that we know in history. " If the career of Jesus Christ is to have a permanent meaning for us, the Cross cannot be regarded as a tragic incident, a regrettable tale, a stormy sunset to an otherwise perfect day. It must be seen to be something inevitable, significant, typical —and, I would add, gracious. The *grace* of our Lord Jesus Christ—to Christians this familiar phrase does not mean a state of mind produced by conscious imitation, but something that involves gift, inspiration from outside. If this belief be given up, Christianity and the Christian experience is ultimately an illusion." [1] This perception, that ' grace ' is necessary to any legitimate reading of the career of Jesus, grace leading to his death and through death to Lordship of life, was an axiom of Paul's preaching, as it was of any preaching in the primitive Church. The categories in which Paul sets the belief are his own, whether drawn from Pharisaism or from some wider contact with apocalyptic religion. Not all his contemporaries shared his views upon the truth. But all would have agreed with him that ·apart from such an attitude towards the life of Jesus there was no effectiveness in preaching the gospel. *The story of the Cross,* i.e. not a mere description of how Jesus was executed but an explanation of why he was put to death and why death was not the last word upon his life—this might be *sheer folly* or nonsense to pagans, Paul admits, *but for us whom God saves it is the power of God.* He was speaking here for the whole Church. The last thing the primitive Christians would have given up was the belief that Jesus their Lord had been ' given ' to them. However they might fail to understand the particular

[1] F. C. Burkitt, *The Modern Churchman* (1928), pp. 357 f.

6

explanation which Paul offered of that Gift, they saw in their own way what was in 'the eye and prospect' of his vision.

How did Paul come to believe that this new world into which Christ had brought him and in which he reigned as Lord was a world in which one must be unselfish and self-sacrificing ? That is the question which the historian has to answer. Why did the otherworldliness of the apostle press such duties on the conscience ? How did he come to interpret the apocalyptic Realm as he did—to say, for example, ' The kingdom of God is righteousness and peace and joy in the Holy Spirit ; he who serves Christ on these lines (ἐν τούτῳ) is acceptable to God ' ? How was he sure that the divine character made these particular demands upon men ? It is not easy to see any answer, if the Christ of his theology was a mythological figure taken over from tradition or some messianic being who dipped into life, was rescued by God, and then elevated to the high destiny of being the future judge of the world. Hellenistic beliefs about a ' Lord ' explain this as little as the synagogue. As for the latter, the traditional messiah, so far as we know, was not expected, for example, to forgive sins on earth nor to teach. Jesus had done both, and his teaching had been part of his gracious mission. His ' mind ' was very different from the ' mind ' of an Attis or a Dionysus of the cults. Only on the assumption that Paul knew this, can we reasonably explain the moral emphasis of his religious message, that is, that he knew Jesus as substantially we know him in the gospels. That Paul's gospel took the form of stressing unselfishness and love as the giving and as the forgiving reality of life, is intelligible in the light of some conviction about the character of him who had inaugurated the new and final realm of God. Not otherwise.

Nor is it simply that apart from the attitude of Jesus Paul's criticism of the Law is unintelligible ; unless the primitive Christians had been convinced of the same freedom on the part of Jesus they would not have fallen in with the main contention of Paul. No argument is required nowadays for the view that in passing beyond nationalism the Christian movement was inspired by more than the apostle's propaganda. " There can be no doubt that in Jesus Paul found justifying support," [1] when he set aside the ceremonial Law. But already there was in the primitive Church some recognition of the emancipating power that lay in the gospel for which Jesus had lived and died and risen. The recognition was hesitating and imperfect, to begin with ; it was the liberal preaching of Stephen which first forced it upon the consciousness of the Jerusalem church. Yet Peter and his group assimilated it in such a way that they were ready, even against the more conservative party of James, to uphold Paul as he insisted not merely on faith but on the freedom of his Gentile converts from any obligation to the Law, except as interpreted in the spirit of love enjoined by Jesus. In other words, the essence of the Pauline teaching on grace may be summed up in the sentence, ' Anyone can be saved by faith ' ; as the emphasis falls on ' anyone ' or on ' faith,' one or another element of grace is brought out, either the universal range or the antithesis to Law. And, even though the term ' grace ' is not on the lips of the primitive Church, these two convictions are implicit in their religious position, a position which is unintelligible, apart from what had gone before in the life of Jesus and had been ratified by his death and resurrection.

In the primitive Church the resurrection was regarded as the divine authentication of the messianic claims of Jesus and as the assurance of his return in glory, but also as an integral part of his saving work. As Peter told the Sanhedrin, *The God of our fathers raised Jesus whom you murdered by hanging him on a gibbet. God lifted him up to his right hand as our pioneer* (ἀρχηγόν) *and saviour, in order to grant repentance and remission of sins to Israel* (Acts v. 30, 31). Or, as he had already told the Jerusalemites, *You killed the pioneer* (ἀρχηγόν) *of life*, choosing a murderer like Barabbas. *But God raised him from the dead. . . . Repent then, and turn to have your sins blotted out. For God raised up his Servant and sent him to bless you by turning each of you from your wicked ways* (iii. 15, 19, 26). Though the last passage refers to the

[1] Klausner, *Jesus of Nazareth*, p. 369.

start of the mission in the historical life of Jesus, the context shows how its range extended to the present ; He who had ' raised up ' Jesus as the prophet of repentance on earth had raised him up in a deeper sense to complete the mission.

The thought recurs in Acts x. 40–43 and is echoed in 1 Peter iii. 18 f., which here answers to the common preaching of the primitive Church, elaborating it but presupposing it in a way which seems independent of the apostle Paul. Paul's statement is ampler, for he widens the range of the belief, but it is not an independent addition of his own to the kerugma, according to which *Christ died for our sins as the scriptures had said, that he was buried, that he rose on the third day as the scriptures had said* (1 Cor. xv. 3, 4). This Paul had taught from the first ; he was only developing this tradition when he wrote afterwards that Christians must *believe in Him who raised Jesus our Lord from the dead, Jesus who was delivered up for our trespasses and raised that we might be justified*, telling them, *confess with your mouth that ' Jesus is Lord,' believe in your heart that God raised him from the dead, and you will be saved* (Rom. iv. 24, 25, x. 9). In the Macedonian letters this uncontroversial view prevails ; salvation is to come at the divine event which is so near, on the apocalyptic scheme, *through our Lord Jesus Christ, who died for us that waking in life or sleeping in death we should live together with him* (1 Thess. v. 9, 10), *since we believe that Jesus died and rose again*. When the full implications of Paul's references to grace in the opening and closing formulas of the letters are fairly estimated, along with such allusions in the body of the epistles, it becomes plain that the common faith of these churches in the Macedonian mission implies the substance of what is afterwards worked out antithetically, viz. that death had come to Jesus as the supreme act of obedience to the will of God in life, and that it was crowned by his resurrection. He had died for men because he had lived and as he had lived for them, this Son and Servant of the Lord. Although it was inflicted upon him by others, it was his own act, freely endured for the sake of the cause and the redeemed. He had chosen to undergo it, Paul argues, as he had chosen to enter life, out of devotion to the interests of men, after the gracious will of God. On this hung all the hopes of the human soul.

This ' kerugma ' or *Christian message* was a scandal to Jews and *sheer folly* to Gentiles, Paul admits, this *message of Christ the crucified*. Not the mere fact that Jesus had been crucified. Such capital punishment for slaves was familiar. Not even the fact that a good man had been unjustly murdered by the authorities. It was not Jesus as a victim or a martyr, it was Jesus as Christ, as the Lord who had risen from the dead, that made Christianity at once a living faith and a shocking offence to Jews and Gentiles. In other words, it was the ' grace ' of this action that constituted the distinctive element in the Christian gospel. The NT is a literature of power because it is written out of belief in this Lord of life, by men who were conscious of his Spirit. The resurrection was a divine action because it was the manifestation of gracious love. Love cannot express itself except through deeds. And in this divine action the early Christians saw God's loving favour creating a new order of things for the world of men. The first interpretation of the cosmic change was offered by Paul, but he was only interpreting a faith common to the whole Church when he argued that the resurrection and all that led up to it in the life of Jesus presented itself as the sign of a creative action of God in history, beside which everything else paled in significance.

It would carry us too far from our subject to trace the ramifications of this central belief. But one illustration may be given, in order to show how for Paul the divine power of grace in the resurrection meant everything. It is his use of language about the resurrection, when he speaks of God working in life. As we see elsewhere, his conception of God the creator is almost concentrated upon the new creation of the Church in the new Era, God is creator as He is redeemer, rather than redeemer as He is creator. The standing marvel is what He calls into existence through faith in His grace. It is hardly surprising therefore to read the strong terms chosen by the apostle to express the unshared power and purpose of God in the religious life, not simply in creating

it but in supporting it.   God, he is fond of saying, makes
life out of death or raises the soul from death to life ; also,
God creates being out of non-being.   How does faith originate ?   By means of *a God who makes the dead live and calls
into being what does not exist* (Rom. iv. 17).   ' Consider your
calling ' (*κλῆσιν*, the ranks in which you stand as called by
God) ;   ' God chose things that are not . . . that no person
may boast in his presence ' (1 Cor. i. 28, 29).   That is, you
were utterly unpromising material, when God selected you.
The former phrase was familiar to Paul in the daily benedic-
tions of the liturgy ; ' Blessed art thou, O Lord, who makest
the dead live.'   The latter was philosophical.   The union
of the two was not unknown in some circles of contemporary
Judaism, if we may judge from an invocation in the Syriac
Apocalypse of Baruch (xlviii. 8), ' With a word Thou callest
into life that which did not exist.'   Paul uses it to bring out
the absolute power of God in creating the Christian experience ; men are helpless and hopeless, to all appearance, when
God intervenes.   But all through life the same trust in God,
not in one's self, has to be maintained.   It is so natural to
rely upon one's own resources, the apostle feels, that we
constantly need to be broken of our self-confidence.   One
great lesson of dangers and emergencies in actual life is to
teach the lesson of utter faith in God, and he puts this in
similar language at one point (2 Cor. i. 8 f.).   Speaking of
some peril through which he had recently passed in Asia,
he tells his friends at Corinth that *he despaired even of life.
But that was to make me rely not on myself but on the God who
raises the dead ; he rescued me from so terrible a death, he rescues
still and will continue to rescue me.*[1]   Doubtless his own faith
was required.   Also, he at once proceeds to admit that the

---

[1] Compare with the last words Agamemnon's confidence in Zeus (*Iliad* ii.
117–118) :

　　　ὃς δὴ πολλάων πολίων κατέλυσε κάρηνα
　　　ἠδ' ἔτι καὶ λύσει· τοῦ γὰρ κράτος ἐστὶ μέγιστον.

intercessions of his friends played a part in the divine deliverance from so serious a crisis. This is a natural rendering of the ambiguous words that follow ; they mean, not that Paul asked for the prayers of his friends when the trouble was over, so that there might rise " to God, as the outpouring of many hearts, a cry of gratitude on our behalf, for the mercy that has been shown to us " (W. Gunion Rutherford), but *that many a soul may render thanks to Him on my behalf for the boon (χάρισμα) which many have been the means of Him bestowing on myself.* He recognizes here, as gratefully as in Rom. xv. 30 f., that God's gracious aid comes to one through the prayers of others on his behalf. There is no slight thrown by this upon the free grace of God, which wrought as it were a resurrection in the life of the apostle, and which, as he recalls it, seemed so utterly generous.

The notion of expressing the thought that religious privilege owed everything to God, by saying that God brings into existence the People of His choice, was not unfamiliar, however. In the LXX rendering of Malachi iii. 17, ' they shall be mine on the day when I make (or, create) them to be my very own' (ἐγὼ ποιῶ εἰς περιποίησιν), ποιῶ has this meaning, though Peter in echoing the phrase does not use the verb (λαὸς εἰς περιποίησιν, 1 Peter ii. 9) ; Paul does not appear to use περιποίησις at all in this sense (see Ephes. i. 14), and prefers to use more philosophical language for the idea of God bringing into existence the Christian Church.

An examination of the elementary and the more advanced theologies of the early Church during this period justifies us therefore in holding that the message of grace was inspired by the resurrection of the Lord Jesus (' grace ' is a meaningless word apart from the resurrection), and that this belief is inexplicable apart from a reading of the life of Jesus on earth such as the gospels imply. Any solid reconstruction of the life and mission of Jesus involves the recognition of two facts ; (*a*) that his consciousness of communion with God meant ' the conviction of a unique vocation ' as God's Son and Ser-

vant, and (b) that his message was more than the teaching
of an individual saint or prophet.   One hesitates indeed to
accept Bultmann's account of Mark's Gospel as " the epiphany
of a god," but it is at least closer to the truth than analyses of
the synoptic tradition which leave little more visible than the
diminutive figure of some Galilean leader of revolt or some
pious peasant who taught an incoherent blend of socialism
and pacifism.   The mission and message of the real Jesus
were followed by a triumph over death which revealed him as
Lord or Son of God in power.   This, the gospels witness, was
the sequel or result of what he had been and done.   And
from this, from this alone, flow the results which we know as
primitive Christianity.

The recent *Formgeschichte* movement has helped to give the coup-
de-grâce to the hypothesis of a ' Galilean idyll ' in the life of Jesus,
which reduced grace to what Renan called, in a truly detestable phrase,
" the adorable indulgence of Jesus."   It has also contributed to deliver
criticism from the notion that the synoptic gospels were a deliberate
or involuntary corrective to the epistles, as though the latter represented
a theological construction which hid some human career of Jesus, whilst
the synoptic sources fortunately preserved the original.   When we read
the epistles we are not reading a palimpsest.   Both gospels and epistles,
it is now seen, sprang from the same worshipping community.   The
early ' disciples ' were not disciples of Jesus in the sense that Greeks
had been disciples of Socrates ; they did not merely adhere to his
teaching and principles, they were men who looked up to a Lord in
heaven.   It is true that this (a) cult-relationship may be exaggerated.
The attitude of the primitive Christians, including the apostle Paul,
is not to be explained wholly in terms of a worship-movement which
posited Jesus as the divine hero of the group.   Nevertheless, it is a
service to bring out the fact that the analysis of the synoptic traditions
does not lead away from faith in Jesus as Lord ; the *Formgeschichte*
movement is welcome as it cuts the ground from under the view that
a religion of Jesus was turned into a religion about Jesus.   Again,
however (b), the scepticism of some of its applications is unwarranted.
Stories about Jesus did not simply arise from the needs of the worshipping

Church. We have to ask more questions than about the requirements of apologetic and catechetical instruction, if we are to understand the origin of the tradition. This is admitted by Bultmann. " Ein geistiger Besitz objectiviert sich auch ohne spezielle Zwecke " (*Geschichte d. Synopt. Tradition*, p. 225). But more than a passing recognition of such a principle is needed ; the principle carries one beyond the position that the bulk of the material about Jesus was created by the imagination and reverence of the early Church. The synoptic gospels are not an objective transcript of historical data about Jesus which the epistles presuppose. There are dark lines of myth and legend in the spectrum. Furthermore we are able to detect a story being improved and adapted in the course of transmission. But this does not evaporate the story itself. For example, the grace-teaching is innate in the historical Jesus, if anything is. Stories about Jesus interested people, apart from the moral which is sometimes attached to them in the tradition. They arose out of more than a cult-interest. And in the stories no less than in the morals the truth of what the Church came to call ' grace ' is enshrined.

The relation of the synoptic gospels to their environment within the primitive Church is a subject on which those most competent to judge are the least eager to-day to pronounce any final verdict, but so far as it concerns the problem of grace this may be said. These documents bring out (i) the human character of the Jesus whom the Church was worshipping as Lord divine, and that character had nothing dictatorial about it, nothing unreluctant or official ; it was authoritative and at the same time unambiguously gracious in dealing with men of all classes and conditions. Then (*a*) the outcome of his life was his death (Mark), for the sake of the kingdom, and (*b*) that kingdom was God's, to be established by God ; it did not depend upon human efforts or plans. Jesus taught men to set their hope on God, Who was more than equal to the forces of evil in the world. The gospels also (ii) emphasize the moral demands of God's gracious purpose, partly because this was innate in the mission and character of Jesus, and partly because it required to be stated against misconceptions or temptations of laxity which were started by the very experience of grace in some circles of the early Church. Thus on the one hand Luke brings out this feature by means of an imaginative delineation of Jesus on the basis of his sources, while Matthew succinctly states the ethical obligations of the Lord's religious message as contemporary needs of the Church seemed to require. Various movements have stamped and shaped the synoptic tradition about Jesus, but the common interest in the apostolic preaching of grace and in the synoptic account sprang from the conviction that the divine generosity to which Christians owed everything must control their lives. To speak of the mind of Christ, or of the grace of the Lord, or of the Spirit of the Lord, was meaningless apart from an intelligent sense of what he had been on earth. Why selfishness and worldliness quenched grace, why any unloving temper excluded the soul from a real experience of the gracious Lord, why nothing mattered but faith and yet why adoring Jesus as ' Lord, Lord ' mattered nothing apart from obedience to his commands, this was inexplicable save from some knowledge of the divine Will which he had revealed with power in his own life ; and this knowledge, implicit in the apostolic preaching, was held up before the conscience of the Church by the gospels as we have them.

From an examination of the gospels we carry forward two conclusions about the mission and spirit of Jesus in what one writer called ' the days of his flesh ' : that the saving initiative is with God, and that no man must think of facing God on the basis of conscious merit. These are held together in a religious unity, but it was not until the genius of the apostle Paul interpreted the mind of Christ that they were expressed in terms of ' grace ' as a category which included both. He re-stated them in a dialectic of his own, full of sharp antitheses and daring paradoxes, which are unintelligible or liable to be misunderstood except against the background of contemporary movements in religion. But he is not interested in them as subjects of detached speculation, even when he discusses them in language which sounds abstract. They are for him vital realities of the Christian faith, in the light of the resurrection of the Lord. What the Lord had done and what the Lord demanded was summed up in 'grace.' It was because he had verified this in his own experience and because he found himself obliged at various points to explain and apply it during the course of his mission, that he wrote as he did upon the subject, always with a more or less practical and direct aim, yet also from a central conviction. In studying 'grace' as Paul used it we are dealing with something which was for him as fundamental as 'ideas' were for Plato. Inevitably we look before and after. What he taught about grace did not always enter into the mind of the later Church, at any rate as he taught it, but in his various discussions of grace he was putting in his own way what was known to have been present in the message and mission of Jesus. The grace-teaching of Paul, in other words, is an interpretation of God's new action as revealed in Jesus the one Lord and Saviour. His gospel as a gospel or message of grace presupposed a decisive movement of God which he for one could only compare to the first creation of the world and man. Standing in the light of this Dawn which had broken upon the deep needs of men through the life and death and resurrection of God's own Son, and watching its effect upon human nature, he could discover no more apt term for its sheer goodness and creative power than 'grace.' Our task now is to ascertain how and why he came to use this pregnant term.

PART C
THE NEW TESTAMENT LANGUAGE OF GRACE

I

THE TWO VERBS

CHRISTIANITY practically created the word ἀγάπη, but it found ἀγαπάω ready to hand. It found χάρις on the lips of men, and all that Paul had to do was to fill it with fresh content ; but there was no corresponding verb in existence, and none was created. (*a*) There is a partial exception, no doubt, in χαριτόω, for this does not occur in the papyri and inscriptions, neither is it used by Philo. Even when it begins to appear in Jewish Greek, for a very brief career, it is without very much religious interest. The Epistle to Aristeas (225) observes, for example, that " the best gift of God is popularity," τὸ δὲ κεχαριτοῦσθαι πρὸς πάντας ἀνθρώπους. Sirach (xviii. 17) uses the participle for a ' gracious ' giver (a man who confers a boon gracefully). Another mention of the word does, however, carry a religious meaning ; we are no longer on the level of ' charis ' as favour or charm when the hero in the Testament of Joseph (i. 6) confesses, " I was in prison and the Saviour (or, my God) showed me favour (ἐχαρίτωσε με)." Yet, even so, it is much further to the NT usage. Paul employs the verb once of God bestowing grace on Christians (Ephes. i. 6) : τῆς χάριτος αὐτοῦ ἧς ἐχαρίτωσεν ἡμᾶς. It was not unnatural for a Greek like Chrysostom to read such a phrase in the light of classical usage, as though the apostle meant that God had not only delivered men from their trespasses but also made them lovable or ' grace-ful ' in the sense of being morally attractive (ἐπεράστους). But the more probable meaning is, ' endowed with grace.' The Vulgate attempted to reproduce the play on the word by ' gratificavit,' which the Rheims version transliterates by ' gratified.' This is as un-English as ' graced ' would be.

There is no means of translating the term except by expanding
it to suggest the idea, and the idea is the same as in the following description of 'charis' as ἧς ἐπερίσσευσεν εἰς ἡμᾶς. In
the only other passage where the word occurs in the NT,
Luke employs it of the Virgin Mary who is addressed by the
angel (i. 28 f), χαῖρε, κεχαριτωμένη. He is aware of the
assonance of χαῖρε and χαριτόω, but he means what he makes
the angel say below, εὗρες γὰρ χάριν παρὰ τῷ θεῷ. Here it is
the divine favour for a special vocation, not as in Paul for the
general position of Christians towards their God ; but the
fundamental idea of human beings as objects of the divine
favour is the same.

Lasserre who follows the Vulgate by rendering the first phrase ' pleine
de grâce ' translates the second by ' vous avez conquis des bonnes grâces
de Dieu,' but ' thou art in favour with God ' (Genevan version) or
' thou hast found grace with God ' (Rheims) is quite adequate. The
Genevan version was the first of the English versions to render the
former phrase by ' thou art freely beloved ' ; both it and the Authorized
version (' thou art highly favoured ') broke away from the literal rendering of κεχαριτωμένη based on the Vulgate ' plena gratia,' for ' full
of grace ' was not only ambiguous but had led to unhealthy developments of mariolatry, as though the meaning had been a source of grace,
not ' highly favoured ' by God as an object of His grace. The sub-
Christian idea current in some circles of the mediaeval Latin Church
that Mary might be invoked as a means of grace to intercede with her
wrathful Son flowed from misconceptions fostered by this unlucky
rendering. Hence, for example, the distressing lines of the hymn,

> Placa, Mater, iram Nati,
> Juste sumus jam damnati,
> Et est opus gratia.

Luke's meaning was ' Hail, O favoured one.' As a literary artist he
put κεχαριτωμένη after χαῖρε, but we have no means in English of
reproducing the effect of the Greek.

An echo of the Lucan tradition is to be overheard in what seems
to be the most natural interpretation of the obscure eleventh Ode of

Solomon (1–2), which Professor Bacon [1] attractively expounds as a canticle of the Virgin Mary :

> My heart was cloven,
>   and its flower appeared ;
> and grace sprang up in it,
>   and it brought forth fruit unto the Lord.

If the verb is scanty in the NT, it is not less scanty in later usage ; neither in Christian nor in non-Christian Greek did the word ever take hold. We come across it once in Hermas, it is true (Sim. ix. 24. 3, ' The Lord was gracious [or favourable] to them in all they undertook '), but otherwise, for some unexplained reason, it never became popular. One remarkable use of it does occur in Clement of Alexandria, who actually substitutes κεχαριτωμένης for εὐμόρφου in citing Sirach's misogynistic couplet (ix. 8) :

> Turn your eye from a graceful woman.

This has been taken to confirm the hypothesis, for which there is other evidence, that Clement used an independent pre-Christian version of Sirach,[2] since " it is inconceivable that a Christian should by choice employ " the participle in such a connexion, when it had been consecrated by the salutation to Mary, χαῖρε κεχαριτωμένη. Even so, however, it remains difficult to understand why he did not change the word (Paed. iii. 11, 83). The fact is, the primitive Christians who spoke Greek were in little better case than moderns who speak English. We have the negative verb ' disgrace,' but no longer have we any positive grace-verb.

(b) Unlike the English, the French have in ' gracier ' a verb for pardoning derived from grace. So vital a part of ' charis ' was forgiveness that Paul required a special verb in this connexion. He finally took over χαρίζεσθαι to denote forgiveness, human as well as divine ; which was a new departure, for up till now this verb had been confined to giving or bestowing, without reference to moral offences. But as God's gift or gracious boon meant pardon of sins for men, so

---

[1] *Expositor*[8], 1911 (September), pp. 247 f.
[2] Hart, *Ecclesiasticus in Greek*, p. 336.

7

it was not unnatural that a verb which denoted ' give,' in ordinary language (e.g. Epist. Aristeas 38), should now mean ' forgive ' as well.   God *forgave us all our trespasses* (Col. ii. 13) is the first use of the term as applied to God ; it is confined in this sense to the later epistles, where it links God's pardon of men with their forgiveness of one another, as e.g. in Colossians iii. 13, ' forbearing one another and forgiving (χαριζόμενοι) one another, if any man have a quarrel (or complaint) against any—even as Christ forgave you, so also ' must you forgive ; or again in Ephesians iv. 32, ' be kind one to another, tender-hearted, forgiving one another even as God for Christ's sake hath forgiven you.'   In these passages, especially in the latter, χαρίζεσθαι means almost to treat generously, forgiveness being regarded as the expression of a gracious nature, as opposed to any unlovely temper like harshness and hard-heartedness.   The verb retained something of its classical nuance, to be obliging or agreeable.   But Paul had begun by using it of human forgiveness in Second Corinthians, where he was dealing with a local case of moral failure.   He pleads for pity towards a penitent.   *Instead of censuring* him at this stage of the proceedings, *you should now forgive him . . . Reinstate him in your love . . . If you forgive the man, I forgive him too ; anything I had to forgive him has been forgiven in the presence of Christ for your sakes* (ii. 7–10, see further xii. 13). The words *in the presence of Christ* (ἐν προσώπῳ χριστοῦ) mean that the apostle identifies himself with the Church as met in the presence of the Lord to deal with the matter.   It is assumed that their forgiveness, their refusal to persist in an unduly severe attitude towards the offender is inspired by Christ and is a ratification of his pardon.   This would be brought out more definitely if the words were rendered ' in the person of Christ,' as e.g. Tertullian does in the *De Pudicitia* (xiii.) : ' I have forgiven him in the person of Christ,' i.e. as Christ's delegate, in virtue of my apostolic authority, repre-senting the mind of Christ in this matter.   But in either case the human forgiveness has a divine forgiveness behind it, though this is not explicitly stated till the later epistles.

The common Hellenistic sense of ' bestow ' or ' present as a favour,' with the suggestion of readiness and cheerfulness, is sometimes visible, but always it is God who is the giver, e.g. of the Inheritance bestowed by a promise on Abraham (Gal. iii. 18), of help and aid to Christians (Rom. viii. 32), of any privilege (Phil. i. 29), and of the spiritual mysteries in revelation (1 Cor. ii. 12). Once the verb is used of God conferring upon Christ the supreme Name (Phil. ii. 9) as his reward. The unusual employment in Philemon 22, of God ' restoring ' Paul to his friends, is paralleled by Acts xxvii. 24 (' God hath given thee the lives of all who sail with thee '), and another general use of the word in its religious sense occurs in Luke's Gospel vii. 21, where Jesus ' granted (the boon of) sight to many who were blind.' Elsewhere in Acts Luke uses the verb of giving up a prisoner (iii. 14, xxv. 11, 16), for which there are ethnic parallels.

In the LXX, where it invariably means ' to give,' the verb is by no means a prominent religious word, only appearing in the later hagiographa ; it is absent from the Psalms of Solomon, though it persisted in Jewish Greek. Thus Josephus (Ant. iii. 36), in telling how Moses brought water out of the rock, writes, " Moses told the people that God would rescue them from this strait and that he had vouchsafed (κεχαρίσθαι) an unexpected relief (σωτηρίαν)." The Hellenistic usage of ' blessing God ' is never present in Paul. Philostratus (Epist. xxi.) asks " How should man win the favour (χαρίζοιτο) of the gods " when they need no sacrifices, and answers that a man may make himself wise and also do good to the deserving, as far as possible. Paul had no thought that the divine favour was to be won, by sacrifices or by moral culture, and for the ethical response to God he preferred equivalents ·like ἀρέσκειν, just as he preferred εὐχαριστεῖν to χαρίζεσθαι when he wished to speak of showing gratitude.

What seems to have led Paul to develop this verb was his consciousness of the divine grace in pardon. When he thought, " God gives," he instinctively thought, " God forgives." Hence the word is not employed of the divine goodness in creation. James (i. 17) spoke of our human faculties as gifts of the good God, just as some gnostics did ; in the Hermetica (xii. 12), for example, " God bestowed (ἐχαρίσατο) on man two boons which are more than mortal animals possess, reason and speech." The same use of the verb appears in 2 Maccabees vii. 22 and 4 Maccabees v. 7. The apostle's concentration of grace upon the moral relations between God and man, however, made him confine the verb χαρίζεσθαι to the same sphere. Probably it was the influence of this Pauline usage that led the evangelist Luke to use the term once in his Gospel (vii. 42, 43) as an equivalent for pardon. When the two debtors in the parable *were unable to pay* what they owed to the money-lender, *he freely forgave them both* (ἐχαρί-σατο. On being asked by Jesus which of the two would love the creditor most, Simon replied, *I suppose, the man who had most forgiven*. The papyri yield one or two instances of the verb in a similar sense of ' remit,' where debts are in question, but not in the religious sense of ' forgive.' What would make it intelligible in this sense to early Christian readers was not so much any contemporary usage in life as the employment of the term already by Paul to denote the action of God as the great Giver, who gave favour rather than favours. Etymologically χαρίζομαι was a grace-word ; Paul made it a full grace-word by his religious setting of it, so that the verb now indicated God's bestowal of favour, with a specific allusion to forgiveness, which even carried it into the human duty of forgiving others.

II

THE NOUN χάρισμα OR ' GRACE-GIFT '

PAUL enlisted another term in the Christian vocabulary, namely, χάρισμα, which had no traditional usage. It never occurs in the LXX, not even in the later sapiential literature ; in the text of Sirach it is merely a mistake for χάρις (vii. 33) and χρῖσμα (xxxviii. 30). The sole sign of its vogue in religion occurs in Philo (see below 114), and apparently the vogue was small. It was by an instinct for its possibilities that his younger contemporary Paul seized the word ' charisma ' and shaped it to suit his interpretation of human nature as the recipient of divine favour. We have thus another instance of the influence exercised over Christianity by the idea of grace, in the terminology which it created during the first century.

Once the apostle employs it as an equivalent for grace itself, i.e. in Romans v. 15, 16, where, like δωρεά and δώρημα, χάρισμα denotes the full saving gift of God in Jesus Christ, as again in vi. 23: *Sin's wage is death, but God's gift is life eternal in Christ Jesus our Lord.* Apart from the general statement of Romans xi. 29 (' the gifts and call of God are never taken back '), however, Paul does not apply the term further in this direction. It serves elsewhere to mark a derived sense, in one or two special references.

(*a*) Any favour of deliverance in his own life is a ' charisma ' (as in 2 Cor. i. 11), a boon from God for which one is grateful, (*b*) The capacity for living a celibate life is also ' a gift,' as we might say ; indeed, whether a man was able to marry and remain a true Christian (perhaps also to abstain from sexual intercourse) or to reach the equally difficult level of remaining pure and unmarried in the service of God, was in either case due to God's will. Each is a vocation, Paul insists. *I would*

like all men to be as I am (i.e. unmarried, for he was by this
time a widower). *However, every one is endowed by God* (has
his χάρισμα from God) *in his own way ; he has a gift for the one
life or the other* (1 Cor. vii. 7). Jesus had already said that
to remain unmarried was only feasible for those who had the
gift (δέδοται, Matt. xix. 11). This was sound Jewish
doctrine ; it had almost been said in so many words by the
author of Wisdom (viii. 21, οὐκ ἄλλως ἔσομαι ἐγκρατὴς ἐὰν μὴ ὁ
θεὸς δῷ). Paul, however, ranks not only abstinence from
immorality and even from marriage as a charisma but also
marriage itself. He does not mean to say merely that one
has the ascetic gift and another has not ; his point is that
there is a providence over man's temperament no less than
over his circumstances, and that marriage is thus included
in the range of God's order for human life.

   The pride of celibates in the primitive Church soon made it needful
for them to be reminded that they must not plume themselves on what
was after all a divine endowment. Thus Clemens Romans xxxviii. 2,
' Let no one who is pure in the flesh be proud of it, let him realize
that Another bestows on him his power of continence ' ; Ignatius *ad
Polykarp*. v. : ' if any man is able to remain pure and continent, let him
do so without boasting of it.'

   (*c*) The meaning of Romans i. 11 is more general. ' I am
longing to see you that I may impart to you some spiritual
gift, that you may be strengthened.' In the light of xv. 29
this seems to denote what Wyclif calls in his translation,
' somewhat of spiritual grace.' If the adjective ' spiritual ' is
to be stressed, the apostle hints that the Romans did not
require any contribution of money. But the obvious interpretation of the whole sentence is that he hopes to impart to
them some fuller realization of the gospel, not indeed to
present them with his own type of Christianity, as though
' my gospel ' was to supplement their inadequate knowledge,
but to let them share what he had received from the Spirit as

an apostle. He is modestly conscious that wherever he goes (see 1 Thess. iii. 2, 2 Thess. ii. 17, 2 Cor. ii. 14 f.), God will transmit through him to any church a richer experience of truth ; some such knowledge as he sketches in this very epistle is the χάρισμα he is to share with the Roman Christians, as part of his debt to them

(d) A similarly general sense occurs in 1 Corinthians i. 7, where after thanking God for *the grace of God that has been bestowed on* the Church, with its *wealth of all blessing*, he declares that they thus *lack no spiritual endowment* (χάρισμα) *during these days of waiting* till the end. It is generous praise, for no one knew better than Paul how far short some of the Corinthian Christians came in the sphere of spiritual attainment ; but he uses this technical term for the religious privileges with which they were endowed as they held fast to their hope, particularly for the shining though somewhat showy gifts of λόγος and γνῶσις, i.e. power to speak of their faith and insight into its meaning. These, no doubt, as he indicates later, were strong points of theirs which at the same time were their weak points. Nevertheless, they are included in the experience of grace.

I

This opens up into a particular use of ' charismata ' in 1 Corinthians xii. and Romans xii. 6 f. The underlying thought is that "if life is to be of any value, it must be disinterested" (Jowett). The experience of grace within the Christian communities involves capacities and responsibilities, without which the life of the community cannot develop. The generous service of man, the active devotion to man's best interests, which grace divine prompts, this must be reproduced, the apostle assumes, in the human relationships created by the God of grace. Grace means for the Christian a certain ministry to others, and to this end ' grace-gifts ' are bestowed.

It is characteristic of the ethical interests of Paul that here as elsewhere he is preoccupied with the risk of men taking

credit to themselves. There is indeed the danger of failing
to use their powers properly, but there is the further danger
of using them wrongly. Thus, in the Romans passage he
begins by warning Christians against the spirit of self-importance, as they did some service to the community. *In virtue
of my office, I tell every one of your number*—the canonical Greek
text runs ὄντι ἐν ὑμῖν, but when τι is supposed to have slipped
out after ὄντι we get a better sense—*everyone of your number
who is self-important, that he is not to think more of himself than
he ought to think ; he must take a sane* (σωφρονεῖν) *view of himself, corresponding to the degree of faith which God has assigned
to each*. All attainments are endowments ; the gifted man
must recollect that his powers are a gift. So Paul character-
istically strikes at the root of subtle Christian Pharisaism.
What these different measures of faith mean, he goes on to
explain ; they are intended for the common service of the
Community or Body, in which each has his special function.
Those sure of their standing in grace should be wise about life,
helpful, and humble. The temptation to take credit to oneself
is countered by σωφρονεῖν, which is the opposite of undue self-
importance. Such exaggerated ideas are removed by the
thought that one's gift is really a divine gift, and also that it
is designed for the good of others, not for vainglory or self-
display. Our ' charismata,' he adds, or, as we might render
it, *our talents are not the same, they differ with the grace that is
given us*, but their use is for the same end ; they were never
intended to let a man give himself airs as he exercised them.
For example, to take what Paul himself regarded as the highest
spiritual gift, *if the talent is that of prophecy, let us employ it in
proportion to our faith*, i.e. the gift of rapturous utterance on
the deep things of God must always be used with faith in
view and as an expression of faith. The gift of speech does
tempt men to say more than God gives them to say, but this
is a warning against employing the gift for vainglorious ends,
not merely against prophesying for the sake of effect beyond

what one had really received as a communication of the Spirit. The informal list of the other charismata does not concern us here. What is important is to note how Paul took this term in a new, semi-technical sense for the various capacities and functions, more or less inspired, which were in operation within the corporate life of a normal Christian group. These are all gifts, he repeats, gifts. And a divine gift must be used humbly as well as for the divine end of human help, like the ' grace ' from which ' charismata ' come and after which they are named. Only thus are they effective, for without the spirit of unselfish humility there is no real service of the Church. Such is the characteristic stamp which he puts on the noun. It designates " either what we call ' natural advantages ' independent of any human process of acquisition, or advantages freshly received in the course of Providence, both alike being regarded as so many various free gifts from the Lord of men, and as designed by Him to be distinct qualifications for rendering distinctive service to men or to communities of men." [1]   Self-seeking in any shape or form is utterly out of keeping with such charismata.

The Corinthians passage goes into more detail, connects the spiritual charismata definitely with the Spirit, who ' apportions them severally to each individual as he pleases,' and posits love as the supreme manifestation of the Spirit, without which no gift has value. But again the unselfish end of the charismata is stressed ; *each receives his manifestation* of divine power or *of the Spirit for the common good* (πρὸς τὸ συμφέρον), though here Paul has to warn Christians to be content with their appointed capacities. His axiom is that the various charismata are not attained by personal choice, though one may rise from lower to higher by faithfulness, but that like the Christian life itself they are the expression of God's grace ; they are all endowments and all needed for the service of the Body, so that there must not be any exclusive importance

[1] Hort, *The Christian Ecclesia*, p. 154.

attached to any one, like glossolalia, as if that or any other
striking gift were specifically Christian.

> *There are varieties of charismata,*
> *but the same Spirit ;*
> *there are varieties of service,*
> *but the same Lord ;*
> *there are varieties of effect,*
> *but the same God who effects everything in everyone.*

The charismata are powers, as grace is power, for the service
of God in His Church ; χαρίσματα, διακονίαι, ἐνεργήματα, in
any aspect they shut out the thought of pride, since they are
from God and for God, not simply the vaunting pride of one
who excels in exercising the higher charismata (τὰ μείζονα in
ver. 31, i.e. better for the corporate life of the Church), but
also the wounded pride of those who are tempted to neglect
their humbler functions because they think the work unworthy
of their noble selves, or perhaps not worth doing at all. It
is such dangers to social fellowship that the apostle has specially
in view here. The charismata were not confined to worship
or to the organization of the Church ; some of them were
exercised outside, in visiting the sick, for example. Renan
is tinged with sentimentalism when he remarks that " sous
le nom de dons du Saint-Esprit se cachaient ainsi les plus rares
et les plus exquises effusions de l'âme, amour, piété, crainte
respectueuse, soupirs sans objet, langueurs subites, tendresses
spontanées. Tout ce qui naît de bon en l'homme, sans que
l'homme y ait part, fut attribué à un souffle d'en haut." [1]
The last sentence is true to Paul's account, but one of his
standards for charismata is precisely that they must have an
object, the object of profiting the Church. Indeed this is the
supreme criterion for the phenomena which went under the
name of charismata ; even the most ecstatic must somehow
be made to further the moral and spiritual health of the Body,
like the grace of God itself. None is ' sans objet.' If it is,

[1] *Les Apôtres*, p. 73.

or if the object is self-display, it is loveless and therefore irrelevant to Christianity.

Some 'charismata' are intrinsically more useful to the Church than others, and Paul does not mean that individual capacity is fixed or limited by its initial range *Set your hearts on the higher talents*, not for any opportunity of self-display, however, but in the spirit of love, which is the secret for gaining and using all 'gifts.' It is implied that our human nature, which is the basis for spiritual service, is capable of improvement and elevation.   There are cases in which a man who uses one gift may be qualified for a higher, and it is a legitimate ambition to seek this larger exercise of one's powers, as a good and faithful servant.

In both passages the variety of grace-gifts witnesses to the extraordinary stimulus of grace in human nature.   The Spirit or power of God is given to men differently, for service, but it stirs every power of human nature, thought, sympathy, moral force, moral discernment, emotion ; the influx of grace thrills every faculty for the common end of furthering the corporate fellowship.   This conviction of the Spirit realized in and through the community, not simply in the individual relationship to God, is one of the features which differentiated the Christian Church from the sodalitates or thiasoi of contemporary religious life in the Empire.   As Reitzenstein admits, there is no exact parallel in the cults to such a reality of common religious life.   " Der ganze Begriff der Kirche im Grunde . . . trennt von Anfang an das Christenthum von den heidnischen Mitwerbern ab und ist nach Sprache und Gedanken nur aus dem Judentum einigermassen zu begreifen " (*Die Hellenistischen Mysterienreligionen*,[2] p. 31.)

When Justin Martyr in his Dialogue (3, xxxix.) mentions the ' gifts ' received by various Christians, ' by each as he is worthy,' Trypho retorts that he must be mad to claim this for the Church. ' But listen,' Justin answers, ' I am not mad ; this has been foretold.' And he quotes Psalm lxviii. 18 :

> When he ascended on high he led a host captive
> and granted gifts to men.

This, he explains, was a prophecy of the Ascension, when

Christ gave us these gifts.   In Ephesians (iv. 7 f.) Paul cites
the same psalm in order to prove the origin of the Christian
ministry in its varied functions.   We expect the term ' charismata,' but the Greek term in the psalm is δόματα, and the
apostle simply expounds it by saying that after the ascension
he gave some men to be apostles, etc.   The rubric of the
passage is that *each one of us is granted his own grace* (χάρις),
as determined by the full measure of Christ's gift (δωρεά).   As
usual he clinches his argument by quoting something from
the OT, which although not strictly a proof will serve as an
apt illustration.   To do this he changes the wording of the
psalm, possibly following some earlier interpretation.   The
second person is altered to the third, the gifts are given to
men instead of received from men, and consequently ' thou
hast received ' becomes ' thou hast granted.'   A psalm which
originally referred to material tribute of homage from conquered foes to Yahweh thus becomes a description of the
spiritual grace bestowed by Christ on the Church which he
has rescued from the evil powers of sin and death, and which
has been equipped by the divine Conqueror for its work.
Paul in short has the charismata in mind, though he omits
the abnormal or ecstatic cases, even healing; to emphasize the
gracious or ' given ' character of all service in the Church, he
turns an OT text into a meaning exactly the opposite of its
original sense,[1] in order to commend his argument.   The
variety of functions is a gracious provision of God for developing the vital unity of the Church in faith and knowledge,
through the due exercise of such ministries by gifted individuals within the corporate life.   The risen Christ *has
granted some men to be apostles, some to be prophets*, etc.   His
real gifts to the Church are gifted men, variously fitted to
promote faith and fellowship.

[1] See Josef Schmid, *Der Epheserbrief des Apostels Paulus* (1928), pp. 317–21,
for a good statement of the data.

2

Two later writers touch the same theme. In language and in thought the allusion to grace-gifts in First Peter (iv. 10 f.) follows Paul. 'As each has received his gift, minister the same one to another, as efficient stewards of the varied grace of God,' from whom the various functions are derived for the welfare of the Household. No self-reliance, no self-glorification ! On the other hand in the Pastorals it is hesitation to use the charisma that is the danger, not vainglory in employing it. In this group of documents ecclesiastical interests are predominant, and the term is exclusively applied to the exercise of the ministerial gift. A contemporary preserves the broader sense. In the only use of the term that he happens to make, Clement of Rome (xxxviii. 1) applies it broadly to all Christians. 'May the Body which we form in Christ Jesus be preserved in all its integrity ; let each be subject to his fellow, according to his position assigned by grace (καθὼς ἐτέθη ἐν τῷ χαρίσματι αὐτοῦ).' The charisma here is the lot of each member : 'Let the strong care for the weak, and let the weak respect the strong' (instead of envying or maligning them), 'let the rich furnish aid to the poor, and let the poor give thanks to God,' etc. The Pastorals, however, concentrate on the ministry ; Timotheus possesses a charisma or special form of apostolic grace which enables a Christian man to take his part in the service of the Church, and this is twice mentioned. *I would remind you to rekindle* (or, to keep alive, ἀναζωπυρεῖν) *the divine gift which you received when my hands were laid upon you ; for God has not given us* (i.e. you and me, as ministers) *a timid spirit but a spirit of power and love and discipline* (2 Tim. i. 6, 7). All ministry depended on personal character. The 'charisma' cannot be any power of ordination, since that could not be said to wax or wane ; it is the spirit of apostolic devotion and brave courage needed for witnessing to the gospel or for preaching the Word, which

Timotheus received at his ordination or commission, when he was consecrated solemnly to the service. The appeal is, never let this spirit be damped by a shrinking from hard duty, by false shame, or carelessness about character. Marcus Aurelius uses the same verb in urging men to revive their fundamental conceptions of life ; ' these it is in your power (however circumstances may be out of your power), these it is in your power to rekindle constantly ' (ἀναζωπυρεῖν, vii. 2). Clement of Rome too writes, ' Let faith in Him be rekindled in us ' (xxvii. 3).

The risk of having this divine gift spoiled by personal neglect is repeated in the counsel of 1 Timothy iv. 13 f., where, after bidding him attend to his scripture-reading, preaching, and teaching (i.e. to the distinctive functions of the apostolic office), Paul reiterates the advice ; ' do not neglect the gift that is yours, transmitted to you by the prophets, when the presbytery laid their hands upon you.' The transmission of the ' gift ' by the laying on of hands is a new feature, though Luke implies that this had marked the first mission of Paul himself from the Church at Antioch (Acts xiii. 3). But both allusions in the Pastorals emphasize the truth that unless such a gift is used, it will be lost. It is this responsibility which is urged, not any warning against vainglory. The implication is that the charisma, however it worked, is an aptitude or capacity granted for the ministerial vocation. As such, it is not to be received in vain ; the talent must be employed.

3

One use of ' charisma ' is absent from Paul and indeed from the NT as a whole. As with love, so with grace, Paul like the rest of the NT writers confines it to the relations between God and man ; consequently ' charisma ' is not a term for God's gifts in creation. It is in human nature not in nature that the expression of God's grace is sought and found by the apostle. Now Philo had traced creation itself back to the gracious goodness of God, and one passage on this truth is remarkable as apparently almost the only one in which he employs the term χάρισμα. The Alexandrian thinker ob-

serves : " the just man makes this supreme discovery, that
the universe is God's gracious gift (χάριν τοῦ θεοῦ) and that
nothing is the mere gift (χάρισμα) or possession of creation ;
hence thankfulness " (τὴν χάριν, note the double sense of
χάρις) " is due to Him alone.   Thus the most correct answer
to the question about the origin of creation would be that it
means the goodness and grace (ἀγαθότης καὶ χάρις) of God,
which He has freely bestowed (χαρίσατο) on the human race,
for the world itself and all that is therein is the boon and blessing and free gift (δωρεὰ καὶ εὐεργεσία καὶ χάρισμα) of God "
(Leg. Allegor., iii. 78).   This truth was soon echoed by
another Alexandrian, the Christian Clement, who pleads that
a Christian may well repay God with some faith for His good
gift of the universe.   ' At the price of a little faith He gives
you such a great earth to till, water to drink, water to sail
upon, air to breathe, fire as your servant, and a world to dwell
in. . . .   All these great works of creation and free gifts
(χαρίσματα).   He has let out to you for a little faith ' (Quis
Dives Salvetur, xi.).   Paul's special conception of grace and
the Spirit does not allow him to extend the term ' charisma '
to such divine endowments.

III

'GRACE' PREFERRED TO 'MERCY' (ἔλεος)

TO be freed and to be forgiven are, for Paul, two expressions of the happy result achieved by grace. However difficult it may be to explain the connexion of the two ideas in the apostle's mind, both are determined by the common end of life. The freed Christian and the pardoned Christian are alike brought into a positive relationship to God which means peace or allegiance or devotion in the form of a living, reasonable service. With regard to the conception of God's gift as pardon, it is to be noted that Paul never uses ἀφίημι, the common term for ' forgive,' in the sense of pardon, except once in an OT citation (Rom. iv. 7) and that he only once (Col. i. 14 = Eph. i. 7) uses the noun ἄφεσις, and then merely as a synonym for ἀπολύτρωσις. His use of ἔλεος and its verb is equally scanty, but it is notable. (a) Twice, apart from the human allusion in Romans xii. 8, the verb implies the favour of God shown to an unworthy recipient, without any specific reference to sin, as in 1 Corinthians vii. 25 (' I give my judgment as one that hath obtained mercy of the Lord to be faithful ') and 2 Corinthians iv. 1 (*I hold this ministry by God's mercy to me*); in Philippians ii. 29, the meaning is slightly widened but it is still the same (*Epaphroditus was ill, nearly dead with illness. But God had mercy on him, and not only on him but on me, to save me from having one sorrow upon another*). In this small group of passages ' mercy ' approximates to ' grace ' in the sense of God's kindly favour or goodness. (b) In another group, where the reference is not to the individual apostle and his mission but to the broad purpose of God, the associations of ' grace ' are equally prominent. Except in Romans xv. 9 (*the Gentiles should praise God for His mercy*), they all occur in the passage upon the historical problem of Israel's election

(Rom. ix.-xi.), and either denote the choice of the Gentiles (ix. 23, xi. 30, 31) or the general grace of God in its free selection and broad sweep (ix. 15–18, xi. 32), suggested by an OT text. A survey of the two terms in Paul's vocabulary shows therefore that the noun and the verb denote pity or favour rather than pardon, and that neither is used of an individual being forgiven.

There is a difficulty in Gal. vi. 16 : καὶ ὅσοι τῷ κανόνι τούτῳ στοιχήσουσιν, εἰρήνη ἐπ᾽ αὐτοὺς καὶ ἔλεος, καὶ ἐπὶ τὸν Ἰσραὴλ τοῦ Θεοῦ. As this is the first time Paul uses ἔλεος in his extant letters, we have no guide to the meaning that he was likely to attach to the term ; but in view of his later use of the word it probably denotes not the final mercy but the present favour of God. He is varying his expression of the same blessing. ' On all who will be guided by this rule which I have just laid down for Christian belief and discipline, may peace (in the full sense of bliss or prosperity) and mercy rest, yea or even upon the Israel of God. As he began the sentence he had in mind the psalm-ending (cxxv.) εἰρήνη ἐπὶ Ἰσραήλ (may Israel prosper; 'salvus sit et maneat,' Rosenmueller), perhaps echoed in the daily synagogue service with which he was familiar. But after ' peace ' he adds ' mercy,' in order to bring out liturgically the source of the welfare or bliss. It is tempting to follow Dr. E. D. Burton's theory that the closing words should read, ' And may mercy be on the Israel of God ' (i.e. the believing Remnant of Jews, even including those who did not see eye to eye with the apostle). But the Israel of God answers aptly to the real sons of Abraham (iii. 7), and on any other interpretation the καὶ after ἔλεος is very awkward. Paul is more likely at this point of his letter to be definitely claiming that true Christians, who followed his principles, were the catholic People of God, than to be making a semi-apology for his previous anti-Jewish outbursts.

It is true that in Hellenistic Greek ἔλεος acquired a wide range of religious meaning, due to the older LXX emphasis which made the term equivalent to ' salvation ' rather than to ' mercy ' in the stricter sense of the word. Thus Sirach (xxxv. 19 f.) describes God vindicating Israel in the world and thereby causing the People to rejoice in His ἔλεος. Such

8

saving mercy, he adds, " is seasonable in the time when He
afflicts them, like clouds of rain in time of drought." But
the narrower sense of ' mercy ' or compassion clung to the
word. There is an apt illustration of this in contemporary
Greek. In A.D. 67 Nero presented the province of Hellas
with local self-government, and in the address which he
delivered at Corinth he speaks floridly of the boon he was
bestowing on the Greeks (Dittenberger's *Sylloge* 376), calling
it a free gift (ἀπροσδόκητον ὑμῖν δωρεάν . . . χαρίζομαι) and
wishing that he had lived in the palmy days of Greece long
ago—ἵνα πλείονες ἀπολαύωσι τῆς χάριτος. As it is, he observes,
be sure that I am not doing this out of mere pity but from
sheer goodwill—καὶ νῦν δὲ οὐ δι᾽ ἔλεον ὑμᾶς ἀλλὰ δι᾽ εὔνοιαν εὐερ-
γετῶ. Note the use of χάρις as a free boon granted by a royal
authority, but also the feeling that ἔλεος was less than generous
goodwill. Nero disclaims the motive of mere pity, which
might convey a certain condescension. He assures the Greeks
diplomatically that they are not pitiful objects for him. He
poses as a Philhellene, who loves the Greeks with genuine
goodwill and desires to treat them as a friend and well-wisher,
even as he acts in an imperial capacity. The limitations of
ἔλεος in ordinary usage are reflected here with a clearness
which is all the more remarkable on account of the non-
religious setting of the phrase. So much was this felt in
Christianity itself that Christian scribes afterwards would
sometimes add ' and salvation ' to ' mercy,' as in Tobit viii.
17 (‫א‬44, 106), to bring out the full sense of the word. This
was evidently before the mind of Paul in the first century,
and it helps to account for his choice of a word like ' charis '
when he desired to express the full generosity and active
goodwill of God to man.

In the Psalms of Solomon it is ἔλεος not χάρις. God is indeed
χρηστός, and His goodness or kindness supplements His saving mercy
towards suffering, persecuted, and sinful Israel. In the former of the
two allusions to ' grace and mercy ' in Wisdom (iii. 9, iv. 15), the Latin

version has ' donum et pax,' but this was an error of translation, due
to the influence of the Christian ' grace and peace,' χάρις being taken
as ' a boon.'   Both Wisdom passages relate ' mercy ' to the elect, not
to frail humanity in general.   It was from this association of the word
that Paul derived his larger belief in God's ' rich mercy ' (Eph. ii. 4,
see 1 Peter i. 3), and yet it was not adequate for all his purposes.

It is Paul's preoccupation with the moral aspect of life that
explains why he prefers a term like ' grace ' to ' mercy,' or at
least why he needed another term than ἔλεος to represent the
relationship of God to men.   Mercy recalled the frail mortal
lot of men ; no doubt, this was due to their sin, but the consideration of life's plight often dwelt more on its pitiful situation than upon its moral evil.   Even when the latter was
recognized, the former was predominant.   Thus in the contemporary apocalypse of Baruch, a product of apocalyptic
piety at its best, on the passive side, the author appeals for
mercy (xlviii. 11 f.) :

> Hear thy servant,
>   and give ear to my petition . . .
> Be not wroth with man ;
>   for he is nothing ;
> take not account of our works,
>   for what are we ?
> Lo, 'tis by Thy gift that we enter the world,
>   and not by our will do we depart.
> We bade not our parents beget us,
>   we send not to Sheol to be received.
> What then is our strength,
>   that we should bear Thy wrath,
> or what are we
>   that we should endure Thy judgment ?
> Protect us in Thy compassions,
>   and in Thy mercy help us.

But on the view of the apostle the deepest word upon God's
mercy is not said when He is sought as a counterpart to the
fading fleeting years of man's mortality.   There is no Welt-
schmerz in Paul, not even in a passage like Romans viii.

19 f. For him men are in a deplorable state, not because
they are soon to die but because they are already dead in
trespasses and sins.   He sees them either as rebels against
God, wilfully defiant, or else as captives of Sin and the Flesh,
deprived of freedom and yet needing above all things rescue,
in order to be truly free for the service of God.   For penitence
indeed he is sure that God has mercy.   But his favourite conception is that of the divine power which deals with the situation of man, either as freely providing reconciliation or as
releasing the prisoners from their captivity. ' Charis ' was
better for this purpose than mercy ; it denoted power no less
than pardon.   The ordinary connotation of mercy limited it
to pity for the unfortunate, and even although the pity of a
great God acted graciously, it did not call up before the mind
the same active and spontaneous intervention as ' grace ' did.
What moved God, in Paul's mind, was not the silence or the
sighing of mortal misery in a short-lived life which had to face
death and the judgment before long, but the initiative of God's
loving purpose which would no longer wait ; he thought
less about the pathos of life than about its desperate moral
plight, and therefore he spoke of the ' grace ' which carried
God freely into the low estate of men who were ' yet sinners '
and enemies of His will.   Mercy moves to deal with the
results of sin ; grace moves to deal with the reason of sin.

After Paul the noun and the verb came more into play among the
churches, sometimes in a mere citation from the OT, as in 1 Peter ii.
10 (*once you were unpitied and now you are pitied*, i.e. taken into favour
as God's People), but also independently, as in the Pastorals, and in the
archaic language of Luke's songs (i. 50–78).   In the synoptic tradition
the verb is freely employed of the ministry of Jesus in healing and
pardoning.   In the apostolic Fathers ' mercy ' is not common ; generally
it denotes compassion or pity, occasionally favour, as e.g. Clem. Rom. 1, 2.

IV

WHY 'GRACE' IS PREFERRED TO εὐδοκία

PAUL preferred ' charis ' to another term which had begun to acquire a similar religious significance in biblical Greek —I mean εὐδοκία, with its verb εὐδοκέω. In this case the noun followed the verb in gaining a derived application to God ; sometimes in the LXX it renders *ratzon*, i.e. the divine will or goodwill, the latter not merely in the sense of approval or satisfaction but as active favour. The idea came to include determination as well as delight on the part of God. The Greek verb had led the way along this line, e.g. in Psalm xl. 13 : ' Be pleased (εὐδόκησον), O Lord, to deliver me,' or better still in xliv. 3, where the full idea of ' grace ' as the free intervention of the Lord on behalf of Israel with generous gifts is emphasized :

> For the land was not won by the sword of our fathers,
>   nor the victory won by their arm ;
> thine was the hand and the arm,
>   thine was the favour that smiled on them—

ὅτι εὐδόκησας ἐν αὐτοῖς. Paul must also have been familiar with the ' gracious ' use of the noun in the hymnbook of his party, for the Psalms of Solomon show precisely this meaning in a passage like iii. 4, where the obscure line ἡ εὐδοκία αὐτοῦ διὰ παντὸς ἔναντι Κυρίου is actually rendered by Wellhausen, ' er bleibt doch in Gnade bei dem Herrn.' Similarly in Sirach the noun denoted not only divine favour but God's independent action in human life which was not to be resisted, as e.g. in the famous passage (xxxvi. 13 f.) [xxxiii] where it is linked to the metaphor of the potter and the clay as in Romans ix. 21—

> As the potter's clay is in his hand,
>   so men are in the hand of their Maker ;
> all the Lord's ways are κατὰ τὴν εὐδοκίαν αὐτοῦ.

That is, He has power to handle human life as He pleases, according to His judgment ; His dealings are just but they are above criticism or comprehension.

In the NT the verb has sometimes the double sense of delight and purpose, as in Luke xii. 32 where εὐδόκησε means " it is the delight or good pleasure of the Father to bestow the Realm upon you " as a gracious boon or destiny.   The same generous purpose is in Paul's mind when he writes 1 Corinthians i. 21 and Galatians i. 15 with special emphasis upon the free action of God in graciously choosing this man or that.   The sense of divine approval, on the other hand, seems more prominent in the description of Jesus Christ ἐν ᾧ (or, εἰς ὅν) εὐδόκησα 'in whom I am delighted,' or ' on whom I have set the seal of my approval.'   Even here, however, the thought of the divine vocation is implied.   Certainly in Luke ii. 14 the noun denotes the gracious choice of God :

> Glory to God in high heaven,
> and peace on earth
> for men whom he favours

(ἀνθρώποις εὐδοκίας).   Here εὐδοκία denotes the gracious choice of God, not any approval or recognition of human excellence but His good purpose in freely singling out those who were to be favoured with the new revelation.   The angel's song (ver. 10) had already spoken of this as a *great joy for all the People* ; i.e. it was grace for all.

Read the nominative (' goodwill to men ') and the meaning remains the same.   The internal evidence is in favour of the genitive, though εὐδοκία soon was read in the sense of ' la grâce divine aux hommes ' (Loisy), and Professor Ropes has recently argued in its favour (*Harvard Theological Review*, 1917, 52–56).   Harnack's ingenious attempt to connect εὐδοκίας with εἰρήνη (' peace, no ordinary peace but the peace of His gracious will ') involves a somewhat harsh hyperbaton ; though Origen took this view, the Greek father was really adopting a tour-de-force of exegesis in order to harmonize Luke's words with the saying of Matthew x. 34.

Εὐδοκία might denote human purpose in a passage like Phil. ii. 13, but not here. Zielinski (*Revue d'Histoire et de Philosophie religieuses*, 1927, pp. 342–347), who admits that the genitive is more original than the nominative, and who is not afraid to see that it implies ultimately a smaller group than ' all the People ' (' c'est juste, pas de morale sans élite '), interprets it of ' la morale volontariste ' ; it is peace for men ' bonae voluntatis.' But however obscure the reading may be, it is clear that Luke intended to speak not of a human quality on earth but of a relationship between God and men which depended upon the divine choice. Men as the objects of such favour or revelation (*ἀνθρώποις εὐδοκίας*) would correspond to Daniel as ' greatly loved ' by God (Dan. ix. 23, x. 11, 19), which in the LXX is rendered *ἐλεεινός*. In the NT this adjective means a ' pitiful ' object, but in Daniel by a remarkable turn it denotes one who is the object of the divine *ἔλεος* or grace (so G. v. Rad in *Zeitschrift für Neutestamentliche Wissenschaft*, 1930, 111–115), i.e. graciously selected by God to receive a revelation, although he deemed himself unworthy of it, for *ἔλεος* does translate the Hebrew *ratzon* at one place (Isa. lx. 10) just as *εὐδοκία* does occasionally in the Psalter. Such a ' gracious ' meaning of *ἐλεεινός* in the Daniel passages is corroborated by the variants *ἐπιθυμητός* and *ἐπιθυμεῶν* (Vulgate, vir desideriorum), especially by the latter, for this reproduces the idea of the Hebrew, that man is the object of the divine affections or interests, not that he is full of desires for God, however true the latter may be.

Paul does employ the noun not only for human resolve but for the divine purpose, as in Philippians ii. 13, and specifically in connexion with ' grace ' at one point (Eph. i. 5–6, 8 f.), as the destiny of Christians in accordance with His eternal goodwill. The verb is employed of the divine will selecting Christians (Gal. i. 15, 1 Cor. i. 21), as well as in relation to the person of Christ, in Colossians i. 19: *it was in him that the divine Fulness willed* (*εὐδόκησεν*) *to dwell*, that the gracious purpose of God might be carried out. ' Haec habitatio est fundamentum reconciliationis,' as Bengel tersely puts it. But otherwise Paul prefers other terms like ' love ' or ' choose ' or ' grace.' Both the noun and the verb lay near to ' grace ' as he understood it ; both meant an utterly free purpose, undetermined by any claim or merit, and both could denote the selection of some by God either for special service or more generally to receive His favour. Yet for some reason the apostle chose ' grace ' rather than εὐδοκία. Whether as the result of this or not, the noun and the verb fade out of the primitive vocabulary of the Church ; neither is at all popular in the second-century literature.

V

(*a*) The last word in Marcus Aurelius is a Greek term for
'gracious.' Why resent death, the emperor pleads ? Why
take it as an unfair interference with life ? You may think
you are being sent off the stage too soon, but surely he who
sent you to play your part knows best when you have done all
that you can. ' Leave then with a good grace (ἵλεως), for he
who dismisses you is gracious (ἵλεως).' As it happens, this
is neither the first nor the last word in Paul's language about
God and human life. He read it in his Greek Bible ; the
LXX occasionally used ἵλεως of God as well as of men in the
sense of ' gracious.' So did Philo. It was widely employed
in the religious world of the day. Yet it never appealed to
Paul or to any NT writer. The writer of Hebrews indeed
happens to cite it once, but it is in a quotation which, like
Clement of Alexandria (*Cohort.* xi.), he makes from the book
of Jeremiah (*I will be merciful to their iniquities*, viii. 12) ; when
Peter remonstrates with Jesus, he uses the colloquial phrase
ἵλεώς σοι, much as we might say, ' Good gracious ! ' or
' Mercy on us ! ' in surprise and expostulation (Matt. xvi. 22).
But apart from these casual allusions there is nothing. From
the Greek of the NT we should never guess that the term was
not uncommon on the lips of educated and uneducated alike
in the first century.

Neither did it make headway in the early Church, for although
Clement of Rome does employ the word once or twice, in the wake
of allusions to the Majesty or Sovereignty of God (ii. 3, xlviii. 1, lxi. 2),
while Hermas avails himself of it twice (Vis. ii. 2. 8, Sim. ix. 23. 4),
very much like Epictetus (iv. 1. 13 ὁ Καῖσαρ οὐχ ἵλεώς ἐστιν), apart
from these two Roman writers it had no vogue whatever in the second

century. Ἔλεος and its verb, or οἰκτιρμός, preferably the former, served most Christians when they wanted to speak about God's merciful favour to men.

Even the cognate terms were little used. Paul does employ ἱλαστήριον once (Rom. iii. 25) in an obscure connexion, and Luke once has the verb, *God have mercy on me for my sins*, where ἱλάσκομαι answers to δικαιοῦσθαι (xviii. 13, 14). But unless we reckon the use of ἱλασμός by the author of the First Epistle of John (ii. 2, iv. 10), this is all.

(*b*) The omission of another group of words about the goodwill or graciousness of God can hardly be accidental or unconscious. The Priene inscription, with its address of the grateful Greeks in honour of Augustus (9 B.C.), announced : " Inasmuch as the Providence which watches over our life with anxious care has adorned it with the perfect boon of Augustus, filled with power divine that he might benefit mankind (εὐεργεσίαν), sent as saviour for us and ours . . . far outstripping all previous benefactors (εὐεργέτας)." Similarly, in the Additions to Esther (xvi. 13) Mordecai is " the bene-factor and saviour " of the Jews. Philo calls God σωτὴρ καὶ εὐεργέτης (*Leg. Alleg.* ii. 15) ; he sometimes connects εὐεργέτης with δεσπότης or σωτήρ. Plainly (*contra Flaccum* 15) δεσπότης, σωτήρ and εὐεργέτης were or might be allied terms, applied to men as well as to God in ordinary usage. ' Sovereign,' ' saviour,' ' benefactor,' were not far apart, though Philo is sensitive to a difference between them, which he expresses by saying that δεσπότης and κύριος have certain slavish associ-ations which do not cling to the higher σωτήρ and εὐεργέτης (*Sobriet.* xi.). Now Paul, who does not share Philo's dis-tinction between κύριος and θεός as divine names, uses only κύριος and σωτήρ. The apostle, followed here by most early Christian writers, passed by terms like εὐεργετέω and εὐεργέτης, εὐμενής and εὔνοια, even although they were in more or less regular use among Jews and pagans who spoke of the divine favour and help.

(i) *Εὐεργέτης* is indeed employed by the Hellenistic Luke in his version of the saying about pagan rulers, who are called *εὐεργέται* (Luke xxii. 25),[1] but it does not seem to be employed of God by any early Christian writer (apart from a possible case in Clement of Rome lix. 3), though it is a favourite word for God in Philo, and widely applied, as coins and inscriptions attest, to kings and benefactors as a honorific title ; Trajan, for example, is addressed as *ὁ παντὸς κόσμου σωτὴρ καὶ εὐεργέτης* (*Inscript. Graeci*, 1895, xii. 1. 978). Even the verb, so familiar in the OT and in Philo, made no headway in early Christianity. Clement of Rome happens to employ it once of the divine providence in the cosmos (xx. 11), but elsewhere we never meet it except in the interesting case of Acts x. 38. In telling how Jesus *διῆλθεν εὐεργετῶν καὶ ἰώμενος*, Luke's Hellenistic style recalls the mystery-cults, where to be *θεός* was almost equivalent to being *εὐεργέτης*, and healing, as in the case of Asclepius, formed a vital part of the divine goodwill. The noun *εὐεργεσία*, popularized by the LXX and Philo, and a synonym for *χάρις* in the vernacular, is occasionally used by Clement of Rome and by the author of Diognetus (viii. 11, ix. 5), but even it failed to rival *χάρις* among Christians of the early centuries.

(ii) It is not so singular that a term like *εὐμενής* or its noun made no appeal to Christians as a description of God the gracious, for, although Philo and Josephus employ it, the LXX does not. And the vaguer *εὔνοια* was ignored, though again Josephus sometimes spoke thus of God's gracious disposition. Ignatius does occasionally use it, but of man's never of God's goodwill, as pre-Christian Jews had done with *εὐμένεια*, e.g. in the Epistle of Aristeas (254) : " It must be understood that God governs the universe with kindness (*μετ' εὐμενείας*) and without anger." The Church did not need such terms to describe God as propitious or beneficent.

---

[1] See Deissmann's *Light from the Ancient East* [3], pp. 253 f.

PART D
ST. PAUL ON GRACE

ST. PAUL ON GRACE

I

WHEN the apostle sought to transmit ' the light of the knowledge of the glory of God in the face of Jesus Christ,' which had dawned upon himself outside Damascus, his good news may be described as a message or proclamation announcing that " All is of grace, and grace is for all."

I

From the outset he seems to have taught, " all is of grace." His emphasis upon this truth of religion was not simply the outcome of controversy with Jews and Judaists ; it would be more accurate to say that this controversy rose out of his teaching about grace. When he began and ended his letters with a prayer for grace, as he did from first to last, he was recalling Christians to their standing before God, and this relationship, with its privileges and its obligations, was conceived as due to nothing else than God's free favour. The first note struck by Paul is always that of indebtedness to God. His hopes for others as for himself went back to the conviction that life lay open to the stream of grace divine from beginning to end. In his own experience and in the course of his missions he had found that faith first turned men to God, faith receiving the gift of a new fellowship and freedom in which the soul owed everything to Him. Furthermore, the man thus saved by grace was not left to himself. He was not started on a career in which he might keep himself obedient and faithful by relying either on the Torah or on moral efforts of his own, inspired by some ethical code ; the faith which originally was response to grace took the standards of the new life from the same source, from the Spirit of the Lord, and drew upon grace for power to fulfil them. The Christian is not to be saved because he is good ; he is to be good because he is saved, and his goodness is determined by the will of the Lord who has saved him by bringing him into a right relationship to God. His insight into that will and his capacity for fulfilling it are alike the gift of God, no matter whether he was born a Jew or a pagan.

Faith therefore is self-surrender or self-dedication to the Lord who has thus come before the soul as the Deliverer from evil. It is the humble acceptance of the Lord's offer on his own terms, by those who are not too proud to be indebted to Him for what they cannot manage to achieve by themselves. Faith, says Goguel, " c'est-à-dire le don du cœur à Dieu en dehors de tout mérite propre de l'homme." [1] But this gift of oneself is elicited by a greater " don de cœur " on the part of God, which has revealed Him as gracious and loving without regard to the strict merits of man. Grace is favour and love to the undeserving. Only those who are prepared to acknowledge that they are unworthy, can put faith in the Giver of grace. Furthermore, it is as men rely upon the divine initiative and goodwill that they come to realize their need of it. An essential element of the apostle's teaching upon grace is that this attitude of receptivity towards the gift of God is not a preliminary phase but a standing condition, and that one form of penitence is vital humility and the sense of obligation to the Lord of grace.

2

Jesus once said that he had never found such great faith, " no, not in Israel," as he found in an army-officer. As faith is human, not to be confined within fences of race and nation, it was inevitable that the revelation of " All by grace," which was made to faith, should involve " Grace for all." Inevitable for a man like Paul, that is to say.

Various explanations have been given of how Paul came by this belief in ' grace for all, grace open to anyone, of any nation or race.' (a) According to some, he had been haunted by a feeling for the widespread range of religion even before

[1] *L'Apôtre Paul et Jésus-Christ*, p. 379.

he became a Christian. It is argued that his consciousness of being a Roman citizen, for example, made him dissatisfied with any exclusiveness or nationality in religion, and that he must have instinctively resented any practice or belief that separated man from man. On this view the Christian faith only deepened, as it was the first to satisfy, such a sense of religion as designed for the broad world of men. The provincialism of Jewish orthodoxy, the nationalist and racial exclusiveness of scribism, he had begun to feel, would never win " the keen Greeks, whose ironic incredulity he felt to his very soul," nor " the stolid Romans, whose utter indifference to all these local superstitions galled him perhaps more powerfully." [1] Just because Christianity seemed to be relaxing Jewish strictness and appealing to the wide world of pagans, he resented it. This heresy irked him because it appeared to be doing what he still hoped that the orthodox faith of his fathers should and might do. Eventually he came to see that the one satisfaction for his universal hope did lie with this new movement and its gospel of faith for all. One of the convictions for which he was instinctively groping, at the moment of his conversion, was that any religious message destined to supersede scribism, as he knew it, " must have far larger affinities for the Gentile world than strict Judaism could ever have had." Traces of such a vague tendency may be found in some circles of contemporary Judaism, short of the cosmopolitan position adopted by Philo. A certain disposition to modify rigid rites in favour of proselytes is evident, for example, in the Diaspora particularly. But we know nothing of Paul's pre-Christian outlook except what he has suggested in casual allusions, and this feeling for a world-wide appeal as essential to true religion cannot be safely attributed to him as an innate element of his religious being before he surrendered to Jesus Christ. (*b*) That he entered on the mission to pagans merely because the unbelief of many Jews

[1] R. H. Hutton, *Theological Essays*, pp. 318–322.

9

left a gap in the elect which had to be filled up,[1] is still more improbable.   He did argue at one point that gentile Christians were replacing impenitent Jews in the ranks of the chosen people (Rom. xi. 17 f.).   But this was a reflection on what had happened.   It is a very different thing to make it the original motive of his preaching to the world outside Judaism. Whatever may have been the time at which he realized that his real vocation lay in the gentile mission (and this never prevented him from offering the gospel to Jews in the first instance), surely we must seek a deeper reason for this conviction than the mere fact that upon the eschatological scheme a definite number of God's elect had to be made up somehow. Paul believed there was room for all, for anyone of any nation, in the realm of God.   Did his distinctive motive for carrying the Word far and wide lie in the happy thought that there were a number of vacancies in that realm which were graciously to be filled up from the ranks of paganism ?   On the contrary, this belief sprang from his realization of what " All of grace " implied.   There may have been a predisposition in Jewish Hellenism or in liberal circles of Judaism to which Paul was indebted for a readiness to accept such a belief, but it went back to more than any theological theory.

In later writers the idea of a fixed number of the elect became part of the grace-belief, as in Clement of Rome (e.g. ii. 4, lix. 2, etc.) ; but this is absent from Paul's speculations about the future.   Even in Romans xi. 25, when he anticipates how one day τὸ πλήρωμα τῶν ἐθνῶν will come into the fold of God, he means by ' the full number of the gentiles ' the gentiles in full force, i.e. all the nations in terms of the apocalyptic hope.   Before the end every nation must have the gospel presented to it (so Rom. xv. 19 f. implies) and be fully represented in the kingdom.   But this collective outlook does not include on its horizon the questions that rise before the mind of a modern :   What of the dead ?   Are all individuals to be saved ?   It is not the exact number of gentile Christians who are elect, that interests Paul.

---

[1] Schweitzer, *Die Mystik des Apostels Paulus,* pp. 179–183.

II

THE LETTERS OF PAUL

THE form in which letters nowadays open and close has become so conventional that a modern reader misses the significance of the words with which Paul begins and ends his epistles. We write, ' My dear so-and-so,' we sign ourselves ' Yours truly, or sincerely,' and the temptation is to suppose that the apostle meant little more when he began by wishing a church ' grace and peace ' and ended by praying that the divine grace might be with them. As a matter of fact, this was a new type of correspondence, and it was charged with a profound religious meaning. In such phrases we have a compressed allusion to beliefs which lay at the heart of the writer's gospel. Sometimes this or that element in the beliefs is discussed in the course of the letter, but what underlies such words about grace and peace is in every case vital to the religious experience shared by writer and readers. Paul can take for granted that his correspondents understand what these words imply. Now and then he has to make their content or context explicit, but they are never conventional. It was a new and true and glad thing for any religious community or group in the first century to be addressed thus.

Paul's letters were read aloud at the worship of the churches to whom they were written. When the local Christians met, it was for worship, and at their informal gatherings the apostle's letters would be read by any church belonging to his mission, either a letter sent to themselves or a copy of some letter to an adjacent church.   It is most probable that he had this ' liturgical ' use in view as he drew them up. The opening of a Pauline letter reads like a call to fellowship and prayer as well as praise. The salutation at the end is like a benediction when service is over. As a matter of fact some of his letters actually end with Amen, and Amen is sometimes added in other cases by later scribes.

The reading of such an epistle was originally an act of worship, not a literary treat. A Pauline letter therefore would serve as a primitive homily. Dryden was right in calling the apostolic letters of the NT the ' absent sermons ' of the apostles, who wrote in order to help churches from which they had to be absent for the time being :

> For all their wants they wisely did provide,
> And preaching by epistles was supplied.

Hence the form of the opening and the close in particular. We know little or nothing of primitive liturgical usages in the Church, during the first century. Doubtless these were beginning to take shape independently of Paul. But it is not unlikely that he created a letter-form, which afterwards fitted into the simple service of worship at which the letters were originally employed. The letters are none the less letters, that they were written with the consciousness of a gathering for worship at which they would be read. Hence the occasional doxologies and prayers with which they are interspersed. The ordinary book was ' published ' by being read aloud at some gatherings of literary friends. Paul's letters came into circulation by being read aloud at meetings for worship, and for this reason they open as they end with words of prayer and blessing.

I

The ordinary Greek opening of a letter was ὁ δεῖνα τῷ δεῖνι χαίρειν, i.e. ' So-and-so to So-and-so greeting ! ' The Oriental and Semitic word was ' peace ' (Shalôm), which in Jewish Greek became εἰρήνη (as in Ezra iv. 17 and v. 7) ; that is, the personal salutation passed into the opening formula of a letter. There were variations in both circles. Thus Greeks might add to χαίρειν a word like ' prosperity,' as the papyri prove. ' Dionysius to Ptolemaeus wishes (or sends) greeting and prosperity ' (χαίρειν καὶ ἐρρῶσθαι) is the opening of a letter [1] from the second century B.C., and numerous cases of this form are preserved. Indeed it passed over into Jewish Hellenism, if we may judge from the contemporary Epistle of Aristeas and the Second and Third Books of the Maccabees. An

---

[1] See Witowski's *Epistulae Privatae Graecæ*, p. 87.

elaborated form occurs in Second Maccabees (ix. 19), where a letter written by Antiochus to the Jews expands the simple χαίρειν into a triple greeting : ' To the honest (i.e. loyal) Jews Antiochus wishes much joy, health, and prosperity ' (πολλὰ χαίρειν καὶ ὑγιαίνειν καὶ εὖ πράττειν). These three terms were all in use. Plato, according to Lucian (*Slip of the Tongue in Salutation*), preferred εὖ πράττειν to χαίρειν, the Pythagoreans preferred ὑγιαίνειν and Epicurus employed χαίρειν in serious letters, using ὑγιαίνειν in private correspondence. Jewish letters incorporated in Second Maccabees preserve the simple χαίρειν, followed by ἔρρωσθε (xi. 27, 28) or by ὑγιαίνειν (i. 10), and also εἰρήνην ἀγαθήν (i. 1), i.e. ' perfect peace ' in the sense of full prosperity ; but outside Judaism ' peace ' was not employed in letter-greetings.

All such combinations Paul passed by. In writing to a Christian church he created a fresh form of greeting by turning the conventional words into a definite prayer in which χάρις was substituted for χαίρειν and ' peace ' retained. Two characteristic terms were thus combined ; although ' grace ' was new in this connexion, it was partly suggested by χαίρειν, and it preceded ' peace ' for a religious reason, even when ' peace ' had acquired a deeper Christian content. This reason is, " All is of grace."

With slight variations the formula is always the same.

> *Grace and peace to you*
> *from God our Father*
> *and the Lord Jesus Christ.*

This the fullest form (in Galatians, Corinthians, Romans, Philemon and Philippians) appears in 2 Thessalonians as :

> *Grace and peace to you*
> *from God the Father*
> *and the Lord Jesus Christ.*

For some reason this is abbreviated in Colossians into

> *Grace and peace to you*
> *from God our Father.*

Finally the shortest form recurs in First Thessalonians :

Grace and peace to you.

To the rule that ' grace ' in a letter-greeting is always first in Christian correspondence, there is one partial exception.   Peace was occasionally put first, during the second century.   Thus Tertullian's *De Praescriptione* ends with ' pax et gratia domini nostri Iesu Christi.'   The text is uncertain ;   Rauschen not only reads ' dei ' for ' domini ' but like Preuschen brackets the whole sentence ; the Migne text ingeniously alters ' et ' to ' ex.'   Still, whether Tertullian did or did not write the text as we have it, the likelihood remains that this form was familiar, for there is a Greek parallel in the earlier Letter of the churches of Lyons and Vienne (Eusebius H.E. v. 1) which opens : ' peace and grace and glory from God the Father and Christ Jesus our Lord.'   The reason for this particular stress on peace is given at the close of the account ;   the faithful are praised for having been free from anything that would mar the harmony of the church, such as apostasy, heresy, sectarian assertion, or unbrotherly harshness.   By their heroic death the martyrs are said to have sealed their testimony to harmony, concord, and unity.   ' Having been ever lovers of peace, they commended peace always, and went in peace to God, leaving Mother Church no grief, no strife or discord to the brethren, but joy peace, concord, love.'   Hence in the greeting ' peace ' is put before the grace which, as the letter repeatedly testifies, produced such Christian fruit.

As Greeks often played on the courteous ' chairein ' at the beginning of a letter or in a conventional greeting, the writer of the Epistle of James begins by linking it to ' charan,' which sounded so like it.   The alliteration enables him to pass at once into the first theme of his homily.   *James . . . to the twelve tribes in the Dispersion ;   greeting* (χαίρειν).   *Greet it as a reason for pure joy* (χαρὰν) *when you come across any sort of trial.*   This is the only epistle in the NT where the conventional salutation is retained, for the sake of a religious truth which it serves to suggest.

Χαίρειν meant to be glad as well as to greet a friend.   Even when it passed into the opening of a letter, it did not wholly lose its cheerful associations. If it sometimes came to mean little more than ' dear ' in our conventional start of a letter, it might mean more and often it did mean more. Thus it has been disputed whether χαίρετε in Phil. iii. 1 is an epistolary phrase (' greeting to you ') or definitely *rejoice*, as in James i. 1.

' Chairein,' however, directly suggested ' charis ' in the sense of thanks. Letters are preserved from pre-Christian and non-Christian sources which show how the conventional habit of beginning a letter with some expression of thanks to the gods took this stylistic form. Sometimes the term is the verb ' eucharistein,' sometimes the noun ' charis ' itself. Thus a pagan Egyptian in the Roman service writes to Epimachus his father and lord, ' Many greetings ! (πλεῖστα χαίρειν) . . . I thank (εὐχαριστῶ) Lord Serapis that when I was in peril at sea he saved me instantly ' (a second-century papyrus in *Aegyptische Urkunden aus den Koeniglichen Museen zu Berlin*, ii. 423). Or again in the third century B.C. we find a letter opening thus : Alcaeus to Sosiphanes ; ' greeting (χαίρειν) ! Many thanks (χάρις πολλή) to the gods, if you are keeping well ' (*Flinders Petrie Papyri*, i. 29). Paul does not use ' charis ' in this connexion, as he begins an epistle, but he followed the custom of opening a letter by using ' charis ' in the greeting and then employing the verb ' eucharistein ' (as in Thessalonians, First Corinthians, Romans, Philippians, Colossians, and Philemon). Twice (in Galatians and First Corinthians) grace itself strikes the keynote of the first theme in the letter. What underlay this phrase was the glad belief that the present blessings and the coming boons of the new order were all due to God's gracious favour. The Age to Come had begun ; in the resurrection of Jesus the Lord the messianic age had dawned, and soon it would be fully revealed at his return to complete the purpose of God. Meantime, during the short interval, believers were not left to themselves but kept in vital communion with the Father and the Lord. In the divine action both are present, and all is of grace. The saving power of God had been manifested decisively in His Son ; the Lord Jesus Christ, Paul believes, has done for men what they could not do for themselves and what they could not do without. For Israel the Torah was the supreme means of grace provided by God, whereby the People might attain life, that is, be righteous before Him by an obedience which, eked out by His kindly mercy, would secure sufficient merit. For Paul this method of religion had broken down and been replaced by a better ; the saving means of grace was Jesus Christ, and the relationship between man and God rested on God's grace entirely, as the gift and power of life. At every mention of ' grace,' he was unbaring the vital heart of Christianity as he understood it ; there is a throb and thrill of thankfulness for an undeserved and absolutely effective religion. The life of all who believed in Jesus Christ lay open now to the gracious power of God which had entered history and was working upon the susceptible in any race until the final aim of love divine was reached.

This opening phrase is therefore an emphatic, pregnant summary of nearly everything that the apostle has to say in the course of his instructions and appeals. For him ' given ' is the deepest note in the relationship of God to man ; He gives, and we view religion rightly when we think of it as given. His equivalent for this was ' grace,' and when ' grace ' is truly used it frees faith from anxious moralism and racial ties. The outlook of the word is to the past, to the initial phase in the crucifixion and resurrection of the Lord, and to the future, for which the experience of grace provides a certain hope. Besides this glad memory and happy prospect, a further expression of the satisfying relationship between a living God and the present needs of men is conveyed by the additional word ' peace.' For ' grace ' determines what ' peace ' means in Christianity. But before the latter term can be fully understood, we must turn to the closing formula of the letters.

2

It was also characteristic of the apostle to close a letter with some reference to grace. This is explicitly mentioned in the postscript to 2 Thessalonians (iii. 17, 18), where, after having dictated the letter up to this point, he takes the pen himself : *The salutation is in my own hand, Paul's ; that* (i.e. the fact of a personally written greeting at the close, what contemporary letter-writers called σύμβολον) *is a mark in every letter of mine. This is how I write : ' The grace of our Lord Jesus Christ be with you all.'* The words *This is how I write*, primarily refer to the handwriting, which was evidently characteristic. It is not needful to suppose that he wrote the word ' grace ' in some picturesque way of his own, as Bengel suggests. Any letter of the apostle could be proved genuine by a glance at the postscript or closing greeting ; but as this would merely apply to the autograph and not to copies of the letter made for other churches, it is probable that an allusion to ' grace ' formed part of his authentication. Some word about grace was vital to the closing salutation of a true Pauline letter, and this I have endeavoured to convey by printing the last sentence here in inverted commas. The use of ' grace ' in this connexion was plainly a new thing ; though we have no specimen of any Christian letter prior to Paul's correspondence, with the possible exception of that in Acts xv. 23–29, we may assume that the grace-salutation was a distinctive feature, unexampled hitherto. The letter of the Jerusalem church actually begins with χαίρειν and closes with the conventional ἔρρωσθε. That Paul struck out a fresh conclusion to the Christian letter was more than a stylistic idiosyncrasy ; it indicates the dominant place of ' grace ' in his religious vocabulary, and also the fact that this was recognized by his churches as characteristic of his own message. As a matter of fact, the only other salutation of this personal kind does include grace, i.e. the closing word to the Colossian letter : *This salutation is in my own hand, from Paul. ' Remember I am in prison. Grace be with you.'*

This closing salutation was in form even more original than the opening. According to Lucian, Ptolemy Lagus the Egyptian king had once reversed matters in a letter to Seleucus " by wishing him health (ὑγιαίνειν) at the beginning and adding Greeting (χαίρειν) at the end instead of Farewell (ἐρρῶσθαι), as is recorded by Dionysodorus who collected his correspondence." This was certainly abnormal,[1] in the fourth century B.C. and afterwards. But Paul's innovation of dropping Farewell for a closing form in which ' charis ' appears, is another feature of his style which proves how central a term ' grace ' had become for him. The ethnic Farewell (ἔρρωσθε) was employed not only by Claudius Lysias the Roman magistrate (Acts xxiii. 30 ἔρρωσο, writing to an individual) but by some Christians. After Paul the most independent writer of letters in the early Church was Ignatius the bishop of Antioch, and he is content to use Farewell with some Christian tinge to it, like ' Farewell in God our Father and in Jesus Christ ' (Ephesians), ' Farewell to the end in the patient endurance of Jesus Christ ' (Romans), or ' Farewell in Jesus Christ ' (Trallians), whilst Polykarp of Smyrna bids goodbye to the Philippian church by writing ' Farewell in the Lord Jesus Christ,' adding either (for the Latin in which alone the conclusion of the letter has been preserved is doubtful) ' and His grace be with you all ' or ' in grace ' (as a parallel to what precedes). This represents a fusion of the conventional ending with an allusion to grace, but it is the latter which is characteristic of Paul's letters. He allows nothing to stand alongside of ' grace,' nothing, that is, of a conventional phrase like Farewell. Grace may draw into its company other words of like significance, but it remains the dominant note of the music as a Pauline epistle dies away. His last word to any church was ' grace.'

---

[1] That is, the use of χαίρειν at the end of a letter, for ὑγιαίνειν was commonly used near the beginning. Paul never employs the term in any sense, but the Presbyter John begins a note to Gaius (3 John) by writing : *Beloved, I pray you may prosper in every way and keep well* (ὑγιαίνειν) *as indeed your soul is prospering.* Light on this as on the meaning of ' sound teaching ' (ὑγιαινούσῃ διδασκαλίᾳ) in the Pastorals is thrown by the fact that Plato uses χαριέντως ἔχειν and ὑγιεινῶς ἔχειν indifferently for being healthy or sound (Phaedo 80 c., Rep. 407 c., 571 d.).

The following are the forms employed :

(*a*) *The grace of our Lord Jesus Christ be with you* (1 Thessalonians, Romans xvi. 20).

(*b*) *The grace of our Lord Jesus Christ be with you all* (2 Thessalonians).

(*c*) *The grace of our Lord Jesus Christ be with your spirit* (Galatians).

(*d*) *The grace of the Lord Jesus Christ be with your spirit* (Philemon, Philippians).

Then, answering to (*a*), we find

The grace of the Lord Jesus be with you (1 Corinthians),

and the shorter form

Grace be with you (Colossians),

which in Ephesians is expanded into

Grace be with all who have an undying love for our Lord Jesus Christ.

The fullest form occurs only in 2 Corinthians :

The grace of the Lord Jesus Christ and the love of God and the fellowship of the Holy Spirit be with you all—

which is an expansion of (*b*) and (*d*).

Grace here is explicitly connected with the Lord Jesus, as it is not in the opening formula. Also there is an absence of any allusion to ' peace.' But this absence is only superficial, for an examination of the letters shows that the apostle hardly ever closes without making some allusion to *peace*, as though the two words chimed together in his mind. Grace may be reserved alone for the actual salutation at the end, but it generally follows a reference to *peace* as the divine blessing which is more than equal to any fears or friction in the Church.

The closing paragraph of First Thessalonians (v. 23–28) opens with the prayer *May the God of peace consecrate you through and through.* So does 2 Corinthians (xiii. 11–14) ; the final salutation is preceded by the counsel and promise, *Live in harmony* (be of one mind), *keep the peace ; then the God of love and peace will be with you.* In Philippians the same assurance that *the God of peace will be with you* is only separated from the grace-greeting at the close by a special paragraph of thanks for the Church's generosity (iv. 9, 10–20, 23). The uncertainty about the original form of the Roman letter makes it difficult to decide whether *The God of peace be with you* (xv. 33) was the last word or not, but at any rate in xvi. 20 the nexus of peace and grace is plain ; *The God of peace will soon crush Satan under your feet. The grace of our Lord Jesus Christ be with you.* In Galatians it is only the passionate outburst, *Let no one interfere with me after this, for I bear branded on my body the owner's stamp of Jesus,* that comes between the grace-greeting at the end and the climax of what preceded : *On all who will be guided by this rule, may peace and mercy rest, even upon the Israel of God* (vi. 16–18). In 2 Thessalonians the grace-greeting follows the prayer, *May the Lord of peace Himself grant you peace continually, whatever comes ! The Lord be with you all* (iii. 16 f.). Still closer is the connexion in Ephesians, where the grace-greeting immediately follows : *Peace and love with faith be to the brothers from God the Father and the Lord Jesus Christ* (vi. 23 f.).

Once or twice this underlining of peace is due to quarrelsomeness within the fellowship. But to assume that such a connotation of peace applies to all the peace-words, for example, to ' peace ' in the opening salutation, is to take a wrong focus. The impression is not unnatural, for the English word ' peace ' conveys merely one side of what the primitive Christians understood by εἰρήνη. Even interpreters in the early Latin Church went wrong at this point. Many moderns who are not Pelagians have thought, as Pelagius thought, that when Paul thus prayed for ' grace and peace ' in his churches he was bidding those who had received God's grace to be peaceable in their common fellowship. The God who had bestowed on them His grace expected and would enable them to keep the peace, instead of giving way to faction and party-spirit. " Commonet pacificos esse debere unam eandemque gratiam consecutos." But the words are more than a reminder that brotherly concord ought to be the outcome of religious fellowship with God. *Peace* here covers a wider truth which is implicit in the Hebrew tradition

of the term. To ' seek the peace ' of another was to seek
his good or prosperity (Deut. xxiii. 6, etc.), and this usage
prevailed down to the first century. Thus in the Zadokite
documents (viii. 17) one of the items of the religious ethic
is that everyone is ' to love his brother as himself . . . and to
seek the peace of his brother.' When we pass on to the NT
and especially to the epistles of Paul, the range of the word is
still more widened. In his peace-words at their deepest
we overhear more than the English term ' peace ' denotes.
In Galatians vi. 16 'tranquillitas mentis' (Aquinas) is not all
that the apostle intended the Galatians to understand. Even
the richer analysis offered by the Cambridge Platonist, John
Smith, in the sixth chapter of *True Religion*, fails to plumb
the depths of Paul's meaning. John Smith makes use of the
language of Romans ii. 9, 10 to illustrate the " vast difference
between the ways of Sin and Holiness. Inward distractions
and disturbances, ' tribulation and anguish upon every soul
that doeth evil ; but to every man that worketh good, glory,
honour and peace,' inward composedness and tranquillity of
spirit, pure and divine joys far excelling all sensual pleasures ;
in a word, true contentment of spirit and full satisfaction in
God." Yet for the apostle and his contemporaries not only
is ' peace ' or prosperity primarily the welfare of the human
soul in relation to God, but the essential peace of life, as it
is to be enjoyed in the present, is bound up with belief in
Jesus as the Christ or Lord. In the realm of messianic hopes
the supreme boon of the final period was peace. A traditional saying attributed to rabbi Jose the Galilean (*c.* 110 A.D.)
may be taken to express a characteristic tenet of rabbinic
piety. " Great is peace ! For in the hour when king
Messiah reveals himself to Israel he begins by speaking of
peace. As it is written, ' How beautiful upon the mountains
are the feet of him that bringeth good tidings of peace ! ' "
It was the conviction of the primitive Church that such
peace was theirs, thanks to the advent of Jesus as the Christ

(see e.g. Acts x. 36, where as in Eph. ii. 17 this very prophecy is claimed for Christ). Their experience of 'peace on earth' meant that the divine order had already begun, and that the hope of Israel was fulfilled for them in the gospel. This consciousness of God's favour and fellowship they traced back to Jesus, and in so doing they differentiated themselves from Judaism, just as from Hellenism, where no such expectation was current. When Paul therefore prays for 'grace and peace from God and from Jesus Christ' he is concentrating in a single phrase the essence of the primitive gospel. The eschatological hope of peace, which he still reflects (e.g. Rom. ii. 10), is no longer for him a wistful anticipation but a present reality, due to the grace of God in His Son. 'Life and peace,' 'righteousness, peace, and joy' (Rom. viii. 6, xiv. 17), are to be enjoyed here and now in the Spirit or realm of God. Only, whereas in Judaism there was no idea of the messiah who brought news of peace being lowly and humble, the Christians knew that their Christ had stooped to a human lot of poverty and suffering in order to bring peace on earth. That, said Paul, is the grace of the Lord, and from such grace alone is peace derived.

How closely grace and peace thus approximate may be seen from the fact that the Christian scribe of Codex Sinaiticus could alter 'peace' into 'grace,' in the text of Canticles viii. 10, just as the Vulgate does in 1 Peter v. 14.

3

This collocation of grace and peace at the end as well as at the beginning of a letter serves to confirm the impression that 'grace and peace' was a creation of the apostle. It is indeed possible that the opening phrase in the Pauline letters was originally a liturgical expression,[1] and that the apostle borrowed it from some opening sentence of worship. But this is guess-work. In the literary criticism of first-

[1] E. Lohmeyer in *Zeitschrift für Neutestamentliche Wissenschaft*, xxvi. 162 f.

class minds, the question, ' Who said it before him ? ' rarely takes us very far. Such an hypothesis cannot appeal fairly to the argument that ' grace and peace ' in this formula do not correspond to the normal usage of the apostle. On the contrary they do. As we have seen, he recalls ' peace ' as he comes to close his letters with a wish or prayer for grace, just as he had begun by placing both side by side. If he was not the first to coin this phrase, he was the first to say it with power, at any rate. For Paul peace had a vital connexion with grace, which is missed unless the complete sense of ' peace ' is realized. This fuller sense had been partly anticipated by Jewish and Hellenistic usage, but it was a creation of the Christian consciousness in its specific content, and, we may reasonably judge, invested by Paul first with its expression. (i) Primarily peace denoted peace with God, the rest of the soul in God on the ground of His saving revelation, i.e. on the basis of grace, as Luke indicates in the songs of his gospel. Thus in the Benedictus (i. 78, 79) it is *the tender mercy (ἔλεος) of our God* whereby *the Dayspring from on high* visits us

> *to shine on those who sit in darkness and in the shadow of death,*
> *to guide our feet into the way of peace.*

Again (ii. 13) the birth of Jesus the Dayspring is hailed thus :

> *Glory to God in high heaven,*
> *and peace on earth for men whom he favours.*

The sense of peace here is a blessing implied by grace, as Wesley was both scholar and Christian enough to know, when he rendered it,

> Peace on earth and mercy mild,
> God and sinners reconciled.

When Paul writes, *There is therefore now no condemnation to them which are in Christ Jesus,* or when he asks triumphantly, *If God be for us, who can be against us ? He that spared not his own Son but delivered him up for us all, how shall he not with*

him also freely give us all things ? he is thinking of the God
of peace who provides for His own and protects them, so
that they are delivered from restless fears and anxieties.
Their standing in grace is secure ; why be disturbed ?
(ii) ' Peace ' further denoted religious bliss and welfare in a
more general sense. The Hebrew *shalôm* which the Greek
term represented in greetings and elsewhere, covered a wide
range ; it included [1] " Peace of external circumstances and
peace of soul, a perfect harmony between the individual and
the world, between Israel and God," as e.g. in the priestly
benediction of Numbers vi. 24 f. (*The Lord be gracious to thee
and give thee peace*). With this meaning of the term Paul
was familiar. It was implied in the colloquial farewell,
Go in peace (ὕπαγε εἰς εἰρήνην or πορεύεσθε ἐν εἰρήνῃ), meaning,
' May you fare well,' as well as in the LXX phrase *Seek peace*,
i.e. the bliss and security of a life under the control of God.

The connexion of this last phrase with grace emerges in Hebrews
xii. 14 f. *Aim at peace* (this religious welfare) *with all* (i.e. in common
with all the other saints) . . . *see to it that no one misses the grace of
God* (on which alone such ' peace ' depends). The profound sense of
εἰρήνη in such a context had been noted by Philo, who declares (in
Quis Rerum Divin. haeres 58) that peace in the Bible, the peace enjoyed
by a man of faith like Abraham, is not the so-called peace of States
which are free from war's annoys, but the deeper bliss of a moral relationship to God as the Cause and Creator of the universe which imparts
stability to life. Similarly Epictetus deepens the term in iii. 13. Peace
was commonly hailed as the supreme boon of the strong Imperial govern-
ment, but Epictetus argues there must be an inward tranquillity, if life
is to be truly stable. " You see that Caesar seems to provide us with
great peace ; no longer are there campaigns, battles, great gangs of
robbers and pirates ; one can travel whenever he pleases and sail from
east to west. But can Caesar provide us with peace (security) from
fever too . . . from the love-craving ? He cannot. From sorrow ?
He cannot. From envy ? No, he cannot secure us against any one

---

[1] Abrahams, *Authorized Daily Prayerbook*, p. lxx.

of these at all." Only the inward peace of a philosophic mind, "proclaimed by God through reason," renders the world a place of peace.

In Paul peace sometimes has indeed a special reference to the feuds and factions of the churches he is addressing. But while the party-spirit which tore some of the communities, the disputes between liberals and conservatives over doctrine and practice, and the friction between individuals like Euodia and Syntyche at Philippi, lent emphasis to some of his words on peace, this is only one element in a thought which is far more comprehensive. And the thought is linked to that of grace. Order, harmony, and fellowship, as well as steady trust and freedom from nervous anxiety, are derived from the controlling consciousness of God. Peace in the full Pauline acceptation of the term is more than tranquillity and ease of soul ; it is the vital spirit of life in individuals and in the community,

> Peace whose names are also rapture, power,
> Clear sight and love ; for these are parts of peace.

It is an inward energy corresponding to grace in this respect. A prayer is a wish breathed in the presence of God, and when the apostle desires at the outset that ' grace and peace ' may be more and more experienced by his churches, he does not mean simply that peace is what may be called the subjective experience of the objective grace of God, though that is in a way true ; he makes both grace and peace come down from God and the Lord Jesus Christ. While grace and peace are equally experienced, they are equally the gift and the power of God, to be realized in life as faith is obedient and receptive.

The nexus between grace and peace is not to be modernized, as it is by Matthew Arnold. Although he had no interest in Paul's antithesis of grace and law, he found some place for grace in his ethical outlook. When he speaks of his brother William in the elegy, he recalls his finely-tempered manly character and asks,

10

> And what but gentleness untired,
> And what but noble feeling warm,
> Wherever shown, howe'er inspired,
> Is grace, is charm ?

More than that, he recognizes this spirit in what Paul termed " the meekness and gentleness of Christ."   In the essay on Modern Dissent, which Arnold found so assertive and ungracious, he praises Jesus for exhibiting this flower of excellence.   " This mildness and sweet reasonableness it was, which, stamped with the individual charm they had in Jesus Christ, came to the world as something new, won its heart, and conquered it.   Everyone had been asserting his ordinary self and was miserable ; to forbear to assert one's ordinary self, to place happiness in mildness and sweet reasonableness, was a revelation.   As men followed this novel route to happiness, a living spring opened beside their way, the spring of charity ; and out of this spring arose those two heavenly visitants, Charis and Irene, grace and peace, which enraptured the poor wayfarer and filled him with a joy which brought all the world after him.   And still whenever these visitants appear, as appear for a witness to the vitality of Christianity they daily do, it is from the same spring that they arise ; and this spring is opened solely by the mildness and sweet reasonableness which forbears to assert our ordinary self, nay, which even takes pleasure in effacing it."   This is true but by no means all the truth of ' grace and peace,' for peace denotes much more than quietness and harmony.   Its position in the Christian experience was once defined by Jowett in a few sentences which leave little to be said on this point.   " We grow up spiritually, we cannot tell how ; not by outward acts, nor always by energetic effort, but stilly and silently, by the grace of God descending upon us, as the dew falls upon the earth.   When a person is apprehensive or excited about his future state, straining every nerve lest he should fall short of the requirements of God, overpowered with the memory of his past sins, that is not the temper of mind in which he can truly serve God or work out his own salvation.   Peace must go before as well as follow after ; a peace, too, not to be found in the necessity of law (as philosophy has sometimes held), but in the sense of the love of God to His creatures.   At once and immediately the Gospel tells him that he is justified by faith, that his pardon is simultaneous with the moment of his belief, that he may go on his way rejoicing to fulfil the duties of life ; for, in human language, God is no longer angry with him." [1]   This transcript of a fundamental experience in personal religion corresponds to much that is most vital in what Paul meant by *grace and peace.*

4

A new and difficult phrase appears in the closing benediction of 2 Corinthians.   ' The grace of the Lord Jesus Christ and the love of God and the communion (*κοινωνία*) of the holy Spirit be with you all.'

> 'Η χάρις τοῦ Κυρίου 'Ιησοῦ Χριστοῦ
> καὶ ἡ ἀγάπη τοῦ θεοῦ
> καὶ ἡ κοινωνία τοῦ ἁγίου πνεύματος
> μετὰ πάντων ὑμῶν.

Paul means, " May you all experience or enjoy the grace bestowed by the Lord Jesus Christ, the love God offers, and the fellowship which the holy Spirit creates or inspires." Grace is put first, since it is through this manifestation that the divine love is realized.   Such is the order of experience, and as Paul commonly spoke of the Lord's grace in his closing salutation he begins with it here ; what grace implied was the divine love, which is the first thing to be said about the living God, but he can put that second without fear of being misunderstood, although in reality it was God's love which expressed itself through the grace of the Lord Jesus. What the third part of the phrase denotes, is the real difficulty. Does it mean, " May you all, who experience the divine love through Christ's grace, form a fellowship of the Spirit," i.e. the true fellowship created by the Spirit ?   Or is it, " May you all experience Christ's grace and God's love as you participate in the holy Spirit " (i.e. share in the Spirit's gifts) ?

The Authorized Version followed Wyclif by rendering ' communion ' ;   the Rheims version translated literally the Vulgate ' communicatio ' ;   Tyndale, who first put ' fellowship ' into the English versions, was followed by Cranmer and the Genevan version.

[1] *St. Paul's Epistles to the Thessalonians, Galatians, and Romans,* ii. pp. 266, 267.

In the nearest approach to the words elsewhere, Paul means 'participation in the Spirit.' Such is the sense of κοινωνία πνεύματος in Philippians ii. 1, where this participation denotes the loving and affectionate spirit of true fellowship in Christ. All Christians as they are Christians share in the Spirit, and the apostle implies that this participation breathes an incentive to unselfish love in the community. Here the primary idea is of the fellowship participating in the Spirit as vital to their experience of the Lord's grace and the love divine. There is a clue to its implication in what he had already written to the Corinthians. *I tell you, no one is speaking in* (i.e. under the influence of) *the Spirit of God when he cries,* ' *Cursed* (ἀνάθεμα) *be Jesus !* ' *And no one can say,* ' *Jesus is Lord* ' *except in the holy Spirit.* The context and content of these words are perplexing, but we may be sure that they meant something special for Paul, and indeed for anyone who had passed through an experience like his. If it is a terrible thing in life to find oneself laughing at what one once loved and admired, there is a special awe in discovering that we now have to adore what once we detested and despised. Paul had cursed Jesus, and had even tried to make others curse Him. This crucified pretender to the glorious messianic crown—this ringleader from Galilee who had been consigned to a shameful and well-deserved death in the holy City—Paul had despised and rejected him with the full force of his Pharisaic faith ! ' God's curse be on him ! ' the young Pharisaic leader had cried with flashing eyes and loud indignation. And now where he had seen nothing but disgrace he saw grace, the grace of the Lord Jesus Christ. Where he had formerly traced God's curse, he realized His love. His eyes had been opened to the risen, living Lord, and only the Spirit of the Lord, he knew, had wrought this change. What, Paul felt, but the power or Spirit of the living God is able to overcome the prejudices of Jew or pagan against Jesus the crucified and risen Lord ?

Dishonoured here thou diest,
Yet here I worship thee.

To call Jesus 'Lord,' the Lord of glory, to realize in this paradox the love of God, was impossible except within the sphere and influence of the divine Spirit.

In the light of this resurrection-faith, which is always axiomatic for Paul and his churches, it is only through the Spirit that Christians can invoke Jesus as 'Lord' at all, or call God 'Father'; i.e. the grace of the Lord Jesus Christ and the love of God are ours as we are in touch with the Spirit, not otherwise. The collocation of the three phrases here would correspond to the truth elsewhere expressed by Paul, when he declared that those who have *received the Spirit of sonship* are thereby moved to *cry 'Abba Father!'* It is in the order of the Spirit alone that such vital experiences become possible. As Christians participate in the Spirit of God, manifested within the new order of messianic blessing which has been inaugurated by Christ, they realize what grace and love mean. Thus, *God proves His love for us by this, that Christ died for us when we were still sinners*, and *God's love floods our hearts through the holy Spirit which has been given to us.* But if κοινωνία is to have anything like the same relation to 'Spirit' that grace has to Christ and love to God, it must mean an active communication of the Spirit, in other words a 'fellowship' or communion created by the Spirit. This is primarily the relation of Christians to God and Christ, but as κοινωνία already signified the divine fellowship of Christians, i.e. the common group of believers in Christ, Paul may well have included in it here this further idea. In this case the phrase would be an anticipation of 'fellowship' as used by the writer of First John (i. 3), where it covers fellowship with the Father and with his Son Jesus Christ as well as the corporate union of Christians. The apostle would therefore be embracing the idea of the Spirit as the creative principle of the new life and experience, as well as the idea that this involves a common fellowship among those who share that relationship to God through His Son. The Greek term for Paul signified generous imparting to others ; he could use it even of a contribution of money, given as the expression of Christian love within the fellowship (as in 2 Cor. viii. 4). It also meant intercourse between Christians and the Lord ; he could tell the Corinthians that they had been called by God *to fellowship with his Son Jesus Christ*. This rich double sense explains the usage here. The ' fellowship ' imparted by the Spirit is intercourse with God and His Son, and as this new life is a life of divine love experienced by human nature, it becomes a fellowship in the sense of a common life of brotherly love corresponding to its source. The Spirit as active within the fellowship communicates the things of God which are the inspiration of any Christian peace with God and man.

It may be that this elaboration of the simpler benediction, ' the grace of the Lord Jesus Christ be with you,' was due to the controversy with the Jews. Paul may be thought to echo this dispute,[1] as it were coining a formula of religion which would present succinctly the distinctive features of Christian belief : the grace of the Lord Jesus, not the Torah, then God under the comprehensive category of love, and finally, as the living proof of this revelation, the Spirit now imparted to all, not to a chosen few. The presence and power of the Spirit in the community was the guarantee that the messianic age had really arrived, as Christians claimed, through the grace of the Lord Jesus Christ, which expressed the love of God. Such is the suggestion offered by this theory. We should expect, however, had this been present to the mind of Paul, some reference to the Son and the Father, as in the confession of faith in Matthew xxviii. 19. It is probably superfluous to posit any such specific background for the saying. As a matter of fact, the saying stands out with equal force against the world of Hellenistic cults. The grace of the redeeming Lord Jesus Christ

---

[1] Harnack, *Verfassung und Recht der alten Kirche*, pp. 187 f. (Eng. Tr., pp. 263 f.).

is organically connected with the love of God in a way unknown to the cults, where, as we have already noted, the ' saving ' god was a subordinate deity who did not occupy any definite relation to the higher god or gods of the world. Also, ' the fellowship of the Spirit ' denotes the Church in a way unfamiliar to the mystery-religions. A fellowship not of the mere individual with the deity but of the community with God, a corporate tie in which the individual was closely bound both to God and thereby to his fellow-believers, a fellowship of communion in which the divine Spirit was active and realized—this was much nearer to Judaism than to Hellenism. What made the fellowship was the character and purpose of God as revealed in His Son ; that determined the nature of the fellowship, as a creation of the divine Spirit holding the members together in obedience to the will of God as their common principle. No thiasus quite approached this conception. Those who were thus conscious of being saved by the divine love in its gracious favour were knit in a relationship to their God which implied a social nexus of quite a novel character, that is, as compared with any cult of the period.

III

I

FOR the first part of his life as an apostle, i.e. for a period of nearly seventeen years, Paul was engaged in missions at Damascus and then in Syria and Cilicia, which were certainly on liberal lines ; from the outset he preached to pagans freely. It was his well-known sympathy with this gospel of ' grace for all ' that led Barnabas eventually to recruit him for the advancing campaign of the community at Antioch. But did he preach freedom from the Law in the trenchant form which is represented later in the letters to Galatia and Rome ? And if so, how did he escape interference from the conservatives in the Jerusalem Church ? These are questions to which no definite answer can be given. Paul may have taken a line similar to that of the Hellenistic preachers at Antioch, without committing himself as yet to a thoroughgoing statement of the principles involved in his propaganda. Liberality in practice may have preceded such a definite statement of principles as is to be found in what we may call his Middle letters, ' middle ' not because they move on anything like a ' via media ' but because they lie between the Macedonian letters and the Later letters in which the sharp controversy over Grace and the Law has ceased to be a dominant issue. It may have been the challenge encountered at Antioch which first made him conscious of the need to state the full truth about grace. " There is an inner freedom which may grow side by side with an allegiance fostered by birth and custom, prejudice and piety. But men first become conscious of this freedom when a demand is made that restricts it, or when it is assailed on account of some consequence already deduced from it by the enemy, but not as yet patent to the mind that cherishes it." Weizsäcker in these words [1] is explaining how the radical reply of Stephen to his Jewish critics had an emancipating effect upon the primitive Church, many of whom by the controversy thrust upon them in so unwelcome a way were forced to recognize that there was a latent antithesis between the gospel of Jesus the Lord and the belief of Judaism that the law and the cultus were God's final means of grace. This had not yet been realized, and the controversy therefore had a liberating result. Similarly the challenge of the conservative Jerusalem party to the Antioch movement may have been even for Paul an occasion to realize the need for presenting the inner principles of the gospel in a fuller form than had as yet been found necessary. Hence the antitheses of the Galatian, Corinthian, and Roman letters.

It is with Paul as with Francis of Assisi, his writings come from the last years of his life. So far as we know, he had been preaching and teaching in the Christian mission for nearly twenty years before he had occasion to write any letters. Whether his first extant letter was sent to the Thessalonians in Macedonia or to the Galatians in Asia Minor, anyhow, it is obvious that he had not then begun to think out his gospel for the first time. Nor again, even when he wrote letters, was it to teach the faith. The Thessalonian epistles, for example, are not a reflection of elementary Paulinism ; Paul in writing to this church has in mind the interpretation which appears in the later epistles where he has occasion to develop certain elements of his religious view. As a rule he took up questions raised by the local situation. It is significant that had it not been for some irreverent behaviour at Corinth, we might never have known what he believed about the Lord's Supper, for instance. If a vital truth is now and then argued, it is not because he feels the need of presenting a protocol or programme of Christianity either as it was common to the churches or as what he sometimes called ' my

[1] See *Encyclopaedia Biblica*, iv. 4796.

gospel.' It is important to bear these considerations in mind as we approach the epistles in a study of grace. When he told the Corinthians *You know the grace of our Lord Jesus Christ*, he was reminding them of something which he had always taught and with which they were perfectly familiar. No doubt in epistles like Colossians and Ephesians (which we may take as Pauline if not written by Paul himself) he does develop the theme of grace in view of fresh conditions. But substantially the main elements of what ' All of grace, and grace for all ' implied, were in his mind when he wrote the Thessalonian epistles. The fact that they are not argued out till he wrote Galatians, Corinthians, and Romans does not necessarily mean that he had then reached a more mature grasp of them than at a former period of his mission-preaching. It so happened that he did not require to write about grace definitely when he was corresponding with Thessalonica. Yet, as the very opening and closing greetings of these letters indicate, grace was already a fundamental conception of his religious preaching to pagans as well as to Jews. The material overlaps, but for the sake of convenience we shall take the letters thus. (i) First the Macedonian epistles, to Thessalonica and Philippi, then (ii) the Middle epistles to the Galatians, the Corinthians and the Romans, and (iii) the Later letters to the Colossians and Ephesians.

By the time Paul reached Galatia and Thessalonica he was preaching grace in a characteristic fashion. The force of his remonstrances with the Christians in Galatia rests on the fact that he had evangelized them with a gospel of grace and freedom and the Spirit, and the language of the letters to Thessalonica implies that ' grace ' was a familiar term. Behind him lay the controversy described in Galatians i.–ii. and Acts xv. If he does not enter into the sharp issues as he writes to the Macedonian churches, it is because there was no practical call for any such discussion. This applies to the Church at Philippi as well. The letter to the Philippians was probably the last of his extant correspondence, but it may be grouped for our purpose with the Thessalonian letters. All were written to the Macedonian churches, where nothing called for a theological discussion of grace ;

although Philippians reflects a situation of its own, the general attitude towards grace is on the whole common to this letter and to the Thessalonian epistles.

I

All three letters close with the prayer that the grace of the Lord Jesus Christ may be with the members of the Church, and open with the prayer that grace and peace may be with them. What this presupposes, we have already seen. As it happens, Paul has no occasion to speak of grace in connexion with the Jewish Law ; the majority of the local church were pagans by birth, and such a problem had not been raised at Philippi or at Thessalonica. But, whilst the letters are not treatises, they imply a definite teaching and belief about God and Jesus the divine Lord, from whom all blessings flow. Christians are reminded that their life lies open to this action of God on their behalf. At the heart of their new religion lies a power of generous help from God. He is *our Father*, not in the vague sense of a benign fatherly Spirit pervading the universe but as the strong Father of those who have accepted His call to belong to the fellowship of His Son the Lord Jesus. Those who own this Κύριος as their Lord need have no fear for the future. In calling the Lord Jesus ' Christ,' the apostle reminds them of his saving strength, for ' Christ ' was a title which implied One sent by God to be what some cults called ' Saviour.' God's grace had been shown in the mission of this Son and in the revelation of His call through the apostolic preaching, thanks to which they had *turned from idols to serve a living and a real God and to wait for the coming of His Son from heaven—the Son whom He raised from the dead, Jesus who rescues us from the Wrath to come* (1 Thess. i. 9, 10 : see v. 9, 10, Phil. iii. 20). Meantime they have the holy Spirit, God's own gift and power of life. They are not left to themselves during the rough interval of waiting. They can call upon a faithful God, who will strengthen and protect them, supplying all their needs from his wealth in Glory in Christ Jesus (2 Thess. iii. 3, Phil. iv. 19). *He who has begun the good work will go on completing it until the Day of Jesus Christ* (Phil. i. 6, so 1 Thess. v. 23, 24). *Spirit, soul, and body, may you be kept without break or blame till the arrival of our Lord Jesus Christ. He who calls you is faithful ; he will do this* (1 Thess. v. 23, 24).

All this corresponds to the primitive view of Jesus as Lord. The resurrection is the miracle which attests the new messianic order and hope, by the manifestation of the Spirit. Christ had been crucified and raised from the dead ; this was the supreme revelation of God's saving power, which ushered in the long-promised era of forgiveness and fellowship, and these boons, it was soon seen, were not confined to believers within Judaism. Whether Christ was viewed as the Prophet or the Servant, it was recognized that the resurrection had accredited him as God's final representative to men. Every saving power is due now to *the name of Jesus Christ the Nazarene*, Peter tells the Jerusalemite authorities, *whom you crucified and whom God raised from the dead. . . . There is no salvation by anyone else, nor even a second Name under heaven appointed for us men and our salvation.* Here the two notes of ' grace ' are struck, that it is free to all and that it depends wholly on Jesus Christ, crucified and risen. It is within a circle of beliefs like this that the Macedonian letters move.

2

In the correspondence with the Thessalonian Church, apart from the opening and closing greetings, grace is never mentioned except twice in the second epistle. These may be the very first allusions in Paul's definite counsels ; at any rate they are significant for various reasons. One occurs in a passage where the moral imperative is followed by a prayer about grace (ii. 15, 16) : *Stand firm and hold to the rules which you have learned from us orally or by letter. And may our Lord Jesus Christ himself* (αὐτός, for you are not left to yourselves) *and God our Father who has loved us and given us eternal encouragement and good hope, graciously* (ἐν χάριτι) *encourage your hearts and strengthen them for all good in deed and word.* Instead of yielding to the fascinations of religious paganism with which they were surrounded or to the godless forces of the age, the Thessalonians are bidden stand fast, loyal to the apostolic gospel. Such is their divine calling indeed, they are 'beloved by the Lord, chosen for salvation by God,' but this does not work automatically; care and courage are required, and to inspire such noble efforts the apostle invokes the gracious help of God. Elsewhere ἐν χάριτι means 'thankfully,' but here it is 'graciously' or 'by His grace.' Probably the words go with what follows rather than with what precedes. To love and to give, is the same as to be gracious, and the sphere of grace is the inner life expressing itself loyally. It does not come in Paul's way, as he writes these letters to Thessalonica, to mention grace in connexion with forgiveness; this was implied, when he spoke of grace and peace as God's fundamental blessing. What moves him to mention grace at all is the thought of the divine love and of the temptation to which loyalists were liable, under the strain of life, of doubting whether that love was really ready and generous in support of them. The context makes this plain. 'He called you to gain the glory of our Lord Jesus Christ. Well then, stand firm. . . . And may God who has given his loving gift of good hope nerve you graciously.' The spirit of brave perseverance is inspired by an assurance that the God who has so graciously rescued them from hopeless paganism will not leave them in the lurch, as they adhere to their vocation. It is, in fact, the same truth as is put otherwise in the words, spoken in view of fears about the future, 'He that spared not his own Son but delivered him up for us all, how shall he not with him also freely give us all things?' The divine grace is a lasting power, able to carry the devoted through the short dark hours before the Dawn.

The apocalyptic or eschatological outlook of the Thessalonian letters may explain why the divine love here, as connected with grace, occurs in a context not of forgiveness but of hope for the future which is based on the loving action of God and Christ in the past and the present. Similarly, in the only other references to the divine love, it is linked to election, and for the same reason, that the ultimate end of grace or election is the original object of that love, which is not to be defeated, whatever appearances to the contrary may suggest at present. But before passing to discuss these allusions to the grace of election we shall look at the other word on grace in the second Thessalonian letter and then at a cognate passage in Philippians.

At one point (2 Thess. ii. 13 f.) the apostle has been encouraging the local church to loyalty under severe trials, assuring them that their sufferings will mean a certain entrance into the Realm of God which is so near. The Lord will punish His foes and yours, when He arrives ; meantime hold on, for this trying discipline of yours will be rewarded ; God is thereby making you worthy (καταξιωθῆναι) of the Realm for which you suffer. So, he concludes, *in view of this* rough, testing time, *we always pray for you, asking our God to make you worthy* (ἀξιώσῃ) *of His calling and by His power to fulfil every good resolve and every effort of faith.* Here the more active side of life is to the front, instead of the passive endurance of strain, but the practical success of the Christian enterprise either in character or in service is referred to the power of God working in the devoted life. Then the chief end of this comes to be noted—*so that the name of our Lord Jesus may be glorified in you (and you glorified in him).* When the end arrives, and the crisis reveals that you have remained faithful, that will mean glory for your Lord and for yourselves.

The end and aim of grace in human experience is the glory of God (2 Thess. i. 12, Phil. i. 11, ii. 11). In technical terms, the τέλος of χάρις is the divine δόξα. " Man's chief end is to glorify God and to enjoy him for ever." The clue to this profound conception lies in the Christian expansion of the OT belief in the divine glory as goodness or graciousness. Since all the dealings of God with man in history and experience are a revelation of His inner self or aim for the world, this is supposed to awaken adoring recognition. But in the OT God is not glorified " when His goodness is revealed to men, and they admire or praise it ; for that would still involve a certain egoism. He is glorified when by revealing His goodness He attracts men unto Himself, and His own goodness is reproduced in them." [1] This is the NT thought of His grace leading up to His glory. As the original source of human bliss and fellowship lies in such free grace on His part, the full exhibition of His gracious purpose and its realization within the lives of Christians who enter into His purpose by faith, becomes a glorification of Him as the gracious God, who is glorified by this reproduction of His Spirit and life. The most explicit statement of this occurs in the repeated εἰς ἔπαινον τῆς δόξης αὐτοῦ of Ephesians i. 3–14, τῆς χάριτος being once added in order to make the meaning clear, but it is a fundamental thought of the apostle from the first.

The closing words κατὰ τὴν χάριν τοῦ θεοῦ ἡμῶν καὶ Κυρίου Ἰησοῦ Χριστοῦ round off the hope and prayer in the spirit of the greeting at the beginning of the epistle, *grace and peace to you from God the Father and the Lord Jesus Christ.* If there is any special significance in them, apart from the general thought that in the immediate future of Christians all is determined by the favour of God, whereas the disobedient (as has been said) will meet His anger and crushing doom, if Paul may be supposed to have put any emphasis on these words, it may be to reiterate the idea that the triumph of loyal Christians in the final struggle between faith and the evil power runs back to the energy of their Lord—in which case ' grace ' would echo ' power ' and also be a gentle reminder that personal good resolves and efforts are not the ultimate source of confidence. The Thessalonians knew that they had been rescued from paganism by the sheer grace of the Lord ; let them further realize that His grace was needful up to the very end, for all their eager courage and activity. The words would thus carry on the thought implied in the double mention of ' worthiness,' whether the verb be taken to

[1] A. B. Davidson, *The Theology of the Old Testament*, p. 174.

mean make worthy or count worthy.   All is of grace, the apostle suggests, both as an encouragement and as a warning, to rid them of undue self-reliance as well as of anxiety about the character and purpose of God in threatening circumstances. Everything works out *by the grace of our God and the Lord Jesus Christ.*

This phrase is of primary importance for the thought of the apostle. In *the grace of God and the Lord Jesus Christ* here, as in the opening formula of the letter, Paul sums up what elsewhere in the later letters he expands, viz. that in the work of grace Christ did not simply carry out a task imposed upon him by the Father but shared actively in it. The apostle can speak as freely of the grace of the Lord Jesus Christ as of the grace of God.   Both are factors in the divine Action.   The Lord Jesus Christ ' gave himself for our sins ' ; ' though he was rich yet for your sakes he became poor.'   He ' became obedient unto death, even the death of the cross.'   This is one side of the truth which is called the grace of God.   That the Son of God ' loved me and gave himself up for me ' is at once described by Paul as God's grace.   Grace like love is common to the Father and to the Son, and in the Son it implies an active, voluntary element in his death ; all this comes to the front when Paul speaks of the reconciling deed, but already it is implicit in the teaching of these Macedonian letters.

3

Twice in his letters the apostle connects grace and suffering, once with reference to his own experience, and once including other Christians.   Although the former occurs in a non-Macedonian letter, it may be grouped with the Macedonian allusion here, for the sake of convenience.   It is the well-known paragraph in 2 Corinthians xii. 7–10, on the disabling ' thorn in the flesh,' an experience which, he reflects, enabled him to verify, as he could not otherwise have done, the grace of the Lord.   ' For this thing I besought the Lord thrice, that it might depart from me.   But he said to me, " My grace is sufficient for thee ; for my strength is made perfect in weakness."   Most gladly therefore will I rather glory

in my weakness, that the power of Christ may rest upon me.'
Ἀρκεῖ (this is the first word and it is emphatic) σοι ἡ χάρις μου:
It is enough for you to have my grace, the reason being that the
divine power is fully realized and felt in human weakness.
The power of Christ, the apostle observes, rests on his life
like a constant, quickening, divine presence, as he is content
to suffer under the will of God. Hence he goes on to explain,
this makes me *satisfied, for Christ's sake, with weakness, insults,
trouble, persecution, and calamity ; for I am strong just when
I am* to all appearance *weak*. ' Under outward handicaps
and hardships I am being sustained by a power not my own ;
it is His grace.'

A still deeper note is sounded in Paul's grateful message
to the Philippian community, when he hails them as ' companions of grace with me.' So Tyndale and Cranmer
render the Greek of Philippians i. 7 ; συνκοινωνούς μου τῆς
χάριτος. The phrase might indeed be rendered ' partakers of
my grace ' ; Paul speaks of *my God* (i. 3) and ' my grace ' might
be a phrase of his no less than *my gospel*, above any misunderstanding, though generally he speaks of grace being given
to him or being in him. But the preferable translation would
be ' sharers with me in the grace divine.'

What this means, the context indicates. No doubt the Philippians
had contributed to his support all through his mission. He was on
such good terms with this loyal affectionate Macedonian community
that he could accept money from them, and they had been forward to
supply him with funds. He has just recalled the joy which he felt
for *what you have contributed* (τῇ κοινωνίᾳ ὑμῶν) *to the gospel from the
very first day* (i.e. from their conversion) *down to this moment* (ver. 5).
But this does not exhaust his meaning. The Church had also shared
with him in suffering for the cause of Christ, and this tie knit him and
them together. *On behalf of Christ you have the favour* (literally ' the
grace,' ἐχαρίσθη) *of suffering no less than of believing in him, by waging
the same conflict that, as once you saw and now you hear, I wage myself*
(i. 29). He and his friends, though separated by land and sea, had this

11

deep common bond.   He himself had been recently on trial, defending the faith before the Roman authorities, and even as he wrote he was a prisoner.   But, he writes, *alike in my prison and as I defend and vindicate the gospel, I bear in mind how you all share with me in*—not in my sufferings but in—*the grace divine* (ver. 7).   What is uppermost is not the dangers and trials which loyal Christians had to encounter but the Grace that bore them through.   He strikes the heroic note.   To have a share in forwarding the gospel at some cost to happiness and quiet, is a privilege.   It is a proof of God's signal favour that Christians are called to such trying service ;   the grace of God comes into play, as His servants openly confess and defend His cause.   It is *the good work* which God had *begun in them* and which He is sure to complete, the apostle believes (ver. 6), on the ground that when Christians put the interests of God first and are willing to uphold His cause at any risk to themselves, His grace is at work and goes from strength to strength.

To no other church does he write with the same confidence. We do not know what were the hardships of the Philippians, in the service of the gospel, but Paul views them like his own as part of God's high calling and privilege and as proof of His grace.   What he stresses here is therefore more than the favour of co-operation in the work of God.   At the end of *The Prelude* Wordsworth cheers himself and his friend Coleridge by the thought that their common endeavours would not be thrown away.

> Though (too weak to tread the ways of truth)
> This age fall back to old idolatry,
> Though men return to servitude as fast
> As the tide ebbs . . . we shall still
> Find solace—knowing what we have learnt to know,
> Rich in true happiness if allowed to be
> Faithful alike in forwarding a day
> Of firmer trust, joint labourers in the work
> (Should Providence such grace to us vouchsafe)
> Of their deliverance, surely yet to come.

This consideration, with its emphasis on the inner joy that no temporary discouragement could damp, is not far from the tone of Paul's words to the Philippians.   But the apostle

thinks of far more than discouragement ; it is actual endurance
of persecution that is the favour bestowed by God, and more
deeply than in his words to the Thessalonians he now speaks
of 'grace' as he thinks of service and suffering together.
Doubtless the Thessalonians too had at an earlier period
shared his experience of persecution.   He gladly recognized
this in his letters (in 1 Thess. ii. 14 f. and specially in 2 Thess.
i. 4 f.), where he declares that their brave, stedfast faith
under persecution was no casual misfortune but *proof positive*
that God was qualifying them for His heavenly realm.   *He
means to make you worthy of it.*   Even as the apostle is certain
that their patient suffering will be justly recompensed, he is
careful to mark the reward as graciously given, not earned
in their own strength alone.   But he does not connect such
loyal suffering with the service of the cause exactly as in his
words to the Philippians.   In the earlier passage he is reason-
ing on the lines of the Jewish belief as stated in the Berachoth
(5A), 'God gave three choice gifts to Israel—the Torah,
the Land of Promise, and Eternal Life, and each was won
by suffering.'   In the latter passage he speaks of the privilege
of suffering rather than of its reward.   The recompense is
not forgotten indeed.   *Never be scared for a second by your
opponents ; your fearlessness is a clear omen of ruin for them
and of your own salvation—at the hands of God* (Phil. ii. 28)—
which is parallel to the argument of 2 Thessalonians i. 6 f.,
and of 1 Thessalonians i. 14 f. where the Jews are said to be
persecuting the Church in order to hinder the preaching of
the gospel as 'grace for all' to non-Jews.   Nevertheless, the
interests of the gospel in the present are more in Paul's mind
as he writes to the Philippians than to the Thessalonians.
Suffering on the part of the faithful is viewed primarily
as the privilege of contributing to the success of the gospel-
cause, not only as a sure token of personal salvation.

'Grace'?   But should we not read 'joy' in Philippians i. 7, "sharers
in my joy"?   The presence of 'gaudii' in some early Latin codices

(Amiatinus, Harleianus, and Laudianus, e.g.) as well as in the fourth-century 'Ambrosiaster' commentary, proves that some Greek copies of the epistle must have read χάρας here instead of χάριτος at an early date, although no traces of it exist in any extant Greek manuscripts. It is hardly surprising that ' charis ' and ' chara,' springing from the same root, should be confused. Either yields a fair sense in certain passages. Here it was the unusual meaning of ' grace ' that led some editors to substitute the easier ' joy,' a characteristic word in Philippians. ' Joy ' is as wrong here in the Latin texts as it is in the Syriac texts of 1 Peter i. 13. The decision in the case of 2 Corinthians i. 15 is more difficult, for either reading here is relevant, and the textual evidence is not un-ambiguous, though probably what Paul wrote, as he explained to the Church why he had intended to visit them first, was that he had meant to let them enjoy *a double delight* (χαράν), not a double favour or benefit (χάριν). There is no doubt that the variant χάριν in Philemon 7 and 3 John 4 is an error for χαράν. Also the likelihood is that Edna's words to her daughter were, ' The Lord of heaven and earth grant you joy for this sorrow of yours ' (Tobit vii. 18) ; yet some pious scribes put χάριν here for χαράν, just as they did in Sirach xxx. 16. In the Easter homily appended to the Epistle to Diognetus (xi.–xii.), after praising the risen Lord 'through Whom the church is enriched and grace unfolded and multiplied among the saints, bestowing understanding, making mysteries clear, announcing seasons, rejoicing in the faithful, etc.,' he adds, ' Then is chanted the fear belonging to the Law, the grace of the Prophets is made known, the faith of the Gospels is estab-lished, the apostolic tradition is safeguarded, and the grace (χάρις) of the Church exults.' Read χαρά, Lachmann argued, ' the Church's joy exults.' An attractive conjecture, which gives an excellent sense ; but the preacher instantly warns his congregation not to ' grieve this grace ' !

A further illustration of the affinity between grace and joy is afforded by their adjectives. Twice ἐπίχαρις occurs in the LXX (Job xxxi. 29, Nahum iii. 4), and in both places ἐπιχαρής is a variant.

4

Nowhere else in the Macedonian letters is ' grace ' men-tioned. The ordinary ideas of the later epistles upon the

' gracious ' determination of life are absent ; there is not a word about ' heirs ' or adoption or the Promise. But the need of rallying some Christians at Thessalonica who were wavering under the strain of persecution led the apostle to speak of election, a truth which for him brought out the sovereign power of God and also the basis of assurance on the part of Christians. In both letters this is emphasized (see 1 Thess. i. 4, God has chosen you, iv. 7, v. 8, 9, 24), but particularly in the second (ii. 11, i. 11, ii. 13, 14), where the apostle is dealing with the bitter troubles that seemed to upset the Christian hope and to deny any purpose in life. Against this doubt he stresses the eternal choice of Christians by God, their invitation from Him, and the triumphant purpose which has begun and is to be completed in Jesus Christ ; once inside this, they need not fear. Since it is all of grace, God's doing and not any aspiration of their own nor any mere dream of a baffled human desire, and since they know God's character as their Father, as One who raised Jesus from the dead to be Lord and Christ, they may well take heart. *God called you by our gospel to gain the glory of our Lord Jesus Christ. The Lord is faithful ; he will be sure to strengthen you and protect you from the Evil One* (2 Thess. ii. 14, iii. 3).

God's love and His election of Christians are organically connected in 1 Thessalonians i. 4: *O brothers beloved by God, we know he has chosen you* (τὴν ἐκλογὴν ὑμῶν), and in 2 Thessalonians ii. 13 : *We are bound always to thank God for you, brothers beloved by the Lord, because God has chosen you as the first* (ἀπαρχήν) *to be reaped for salvation*. In the latter passage if ἀπ᾽ ἀρχῆς be read, the meaning is ' chosen from the beginning, i.e. from all eternity.' The thought in any case is that grace is for all ; Christians are now the Chosen People, whose tie to God goes back to His eternal will of love, and what the Jews had once claimed as their prerogative is now shared by gentile Christians who have accepted the Christ as their Lord. But this is not argued ; it is implied as a current belief, of which it is only needful to remind the faithful.

The term ἐκλογή was familiar to Paul in the Pharisaic Psalms of Solomon, where it does not mean ' election ' (not even in xviii. 6 ; in ix. 7 it denotes human choice) ; Paul never uses it except of the divine selection, here and four times in Romans ix.–xi. Apart from a solitary mention of the word in 2 Peter i. 10 (τὴν κλῆσιν καὶ ἐκλογήν), it happens only to be once used elsewhere in the NT, and there of Paul himself as selected by God for the gentile mission (Acts ix. 15, σκεῦος ἐκλογῆς).

In Philippians he only speaks of the divine call once, in relation to himself as pressing forward *to the goal for the prize of God's high call* (τῆς ἄνω κλήσεως) *in Christ Jesus* (iii. 14). But this is a special use of the term and idea. He does not mean the supreme reward held out by the heavenly call which had singled him out on earth, but rather the summons at death to enter heaven. So in the Greek Apocalypse of Baruch (iv.) it is argued that by drinking the sacramental wine the human race will ' receive in Jesus Christ the high calling and the entry into paradise ' (ἐν αὐτῷ μέλλουσιν τὴν ἄνω κλῆσιν προσλαβεῖν καὶ τὴν παράδεισον εἴσοδον). The prize is this divine summons at the end for a faithful follower. Thus κλῆσις here is nearer to a passage like 2 Peter i. 10, 11 (where κλῆσις and εἴσοδος are close together) than to Paul's ordinary use of the term. But in iv. 3 there is a side-allusion to election. By a charming touch, he apologizes for not mentioning by name some excellent local Christians, remarking that *their names are written* in a better place, *in the book of life* (iv. 3). The vivid metaphor had been commonly used in apocalyptic for assurance of one's election to share the heavenly citizenship, though here there is no reason to suppose that these comrades (αἵτινες ἐν τῷ εὐαγγελίῳ συνήθλησάν μοι) are dead. The most characteristic expression of election in Philippians is the political metaphor of iii. 20 (ἡμῶν γὰρ τὸ πολίτευμα ἐν οὐρανοῖς ὑπάρχει), which would be telling for citizens of a Roman colony like Philippi. *We are a colony of heaven*, set here to hold the fort, knowing that we are not forgotten at headquarters in the Homeland to which we owe our very existence. The context of the saying makes the point clear. As a colony was a body of citizens in a foreign land, retaining their rights of citizenship in the mother-country and maintaining the home-traditions among aliens, so Paul hints that Christians must live true to their origin and that their lot is safely determined by a power not in themselves. The phrase sums up therefore in non-theological language two aspects of election by grace, as a source of hope and as an ethical incentive. When Polykarp writes to Philippi a century later, he reproduces in his own way the same idea by addressing them as τῇ ἐκκλησίᾳ τοῦ θεοῦ τῇ παροικούσῃ φιλίππους.

Twice, in speaking of his own experience (i) Paul glorifies the divine initiative or election by grace. ' I am pressing on (διώκω) to appropriate (καταλάβω, grasp, lay hold of) it (i.e. the full Christian experience), because I have been appropriated myself by Christ Jesus.' He finds his own attainments inspired and intelligible in the light of what he had experienced at the hands of Christ, who had arrested him, as it were, taken possession of him. That for Paul was the beginning of everything. He was conscious that the Lord had taken hold of him, and this relationship therefore had a divine purpose in it which encouraged him to go on. It is the thought of the psalmist,[1]

> My soul clings to thee,
> thy right hand holds me fast.

Indeed, in Philippians iii. 12, Paul is repeating the truth he had already put otherwise in ii. 12, 13. The arrest of his life by the Lord had stirred eagerness of will and mind to enter into the new experience and calling ; διώκω, διώκω, he repeats, ' I press forward . . . I press on to the goal.' Every power of his being is alive ; in taking the initiative by putting him upon the right track, the Lord had revealed a love and purpose for him that moved him to do or suffer anything in order to make this his own. What I am out for, he protests, is a religious position which is not of my own making, a

---

[1] Psalm lxiii. 8, ἐκολλήθη ἡ ψυχή μου ὀπίσω σου, ἐμοῦ ἀντελάβετο ἡ δεξιά σου.

religious venture depending on my moral achievements.   It is, he reiterates, not of the law (not based on moral obedience to the Torah) but *the righteousness of faith in Christ, the divine righteousness that rests on faith* (τὴν ἐκ θεοῦ δικαιοσύνην ἐπὶ τῇ πίστει), faith which is a response to the Lord's purpose and offer of grace.   This faith is a vital energy, for whilst human personalities have nothing they have not received, neither have they anything that they have not acquired, in the sense that endowments must be made their own by moral co-operation.   Yet Paul derives such faith from the inspiration of its Object, and therefore for ' righteousness ' he even uses the more personal expression ' the knowledge of Christ Jesus my Lord.'

This truth is echoed in another word upon the ultimate ground of religion, in 1 Corinthians xiii. 12.   One day, he writes, when this life is over, ' I shall understand the full truth, as all along I have been myself understood ' (καθὼς καὶ ἐπεγνώσθην). That God has taken knowledge of him is the deepest fact in life.   For ' know ' here means as usual the personal interest of the Lord in those whom he has chosen and to whom he has given his Spirit.   As a Pauline disciple put it, ' *the solid foundation laid by God* has a double *inscription* ; one is, *The Lord knows who are his*, the other is, *Let everyone who names the name of the Lord give up evil*,' and the former means selection and personal care, not simply that Christians are known or distinguished from other men but that they enjoy an intimate control and care from their Lord.   So here, Paul recalls the basis of the Christian life.   All his efforts to learn the lesson of life as love rest on the revelation graciously made to him.   The more one is conscious of the need for acquiring fresh knowledge of the love-life, the more one recalls the divine purpose of love which has no limitations in its personal hold of one's character.   Ἐπεγνώσθην.   The Lord has had a mind to me.

(ii) The fact that the truth of election is presupposed in

these earliest letters as familiar (he does not argue it ; he argues from it) proves that it formed a salient element of the apostle's teaching. The religious reasons are obvious. When the experience of God's grace reflects upon its origin in the will of God, the instinctive result is a doctrine of election ; Christians realize that they owe their position not to any insight of their own into the faith but to the call and choice of God Himself, who singled them out for this privilege. They are conscious of having been *selected by grace, and therefore not for anything thay have done ; otherwise grace would cease to be grace* (Rom. xi. 6). The first step was taken by God, and taken long before the Christian awakened to his need of salvation ; it was a free, gracious movement within the eternal Will. In no other way could Paul explain why he or anyone else had ever been selected for membership in the Church of God. It must have been God, and God moved by love. The belief was therefore one expression of practical experience as the Christian mission developed. Though taken over from the OT, it marked the Christian consciousness becoming aware of itself in relation to providence in the past and in the future.

What forced this upon the mind was at first the sense of security, or rather the need of being sure that the new experience was not a passing mood of the human spirit, not even a temporary fit of favour on the part of God. Pagan deities might show favour in a capricious way, but Christians, particularly converts from paganism, desired to know that they had been taken up into the lasting purpose of their Lord. Sudden the experience had been for most of them ; the visit of some missioner, hitherto a stranger, had meant an utter change of life which by baptism had enrolled them in a new fellowship. Through the preacher's Word of God the Call had arrested their careless, undeserving lives. But though sudden, it could not be a sudden thought upon the part of God. He must have thought of them before they thought of Him. Such was the overpowering conviction of these primitive believers.

The moral ends and interests of belief in election were in the main that Christians thereby were moved to be hopeful, honest, and humble. (*a*) Hopeful, because their future was assured, guaranteed by the eternal character and purpose of a Lord who was reliable. It is to encourage patience and loyalty under the strain of the present and in face of the future that Christians are reminded of the past, i.e. not of their past but of God's. There is no fear of a break-down on His part, and the assurance of this serves to keep His followers from breaking down as they await the end. (*b*) Only, this hope is pressed as a motive to honest living invariably. ' Never let us rest on our oars on the pretext of being " called " (κλητοί), never let us go to sleep in our sins, lest the evil Prince get hold of us and thrust us out of the Lord's kingdom ' (Barnabas iv. 13). So one early preacher wrote, and the spirit of his warning pervades the NT. When election is spoken of as a supreme encouragement, it is instantly connected with the obligation of personal loyalty to the purpose of God. (*c*) As Christians owed everything to this grace of God, pride was out of the question. The greatness of this love to people who had not deserved it to begin with and who could only obey its very demands by help received from heaven, was felt to leave nothing open but a grateful humble spirit as its correlative. No one who truly understood what this grace meant could pride himself either as he looked towards God or as he looked round on outsiders.

So far as ' charis ' meant generous giving on the part of Christians within the fellowship, the Macedonian churches had little to learn. They had caught from the first the ethical inspiration of grace as a motive for helpfulness and self-sacrifice. When the collection for the Judaean poor was started by their apostle, the Macedonians, as he gratefully declared, were forward to send contributions ; they needed no pressing, these warm-hearted communities in Macedonia (2 Cor. viii. 1 f.). God's grace in their experience elicited an immediate and spontaneous response in the shape of liberal aid to their starving fellow-

Christians, at some cost to themselves. On the other hand, Paul evidently felt that they required, at Thessalonica anyhow, a warning against loose morals. They had no help on this point from their local associations, for in the cult of the Cabeiri, whose cathedral was at Thessalonica, phallic obscenities were part of the mystical worship. These Phrygian deities, so widely popular in the Ægean and in Macedonia, had their rapturous appeal ; indeed Kern [1] thinks that the thirty-ninth Orphic hymn may have belonged to this mystery-religion. But its basis in the reproductive powers of nature did not make for moral cleanliness. There was a disconcerting blend of mystical excitement and licentious suggestion in its rites. Paul therefore has to remind the Thessalonians that the cult of Jesus the Lord, with its Spirit-raptures and ardent fellowship, is for those who are prepared to be clean. Election, the other side of grace, is linked to this particular demand. Our *God did not call us to be impure*, like these Cabeiri devotees, *but to be consecrated*. The deep Hebrew tone of *holy* is sounded, in its fully moral implications, in order to train the Thessalonians to conceive and practise the Christian life of grace as a good life.

In the Macedonian letters the third aspect is absent ; these good Christians were not tempted to indulge in spiritual pride and they had no problem of the Law in their religious life which might have led to any feeling of complacency or of reliance upon their own efforts. Theirs was a simple Christianity, unvexed by speculative difficulties, and characterized by a natural disposition which did not make for religious self-conceit. It is the two former aspects of election that Paul has occasion to mention. The Philippian Church indeed was exposed either to some challenge from local Jews or to a propaganda of the judaizing party, which led Paul to protest that real Christians like himself relied on no outward privileges of birth within the chosen people but solely upon Christ Jesus ; he does contrast legal righteousness or a self-made religious standing with ' the righteousness that comes through believing in Christ, the righteousness which is from God and bestowed upon faith '; he utters incidentally the pregnant

[1] In Pauly-Wissowa's *Real-Encyclop.* (1919), pp. 1399 f.

saying upon the grace-initiative of God which we have just
noticed. But he does not enter into the matter so earnestly
as in Galatians and Romans, plainly feeling that the local
church was not in need of specific counsel on the subject.
His words are rather an illustration from his own life than
an anxious warning. In Philippians as in the two Thessalonian letters the references to election are confined to the
practical issues of perseverance and the good life. The
former (*a*) has been already noted. The latter (*b*) is prominent in the reminder that the position of the called involves
ethical purity answering to the character and purpose of the
Lord who has graciously taken them into His own life. *God
has chosen you as the first to be reaped for salvation, by consecration
of your spirit* (ἀγιασμῷ πνεύματος, i.e. of your whole personality)
and by faith in the Truth (2 Thess. ii. 13). Ἀγιασμός here is
wider than in 1 Thessalonians iv. 7 (*God did not call us to be
impure but to be consecrated ; hence, he who disregards this, disregards not man but God who gave you his holy Spirit*), where the
Spirit is the power of God put into the elect life as the motive
and power for clean conduct instead of licentiousness, though in
both, it should be noted, the call is not to self-sanctification
but to refrain from anything that would thwart God's purpose.
Hence the rendering of ἀγιασμῷ πνεύματος as ' consecration by
the Spirit ' would bring both passages into line.   In any case
the Spirit as the mark of the new messianic era is conceived
not as an ecstatic fervour without moral discipline, as in some
of the cults, but as the inspiration of right living after the will
of God revealed in the gospel of His Son.   What election
means is not a mere safe passage to heaven but the obligation
of good behaviour on board, if life is not to be shipwrecked,
good behaviour as obedience to sailing orders.   God's choice,
the forgiveness of sins through the death of Jesus Christ,
and His indwelling power, all point to a hope which implies
moral alertness on the part of those who are thus favoured.
We must not sleep like the rest of men, but be wakeful and sober

. . . we who belong to the day . . . for God destined us not for Wrath but to gain salvation through our Lord Jesus Christ, who died for us that waking in life or sleeping in death we should live together with him (1 Thess. v. 6–10). At Thessalonica the besetting dangers were evidently a moral laxity due to (i) the tone of their pagan traditions ; (ii) an excitable temper of restlessness which was stirred by the eschatological outlook of the new faith in its intensity ; and (iii) the idea, fostered by the mystery-religions, that anything done in the body surely could not make much difference to those who had been safely initiated into the Christ-cult.

Some words as well as the idea of these Macedonian allusions to election recur in the appeal made by Clement of Rome (xxix.–xxx.) : ' Then let us draw near to Him in holiness of soul, lifting to Him hands pure and unstained ; let us love our gracious and pitiful Father who has made us His chosen portion (ἐκλογῆς μέρος').' After quoting some OT verses, from Deuteronomy xxxii. 8, 9, iv. 34, etc., which are taken to apply to Christians as the elect of God, the writer continues : ' Since then we are a holy portion, let us do all the works of consecration (τὰ τοῦ ἁγιασμοῦ πάντα).'

In the *Martyrium Agapes*, etc. (i), an account of some Thessalonian women who were put to death in the later persecutions, ' grace ' is connected with the first Advent, παρουσία and ἐπιφάνεια being taken to refer to this, not as in Thessalonians to the second. The Martyrdom begins ἐπὶ τῆς παρουσίας καὶ ἐπιφανείας τοῦ δεσπότου καὶ σωτῆρος ἡμῶν Ἰησοῦ Χριστοῦ οσῳ πλείων ἡ χάρις τῶν πάλαι, τοσούτῳ μείζων ἡ νίκη τῶν ἁγίων.

IV

THE MIDDLE LETTERS

THE letters of the Middle period reflect a situation in which Paul's teaching on grace is challenged.   Galatians answers the question, Is deference to the Law necessary in order that a Christian may enjoy complete salvation or indeed be a Christian at all ?   Romans discusses the question whether the Law has any rôle in the Christian religion.   The Corinthian letters reflect the same antithesis between grace and the Law, but the problem raised by the new consciousness of freedom is not exactly the same as in Galatians ; the references to grace are less controversial here, and they touch a wider circle of interests than in any of the earlier letters, probably because in these letters we have a fuller disclosure of the apostle's mind towards a church or group of churches than was possible in the case of Galatia or of Rome.

The breadth of survey in Romans marks it off from the others.   The word ' all ' is a keynote of the epistle. $Πᾶς$ occurs over seventy times.   Indeed Paul inserts it in one of his OT citations in order to bring out his point better (x. 11). The gospel is ' for everyone who has faith,' ' all have sinned,' ' the same Lord over all is rich to all that call upon him,' ' God hath concluded all in unbelief that he might have mercy upon all,' ' Every one of us shall give account of himself to God,' and so on.   This is due in part to the problem of Jew and gentile within the scope of Christianity, which engages the apostle's mind, and which is so fully and antithetically discussed that it differentiates the letter from any other.   To make explicit what is contained in an intuition like that of grace may lead to some formal statement which does not do complete justice to the intuition itself, either because it tends to isolate the intuition as experienced from its living context, or because it attempts to rationalize an ultimate issue involved in that experience. A religious instinct may well be stronger than the reasons given for it by thought. This is true of such statements about grace as we find in Romans. On the other hand, controversial arguments are helpful in their own way. Though they are put sharply, in the form of antitheses, they are here as elsewhere useful as they exhort people to believe in their intuitions ; they are one method of persuading men to see the consequences of what they are doing and believing. It is an invariable service to faith, to show men that their present position is opposed to faith, although they may imagine that both are compatible.

But it must not be supposed that disputation drys up devotion. On the contrary, these Middle Letters reveal for the first time the thrill which is evoked in Paul by the thought of grace. He was conscious that he and his fellow-Christians were living in an order in which a full tide flowed into their little lives from the great ocean. Over and again he speaks of ' grace abounding,' far surpassing in power any contrary force of evil, flooding life with a lavish wealth of hope and strength. Or he will speak of it as an amazingly liberal gift, ' the riches of his grace,' ' the surpassing riches of his grace,' the ' unspeakable Gift,' of which one cannot say enough, so wonderful is its generosity, not merely to the undeserving but in its wealth of unfolding treasure as it is experienced by faith and need. When Paul thinks of grace, it calls up before his mind God pouring into human life His marvellous favour ; his language vibrates with passionate gratitude as he surveys the working of it amid the poverty and weakness of life.

This sense was by no means confined to him. One NT writer speaks of Christians receiving ' grace after grace from His fulness,' another of ' the manifold grace of God,' so rich in its variety. Indeed, words like ' abundant grace ' or ' rich grace ' are specially characteristic of the NT, and the hymns of the Church, which often preserve more traces of its real faith than the creeds, corroborate this conviction of the primitive age. ' Sovereign grace o'er sin abounding,' ' Plenteous grace with Thee is found,' and Dryden's ' Plenteous of grace ' in his version of the *Veni Creator Spiritus*, are modern instances. But the intuition is older ; it recurs in Luther's massive hymn ' Aus tiefer Noth,' which is a version of the hundred and thirtieth psalm :

> Ob bei uns ist der Sünden viel,
>   Bei Gott ist viel mehr Gnaden,
> Sein Hand zu helfen hat kein Ziel,
>   Wie gross auch sei der Schaden.

The closing stanza of the eucharistic hymn by Thomas Aquinas runs,

> Iesu, quem velatum nunc aspicio,
> Quando fiet illud quod tam sitio,
> Ut te revelata cernens facie
> Visu sim beatus tuae gloriae.

But in the version by Dr. Neale this becomes—

> Jesus, Thou whom thus veil'd I must see below,
> When shall that be given which I long for so,
> That at last beholding Thy uncovered face,
> Thou wouldest satisfy me with Thy fullest grace.

It was not merely exigencies of rhyme that led to the last words.

This intuition is not stirred by the revelation of grace in pardon alone, although the consciousness of forgiveness forms normally its primary source ; it extends to the experience of grace throughout the Christian life, for Paul as well as for others in the first century. A characteristic expression of grace entering into the practice of common life, with an impetus derived from its upper source, occurs in the following appeal to the Corinthian Christians on the subject of charity and liberality to their starving fellows in Judaea (2 Cor. ix. 7–15). *There is to be no grudging or compulsion about it, for God loves the giver who gives cheerfully. God is able to bless you with ample means* (πᾶσαν χάριν), *so that you may always have quite enough for any emergency of your own and ample besides for any kind act to others ; as it is written* (of the generous man in the OT),

He scatters his gifts to the poor,
his charity lasts for ever

(i.e. this liberal man's charity or beneficence is unfailing, or, if Paul for once uses the language of ' merit ' without fear of being misunderstood, it is an eternal credit to him in the sight of God). *He who furnishes the sower with seed and with bread to eat will supply seed for you and multiply it ; he will increase the crop of your charities—you will be enriched on all hands, so that you can be generous on all occasions, and your generosity, of which I am the agent, will make men give thanks* (ἐυχαριστίαν) *to God ; for the service rendered by this fund does more than supply the want of the saints* (the poor in the Jerusalem Church), *it over-flows with many a cry of thanks* (εὐχαριστιῶν) *to God. This service shows what you are, it makes men praise God for the way you have come under the gospel of Christ which you confess, and for the generosity of your contributions to themselves and to all ; they are drawn to you and pray for you, on account of the surpassing grace* (χάριν) *of God which God has shown to you. Thanks* (χάρις) *be to God for His unspeakable gift* (δωρεᾷ)! The climax of the passage is the free ' gift ' of God's ' grace ' in the gospel, which produces a gracious temper of generosity in Christians. But this rich favour of God includes worldly means, as used for His ends, namely for self-support and for charitable pur-poses. And the outcome is thanksgiving to Him on the part of the recipients.

I

' All is of grace ' means the gospel. This is definitely assumed in the context of Galatians v. 4. *You are for justifica-tion by the Law* (δικαιοῦσθε is conative) ? You listen to these missioners who persuade you that salvation requires an accept-ance of circumcision and all the rest of the Law ? *Then you are done with Christ, you have deserted grace,* for it is by *faith* that ' we ' (ἡμεῖς, emphatic) *wait in the Spirit for the righteous-ness we hope for ; in Christ Jesus circumcision is not valid,*

12

neither is uncircumcision, but only faith active in love. The saving order of God revealed in Christ is an order of grace, entered by faith, and faith is morally vital by itself ; it does not need to be eked out by supplements from the rival system which it supersedes. It is assumed that this order commits Christians to a life of love, answering to the loving grace of Him who has created the relationship, and this assumption throws light on the meaning of grace ; Paul proceeds to argue that the Spirit produces the real ethical guarantees of true religion, as it produces loving unselfish life, because that corresponds to the character and purpose of Christ Himself. But meantime he declares that the one object of belief and confidence is Christ or grace.

He is meeting here the person who might say, " Well, the Law may be hard, as you point out, but I'm prepared to undertake all these extra requirements of religious discipline, even if need be to be circumcised, if thereby I may assure myself of salvation." The apostle's reply is, " But it is not a question of completing your salvation ; if you submit to the Law you are shifting the entire basis of your religious faith, from Christ as grace to ' merit ' or ' works,' " Law and Grace are viewed as incompatible systems of religion. To toy with the former is to invalidate the latter, from which Christ came to free the soul. " I would ask you one question," the apostle writes ; " did you receive the Spirit by doing ' works ' of the Law or by having faith in the gospel message ? " The experience of the Spirit is the mark of grace, that is, of the new era. To relapse from it is fatal, and any rehabilitation of the Law, however plausibly it may be urged on spiritual grounds, is a relapse.

(*a*) The grace with which he thus identifies the gospel is, as we have already seen, divine action on the part of God and of Jesus Christ. So closely are God the Father and Jesus Christ associated in Paul's mind, when he is thinking of grace, that not only can he speak of grace coming from both, and of *the grace of God* as well as of *the grace of Jesus Christ*, but even in one passage of God's call becoming effective through the grace of Christ. This is in the opening words of Galatians. It is the only place where he expands the greeting, for a reason that comes out in the sequel. After the customary *grace and peace to you from God our Father and the Lord Jesus Christ*, he adds—*who gave himself for our sins to rescue us from the present evil world—by the will of our God and Father, to whom be glory for ever and ever ; Amen.* *I am astonished you are hastily shifting like this, deserting Him who called you by Christ's grace.* It was gracious of Christ, he means, to give himself for our deliverance from sins ; thereby God's call or choice of us became effective. By God's will Christ sacrificed himself for us, and God *raised him from the dead* (ver. 1). The divine purpose and power of redeeming love thus came into play. In the experience of the Galatians, to which Paul appeals, the Will had become a Call which picked them out of their desperate condition and put them in a right relationship towards God ; nothing could affect this relationship except a move on the part of the Christian to shift the conditions, and it is against this mistake that Paul is protesting. As he puts it, from a slightly different point of view later on, ' my life depends on *faith in the Son of God who loved me and gave himself up for me.*' *I do not annul God's grace* (as my critics allege. No) *but* (what I do hold is that) *if righteousness* (i.e. the salvation of which I have spoken already) *comes by way of the Law* (and not by the gracious action of God and Christ), *then indeed Christ's death was useless.* The divine labour of love is not lost unless men try another way of salvation or rescue or righteousness ; and Paul in speaking of this instantly passes from Christ's love to God's grace as factors in the saving action, just as he does above in speaking of God's call and Christ's grace.

The Greek text is certainly susceptible of another interpretation (i) *Τοῦ καλέσαντος ὑμᾶς ἐν χάριτι Χριστοῦ* might mean *the Christ who called you by (His) grace, ἐν χάριτι* being perhaps equivalent to *graciously* (as in 2 Thess. ii. 16). That *Χριστοῦ* or *Χριστοῦ Ἰησοῦ*

or *Ιησοῦ Χριστοῦ* and *καλέσαντος* went together was often the interpretation of those who followed one or other of these ancient textual
forms, and so later editors have sometimes judged.   But elsewhere it
is usually God who calls, e.g. in ver. 15 (*God called me by his grace*).
Indeed the simplest form of the text undoubtedly would be the early
second century *ἐν χάριτι* (so e.g. Tertullian *De Praescript.* 27 qui
suos vocavit in gratia), without anything to follow.   Furthermore (ii) *ἐν
χάριτι* might be rendered *to* or *into* (Christ's) *grace*, as is certainly the case
in the similar phrase of 1 Corinthians vii. 15 (*ἐν δὲ εἰρήνῃ κέκληκεν
ὑμᾶς ὁ θεός*) : ' God called you into a or into the sphere (relationship)
of grace,' summoning you to His own order of grace as the one safe
position.   So the Vulgate, Wyclif, the Rheims Version, and the A.V.
render the words, the main exception being Cranmer's ' Christ who
called you by grace.'   Such a rendering gives a good sense.   In reality
it does not matter very much for our purpose which view of *ἐν χάριτι*
be taken, but there is something to be said for the instrumental use of
ἐν here, in view of the context with its argument that the authentic,
original gospel went back to a divine Call which was bound up with
divine Grace, and that this Power of Love required no supplement ;
it is effective, Paul contends, on account of Him who intervened with
power.

(*b*) In Galatians ii. 11–14, 15–21 the positive value of grace
is brought out by means of a statement upon the issues arising
out of the well-known difference of opinion between Paul
and Peter, which is recalled for the sake of illustrating the
principle at stake.   To what extent Peter and his party sym-
pathized with Paul's view about grace, our sources do not
permit us to be certain.   Luke does make the supersession
of the food-laws, in the case of Peter, a precedent for Paul's
larger position.   Indeed, on the basis of his sources, he makes
Peter admit that even for Jewish Christians salvation was not
bound up with observance of the Torah.   He asks the conservatives at Jerusalem, *Why are you trying to impose a yoke on
the neck of the disciples which neither our fathers nor we ourselves
could bear ?   No, it is by the grace of the Lord Jesus that we
believe and are saved, in the same way as they* (i.e. Gentile

Christians) *are* (Acts xv. 11, 12). This is Luke employing
Paul's language and his liberal spirit. But it is not improbable
that he was correct in attributing such a position to Peter.
The very fact that elsewhere in Acts he does not draw the
logical conclusion, but allows that Jewish Christians still kept
and were entitled to keep the Torah, tells in favour of this, for
his apologetic desire to represent Christianity, as far as possible,
as the continuation of Judaism, determined the latter tendency.
It was his interest to minimize the sharp issues of the conflict.
But in describing Peter's position it is not necessary to suppose
that he is reading back a liberal idea. How such an idea of
Jewish Christians being free from the food laws and indeed
from observance of the Torah could be worked out, he does
not explain. He simply states the fact that such was the view
of Peter and his group, using the very term ' grace ' to express
it. As the account in Galatians implies, this was the position
which differentiated Peter from James and his group and in
principle set the former not very far from Paul.

In ii. 11–14 Paul has been describing how he took Peter
to task at Antioch for inconsistent conduct. Peter had not
been true to his own principles, and Paul recalls how he had
had to rebuke the senior apostle for having implied that Gentile
Christians were really bound to conform to the Law. He
puts his own conviction forward. But he is no longer recalling
the discussion at Antioch so much as meeting the same issue as
it confronted the Galatians. In what follows (15 f.) he is
thinking aloud, as it were. It is a soliloquy or a summary of
his religious position. The question raised at Antioch was
so fundamental that he answers it rapidly and decisively, in
order to bring his argument to bear upon a church which in
its own way was also being tempted to compromise on what
was for Paul the vital issue, namely, ' For salvation is it enough
to have faith in Christ, or does the Law require to be brought
in as a supplementary saving principle, if not as an alternative ? '

The paragraph is compressed and rather difficult to follow, partly because he presupposes the fuller statement as we have it afterwards in Romans, partly because it is not quite clear what misrepresentations he had in view ; but the sentences vibrate with power and intense conviction. As Lütgert argues, if we had nothing of Paul but these words we should nevertheless be able to grasp his gospel in its essence ; all else is a commentary on them. The clue is supplied by the climax, ' I do not frustrate the grace of God ; for if righteousness come by the law, then Christ is dead in vain.' With these words he sweeps into the main argument of the epistle. But we are concerned with them as they stand. They reflect an objection to his teaching of grace. He is meeting some criticism of it, or some misunderstanding of it, on the part of others. Objections taken to some truth by contemporaries are always important, for they bring out its challenging element. Historically we understand a new movement in religion or in any other sphere of life as we enter into the way in which it was misunderstood. The opposition it provokes at the outset is illuminating ; such criticisms point either to an element of the new truth which is being exaggerated or inadequately stated by those who support that truth, or else they reveal that weakness in the current situation at which the new truth has struck with uncomfortable force. What was it, we ask, in the case of Paul ? What was the objection which roused this protest, and who were the critics of his grace-gospel ?

We may be Jews by birth (we Jewish Christians, I speak for those like myself who were born under the Law), *and not ' gentile sinners '* (the current phrase used by Jews, which was heard at Antioch from some of the conservative Jewish Christians, much as a Moslem might speak of these ' dogs of Christians '), *but since we know* (Peter and his party included) that *a man is justified simply by faith in Jesus Christ and not by doing what the Law commands, we ourselves* (for all our privileged position under the Law of God) *have believed in Christ Jesus so as to get justified by faith in Christ and not by doing what the Law commands—for by doing what the Law commands ' no person shall be justified'* (quoting freely from Psalm cxliii. 2). So far the argument seems clear. Even we Jewish Christians had to leave the Law for Christ, or (to put it subjectively) to turn from Law-obedience to faith, in order to be right with God. That was the result of God's revelation to us in Christ ; we recognized in the crucifixion of Christ this higher revelation of God's saving purpose. Even such of us as were ' exceedingly zealous of the traditions of our fathers,' perhaps with a just claim to be considered ' blameless touching the righteousness that is in the law,' even we humbly admitted that there was no way of being saved except by turning to Christ. Well then, *if it is discovered* (if it turns out) *that in our quest for justification in Christ we are ' sinners ' as well as the gentiles* (καὶ αὐτοί), *does that make Christ an agent of sin* (ἁμαρτίας διάκονος) *? Never.* It is true, Paul admits (see Rom. i.-iii.), that we are all on the same level ; ' all have sinned and come short of the glory of God ' ; Jews with the divine Law are sinners needing salvation as much as gentiles outside the Law (ἄνομοι). But does this imply that to ignore the Law's distinction between things clean and unclean, for example, as Christ requires us to do, is ' sin ' ? The position taken up by Peter and his group at Antioch really involved this. Paul pushes their action back to its principles, arguing that it practically meant a retrograde movement, as though acting on the principle of freedom in Christ and eating with gentile Christians who had not been circumcised were a ' sin.' In that case, from the conservative standpoint, Christ had indeed led them for the time being to commit what, according to the Law, was a real sin or breach of God's will. But, Paul retorts, if you are talking about sin, the true sin would be to relapse from Christ to the Law. *I really convict myself* (ἐμαυτόν, not Christ) *of transgression* (and he uses a forcible word παραβάτης deliberately, instead of ἁμαρτωλός, since the latter had been used ambiguously of gentiles), *when I rebuild what I destroyed.* One does that, if one proposes to fall back upon the Law as the basis and standard of life. Why ? Is it because Paul means that in that case the Law is again set up, the Law which we confess we cannot keep and which therefore will make each of us a ' transgressor ' ?   This is a possible interpretation, but it is better to understand the sentence as an assertion that for Christians of Jewish birth to revive the Law or to adhere to it in their new life is the real transgression in God's sight, since the death of His Son was a divine discarding of the Law. Discarded it is, Paul continues, by those who share my position. *For* (and here he speaks out of his own heart, using ἐγώ for the first time) *through the Law I* (ἐγώ) *died to the Law that I might live for God* (ἵνα θεῷ ζήσω).   Salvation or life in the interests of God, life right with God, this is what breaking with the Law means, not any transgression or real sin, such as you imagine table-fellowship with your gentile brethren to be.   *I have been crucified with Christ, and it is no longer I that live, Christ lives in me ; the life I now live I live by faith in the Son of God who loved me and gave himself up for me.*   After this glowing outburst or confession of faith, he then returns to the argument.   You would insinuate that faith in this Christ means a depreciation of the divine Law so graciously given for obedience as a means of acceptance with God ?   You imply that my preaching annuls this ?   But *I do not annul* (' not ' is the emphatic word, not ' I ') *God's grace*.   His grace for me is summed up in Christ ;   *if righteousness* or salvation *comes by way of the Law*, as you imply, if legal distinctions still count in the matter of salvation, *then indeed Christ's death was useless ;* God's grace is rendered superfluous and meaningless, if life with Him is attainable ' *sub lege*.'   Such is the argument. What Paul meant by God's grace he had already indicated (in i. 3 f.) ;   it was the saving purpose by which *the Lord Jesus Christ gave himself for our sins to rescue us from the present evil world*.   This grace included gentiles as well as Jews, and instead of working through the previous divine Law it has superseded that Law as the saving principle or power for Jews as well as for gentiles.   The full and final expression of grace, the apostle concludes, is through Christ as the object of faith, not through the Law as eliciting obedience to its precepts. Indeed, in order to bring out the sharp point of this argument, the apostle uses the term δωρεάν. Had the Law been a saving power, then Christ would have died ' for nothing,' in vain ; his death would have been wasted, since there was no need for it. Elsewhere the same word ' for nothing ' is used in a high sense, of Christians being justified by God's grace for nothing (δωρεάν, Rom. iii. 24). But here it is paradoxically employed. So certain is Paul that nothing except the death of Christ could save the soul, that he declares the Lord's life would have been thrown away, had it not ended in a death of grace. His gospel is summed up in that conviction.

Two other interpretations differ slightly from this. (i) ' If while we seek to be justified by Christ, we ourselves also are found sinners,' is taken to refer to real sins committed by Christians after conversion. Is that Christ's fault ? No, these moral lapses are our own fault. The remedy is not to go back to the Law as the ethical safeguard—that would be sin ; the Law is not needed, indeed it has been superseded as a matter of fact by Christ, who instead of producing any effect of moral carelessness has broken with sin and thereby enabled believers to break with its power. Christ is adequate ; failures in the Christian life are not to be referred to any defect in his revelation, as though it had to be supplemented by the Law. This interpretation is more explicitly developed in (ii) the old view, restated forcibly by Lütgert (*Gesetz und Geist*, 1919, see especially pp. 35 f., 57 f.) and Professor Ropes (*The Singular Problem of the Epistle to the Galatians*, 1929), that the objectors to Paul's grace-gospel were not only conservative Jewish Christians, who were alarmed at the risk of ethical laxity, but also radical spiritualists who charged Paul with adhering to the Law instead of trusting altogether to the Spirit's impulses. Once, they sneered, Paul had indeed been a ' free spirit,' but under pressure from the Jerusalem authorities he had compromised his gospel of the Spirit. It is this misrepresentation which he has in mind. Lütgert takes ' transgressor ' to be the same as ' sinner,' i.e. law-breaker ; Paul is supposed to argue, " We Jews did indeed believe in Christ, not because we were sinners like the Gentiles but because we recognized the futility of Law-obedience as saving, but this does not mean that Christ made us lawless people, as he detached us from the Law." The apostle denies the radicals' inference that he was thereby depreciating the grace or freedom of the gospel. No, he retorts passionately, all I say is that salvation is not by way of the Law. That such antinomian extremists existed, is fairly clear from this epistle as from Romans and Corinthians, whether they were the left wing of the Pauline party or, as Lütgert thinks, at Galatia, Christians affected by the ecstatic spirit of mystery-cults like Cybele or the Magna Mater. But it is another question whether the argument of Galatians ii. 15 f. refers to them. It may, so far as the last three verses are concerned. Paul would then be defending himself against the perfectionists. Paul, they said, you profess to have disavowed the Law, and yet by deferring to Peter and the other apostles and by your ethical demands you are leaving a place for it ; you are inconsistent. No, Paul retorts, if I took the Law as a saving principle, indeed I would be inconsistent ; but I do not. Christ is my Saviour ; I leave no room for the Law as a means of salvation, for if I did I would not be giving free play to grace. While this may have been in the background of his mind, I think that the argument here is in the light of the context more intelligible when the Jewish Christian criticism is presupposed.

2

Twice the grace of the Lord Jesus Christ is explained in terms of the incarnation.

(a) The first passage occurs in the plea for liberality which we have already mentioned (see above, p. 174). Paul has been speaking of the grace or generous liberality (χάρις) with which God had inspired the Macedonian churches to sub-scribe to the fund for relieving the starving Christians in Judaea. In that movement of ready help he traced the hand of God. The gentile Christians of Macedonia are held up as an example to the Achaian and Corinthian churches, but with characteristic depth Paul reminds the latter that they have more than this ; they know, as all Christians do, the supreme example and inspiration of Christ, whose coming had meant the enrichment of life by his self-sacrifice (2 Cor. viii. 7–9). *Do come to the front,* he pleads, *in this gracious enterprise* (ἐν ταύτῃ τῇ χάριτι). *I am not issuing any orders, only using the zeal of others to prove how sterling your own love is.* And wherever there is love, there is grace or giving. Why, *you know how gracious our Lord Jesus Christ was ; rich though he was, he became poor for the sake of you, that by his poverty you might be rich.* This was what 'the grace of the Lord Jesus Christ' involved for Paul, a self-renunciation which began by his surrender of heavenly privilege in order to carry out God's saving purpose for men. *You know* this, he writes. From the first it had been part of his gospel, though this is the earliest specific allusion to it. Γινώσκετε τὴν χάριν τοῦ Κυρίου ἡμῶν Ἰησοῦ Χριστοῦ, you are well aware of " what our Lord Jesus Christ has done as an act of pure grace " (Gunion Rutherford), or, as Tyndale rendered it, " You know the liberality of our Lord Jesus Christ." The wealth of the Christian experience, its reconciliation to God, its enlightenment, its gifts of the Spirit, its hope for the future, all is due to the self-sacrifice of the Lord, who is ' rich unto all that call upon him ' (Rom. x. 12). *He became poor* (ἐπτώχευσε) is not " he lived as a poor man, in poverty and need " ; the aorist (like ἔζησε in Rom. xiv. 9) denotes an act of becoming. On the margin of the English Bible two references are printed, John i. 1 and Luke ix. 58. The former is relevant, the latter is at best secondary. What the metaphor suggests is a wealthy man giving up his possessions in order to benefit poorer persons in whom he is interested. Paul knew some who had actually given up wealth for the sake of poorer men. Indeed the Corinthians themselves must have been familiar (see 1 Cor. ix. 6, Acts ii. 45, iv. 36 f.) with the extraordinary generosity of a man like Barnabas, who had surrendered his property, not because it was detrimental to his spiritual good but in order to enrich the needy with whom he loved to be in fellowship and for whom he was ready to forego anything. More vital than the sight of any such zeal or readiness on the part of other Christians ought to be the consciousness of how ready and unselfish the Lord had been ! Show ' grace ' or liberality, the apostle means, as you have received grace. That is the supreme motive. It is a remarkable illustration of the apostle's religious ethic. The collection, which in 1 Corinthians he had called by the ordinary term λογία, appears in 2 Corinthians as διακονία, εὐλογία, κοινωνία, ἁδρότης, or even χάρις. The question of money is raised to a high level, as the current usage of the Greek word ' charis ' made it possible to do. It is treated in the light of the deepest truth known to the apostle about the divine nature. Do be generous to one another without grudging, he pleads, for the very basis and spirit of your whole life in the Church is unintelligible apart from generosity on the part of the Lord.

When Jesus promised, ' Blessed are the poor in spirit, for theirs is the kingdom of heaven,' his grace-word implied that full provision was made for those who felt beggars before God, instead of feeling self-satisfied and in need of little or nothing. He sees no future for those who rest on their own resources. It is those who are conscious of incapacity to help themselves or to nourish their ' spirits,' it is they to whom God's bliss is promised. Paul declares that the Lord provided what he promised. He put men in the way of becoming rich in faith and hope. By his self-sacrifice, he brought within reach of humble, believing folk an experience of God and life such as otherwise they could not have possessed.

(*b*) A similar motive underlies the second passage, though here it is the truth and not the term of grace which we encounter. In exhorting the Philippian Christians (ii. 5–11) to be humble and unselfish, he bids them treat one another as Christ had treated them, drawing from the saving action of Christ a motive for their common relations. *Treat one another with the same spirit as you experience in Christ Jesus :* τοῦτο φρονεῖτε ἐν ὑμῖν ὃ καὶ (φρονεῖτε) ἐν χριστῷ Ἰησοῦ.

It is not natural to bisect these words, as though ὁ καὶ ἐν Χριστῷ Ἰησοῦ were an introductory formula for some pre-Pauline eucharistic hymn,[1] to which the apostle added θανάτου δὲ σταυροῦ in order to link to his own gospel of the Crucified an original psalm of the primitive Church where the death of Jesus was viewed in a pre-Johannine sense as a mysterious event which in God's good providence was followed by the resurrection. Rhythmically the passage falls into a form not uncommon in Paul :

Who, though divine by nature,	ὅς ἐν μορφῇ θεοῦ ὑπάρχων
did not snatch	οὐχ ἁρπαγμόν ἡγήσατο
at equality with God,	τὸ εἶναι ἴσα θεῷ,
but emptied himself	ἀλλὰ ἑαυτὸν ἐκένωσε
by taking a servant's nature ;	μορφὴν δούλου λαβών.
born in human guise	ἐν ὁμοιώματι ἀνθρώπων γενόμενος
and appearing in human form,	καὶ σχήματι εὑρεθεὶς ὡς ἄνθρωπος
he humbly stooped	ἐταπείνωσεν ἑαυτόν,
in his obedience even to die,	γενόμενος ὑπήκοος μέχρι θανάτου
to die upon the cross ;	θανάτου δὲ σταυροῦ.
therefore God raised him high,	διὸ καὶ ὁ θεὸς αὐτὸν ὑπερύψωσε
and upon him bestowed	καὶ ἐχαρίσατο αὐτῷ
the Name above all names,	τὸ ὄνομα τὸ ὑπὲρ πᾶν ὄνομα.
that before the Name of Jesus	ἵνα ἐν τῷ ὀνόματι Ἰησοῦ
every knee should bend	πᾶν γόνυ κάμψη
in heaven, on earth, and under earth,	ἐπουρανίων καὶ ἐπιγείων καὶ καταχθονίων,
and every tongue confess,	καὶ πᾶσα γλῶσσα ἐξομολογήσηται
' Jesus Christ is Lord,'	ὅτι Κύριος Ἰησοῦς Χριστός,
to the glory of God the Father.	εἰς δόξαν θεοῦ πατρός.

Paul may be thought to interpret the grace of the Lord thus. "The Spirit of humble unselfishness that has made Jesus Lord, and in making him Lord has made you what you are, a fellowship of God, let that spirit determine your relations to one another. As he never thought of himself, neither must you think of yourselves first and foremost." In other

[1] Lohmeyer, *Kurios Christos* (1928), p. 45.

words, ' No self-seeking ' is the clue to the divine Lordship
which has made the Church what it is.   Christians are called
in their own way to reproduce the spirit of their Lord.   It is
the same argument as in Rom. xv. 3 f., where, in pleading for
mutual consideration instead of insisting upon one's own
rights, he writes *Christ did not please himself* . . . *Welcome one
another as Christ has welcomed yourselves, for the glory of God*.
That is, ' be prepared to treat weaker fellow-members with
the same generous spirit as you have all experienced from
Christ, when you believed in him.'   In our passage it is not
a call to imitate a human Jesus ; the motive pours from the
experience of a Jesus who entered human life with all its
limitations and weakness, shrinking from nothing in order
to fulfil his obedience to God's will.   Paul develops the
thought at greater length than in the other passage.   He is
carried away by the conception of what the Lord gave up,
and the rhapsody rises far beyond the immediate occasion.
But it is significant that in speaking of the resurrection he uses
a word like that in the primitive apostolic confession (Acts v.
31) : *the God of our fathers raised Jesus whom you murdered by
hanging him on a gibbet ; God lifted him up* (ὕψωσεν, see ii. 33)
to his right hand.   This term had been used of the Servant
of the Lord (Isaiah lii. 13) being exalted, and the Servant-
contrast between degradation accepted in the course of the
divine mission and a sequel of divine exaltation is in Paul's
mind.   Hence the employment of this word ' raised him
high,' where normally ' raised ' would have come to his lips.
Humiliation freely endured in God's service leads to the real
exaltation of life.   So Jesus had taught.   So, Paul here
shows (in terms drawn from some familiar myth), it had been
in his own case.   Self-abnegation, self-sacrifice lies at the
heart of the divine nature ; this is the thought underlying all
such allusions.   As Paul thinks how Christians ought to
imitate this spirit of their Lord, he is swept into the thought of
how much they are indebted to it in their fellowship with him.

Already there are Christians confessing, " For us the real meaning of ' Lord ' is to be found in Jesus Christ," " He who has thus stooped to our low estate, he is Lord, not Serapis or any other." And this confession, not in words alone, is the proof that the divine action had not been in vain ; the more faith, humble, adoring faith, there is on earth, evoked by the heavenly Servant and Saviour, the more is God the Father seen to be what He really is, as the living God of heaven and earth.

It is no longer natural for us [1] to speak of this grace of the Lord Jesus as ' condescending ' or of ' condescension ' upon the part of God. We may still sing with Lyte of the Lord as " familiar, patient, condescending, free," but we do so with an inward discomfort ; indeed even those who share his faith would not be prepared to avail themselves of Watts's language in the hymn,

> How condescending and how kind
> Was God's eternal Son !

In one of the shifts that befall language, the English term ' condescending ' has come down ; it now suggests superiority in a bad sense, not only self-display or self-importance but a patronizing attitude which in human beings is very properly resented. " Condescension is an excellent thing," Stevenson remarks ironically in *Weir of Hermiston*, " but it is strange how one-sided the pleasure of it is. He who goes fishing among the Scots peasantry with condescension for a bait will have an empty basket by evening." The loss of the term to the vocabulary of religion is unfortunate, for, before it was spoiled by later usage, it connoted two vital elements in the idea of grace, i.e. generosity and reconciliation. To ' condescend,' in older English, was a noble action. It meant generally to waive one's rights and claims, or to forego some privilege for the sake of others. That, and coming to an agreement. Condescension was a genuine favour, the yielding of a higher power or authority to some request, the generous consideration which made

[1] Barth still employs it, however, and from the Lutheran point of view Dr. Lauerer analyses the truth conveyed by the term, in an essay (pp. 258–272) contributed to the Ihmel-Festschrift, *Das Erbe Martin Luthers* (1928).

strength agree or consent to a plea from weakness.   The Authorized
Version could use it as a term for what we call associating freely with
those on a lower level ; thus in Romans xii. 16 ' condescend to men of
low estate ' renders the Greek συναπαγόμενοι.   There is nothing
patronizing about the idea in Elizabethan English, and therefore it
could be employed of the divine grace coming down generously to
man's low estate and making terms in his favour.   That is, it struck
the two chords of reverence and reconciliation which are vital to the
consciousness of ' grace,' as the New Testament understands the term.
Unluckily, thanks to iniquity abounding, the word has been deprived of
its noble significance in modern speech, at any rate in English.   We
are no longer able to command its services in expressing the full truth
of grace.

3

In such conceptions of Christ as pre-existent, it is assumed
that being at the centre of the divine order he is somehow
connected with creation.   Paul had always this in mind.
Thus, in 1 Corinthians viii. 6 he writes, *For us* Christians

> *there is but one God, the Father,*
> *from whom all comes,*
> *and for whom we exist ;*
> *one Lord, Jesus Christ,*
> *by whom all exists,*
> *and by whom we exist.*

In the later letters this is for the first time developed into an
argument that the universe was created by him and for him ;
not only is Christ the complete revelation of reconciling grace
to men but the ground of the cosmic system.   In other words,
he is the vital centre for nature as well as for human nature.
It might be expected that in this statement of Christ as furnish-
ing the ultimate meaning of the universe, there would be
some reference to the providential purpose of the world in
terms of grace, seeing that one fundamental element in the
argument is the co-ordination of redemption and the created
order.   But Paul steadily avoids this.   As with love, so with

grace ; it is definitely confined to the relationship between God and man through Jesus Christ. When in the climax of the world-order Christ appears, then, and not till then, does Paul mention grace. He does not even use it in its Hellenistic sense of beauty as a feature of the natural order. That the world was God's world, and alive with reminders of Him, the apostle assumed. Occasionally he mentions this. But the grace of the Lord Jesus Christ is not deduced from any phenomena of the universe, nor is it illustrated by nature's bounty and beauty. ' The invisible things of Him from the creation of the world are clearly seen,' but it is in the face of Jesus Christ that men for the first time see what alone deserves the name of grace divine. The apostle's real interest in the pre-existence of the Christ starts from his conviction that in Jesus God did come to the world of men.

When in the later letters Paul describes the Redeemer of men as the eternal Son *born first before all the creation (for it was by him that all things were created)*, and as the realizer of the new order of the divine secret or reconciling purpose for the universe which God the creator of all had concealed hitherto, he implies that the reconciling aim had been, as we might say, implicit in providence ever since the world began. Nothing is more important to the apostle than the conviction that Christ's redemption is not an after-thought on the part of God. He never thought of it as an intervention of the good God in a world which was essentially alien to the divine love.

> Good cause it is for thankfulness
> That the world blessing of his life
> With the long past is not at strife ;
> That the great marvel of his death
> To the one order witnesseth,
> No doubt of changeless goodness makes,
> No link of cause or sequence breaks,
> But one with nature rooted is
> In the eternal verities.

The truth in these lines was part of Paul's gospel. But he refrains from expressing it in terms of grace. It is in terms of Hellenistic

speculation within Judaism that he presents this belief in a glory belonging
to Jesus Christ not only after the resurrection but before the incarnation,
but his emphasis upon the divine Lordship and love in relation to human
nature is true to the Hebrew tradition, where the specific trend of
religion was to verify the divine Will specially in men rather than in
nature (see Baudissin's *Kyrios als Gottesname*, ii. 455 f.).

The same concentration upon Jesus Christ explains why
grace is omitted from another phase of God's dealings with
life.   Chrysostom in commenting on ' grace for grace ' in
the prologue to the Fourth Gospel regards the words as meaning that the Jews once had grace but that Christians have now
more, far more, in the course of God's providence.   " There
was grace, there is grace."   There was grace when the Jews
received the Law and were chosen to be God's people.   He
cites quite aptly the words of Deut. vii. 7 : ' The Lord did
not set his love upon you nor choose you because ye were
more in number than any people, but because the Lord loved
you and because he would keep the oath sworn unto your
fathers.'   Which shows that " the Jews were saved by grace.
Even the gifts of the Law were of grace."   Nay more, the
very fact that God created us out of nothing, bestowing moral
instincts and conscience too, this surely was a supreme act of
grace.   And then there are the rich privileges of the Christian
calling ;   there is grace, arising out of the previous order of
grace in creation and in the Old Testament.   Now Paul does
not follow this line, in handling the pre-Christian period of
God's relations with Israel.   He never cites any OT text for
grace.   For other elements in his interpretation of the gospel
of grace he can appeal to scripture, e.g. for faith, election, free
forgiveness, the call of the gentiles, the death and the resurrection of the Lord ;   he was certain that the gospel of righteousness by faith was attested by the law and the prophets.
But, just as he never cites even the prophecy of Joel about
the Spirit, concentrating the idea of the Spirit upon the revelation in Jesus Christ and ignoring the traditional range of

the Spirit in nature and human nature, so he finds grace written for him in Jesus Christ alone, as though the Lord were God's living letter of grace to the world. Grace like love is verified by him in the Christian order with such exceptional intensity that he never speaks of it until in his survey of human history he comes upon Jesus Christ.

The nearest approach to any quotation occurs in 2 Corinthians vi. 1 f. In appealing to the Corinthians not to ' receive the grace of God in vain,' the word ' receive ' (δέξασθαι) suggests to him a prophetic passage upon God receiving men into favour. *For he saith*

> *I have heard you in the time of favour* (καιρῷ δεκτῷ)
> *and helped you on the day of salvation.*

Well, here is the time of favour (καιρὸς εὐπρόσδεκτος), *here is the day of salvation.* The OT passage (Isaiah xlix. 8) refers to the mission of the Servant of the Lord which embraces the gentiles, but Paul cites it here to clinch his argument that the God who hears and helps is present in Jesus Christ with decisive force for the saving of men ; in Christ God reconciles the world to himself, and this is the year or era of grace. It is the thought of Luke iv. 19, and the strong term εὐπρόσδεκτος, which Paul is the first to employ, at any rate in Christianity, brings out the meaning aptly ; it is an offer of high favour from God that is characteristic of the order of grace inaugurated by Christ. Here, now (νῦν) the hour has struck ; God is willing to receive men to His favour, the offer which has cost so much is open, and men must not treat it casually. Erasmus thought there was a warning contrast between the day of salvation and the day of doom. " Sequetur formidabilis ille dies, quo frustra quaereretur reconciliatio." But though Paul had spoken not long before about the day of judgment, it is not certain that he had it in mind here.

In this connexion it is important to notice how he handles the foreshadowing of grace in the historical faith of Abraham (Rom. iv., Gal. iii. 6–21). Though he draws the antithesis sharply, so sharply that he will not recognize grace or the Spirit in the older system of the Law, he finds hints by way of anticipation, not only in the saying that ' the just shall live by faith,' but in the Promise or Promises made by God to Abraham, prior to the Law.   Here a divine promise is made to faith ; this therefore constitutes a religious order incompatible with Law, a religious order which is taken up and fulfilled in the gospel of Christ.   For promise is a gracious act or attitude, which elicits faith from man, and as faith is non-racial, Paul sees in such a relationship the two cardinal features of his gospel, ' All is of grace, and grace is for all.'

It is a precedent however, not a model for the faith of Christian men.   Not only does he ignore the midrashic interpretation of Genesis xv. 6, according to which Abraham's faith was accounted a meritorious work, but he does not say, Have faith like Abraham's, for that would have left out Christ.   It is not by imitating Abraham's intuition of faith, pure and simple, that Christians are saved, but by exercising faith in what for them is the final revelation of God's character and purpose. *Faith will be ' counted ' to us* as long ago it was counted to Abraham, *as we believe in Him who raised Jesus our Lord from the dead.*   With Christ faith receives for the first time its adequate and absolute object. The faith of Abraham is employed in order to show that human faith is the only and the original condition appointed by God for life with Him, and it is in the light of the fulfilment in Jesus Christ Paul interprets that far-off faith as an anticipation of Christian faith which is conditioned by Christ's resurrection from the dead and which implies a world-wide scope for the gospel.

One feature in the scripture about Abraham's faith that particularly appealed to him was its corroboration of the truth, so fundamental to his view of grace, that the basis of the religious life is not what men think about God but what God thinks of them.   The determining fact is His judgment about the relationship of men to Himself.   This is one reason why Paul welcomes the phrase of Genesis about Abraham's faith being ' counted to him as righteousness.'   It was originally a ' legal ' phrase employed by a religious conception that had gone beyond legalism ; the meaning was that the Lord admitted Abraham to a real and intimate relationship with Himself in recognition of the implicit trust which he had shown. That religious fellowship rested on the divine reckoning or determination was an axiom of Hebrew piety. It was an anticipation of grace that the condition of such fellowship had been made faith, in days of old, Paul teaches ; and this was realized in Jesus Christ, where for the first time men saw how such faith was the natural response to God's real character and purpose. In view of sin the one status was a relationship determined by gracious love, and as that Will of love met men in Christ, all they were asked to do was to believe. Men might argue that things were not so desperate ; might they not make a shift for themselves by means of moral obedience and having done their best rely on God's kindly favour ? For Paul, however, God read the situation differently ; the life and death and resurrection of Jesus Christ seemed to him inexplicable apart from a gracious action of God being required on behalf of men. This judgment of life implied a status in which grace divine appealed to faith alone.

The nexus between this and the good life is sometimes described by moderns in terms of God's faith in us. Our trust in God is stirred and sustained by His trust in us, and so is our moral response. Paul does not use this language, but the thought is his. For in treating the ungodly with such amazing grace, so undeserved and generous, in giving them the assurance that His judgment of them is gracious, He inspires them with an answering capacity and desire to please Him. As they are trusted, as they are reckoned His, they are brought into a fellowship and intimate confidence which creates the new life by moving them to adoring obedience. They are, as it were, honoured by His grace or faith in them. To be forgiven is an experience which, if truly realized, cannot leave a man as he was. The God who counts faith as justifying, the Lord whose love so suffered for our sakes, the apostle teaches, is One for whom too much cannot be done. All He asks to begin with is faith, but it is a faith which from the first means fellowship with a reconciling Lord.   If men have been unable to deserve His initial grace, they are inspired to deserve His confidence, once they have been admitted to His inner life of favour.   This aspect of faith was not, however, characteristic of the faith of Abraham.   For Abraham was not a sinner, at any rate as Paul viewed normal human beings.   Hence in Romans iv. 6 f. the apostle adds to the illustration from Abraham's faith another from the thirty-second psalm, about the bliss of the man ' to whom the Lord will not impute sin.'   So, believing in Him who justifies the ungodly, a man has his faith counted as righteousness.   This truth comes in the wake of the larger statements upon grace and revelation, to which we now must turn.

4

Three times over, Paul rapidly explains how the course of God's revelation in the history of Israel led up to the grace of the Lord Jesus Christ.   The mere fact that gentiles were admitted to the People of God required a new interpretation of history.   Also Paul had to explain, as best he could, how his gospel was really anticipated in the OT, instead of being a novelty, unrelated or even opposed to the long purpose of the living God.   Of these three surveys the first (*a*) is in Galatians (iii. 6–iv. 7), and the other two are in Romans, in (*b*) i. 18–iii. 26, iii. 26–iv. 25, and (*c*) v. 12–21.   The first and second are in some respects parallel, but in Galatians the anticipations of grace in the OT are partly explained by means of two grace-ideas, Promise and Covenant.   The former re-appears in the second survey ;   the latter is only used in Galatians as a category of grace, and used in a particular sense.

(*a*) Like Stephen in Acts Paul argues in a way that runs counter to the notion that all developments in religion are for the better.   Fixing on God's promise of a son to Abraham, he deduces from it that since God reckoned Abraham's simple faith as righteousness, those who had the same faith in God to-day were the real sons of Abraham, whether they were Jews or pagans ;   also that the Mosaic Law, which only emerged later, did not supersede the earlier relationship of Promise and Faith, the latter indeed being realized when Christ came and the gospel of faith began. Now 'covenant' as applied to Abraham or to anyone else denoted the entrance of the gracious purpose of God into the history of the People ; it involved the free favour of the Lord. But the Greek term conveniently bore a double sense ; it covered not simply the voluntary gracious relationship into which God brought men, but also a disposition or will ('or testament). Paul takes it in this juristic sense, in order to drive home his point. *To take an illustration from human life. Once a man's will is ratified, no one annuls it or adds a codicil to it. Now the Promises were made to Abraham . . . My point is this : the law which arose four hundred and thirty years later does not repeal a will previously ratified by God, so as to cancel the Promise. If the Inheritance* (i.e. the full spiritual blessing bestowed by God in His will) *is due to Law, it ceases to be due to promise. Now it was by a promise that God bestowed it on Abraham . . . Scripture has consigned all without exception to the custody of sin, in order that the promise due to faith in Christ might be given to those who have faith . . . Faith has come, and we are wards no longer, you are all sons of God by your faith in Christ Jesus.*

Paul does not raise the question of the testator's death, as the author of Hebrews does. He merely employs this legal metaphor of διαθήκη in order to bring out the truth that all depends on God's favour ; this free favour preceded Law, and the disposition came into force under Jesus Christ, depending on nothing like circumcision or observance of the Law, things which were not in existence when the will was drawn up. Whether διαθήκη be taken as covenant or as disposition (will), it implies that the initiative is with God. Which is the religious interest of the apostle in his argument, as well as the contention that no subsequent phase of religion in Israel could invalidate the original and absolute order of things which had been introduced when divine Promise appealed to human faith.

Unlike the author of Hebrews, Paul makes little use of the covenant idea elsewhere. Luke employs it occasionally to bring out the nexus between the Old and the New, the original covenant with Abraham being fulfilled in Christ (Luke i. 72, Acts iii. 25), but beyond a few casual allusions, such as in Romans xi. 27 (the essence of διαθήκη being forgiveness and fellowship with God) and Ephesians ii. 12 (the covenants of promise), Paul's sole reference is to the sharp antithesis between the Sinai covenant and the gospel covenant. It is not the thought of any continuity but the absolute contrast between the old and the new that inspires 2 Corinthians iii. 6 f. (see Gal. iv. 24); the one is transitory and unspiritual, the other is eternal and of the Spirit. Life, instinct with pardon, is the supreme boon of the New Covenant. Strictly speaking, we need not discuss the passage, as it is not couched in terms of grace. But it serves to bring out the predominant interest in ' life,' which characterizes Paul's message upon forgiving grace. The Spirit makes for life, generates life (ζωοποιεῖ) and so is glorious. Here as elsewhere the divine nature of the Lord is expressed by glory and Spirit, the former denoting His fullness, the latter His power. Hence it can be said, ' we are being transformed into the same likeness as Himself, passing from one glory to another (i.e. into ever deeper experience of His life) —for this comes of the Lord the Spirit.'

Why Paul did not use ' covenant ' more freely, is probably because he preferred juridical and metaphysical categories to those of ritual, in explaining the significance of Christ's death. ' Covenant ' implied an atoning sacrifice at the heart of the relationship of favour and fellowship which it guaranteed for the People of God, whose access to His presence was ensured by God's gracious provision for their shortcomings. The truth of this was conveyed by the apostle in other ways, however.

True to the spirit of the OT, where ' covenant (berith) ' and promise overlap, Paul in Galatians employs, for the first time in his extant letters, the category of the divine Promise, as he justifies the truth of grace over against the Law. For Abraham's faith was faith in God's Promise or Promises. *Scripture*, he argues, *anticipated God's justification of the gentiles by faith when it announced the gospel beforehand to Abraham in these terms : ' All nations shall be blessed in thee.'* So that those

*who rely on faith (ἐκ πίστεως, emphatic) are blessed along with
believing Abraham. . . . The Promises were made to Abraham
and to his offspring. If you are Christ's, then you are Abraham's
offspring ; in virtue of the Promise, you are heirs.*

'Promise' was a great term and truth of the Pharisaic
party, almost a technical expression for their vital piety, as we
see from Ecclesiasticus [1] and the Psalter of Solomon, where
devout Israel is the People to whom God makes promises or
gives the Promise :

> May sinners all together be destroyed from before the face of the Lord,
> and may the Lord's saints inherit the Lord's promises !

Neither ἐπαγγελία nor its equivalent ἐπάγγελμα is much used
by Philo, as it happens. But it served Paul as an apt grace-
word. Indeed he calls Christianity the Promise now ; the
gospel of God was promised long ago in the prophets (Rom.
i. 2), and gentiles are described as strangers to the covenants
of the Promise (Eph. ii. 12). For (i) a promise is an act of
sheer grace ; God's promise is a free pledge of His favour,
due to His unconditioned affection. All promises are given,
not earned, and as the Promise to Abraham came before the
Law of Moses, Paul infers that priority is superiority in the
order of God. The true manifestation of His good nature
lies in giving a promise, not in imposing a law. (ii) No
doubt, its correlative is faith on the part of man, a faith that
obeys, but it is not obedience to a code of laws. One trusts
a promise, trusts God to fulfil it, and relies upon Him ;
Abraham felt convinced that He was able to do what He
promised (Rom. iv. 21). Paul, unlike the author of Hebrews,
dwells on the pure faith required, not on the practical outcome
of such faith in action and patience ; he concentrates upon
the opposition of such faith to the ἔργα required by the Law.
(iii) God keeps His word. For Paul, He has made it good in
the gospel, since all the promises of God are fulfilled in Jesus

---

[1] J. H. A. Hart, *Ecclesiasticus in Greek*, pp. 306 f.

Christ (2 Cor. i. 20).   Faith has come to its full rights in Him. This is particularly brought out by the resurrection ; like other writers of the NT (e.g. 1 John ii. 25, 1 Tim. i. 1, iv. 8, Titus i. 2, 2 Pet. i. 4), the apostle recognizes that life eternal is the full content of the Promise.   Hence the gift of the Spirit becomes central to the fulfilment of the Promise (Eph. i. 13, as in Acts ii. 33).

Apart from James (i. 12, ii. 5) the only other NT writer who avails himself of this conception is the writer of Hebrews ; he spiritualizes the OT promises more widely.   Paul practically fixes attention on the promise to Abraham as a shining proof of the gospel.   Once he does quote two general promises as a motive for Christians keeping clear of worldliness and contamination (2 Cor. vi. 16–vii. 1).   But elsewhere the Promise-conception is usually employed in order to develop the antithesis between grace and Law.   It had the double merit of suggesting the connexion between the OT and the Gospel, and also of illustrating the difference between the Law and the revelation of grace.   And the special feature of Abraham having received the Promise when he was still uncircumcised, and long before the Law of Sinai, furnished the apostle with the double corroboration of faith as essentially the religious attitude of man and of the gentiles as predestined to their place among the sons of Abraham.   What he told the Galatians, he repeated to the Romans (iv. 13 f.).   *The promise made to Abraham and his offspring that he should inherit the world, did not reach him through the Law but through the righteousness of faith.   For if it is adherents of the Law who are heirs, then faith is empty of all meaning and the promise is void. . . .   All turns upon faith, to make the promise a matter of favour, to make it secure for all the offspring, not simply for those who are adherents of the Law but also for those who share the faith of Abraham.*

The religious weight of this category of Promise depends upon its gracious character.   No doubt a promise is a promise to act, not an action in itself.   Hence the covenant-idea was more adequate to the active side of grace divine.   Yet a promise binds the promiser to take action, and Paul freely uses the conception for the gracious attitude of God who consents to be thus bound by His word to man, out of pure interest in man, and who, it is assumed, will always be faithful to His engagement, even though patience may be required on the part of men. Furthermore a promise is a personal thing ; what is promised, whether it be a gift or an intervention of aid, comes from the Giver of the promise ; He promises what He possesses or what He alone is capable of bringing about, not anything outside His own life. Thus the various elements of grace re-appear in the idea of the Promise, the free favour of God, His right to determine the terms and conditions of receiving what He promises, and at the same time the generosity with which He binds Himself to carry out His purpose. This third element is rather implied than argued, however. For the purposes of controversy, the two former are to the front in the grace-idea as conveyed through the conception of the Promise. Yet it must not be supposed that God the Promiser is merely valuable to the apostle as he argues against critics of his gospel. The deep religious significance of the idea is present to his mind as a positive clue to the real nature of God. He knows that faith is the fundamental attitude of man towards God, that the saving God needs only faith in order to work upon the distress of the human heart, and that the promises of God are already made, already present as realities which will evoke moral reality in man, if he will but trust them. As the old Scotsman Edie Ochiltree told his young friend in *The Antiquary*, " Sinfu' men are we a' ; but if ye wad believe an auld grey sinner that has seen the evil o' his ways, there is as much promise atween the twa boards o' the Testament as wad save the warst o' us, could we but think sae." " Could we but think so " is the same as " if you will but believe and receive the promise of God in Jesus Christ His Son."

Twice in Romans Paul outlines the situation which led to God's grace being revealed in Jesus Christ. In both passages he sets himself to show how the plight of man was so desperate that nothing else would have saved him. They are not speculative philosophies of history but surveys of the moral position of men based upon the writer's experience of grace ; from this experience he argues back to the past.   As God's grace met a human need, and a human need of urgent necessity and tragic seriousness, he seeks to explain why and how this divine favour came to men.   Why had it to be ' grace ' ? And why did ' grace ' take the form it did in Jesus the Christ ? The surveys are from different angles, but they are agreed on this, that God had to come to the rescue.   Paul had already touched this question, in writing to the Galatians (iv. 4) : *When the time had fully expired, God sent forth his Son.*   But this vague allusion is now filled out.   Why the world was, as we might say, ripe for the gospel of grace, is first described in these passages from Romans.

(*b*) Yet in Romans i. 16–iii. 20 (which forms the negative basis for the more positive statement of iii. 21–iv. 25) grace is never mentioned.   In the gospel, Paul begins by declaring *the righteousness of God is revealed by faith and for faith* ; but we have to wait until iii. 21 f. for any word about faith, since ' righteousness ' at once suggests its sombre antithesis ; the result is that a survey of the moral order in history follows, in which all men, Jews and non-Jews alike, are shown to have come short of God's law or righteousness.   ' They are all under sin.'   Then and only then, as he proceeds to speak about faith and the new, true righteousness offered in Jesus Christ, does the word ' grace ' occur.   It is striking, though it does not seem to have struck many of those who discuss the passage, that the apostle is silent for so long about Christ. No other passage of equal length in all his letters is without some mention of the Lord.   But the reason is that he is analysing the moral and historical conditions for the coming of Christ.   At last he turns from the negative to the positive side of the issue.   And it is at this point that he mentions ' grace.'   *Now* at last *we have a righteousness of God which comes by believing in Jesus Christ.   And it is meant for all who have faith . . . they are justified for nothing* (δωρεάν) *by his grace through the ransom provided in Christ Jesus.* Then again the writer proceeds to discuss the position of Jews (iii. 27 f.), on general principles, and the same thing happens ; there is no further mention of Christ till at the end of the long discussion he comes to speak of Christian faith *in Him who raised Jesus our Lord from the dead* (iv. 24 f.) ; this at once calls up the thought of ' grace,' for it is through the Lord Jesus Christ, as he tells Christians to whom he now turns, that ' we have access by faith into this grace wherein we stand ' (v. 2). It is not, of course, that Paul conceives of God as ungracious during the pre-Christian period ; Israel, he admits freely, had always had its religious privileges, and pagans were not without His range of interest. But ' grace ' is so distinctively the mark of the revelation in Jesus Christ that he reserves it exclusively for the experiences of Christian men. In other words, ' grace ' belongs to the years A.D., not to B.C.

> Strikes for us now the hour of grace,
> Saviour, since thou art born.

This is a truly Pauline couplet.

The exception proves the rule. In ii. 16 he tells how God will judge the secrets of men at the last day, *as my gospel holds, by Jesus Christ.* This anticipation of the end leads him to speak of Christ, but never elsewhere in any connexion.

In describing the dealings of God with mankind, prior to the coming of Christ, the apostle therefore falls back on the term ' righteousness.' The discovery that the word here meant not punitive justice but gracious power threw open paradise to me, Luther confessed ; my anguish of soul was turned into hope and happiness by finding that ' righteousness ' denotes " salus et consolatio nostra, significat enim justitiam dei qua ego justificor divina misericordia." This was indeed the original connotation of the term. *I am proud of the gospel ; it is God's saving power for everyone who has*

faith . . . God's saving power (for so we might venture to
render δικαιοσύνη, which is equivalent in this connexion to
δύναμις θεοῦ εἰς σωτηρίαν) *is revealed in it by faith and for faith
—as it is written, ' Now by faith shall the saved man live.'*
Only, Paul never takes over material without assimilating it,
and he puts a special stamp on the word. In the OT it
denoted often the active grace by which God righted His
People or vindicated their cause, delivering them from pagans
and granting them success or victory. When they were
wronged by foes, they had the right to appeal to Him for
deliverance. He proved Himself the ' justifier ' of the People
as He championed their interests against threats and accusa-
tions.[1] If any punishing had to be done, it was not Israel
but its enemies who suffered ; as the People were penitent
and anxious to be loyal, God succoured them graciously and
routed those who thwarted the divine cause. But the apostle
is dealing with a different situation, and therefore, even as
he uses a word from the old order, it is in a new and keener
sense. The problem of sin confronted him. It was no longer
any question of a nation needing vindication before a hostile
world, but of humanity requiring reconciliation to God Himself. The two parties are God and sinful men. God's saving
power or ' righteousness ' was needed by men who were
wrong, not wronged. They were, as the apostle says, enemies
of God, alienated from Him, men who could not count upon
His protecting favour or upon His loyalty to their interests.

Why does he choose this Greek word which is so inadequately rendered
by ' justitia ' or righteousness ? What he means is the saving power
of God, but in speaking of this in the world before Christ he would
not use ' grace ' or ' salvation.' He took a classical term of his Greek
Bible, which had several advantages ; it had an adjective and a verb
to correspond, it could denote not only God's free action and moral

[1] See Baudissin's *Kyrios als Gottesname*, ii. 403, 422 f. " My righteousness
is near " (Isaiah li. 5) means, as Rosenmueller observes, " tempus liberationis
populi mei, quae justitiae et fidelitatis meae effectus est."

concern but the relationship between Him and men as well as men's moral response ; finally and especially at this point it was suggested by a great prophetic word about faith—' The just (ὁ δίκαιός, i.e. the man who is in right relations to God) shall live by faith.'

Behind all his arguments there also lies the consciousness of what the Servant of the Lord was appointed to do, to ' justify many ' by bearing their sins and being wounded for their transgressions. In the OT God is indeed 'righteous' as He punishes wrong-doing on earth (Isa. li. 5), but more often as He vindicates His people. Yet the latter was not understood by the deepest minds as an obligation on the part of God to Israel so much as the manifestation of His goodness. Thus in the Servant-prediction (Isa. xlii. 21) God is pleased to carry out His purpose for the world by magnifying the Torah in Israel. The Servant by his undeserved suffering and death somehow obtains for the people reconciliation ; their right relationship to God is restored, and their ' righteousness ' preserved. Though disgraced and discredited, they regain His fellowship. It was not difficult for the apostle to carry over suggestions from this line of faith to the view that men on earth, who are not simply wronged but wrong, receive God's saving help through one whom He appoints to ' justify ' them, and to justify them by means of a divine action which the Servant never knew, viz. resurrection from the dead.

The antithesis to ' righteousness ' is therefore not love or grace, it is wrath ; yet the divine wrath is also part of the providential order. Here, just as earlier (see above, p. 159) and later (in ix. 22 f.), Paul regards God's wrath as the reaction of His holy love against the defiance of sin; the saving purpose includes the punishment of evil. Primarily this wrath is eschatological ; indeed, it is often a concept of the end in Paul, though premonitions of it are experienced already in history. The insubordinate and perverse are to be visited by doom, when the last act of the human tragedy of disobedience is played out. But meantime, just before the end, God intervenes with His offer of grace to faith, and believers in Christ are assured of acquittal ; nay more, they are already taken into right relations with God or, as Paul loves to call it, into life, which frees them from death

and condemnation.   In a deep sense, all men are under Law
or ' law.'   Jews and gentiles alike meet God on this common
basis, and all have failed to satisfy the moral requirements of
God.   Looking round on the debased and degenerate state
of the race, Paul sees men exposed to the wrath of God for
this failure, for their violation of His demands ; all are liable
to doom, for their incapacity to keep the divine law, and
therefore are in desperate need of relief.   This is the argument of i. 18–iii. 20, the revelation of the divine anger as
incurred by the general failure of men to obey the Law.[1]
The confession of men that they are perverse and foolish
goes to the root of life ; it proves that they are alive to a
deep-seated liability of error from which they need to be
delivered and for which they need to be pardoned.

As God's loving grace or ' righteousness ' works in the moral order,
it redeems men at the end from His wrath against the Evil Powers
and their adherents or subjects.   God is not ἀπαθής, like the Stoic
deity.   Neither is His anger fitful or vindictive, as often in the OT.
When His purpose is presented and rejected, it becomes wrath, and
the redeemed alone are sure of deliverance from this doom of final judgment on the anti-divine cosmic powers and their sway over men.   The
preaching of judgment which was so vital an element in primitive
Christianity was the other side of the preaching of grace ; [2] the moral
reality of the latter was bound up with the former, on the lines of the
prophetic teaching, and this made the gospel both hopeful and serious
for the pagan world.   Sin to God must be morally hateful ; if it were
not, it would not be sin, and He would not be in any sense the living
God, but either passive or indulgent.   The wrath of God was therefore
one of the strong anthropomorphisms which were demanded by faith
in the reality of grace, which was anything but sentimental.

God 's wrathful said to be, when He doth do
That without wrath which wrath doth force us to.

[1] See *Love in the New Testament*, pp. 138 f.
[2] See on this, Preisker's *Die urchristliche Botschaft von der Liebe Gottes
im Lichte der vergleichende Religionsgeschichte*, pp. 62 f.

The double hope for men was a God who was more than equal to the domination of Evil in the world, a living God whose Son delivered *from the wrath to come*, and also a God who would never be reconciled to Evil. In a world where it was easy, even in some religions, to take moral evil lightly, the gospel of grace and wrath was the one message which held the conscience. Both grace and wrath implied that in the relations between man and God here an ultimate issue was present. They were set in an eschatological context of the messianic kingdom ; at the consummation God was to judge the world by a Man, Jesus the Christ, as Paul told the Athenians (Acts xvii. 17), and the resurrection was proof of this. What annoyed the Athenians was this assertion of a real and recent resurrection, not resurrection as a vague symbolical phenomenon like that of Osiris or other cult-deities but as the divine action which in Jesus Christ had really happened and was to lead to the judgment. The judgment also was to be passed not on cult-practices but on the moral life. This was one reason why Paul never gave up the belief (see below), even though it might seem to conflict with some of his categories of grace ; his real religion was other than a cult-relation to the Lord, it never ceased to be nearer to Hebrew thought, in its ultimate interests, than to Hellenistic. Unless the wrath of God on the disobedient and defiant was real, reconciliation could not be real, and with the Wrath on sinners went the judgment on both saints and sinners. The denial of God's loving purpose or gracious will means for him the manifestation of His absolute Will as wrath against those who are obstinate and hostile or apostates.

In this survey Paul has not forgotten the moral instincts and achievements of man, the evidence for souls who show ' patient continuance in welldoing ' and the moral convictions of honest pagans ' who do by nature the things contained in the Law,' but for the purpose of his argument he concentrates upon the sombre lower side of life. There are indeed other data in the case ; there is the divided life, torn between the good it would fain do and the evil that thwarts it, and the gropings of sincere spirits after God in the great world. But in the present passage the apostle sums up the general position of the human race, both Jews and pagans, till their corporate blame and shame leads to the one verdict of ' Guilty before God.' All the world is ὑπόδικος τῷ θεῷ ; it is answerable to God, and it has no answer to give for its failure to obey His Law. ' Guilty before God ' is the verdict upon men. The attempt to please God by keeping His Law has resulted in a world-wide failure, which leaves men hopelessly in need of help, of relief from moral incapacity and pardon for their offences. God does bestow this relief now by Jesus Christ, the apostle proclaims. It is pardon and more than mere pardon, for He reinstates men in His favour, treating them as worthy and accepting them in spite of the past. This is the marvel of His grace. Indeed Paul now can use the word ' grace ' for the revelation of the divine δικαιοσύνη in Jesus Christ : it is the only adequate term to describe this saving action and attitude of God, as He treats men better than they deserve, moving on His own initiative to rescue them, and to rescue them from their plight so generously, at such a cost. For this supreme manifestation of God's ' righteousness ' the apostle requires a new term, and it is none other than ' the grace of God.' That God should justify the ungodly, that He should accept offenders on the score of faith and not on the score of their miserable record, is a revelation so amazing that ' grace ' is the one word for it, for this ' righteousness ' or right relationship between sinful man and God, which has been brought about by God alone, by a God who took the initiative in dealing with man's situation. *Now* that Jesus Christ has come *we have a righteousness of God disclosed . . . a righteousness which comes by believing in Jesus Christ.* It is God who wills and bestows this new order of life. *It is all the doing of the God who has reconciled me to himself through Christ.* The change by means of which men were freed from the power and penalties of sin and made God's own People, was His doing, not theirs. *All have sinned, all come short of the glory of God, but they are justified for nothing by his grace.* The full significance of the Greek words δωρεὰν τῇ αὐτοῦ χάριτι is brought out by the Latin ' gratis per gratiam ' or by the French ' gratuitement par sa grâce ' better than our English can do. God's doing or God's free gift, not any effort on the part of man—that is the beginning of new life and hope for men.

Pardon as deliverance and new life is for the ' guilty.' The evidence for this verdict of ' guilty ' is drawn from his observation of mankind, both Jewish and pagan. It is argued with illustrations from scripture which for that age were convincing. But the real basis lies in his experience of grace. Just as it was the actual experience of seeing pagans converted to the faith and thus admitted to the fellowship of God's people, which led to the search for proofs of this from scripture, so it was the fact of God's utterly gracious aid in Jesus Christ which made the apostle convinced that the need for this must be widespread. Such a divine intervention could not but be required by all. The entrance of this new power of saving love meant not something but everything for Paul ; he saw in it a revelation of world-wide significance, not simply an additional succour from God to the chosen People, much less a favour granted to them alone, but a gift of life without which men would be hopelessly poor and lost. The powers of sin and the flesh operated so tragically in human life, within and without Israel, that Paul could not see any other way of relief than that provided so freely and fully by Jesus Christ. To bring out the saving significance of this gracious Action, he sets it against a dark background of history and experience which, as he read it, made Jesus Christ the one hope for the world.

> God giveth no man quarter,
>   Yet God a means hath found,
> Tho' faith and hope have vanished,
>   And even love grows dim,
> A means whereby His banished
>   Be not expelled from Him.

The ' means,' as Paul here describes it, is the self-sacrifice of the divine love, which will neither let man off nor let him go. 'All the world guilty before God. . . . But now,' though ' all have sinned and come short of the glory of God,' though they have undone themselves, He does for them what none else could do. They are *justified for nothing by his grace through the ransom provided in Christ Jesus, whom God put forward as the means of propitiation by his blood to be received by faith. This was to demonstrate the justice of God in view of the fact that sins previously committed during the time of God's forbearance had been passed over ; it was to demonstrate his justice at the present epoch, showing that God is just himself and that he justifies man on the score of faith in Jesus.* ' All is of grace.' Instead of standing aloof from sinners, leaving the race to itself, to await the punishment of death and doom, God takes action ; by the sacrificial death of Jesus His Son He breaks the power of Sin, liberating men from their bondage, and enabling them to enjoy the ' righteousness ' of life with Himself. There is a vicarious expiation in Christ's death " for us " or " for our sins." The reconciliation was some-how effected through the self-sacrifice of the sinless Son and Servant, entering human life and dying an undeserved death for the sake of men. His vicarious suffering atoned for the race he loved. But here the apostle states the other side of the action ; God in His pure grace provided the ransom, by putting forward Jesus Christ ἱλαστήριον, as the votive offering of His love for men.[1] He did not condone sin ; the death of Christ proved that He took account of guilt. But it revealed the heart of God, at once condemning iniquity, providing release for men, who are thus emancipated from all

---

[1] So Deissmann in *Encyclopaedia Biblica*, 3027–3035. The inscriptions prove that ἱλαστήριον meant not a sacrifice of expiation so much as an offering made by men to appease some deity. Only, Paul implies, in this case it was " not human hands that set up a lifeless image of the deity as a propitiation for guilt," but God Himself who has made the sacrifice needed to remove guilt.

their liabilities, demonstrating His justice and manifesting His saving purpose of restoring men to life and favour. All this depends upon man's faith. The revelation of the Son of God thus taking upon himself their responsibilities, dying and rising for them, is the supreme object of faith. Those who trust themselves to this gracious God are taken into His 'righteousness,' i.e. justified or treated as right with Him. As Paul sums it up, *God is* thus *just himself and he justifies man on the score of faith in Jesus.* What this 'faith' means, he then proceeds to explain (iii. 27–iv. 25), before unfolding the rich grace of the new position thus opened up by God to believing men.

This implies that in verses 25 and 26 Paul is using 'righteousness' in its special and specific sense of moral energy, almost as punitive. What justifies Him as the righteous God in justifying the ungodly is the propitiation in the death of Christ, which proves that He is just, i.e. the God of absolute integrity, who treats sin seriously. His moral passion is as real as His gracious favour ; and it is through the awful sacrifice of His Son that He as δίκαιος exhibits the attitude and activity of a δικαιῶν. The vicarious suffering and death of the Lord was the divine sacrifice, offered by God Himself, in order to deal effectively with the power and guilt of sin. Commonly men spoke of propitiating an angry god by some sacrifice of their own devising. It is just because Paul moved on a higher level that he can boldly use a term from that religious belief, in order to convey the truth that whilst a sacrifice was needful, God Himself provided the means. The term ἱλαστήριον is used in the higher sense of the Christian faith, just as elsewhere a legal term like παράκλητος is employed, simply because the faith is not legal at all.

The Greek of verses 25 and 26 is patient of another interpretation, however. It might mean that God put forward or set forth Christ Jesus ' *as the means of propitiation by his blood, to be received by faith,* with a view to the exhibition or communication (εἰς ἔνδειξιν) of His own saving power (δικαιοσύνης αὐτοῦ), as in His forbearance God overlooked (διὰ τὴν πάρεσιν) *sins previously committed,* that is, with a view to exhibiting (πρὸς ἔνδειξιν) His saving favour *at the present epoch*, showing that He is saving as He saves (δίκαιον καὶ δικαιοῦντα) the man who believes in Jesus.' This rendering preserves the ' saving ' sense of δικαιοσύνη throughout, assumes (as it is grammatically possible to do) that πάρεσις does not differ from a term like ἄφεσις, and reads δίκαιος of God as in 1 John i. 9, i.e. of God as the God of saving power (δικαιοσύνη) not as ' just ' in the sense of vindicating His moral justice ; the revelation in Jesus Christ shows that God is δίκαιος as He acts along the line of His saving power by making faith in Jesus Christ the condition of receiving His deliverance, not that in dealing with sins through the crucifixion of Christ He is also demonstrating the truth that He does not treat sin lightly. On the one view, Paul explains that the sacrificial death of Christ is not only the sole means of forgiveness and fellowship with God but also a vivid object-lesson upon the seriousness with which sin has to be treated. The other view denies any reference to such a misunderstanding, and singles out the gracious purpose of the crucifixion, which Paul is supposed to reiterate for the sake of emphasis in two parallel clauses εἰς ἔνδειξιν . . . πρὸς τὴν ἔνδειξιν).

No longer treated as guilty, no longer estranged, believing men thus enter upon the great experience of grace. For ' grace ' is not merely the action of God in generous favour shown to the undeserving, whom He ' rights ' through Jesus Christ ; it also represents the new relationship and order into which men are admitted, as their faith answers to the divine revelation. Hence in v. 1 f. ' grace ' is more inclusive than in a passage like iii. 24. It denotes the position as well as the power and purpose which created this position. At this point indeed the apostle's language is tinged with lyrical rhythm and assonance :

So justified by faith	δικαιωθέντες οὖν ἐκ πίστεως
let us enjoy peace with God	εἰρήνην ἔχωμεν πρὸς τὸν θεὸν
through our Lord Jesus Christ,	διὰ τοῦ Κυρίου ἡμῶν Ἰησοῦ Χριστοῦ,
through whom we have our access	δι' οὗ καὶ τὴν προσαγωγὴν ἐσχήκαμεν
to this grace wherein we stand.	εἰς τὴν χάριν ταύτην ἐν ᾗ ἑστήκαμεν.

' Justification ' is not permission to wait in an antechamber, it is admission to the inner presence of God. Grace looks forward to the complete experience of this life at the end, but already the reconciliation is an actual experience. All its expectations rest upon the consciousness of a present fellowship. No estimate of Paul's religious teaching is adequate unless it takes full account of faith, and no account of faith is adequate which regards it as elicited by some formal declaration of pardon or acquittal, to be followed up by a second act of grace in the shape of the gift of the Spirit. Justifying faith for the apostle seems to be more than any such pale preliminary to fellowship. It is a gift of divine favour aiming at the creation of moral personalities answering to God's aim and purpose. He who thus treats erring penitents in their weakness has in mind their sonship and freedom as the object of His loving favour and saving purpose. It was for this end that Christ was sacrificed and raised from death, inaugurating the new order of life.

In all the three surveys this end of ' life ' is presented, in (c) most definitely, in (a) more under the concept of freedom, and here (b) in the underlying idea of justification.

Here, Paul declares, is Life ! As a quondam Pharisee he may choose to express this in terms of ' righteousness,' not of the Realm or kingdom, as Jesus had done ; in technical language, he worked with the category of *zecuth* or righteousness, not of *malcuth*. But he is feeling for the same truth as is implied in the preaching of the kingdom of God by Jesus. In both conceptions God is the giver of Life, and God as the gracious Father ; man receives what He bestows, and receives it just as he is, without attempting first to earn the boon. To be receptive as children, to be humble enough to take what is offered, this was what Jesus had taught as the essential attitude on the part of men ; Paul states this in his own way when he speaks of faith as the response to grace, ruling out ' works ' from the religious life.

To ' justify ' (δικαιοῦν) includes forgiveness, but it is wider than
' to pardon.' It is equivalent to salvation as a rescue from Sin and
the Flesh which brings life into the living presence of God. The
reconciliation thus effected, the status of ' righteousness,' to which
acquittal on the score of faith in the sacrifice of Christ admits men, is
a relationship of life, the final and full phase of which is ' glory,' the
immortal life to be enjoyed by the faithful ; salvation (σωτηρία) is an
equivalent for the realization of such ' glory ' at the end, as opposed
to the doom of death or exclusion from the presence of the living God.
In Paul's terminology δικαίωσις or ' justification ' is ζωοποίησις,
' making alive.' This positive connotation of ' save ' and ' salvation '
was present in the Aramaic terms rendered into Greek by σώζειν and
σωτηρία. The Syriac usage goes to prove this. It is the significance
of the terms in the gospels where, for example, σώσει becomes ζωογονήσει
in the Lucan doublet (ix. 29, 33).[1] As the Realm of God announced
by Jesus meant Life, so Paul's equivalent of ' righteousness ' was a
divine promise and purpose which aimed at the same result. His very
use of a term like σώζειν suggests that it has more affinities with Hebrew
thought than with Hellenistic. The positive imparting of life as the
effect of rescue lies at the heart of ' save ' and ' salvation ' in his
argument.

(c) The third survey arises out of the same situation.
*Now . . . all who have faith are justified for nothing by God's
grace . . . we have got access to this grace where we have our
standing . . . through our Lord Jesus Christ, by whom we now
enjoy our reconciliation* (iii. 21–24, v. 2, 11). Against this
bright Now stands a dark Then. Once more the apostle
shows how this new and final era of grace has been prepared
for in the past, but this time it is in terms of a contrast between
the long era opened by the disobedience of Adam and the
present era of grace inaugurated by God in Jesus Christ,
between the reign of Sin and Death and the Law over humanity
and the reign of Grace ending in life eternal. In form this
survey (v. 12–21) is a digression, but it is adduced as fresh

[1] See P. Joüon in *Recherches de Science Religieuse* (1927), pp. 225 f., and,
more broadly, M. A. Canney in *Theology*, xv (1927), pp. 64–73.

proof of the glorious certainty of that experience and attitude towards God of which the apostle has just spoken.

It is assumed (i) that the end resembles and answers to the beginning. Paul does not speak of any original purpose of God, however; he compares the first Disobedience of man to God with the great Obedience of Jesus Christ which more than met the tragic results of the former. His central faith in ' the living God ' implied that the end of the divine Will must be Life, and that the moral order corresponding to this had not been broken by the Sin and Death that intervened. (ii) Hence Adam prefigures Christ, but how blessed is the difference ! One man's sin in the remote past affected the whole race, millions of whom had never known or heard of him; one Man's fulfilment of God's will now brings acquittal and life, offered directly to all, as God's grace takes us by the hand into personal relations. (iii) This ampler reign of grace, with the contrast thus implied, rests upon the Hebrew idea of solidarity. It is ' grace for all ' that the apostle has in mind, and this is expressed in terms of the ancient idea that the community or race suffer and succeed with him who is their head or representative.

Sin came into the world by one man, and death came in by sin ; and so death spread to all men, inasmuch as all men sinned Sin was indeed in the world before the Law, but sin is never counted in the absence of law. Nevertheless, from Adam to Moses death reigned even over those whose sins were not like Adam's transgression. Adam prefigured Him who was to come, but the gift (τὸ χάρισμα) *is very different from the trespass.* (Paul is trying to show that Christ is like Adam and at the same time that he is far more than Adam. So he proceeds.) *For while the rest of men died by the trespass of one man, the grace of God and the free gift* (δωρεά) *which comes by the grace of the one man Jesus Christ overflowed* (ἐπερίσσευσε) *far more richly* (πολλῷ μᾶλλον) *upon the rest of men. Nor is the free gift* (δώρημα) *like the effect of the one man's sin ; for while the sentence ensuing on a single sin resulted in doom, the free gift* (τὸ χάρισμα) *ensuing upon* (i.e. coming from God in gracious response to the appeal of) *many trespasses issues in acquittal. For if the trespass of one man allowed death to reign through that one man, much more* (πολλῷ μᾶλλον) *shall those who receive the overflowing grace* (περισσείαν τῆς χάριτος) *and free gift* (δωρεά) *of righteousness reign in life through One, through Jesus Christ. Well then, as one man's trespass issued in doom for all, so one man's act of redress* (or righteous Act, δικαίωμα) *issues in acquittal and life for all. Just as one man's disobedience made all the rest sinners, so one man's obedience will make all the rest righteous.* (Then, picking up the argument about Sin and the Law in the historical purpose of God, from which he had been carried away by the parallel between Adam and Christ, he weaves this into the triumphant conclusion.) *Law indeed slipped in to aggravate the trespass ; sin increased, but grace surpassed it far* (ὑπερεπερίσσευσε), *so that, while sin had reigned the reign of death, grace might also reign with a righteousness that ends in life eternal through Jesus Christ our Lord.*

As in i. 18–iii. 20, Paul assumes that somehow the ' all ' who die must have deserved to die by their sin. The vivid picture of Sin and Death as daemonic powers tyrannizing over human life is his way of expressing the conviction that the fact of death being everywhere is a dreadful proof of sin. He does not explain the origin of evil by any recourse to mythological theories of angels or of Satan, for example. The argument is that death got hold of men through their sins, as descendants of the first man. Their plight is connected with his fall, but it is not explained or defined. His solution, so far as it is a solution, is nearer to that presupposed in Fourth Esdras (iii. 26 : ' the inhabitants of the City committed sin, in all things acting as Adam and all his generations had acted ; for they too had clothed themselves with the evil heart '—the ' cor malignum ') ; men are morally responsible for their sins and yet somehow involved in Adam's transgression. But the Christian experience of Paul lifts him far above the melancholy of the apocalyptist. In terms chosen from current speculation he expresses the contrast between the dark past and the bright present. His aim is to exalt the grace of God. As everywhere he saw sin and death triumphant, and referred them to a single source, so he saw the greater triumph of reconciliation flowing from the single source of Christ. But he does not mean that Christ merely reverses the consequences of the fall. There is no idea of restoring man to some primaeval state of innocence and immortality. Grace is infinitely more rich than any prospect of original man.

This argument on grace as opposed to sin and death, its defeated rivals, becomes more intelligible in the light of Paul's predecessors and contemporaries than in the light of subsequent Christian speculation. The question of sin's relation to death was almost the only problem on which the practical genius of Jewish religion had become speculative. Paul knew how in one circle the envy of Satan had been employed to explain man's tragic fate :

> God created man for immortality,
>   and made him the image of his own being,
> but by the envy of the devil death entered the world
>   and they who belong to him (to his party) experience death.

There was also the mythological theory of Enoch, Jubilees, etc., which referred the moral corruption of the race to the fallen angels of Genesis vi. 1 f., with their illicit incitement to lust. Against such supernatural daemonic views there was the idea of the evil ' yetzer ' or impulse in man, which was not original sin, not inevitable, but universal ; to counteract this the Law had been given. Paul reverses that view when he remarks that the effect of the Law was to aggravate the sense of sin, but otherwise he does not use such a theory in the present connexion. Contemporary religious thought shows two opposing emphases. One stressed the solidarity of the race. Thus the author of Fourth Esdras is at his wits' end to explain how sin originated ; he feels the bitter consequence of Adam's sin, and explains the sinful domination which experience revealed, by postulating a hereditary tendency to sin derived from Adam, which is called the ' cor malignum ' or evil heart. " A grain of evil seed was sown in the heart of Adam from the beginning, and what fruit of ungodliness has it produced up till now and will yet produce ! " (iv. 30). This became a permanent handicap. " For the first Adam, clothing himself with the evil heart, transgressed and was overcome ; and likewise all who were born of him " (iii. 21 f.). The author cannot explain the origin of sin, but he bewails its pre-valence. " O Adam, what hast thou done ? For though it was thou who didst sin, the fall was not thine alone but ours also who are thy descendants " (vii. 118 f.). On the other hand a sturdy individualism voiced itself in circles represented by the Apocalypse of Baruch. The fall of Adam is admitted, but the consequences are merely physical death and a certain acceleration towards evil in men, which is not inevitable. The moral nature remains practically unimpaired. " If Adam did sin first and brought untimely death on all, yet those who were born of him each prepared for his own soul its future torment, each chose his future glory . . . Adam is therefore not the cause, save of his own soul. Each of us has been the Adam of his own soul " (liv. 15 f.). Even when supernatural views were accepted, such a protest in favour of freewill and moral responsibility was often echoed, as in Enoch xciv., xcviii. 4. There was a wholesome desire to preserve this truth, even as the solidarity of the race in sin was recognized.

In Romans v. 12 f. Paul states the one side of the truth, inclining more to the position of Fourth Esdras than to the opposite view, though he ignores the ' cor malignum ' theory. The correlative truth of individual responsibility comes out in Romans vii. 7 f. ; there again he avoids any reference to Satan, and reaches a more hopeful view than in Fourth Esdras, where relief from the sinful heritage is postponed till the next world, when God will eradicate the evil heart.

5

After the exulting conclusion of v. 12–21 that Grace reigns, Paul reverts to an objection from the side of ethics. He was sensitive on this point, but up till now he had brushed aside the objection, as a calumny upon his gospel. When people ask, ' If sin gives the opportunity for God's grace to display its power, *why should we not do evil that good may come out of it ?* ' the apostle retorts, *such arguments are rightly condemned,* and passes on (iii. 7–8). But now he takes up the criticism. Why is it right for us to condemn this Jewish slander ? *Now,* he asks, in beginning his answer, *what are we to infer from all this* (i.e. from the conclusion that we are freely forgiven by God's grace and sure to be saved at the end) ? Are we to infer *that we are to ' remain on in sin, so that there may be all the more grace ' ? Never !* And the negative is supported by a series of illustrations or arguments, mystical (1–14), moral (15–23), and juridical (vii. 1–6). They are indeed appeals, for Paul is conscious that " in the last resort the objection can only be practically refuted ; it must be lived down, not argued down." [1] He would have agreed with Fichte that the real atheist is the man who would do evil that good may come of it. But to be lived down, this must be felt to be irrational, and the apostle seeks to produce this feeling by explaining the inconsistency between real faith in grace and any moral carelessness. " Free to sin ? " He is horrified at the thought. " Free from sin " is the rubric of grace. He was distressed by moral laxity in his churches, but he was more shocked to find moral laxity being condoned and even justified by an appeal to his teaching upon grace. Sometimes, as at Corinth, the liberals in a spirit of ' hybris ' seem to have acted as though those who had ' communicated ' could indulge freely in pagan cult-feasts, owing to their possession of a superior divine power. Elsewhere we find that either the sacraments or the specific teaching of the apostle on grace was employed to relax moral obligations. " Is not the Christian-cult like the others ? Why should the baptized be bothered by advice on morals, when they are never to be condemned by God ? Is the welfare of the redeemed spirit, under grace, really imperilled by bodily excesses ? " The apostle's difficulty with Jewish converts was to prevent them from letting moralism infringe the truth of grace, but he had another difficulty when he met converts whose associations with the cults made them ready to accept grace but averse to recognize that grace, as the grace of the

[1] Denny, *The Death of Christ*, p. 185.

Lord Jesus, involved much more than a happy hope of escape from the wrath to come, or at any rate averse to believe that the freedom of the Spirit should be compromised, as they thought, by any ethical requirements and restrictions.

Even where in other passages he connects grace and the good life more simply and effectively, it is not his habit to employ the term ' grace.' Perhaps it was the absorbing sense of ' grace ' as divine that made Paul instinctively avoid current phrases which might have served him as expressions of man's moral response to grace.   For example, as we have seen, he avoids χαρίζομαι of man ' pleasing ' God, and also the good Greek phrase ποιεῖν ἐν χάριτι.   Socrates tells his disciples, " If you take heed to yourselves, you will always be doing a service (ἐν χάριτι ποιήσετε) to me and mine as well as to yourselves " (Phaedo 115 B). Paul might well have taken this phrase for the ethical answer of life to the Lord, but he does not.   The reason is that for him 'grace' is predominantly divine ; it is God acting, not man.   He reserves the term for the Lord.   When it comes to faith's activity, as inspired by grace, when he desires to show how the goodwill of God produces a goodwill in man, he chooses other expressions than such a Greek set of grace-words.   Apart from employing ' charis ' in the sense of thanks, he seems reluctant to associate it with any activity save that of the Lord.

In the sequel (Rom. vi. 1–viii. 2) he first (i) uses the cosmical and metaphysical argument, that as Christ by his death and resurrection has broken with Sin and the Flesh, so those who believe in him and are baptized into him are lifted thereby into a new order of being, where they are free and bound to serve God.   This incorporation into Christ generates the good life.   In organic mystical union with the risen Lord, Christians cannot but rise above their lower nature.   But it is not automatic ; *consider yourselves dead to sin and alive to God in Christ Jesus our Lord.*   Just as else-where, in deducing the good life from the power of the in-dwelling Spirit, he reminds Christians, ' As we live by (ἐν) the Spirit, let us be guided by the Spirit,' so here.   (ii) Another motive for the good life is adoring gratitude to the Redeemer, since *he died for all in order to have the living live no longer for themselves but for him who died and rose for them*. But this is worked out in indirect terms of grace by the use of εὐχαριστία and other terms for thankfulness (see above, pp. 139 f.).

In some of the later documents (e.g. in Titus ii. 11), grace is definitely linked to the moral ends of life. Paul generally employs the conception of the Spirit, but there are two points, however, at which the conception of grace as divine power is employed in order to bring out the activities of the Christian vocation. One is with reference to the apostolic calling, and the other occurs in the sphere of what may be termed the Christian graces.

(a)

Grace is more than pardon, it is power, the divine power which redeems life and also uses it, rendering a man efficient for service. Twice, in the First Epistle to the Corinthians the apostle employs the term in this sense for the apostolic mission, implying that all we do as well as all we are, we owe to God Himself. *I am the very least of the apostles* (he writes in xv. 9 f.), unfit indeed, I admit this freely (repeating a sneer of his opponents), quite unworthy *to bear the name of 'apostle,' since I persecuted the church of God. But by God's grace I am what I am*, turned from a persecutor into an apostle, freely forgiven and re-shaped in my nature. *And the grace he showed me did not go for nothing ; no, I have done far more work than all of them—though it was not I but God's grace at my side* (σὺν ἐμοί). The last to be called to the ranks of the apostles, he claims to have outstripped any or all of the others in efficiency. *I have done far more work than any of them* is a naïve trade-metaphor of humble pride, derived originally " from the joyful pride of the skilled craftsman who, working by the piece, was able to hand in the largest amount of goods on pay-day." [1]   But instantly he adds, 'yet it was not I but God who inspired me.'   The Greek phrase means more than co-operation, as though God's grace and Paul's energy were equal factors in the process.   It is not a common expression of his, but he could use it without fear of misunderstanding for divine inspiration as the source of a hardworking servant's success ; 'no man can do these Signs that thou doest, except God be with him' (John iii. 2, so Acts x. 38) gives the idea of the phrase.

The pious phrase σὺν θεῷ or σὺν θεοῖς, 'by the favour or help of the gods,' which the papyri and inscriptions attest as common in the outside world, Paul never uses.   His unique phrase here for the presence of God as the power in his life seemed to later scribes to require the addition of the article (ἡ σὺν ἐμοί, which is with me), in order to make it clear that he referred all the credit to God's grace.   There was a similar change in the tenth Article of the English Church (" we have no power to do good works pleasant and acceptable to God, without the grace of God by Christ preventing us, that we may have a good will, and working with us, when we have the good will ").   Originally, as written by Cranmer, ' co-operante ' was rendered ' working in us,' but Jewel in 1571 altered it to its present form.

Again, in iii. 9, 10, the apostle writes : *We*, Apollos and myself, *work together in God's service.* . . .   *In virtue of my commission from God* (κατὰ τὴν χάριν τοῦ θεοῦ τὴν δοθεῖσάν μοι) *I laid the foundation.*   The words θεοῦ συνεργοί include the thought of being God's helpers in the mission, but the primary idea is of co-operation between himself and Apollos in the divine service.   The reason why he stresses the ' grace ' of his commission, when he comes to speak of his own work, is not that he feels it needful to correct or supplement the former idea but because he desires to insist that his work had been valid and effective.   It had not been an irregular, independent adventure.   ' Grace ' here denotes the authority of the commission, the power behind the service.   In narrating

[1] Deissmann, *Light from the Ancient East*, p. 313.

how the apostles at Jerusalem cordially recognized his orders,
as we might say, Paul also uses grace ; *they saw that I had
been entrusted with the gospel for the benefit of the uncircumcised . . .
and they recognized the grace that had been given to me* (Gal. ii.
7–9). They acknowledged that he waˢ an apostle, having
seen something of the genuine effects of his mission. Here
again grace includes both authority and power, just as a term
like ἐξουσία could do in the religious sphere ; but in the
present case it further refers to the gentile mission,- as it
may do in the earlier words of i. 15, 16 : *the God who had
set me apart from my very birth called me by his grace* (in the
exercise of his loving favour to my undeserving self) *and
chose to reveal his Son to me, that I might preach him to the
gentiles.* Once again, his authority for issuing directions to
a church which he had not himself founded, is traced back
to the same grace. ' In virtue of my office (as we may render
διὰ τῆς χάριτος τῆς δοθείσης μοι), I give the following orders
to you ' (Rom. xii. 3), not presumptuously but as one who
has been commissioned by God and empowered by Him to
advise and counsel the Church.

(b)

A contemporary inscription (Dittenberger's *Sylloge Inscription Graecarum* 365), referring eulogistically to some refugees
whom Caligula had reinstated in the ample generosity of
his ' immortal favour,' addresses the emperor as a sort of
divine source of grace and observes that the favours of the
gods are as far above human favours as the sun is above the
night and immortality above mortality (θεῶν δὲ χάριτες τούτῳ
διαφέρουσιν ἀνθρωπίνων διαδοχῶν ᾧ ἡ νυκτὸς ἥλιος καὶ τὸ ἄφθαρτον
θνητῆς φύσεως). Like the other NT writers, Paul avoids
using ' grace ' thus in the plural, even when speaking of the
abundant grace of God. The Hellenistic χάριτες is absent
from the NT literature (except as a variant in three ninth-
century MSS for χάριτα in Acts xxiv. 27). Hence we do

15

not find the apostle speaking of what we call the Christian graces. But at four points he uses the vocabulary of grace in order to explain some phases of the Christian ethic. Two of these have been already noticed, (*a*) the ' gracious ' spirit of forgiveness between Christian and Christian, for which the verb χαρίζεσθαι (see p. 101) is employed, and (*b*) the grace-gifts or χαρίσματα of the Church (see pp. 105–114), covering the larger duties of the common fellowship. But there are two other points which, although of minor importance, deserve mention ; one bears upon practical generosity and the other upon the unselfish, disinterested temper which grace evokes in life. Both, as it happens, emerge in the Second Epistle to the Corinthians, the first in viii. 7, the other in i. 12.

(i) He had been so encouraged by the liberal response of the Macedonian churches that he ventured to use their example as a stimulus to the Corinthians or Achaians, just as he had stirred up the Macedonians by praising the willingness of the Achaian churches. *Now then*, he writes, *you are to the front in everything, in faith, in utterance, in knowledge, in all zeal, and in love for us* (or, as τῇ ἐξ ἡμῶν ἐν ὑμῖν might be rendered, in love caught or learned from us)—*do come to the front in this gracious enterprise* (χάριτι) *as well*. He is not speaking ironically, as though the Achaian Christians were more ready to discuss their faith than to part with money for the sake of other Christians ; he fully recognizes the hearty desire of the Achaians to do something practical (ix. 1–2). It is simply a call to exercise ' grace ' in all its departments. Here, he declares, is an opportunity for you to be as distinguished in liberality as in other gifts of the Spirit on which you pride yourselves. He had congratulated them on their *power to speak about* their faith and their *insight into its meaning*. But grace enters into the relationships of rich and poor, if it is anything. Grace means giving, at the heart of it, in man as well as in God. Indeed the whole range of human kindness is covered by an argument like this, for we may take in the broadest sense the apostle's maxim, in the same connexion, " God is able to make all grace abound towards you that ye may abound to every good work."

(ii) Some misunderstanding had arisen, and the Corinthians thought they had reason to suspect him of not being quite straightforward in his dealings with them. This ugly spirit he seeks to exorcise in the argument of i. 12 f. He has just been appealing for their sympathy and prayers in the grave situation which still threatened him—*so that many a soul may render thanks to Him on my behalf for the boon* (χάρισμα) *which many have been the means of Him bestowing on myself.* For, he continues, I am surely justified in asking this from you ; I have a right to claim it, owing to my sincere conduct towards you. *My proud boast is the testimony of my conscience that holiness and godly sincerity* (εἰλικρινείᾳ τοῦ θεοῦ), *not worldly cunning but the grace of God* (χάριτι θεοῦ), *have marked my conduct in the outside world and in particular my relations with you.* By a deliberate and telling paradox he uses the term ' boast ' (καύχησις) here, even in speaking about grace. It is not that ' grace ' is employed as a foil to ' boon,' as though to disavow any further credit for a personal achievement on his own part. Grace is the foil to astuteness or calculation ; primarily it is opposed to any consideration of self in his ministry. On one side he can truly speak of his *holiness and sincerity,* εἰλικρινεία being in T. H. Green's happy definition " perfect openness to God, that clearness of soul in which nothing interferes with its penetration by the divine sunlight " ; that is to say, he disclaims proudly any conceit or private ends in his ministry. But as he speaks of the human conditions in which the grace of God works, he proceeds to contrast any such *worldly cunning* with it. Consequently *the grace of God* here is not His kindness but grace as the ruling and controlling principle by which the apostle's ministry is inspired. To this grace he owes not only the holiness and sincerity he has displayed but the power of living by these qualities in a career of devotion to God ; unselfish care for others, as inspired by the thought of God's grace, has been the determining power of his life, not any selfish end or side-effort to use other people as instruments for private ambition. Such is the underlying thought of this reference. Negatively the grace of God has kept him from inconsistent conduct ; positively it has enabled him to carry out his mission on the lines of God Himself, without being deflected by any " unconquered selfishness." God's grace is a power, and grace is disinterested in its working ; these two ideas are combined here.

The sensitiveness of the apostle on this point and the need he feels for justifying his conduct are significant proof that the grace or Spirit of God was understood to be the principle of divine unselfishness as the controlling motive of life.   In her biography of *John Knox* (p. 124) Mrs. Florence MacCunn notes that

" those whom we recognize as saints differ from other zealous and righteous men in virtue of a certain aloofness. They may associate with the vilest, loving them with a pure passion unknown to other men ; they may wear out heart and brain contending with triumphant worldliness, but they keep their souls anchored in the Eternal Calm, and thus escape the deadliest danger of the conflict, the temptation to use in God's quarrel weapons forged by craft or violence."

Here it is craft which Paul disclaims. Charged with being underhand, he protests that he was straightforward and transparent ; his motives and methods had been determined by a disinterested concern for men, even for those who were actually impugning his behaviour.

(c)

The moral obligation of grace emerges in 2 Corinthians v. 20 f. *I am an envoy (πρεσβεύομεν) for Christ, God appealing by me, as it were—be reconciled to God, I entreat you on behalf of Christ. For our sakes He made him to be sin who himself knew nothing of sin, so that in him we might become the righteousness of God. I appeal to you too as a worker with God, do not receive the grace of God in vain (εἰς κενόν).* But why ' too ' ? Why

this further appeal ? It is as if he said, ' I beseech you not
merely to accept the gracious offer of a new standing with
God but also to be diligent in living up to it.' The words εἰς
κενόν are put first in the Greek sentence for the sake of emphasis. It sounds at first as though Paul were addressing
people still outside the Church ; the language recalls his
mission-preaching, especially in the light of Greek usage, for
to receive ' charis ' denoted naturally the reception of pardon
from an offended authority, as in Plutarch's Life of Themis-
tocles (xxviii.), where the suppliant statesman humbly tells
the Persian king, παρεσκευασμένος ἀφῖγμαι δέξασθαί τε χάριν
εὐμενῶς διαλλατομένου. Yet the stress here is upon the duty
of using the favour as God meant it to be used. He had
already told them that *Christ died for all in order to have the
living live no longer for themselves but for him who died and rose
for them*, and he reminds them that, to ' become the righteousness of God in Christ ' involved a serious life of devotion ; to
treat the privilege casually as though it did not bear upon the
ethical responsibilities of life was to receive the favour in vain.
It is tempting to imagine that one of the reasons which led
the apostle to add the citation from Isaiah about the acceptable
time was the cry of the discouraged Servant of the Lord in the
immediate context (Isa. xlix. 4) : κενῶς ἐκοπίασα. But it is of
the Corinthians not of himself that he is thinking primarily
in these words. Their sense is excellently conveyed by
Pelagius : ' in vacuum gratiam dei recipit qui in novo testa-
mento non novus est, hoc est, nihil in illo proficit.' Grace
meant the truth that the forgiven man was now the possession
of the God who had thus delivered him, and consequently
that life must be devoted to God's purpose ; to take it on any
lower level, as though it involved serious relief but not an
equally serious obligation, was to receive it to no purpose at
all.

Paul as an apostle was commissioned to announce this ' grace,' not
to exercise it, for it is more than a gracious temper which Christians

ought to evince towards one another or towards the world at large. This becomes clear from the introductory words of v. 18 f. When he writes that *in Christ God reconciled the world to himself instead of counting men's trespasses against them, and he entrusted me with the word of message of reconciliation,* he does not mean that he and others, even though they were apostles, were to share in this reconciliation, by overcoming the antagonisms that spoil human relationships and re-creating a new world through a friendly spirit and unselfish temper, such as Christ had exhibited ; the apostolic task was to proclaim the power of the living, loving God in Christ, or, as he puts it, to persuade men to accept this grace. The ministry of reconciliation begins with the announcement of the revelation that God had reconciled men. This had been a revelation of grace to Paul himself ; he sometimes calls the very commission to proclaim it, a grace or favour of God. And it was a revelation still to those who accepted it. No doubt, the forgiving, friendly spirit which he called love, the mind of Christ which by producing in Christians unselfishness and mutual service moved outsiders, no doubt, this did help to create an impression of the reality of this divine Spirit. By being gracious and helpful, by living for others in a spirit of service and self-forgetfulness after the example of Jesus, his followers carried on the good work, overcoming in their own lives every racial and social prejudice that set men one against another and thus darkened the vision of God's purpose. Such an attitude did go to make a new world. Paul was never tired of urging this upon his churches. If we are faithful in following Christ, he told them, as John Woolman told his readers, " our lives will have an inviting language." Certainly it was in this spirit alone that the gospel of reconciliation could be preached. But such qualities were all effects of what God had done. These healing waters flowed from a fountain of life, and the fountain lay in a Rock that had been struck, not in striking words about harmony among men. The only fellowship of reconciliation which Paul recognized was the Christian Church living in the consciousness of having been reconciled by the Lord to Himself.

(d)

Paul never spoke of requirements without speaking of resources in religion. *God has done what the Law, weakened here by the flesh, could not do ; by sending his own Son in the guise of sinful flesh, to deal with sin, he condemned sin in the flesh, in order to secure the fulfilment of the Law's requirements in our lives, as we live and move* (περιπατοῦσιν) *not by the flesh but by the Spirit* (Rom. viii. 3, 4). These requirements are summed up in brotherly love, for he does not imply that the redeemed man, once equipped with power from God, goes back to carry out the old Law in its ceremonial or even in its ethical details. But the point here is that the aim and end of deliverance is a religious life which means obedience or service, and that without the grace of God this is impossible. The trend of thought throws light on the remarkable introduction of ' weak ' in the previous argument of v. 6–10. ' When we were yet without strength (ἀσθενῶν ἔτι) in due time Christ died for the ungodly . . . while we were yet sinners (ἔτι ἁμαρτωλῶν) Christ died for us . . . when we were enemies (ἔχθροί), we were reconciled to God by the death of his Son.' The moral weakness here is an inability to help ourselves. But the consciousness of this powerless position implies that the end of life is a free active relation to God and His Will or Law. When elsewhere Paul speaks of the ' weak,' it is commonly in connexion with scruples felt by some members of the Church. But here ' weak ' describes from one point of view the position of those who need the grace of God in order to have strength for doing His will. They are not only estranged but they have lost their vital powers. Salvation is life. To be saved is to gain or regain life. And as life is not merely existence but a relationship to God in which His will is to be known and done, the apostle can even speak of ' the law of the Spirit.' His highest category is that of law, since the essence of law is the will of God for His people. In the light of His revelation through Jesus Christ, it is plain that the only obedience with which He is ultimately satisfied is that rendered by love to Love, by grateful trust to the Grace which endows life with a heavenly freedom whose other side is a higher control.

When the heart of Christian faith comes to the lips, as in some of the classical prayers and hymns, it is—

> Plenteous grace with Thee is found,
>   grace to cover all my sin ;
> Let the healing streams abound,
>   make and keep me pure within.

The sinful heart requires to be kept no less than made clean. Therefore, unless grace be restricted to pardon—which is not the case in Paul—there is no meaning in " a higher gift than grace." In the religious outlook of the NT there is nothing higher than grace, for grace is the gift of God Himself in His fulness, the gift of His power and presence no less than His pardon. *God sent his own Son in the guise of sinful flesh to deal with sin* (περὶ ἁμαρτίας) not to deal with ignorance. More than moral enlightenment was required, more than the removal of wrong ideas about God. The root of the trouble lay deeper. And the remedy was larger than forgiveness. For, Paul continues, *he condemned sin in the flesh in order to secure the fulfilment of the Law's requirements in our lives, as we live and move by the Spirit.* The supreme end of this gracious favour or action of God is therefore to secure the moral vitality and obedience which answers to His eternal requirements. In other words, the good life is the outcome of a new relationship to Christ. Like Jesus, Paul conceives life as a service, however it is lived. ' God or Mammon ' becomes for Paul ' God or Sin,' ' the Spirit or the flesh.' The categories are less simple, but the counsel is the same. It is most appealing in the famous ' divided-self ' passage (vii. 7–25), most technical in the arguments of viii. 1–11, and most direct in the appeal of vi. 15 f., which swings from the position that *sin must have no hold over you, for you live under grace, not under law.*

In mediaeval liturgies one of the prayers of the priest before mass begins, " Domine, non sum dignus ut intres sub tectum meum, sed confisus de tua pietate ad altare tuum accedo." [1]   But this confession

---

[1] See *The Sarum Missal in English* (ed. Vernon Staley), i. 18.

was not originally spoken by a priest. It is the word of a layman.
" I am not worthy " was spoken by an army officer, who was considered
extremely worthy by his neighbours. Judged by the standards of
contemporary religion he had done well and deserved the favour of
God ; but in presence of Jesus he knew that another attitude to God
was required. This great grace-word illustrates an ethical truth which
is characteristic of belief in grace. The leading Christians who have
upheld such a conviction as essential to Christianity have been generally
strong men, like Paul, Ambrose, Bernard, Luther, Bunyan, and Wesley,
strong men in the sense that they came to their consciousness of grace
from a keenly moral consciousness of religion. Grace has its deep
message for the guilty. It is a gospel that reaches the vile and the
vicious. It is for broken lives, for souls oppressed by the blame and
shame of sin. It touches outcasts and outcastes. But this is by no
means all. From the first it has appealed to eager spirits, who have
found themselves hampered and handicapped by religious principles
that failed to release the powers of life. Paul as a Christian was
conscious of being ' alive ' as he had never been until he met the
Lord Jesus. Fresh resources for obedience were unlocked. He
assumes that this is a normal experience of Christians, though it is
evident that many converts from the pagan world cannot have had
anything like his moral training or deep zeal for religion. Nevertheless,
even in speaking of grace on semi-metaphysical lines, he interprets the
vital effects of faith on personality by co-ordinating grace with relief
from the bondage of evil in the world, with the sense of a new vocation,
with a fresh vision of duty and devotion, with power to endure suffering
for the sake of the cause, and with loyalty to the welfare of the Church.
All this is derived from the primary experience of vital communion
with the Lord, which he owed and wished others to know that they
owed to grace.

(e)

The mind of the apostle moves naturally from the thought
of indebtedness to God for all in life to the thought of the
obligations under which this privilege lays the believing man,
as may be seen in the argument of Romans viii. 15 f. : *You
have received the Spirit of sonship* (put into the position of sons,

at the start and source of your Christian life). *And when* (whenever in our prayers) *we cry ' Abba ! Father ! '* (which was a new invocation in prayer even for those who had been trained as Jews) *it is this Spirit testifying along with our own spirit that we are children of God.* The very prayers in which life seems most instinctive and spontaneous are inspired by the divine Spirit, Paul means. Then he adds, *And if children,* then *heirs as well, heirs of God.* Again the note of grace is struck, as against merit ; we come into an inheritance provided for us, not won by our own efforts. But to emphasize the companion thought of obligation, as he repeats *heirs* (for the third time) he adds *heirs along with Christ—for we share his sufferings in order to share his glory.* As Jesus had said, we reach the kingdom by taking up the cross and following him, not otherwise. The moral conditions of the great hope are stressed. Paul glances at them again, when he declares : *even we who have the Spirit as a foretaste* (ἀπαρχή) [1] *of the future, even we sigh to ourselves as we wait for the redemption of* (not, from) *the body that means our full sonship* (υἱοθεσίαν). The note of grace sounds in υἱοθεσία, for sonship implies adoption by God, the free favour to which we owe our standing in His order ; the full realization of this favour is only attained at the end, as the inheritance reserved graciously for those who have been true to their sonship. Christians are sons and they are to be sons completely in the glory of the heavenly realm where the flesh is no more a handicap. Both the present experience and the future hope are grounded in grace, but one is not carried to glory on a tide of privilege, the apostle reminds his readers. The Christian hope involves a dis-

---

[1] It would sharpen the force of the argument if ἀπαρχή could be taken in the sense of birth-certificate ; in some contemporary papyri it is a legal word for the birth-certificate of a free person (see H. S. Jones in *Journal of Theological Studies,* xxiii. 282, 283), and here it might be used metaphorically, the possession of the Spirit being viewed as our title from God the Father to the full status of sonship at the end.

cipline. Here he touches the passive side of this. But even elsewhere, in speaking of the more active aspect, he conceives the goodwill of God as no fiat or force of irresistible power but as the inspiration of the moral personality. He always does his best to hold together two factors which were often isolated and therefore misunderstood by some of his later interpreters. Sonship or the justification wrought by God's grace was for him both an act of God and an experience of man. In emphasizing the former he was not afraid to appreciate its consequences in human life. ' It is all of grace ' did not mean an abstraction ; the justification of man is a nucleus in which the divine grace and human faith interpenetrate, and whilst Paul would never allow that this faith was to be taken as any ground for grace, nevertheless he does not seem to have conceived it possible to think of faith apart from the aim of grace, that is, a right relationship to God in which faith was the motive and instinct of ethical obedience. *Work at your own salvation with reverence and trembling, for it is God who in his goodwill enables you to will this and to achieve it.* This is a paradox only upon paper. It was a reality of religious experience in the sphere of grace, which caused Paul no more difficulty than it did for the prophet of old, who prayed in the name of the People :

> Oh maintain our welfare ;
> for whatsoever we achieve
> is all thy doing.[1]

Omnia enim opera nostris operatus es in nobis.

But his experience of missions and church-life made him aware of the tendency which either bisects the universe into grace and nature, as though God were apart from the common life of men, or deceives the mind by conceiving God as a genial, friendly person, with Whom there is no reason why the well-meaning soul should not be on good terms. This latter was the danger against which the apostle put his

[1] Isaiah xxvi. 12.

churches on their guard, just as he assured them of God's saving grace. Awe in the shape of reverence before the great God may indeed become superstitious. It readily becomes an unreasoning dread of the lower order before what is felt to be the majesty and the mystery of the world. But from this obsession which the contemporary astral fatalism was apt to engender, the gospel released men ; Paul was not seriously afraid of a recrudescence of such baser emotions within his churches, provided that they lived conscious of the grace of the Lord Jesus Christ which inspired a certainty about God's character that freed life from the old terror. What he feared was rather the lack of reverence and awe in people who allowed themselves to be presumptuous and forward, as the experience of God's favour met them. The very privilege of grace exposed the soul to risks. Let not slaves who had become Christians spoil their service by giving themselves airs and taking liberties, let them do their work thoroughly ' fearing the Lord ' (in the good sense of reverent awe, Col. iii. 22). So indeed with all social relationships ; ' be subject one to another as you stand in awe of Christ ' (Eph. v. 21). Such is the only atmosphere for the strict discipline of character (' perfecting holiness in the fear of God,' 2 Cor. vii. 1), the surest check upon the tendency to presume upon God's favour as though His favourites could afford to take life easily, to imagine that they knew all about His mysteries, or to be at ease in their new Sion of grace. ' Be not wise in your own conceits.' ' Be not high-minded but fear.' ' Work out your salvation with fear and trembling.' In this deep reverence for God the apostle saw not only the beginning of wisdom, that is, insight into the mystery of life, but the condition of sound energy in the service of God.

He is so impressed by the need for stressing moral responsibility that he retains the conception of a final judgment upon Christians, even on those for whom ' now there is no condemnation.' Logically this seems incompatible with the juridical categories in which at one point he had conveyed his assurance of present favour and acquittal. But these categories did not do full justice to his thought. He never regarded justifying faith as either morally indifferent or as a mechanical guarantee of goodness. It was his dread of any temper which lightly counted on God's final favour that made him insist upon the truth of a scrutiny at the end. Formally this is in contradiction to the juridical statement of assurance, but as he refused to believe that even sacraments guaranteed salvation apart from moral earnestness (1 Cor. x.–xi.), as he admitted that if he himself was not careful he might be disqualified at the end (1 Cor. ix. 23–27), so he was not afraid to declare : *We have all to appear without disguise before the tribunal of Christ, each to be requited for what he has done with his body, well or ill.* The conception of a loving God Who made personal faith the condition for receiving His gift of grace, and the interpretation of this grace as fellowship of moral personalities with Himself, implied that believing men must be responsible for their use of the gift. Why "all men have not faith," why some rejected and others accepted the offer of grace, was one problem. The latter fact was explained by predestination ; it is a further problem why the elect needed the sacraments, on Paul's view. Here his Hellenistic factor crosses the Jewish factor. But his deeply religious conception of what faith demanded from the moral life evidently prevented him from positing a merely logical notion of salvation for the elect or for those who used the sacraments, as though this relieved the faithful from God's strict judgment at the end upon what they had done with His gift. He carried on this conception at any rate from the 'Son of Man' tradition, that the Lord as the heavenly messiah or Christ of God was to judge the world at the final crisis.

Paul does not extend his use of ' grace ' to cover the end ; for that final event he prefers to employ other terms. But the problem of grace and judgment was raised by the eschatological outlook of his forensic categories. Originally the boon of ' justification ' as the work of grace referred to the end ; it was the assurance that having been saved by grace the believer would be right with God at the final judgment, delivered from the Wrath or doom assigned to the unrighteous. The position of those who were now and here under grace relieved them

GRACE IN THE NEW TESTAMENT

from any fear of the last judgment ; they could anticipate the future with confidence, sure of being acquitted.   Christ who had inaugurated the new order and brought believers into their right status before God would return before long to complete his work, but Christians could await the consummation hopefully ; all they had to do was to expect the coming of God's Son from heaven, the Son whom He raised from the dead, *Jesus who rescues us from the Wrath to come.*   Nevertheless, God was to judge the world at the end by Jesus Christ.   This was as vital an affirmation of faith as the message of grace with which it was bound up, and Paul strove to hold both together, conscious that if either were dropped there would be a defective gospel (see above, p. 213). The need for establishing a nexus between the experience of grace and the good life which could alone entitle a man to heaven, was native to him as a religious Jew, but it was forced upon him by experiences in his gentile mission.   Converts who were acquainted, for example, with such a cult as that of the Eleusinian mysteries, had to be taught the elementary truth that bliss was conditioned by faith and obedience, for the Eleusinian rites did not lay this on their initiate after his purification.   " So far as we know, it was at no time enjoined that, in a moral sense, he should thereafter walk in newness of life.   It cannot, indeed, be doubted that a ceremonial so impressive must often have produced a more or less enduring moral effect ; but the nature of the effect was left to the pre-disposition of the initiate ; it was not prescribed by the religion itself." [1]   Some cults were more careful, but the truth could not be taken for granted.   Is it any wonder that Paul had to say, and to surprise those who heard him say, " This is the will of God "—not to be precise in ritual but—" sanctification," a clean, moral life ?

In Paul's dialectic Law is opposed to grace or the Spirit of Christ as the religious principle.   He does not distinguish between essential and non-essential elements in the Law as Jesus had done ; for him the Law as a unity is bound up with belief that salvation is secured through deeds of obedience which merit reward.   Speaking from his experience as a Pharisee he sums up the position thus: *A worker* (i.e. one who who sets himself to keep the items of the Code) *has his wage*

---

[1] F. M. Cornford, in *The Cambridge Ancient History*, vi., iv., pp. 531 f.

counted to him as a due, not as a favour. And that moralism, with its outlook on the last judgment, he would not tolerate, eagerly as he pressed moral demands upon his churches. It is another point at which he is true to the spirit of Jesus. Nevertheless, as Jesus had taught,[1] Paul expected a judgment of God on the relative records of Christians who have lived and worked by grace. Sound work or loyalty is rewarded (2 Thess. i. 5 f., 1 Cor. iii. 14). *The hour of reckoning has still to come, when the Lord will come to bring dark secrets to the light and reveal life's inner aims and motives. Then each of us will get his meed of praise from God* (1 Cor. iv. 5). The final scrutiny is passed on the whole of life under grace, and deeds done in the Spirit are rewarded in proportion to their value. Again, the principle of judgment on good conduct is not a mechanical equivalence of reward and service, but all of grace. Furthermore, faith is not mere fidelity; it is not one of the good deeds, but the inspiration of all good deeds that win God's approval or praise. Such considerations are relevant. Hebrew had one word which meant either work or recompense, and Paul had inherited a religion in which, as Wellhausen shows, the demand for goodness being rewarded even on earth was one expression of the craving for religious reality. True piety " cannot maintain itself if God makes no difference between the godly and the ungodly and has nothing more to say to the one than to the other." No juridical categories hindered Paul from reaffirming the ethical message of evangelical faith in the wrath and judgment of God (see above, p. 211 f.), for even the life of the saints was to be judged by the revelation of God's will in Jesus Christ, as the early Church believed (see Matt. xxv. 31 f.). And in holding that this judgment was of grace he was undoubtedly helped by the finer element in contemporary Judaism. He had the advantage of having been trained to acknowledge the merciful

[1] On rewards in the ethic of Jesus, see Dr. Wauchope Stewart's admirable papers in the *Expositor*[7], x., pp. 97 f., 124 f.

grace of God in dealing with human shortcomings. He was familiar with the prayer, " Sovereign of all worlds, not because of our righteous deeds do we present our supplications before Thee but because of Thine abundant mercies " ; which meant, as Dr. Abrahams puts it (*Daily Prayer Book*, p. xxi.), that while " reward and punishment were meted out in some sort of accordance with a man's righteousness and sin," yet " nothing that man, with his small powers and finite opportunities, can do constitutes a claim on the favour of the Almighty and the Infinite. In the final resort all that man receives from the divine hand is an act of grace." It is not difficult to understand how a devout tradition like this was some preparation for the apostle's recognition of moral recompense side by side with belief in a gracious God at the end.

Not that his attitude towards the judgment corresponded to the outlook of popular scribism as afterwards reflected in a well-known passage of Pirke Aboth. iii. 22 f. : " The world is ruled by goodness (or, grace), yet all is according to the amount of work." It is not quite certain whether this saying belongs to rabbi Akiba, who was executed for complicity in the messianic rebellion of A.D. 135, but it may be taken as reflecting one current of opinion in second-century rabbinism. If it refers to the present world,[1] it means no more than that God is generous rather than strict. Later rabbis were not sure of the precise sense of the saying. Indeed, so vague was rabbinism on the subject that the aphorism sometimes ran, " and not according to the amount of work," an optimistic hope based on the feeling that sins were sure to abound, whereas the text without the negative would apply to the individual who was to be judged, acquitted or sentenced, as his life showed a surplus of good or unlawful deeds. That the saying referred to the final judgment is probable in the light of the following parable or allegory, also attributed to Akiba. " Everything is given on pledge (i.e. of repayment),

[1] Schechter, *Some Aspects of Rabbinic Theology*, pp. 15 f., 306.

and the net (i.e. of providence or destiny) is spread over all the living. The shop is opened and the Shopman (or, money-lender) gives credit ; the accountbook is opened and the Hand writes ; everyone who desires to borrow comes and borrows, but the collectors (the angels) go round continually every day and exact payment from a man whether he knows or not (i.e. whether he is content or not, or whether or not he is aware that his sickness or calamity atones for his debt) ; and they (the collectors) have that on which they rely. And the judgment is a judgment of truth (i.e. quite accurate and fair ; men have to pay what they owe but no more). And everything is prepared for the Banquet " (which in the next world a man enjoys once he has paid off his moral debts incurred in this world). It would be unfair to describe this as a commercial view of religion ; after all it is less commercial and charged with more moral vigour than the ' Treasury of Merits' notion, for example, which the mediaeval Latin Church popularized, and it breathes a wistful, charitable idea of God's leaning to mercy at the end. But it presupposes a quantitative estimate of obedience to the Torah, which substantially relieved the masses at the expense of a thorough-going insistence on inwardness.

In theory and practice the rabbinic view is a parallel to the later Latin conception, according to which the grace of God, instead of bearing wholly on the personal relationship of God and men, as implied in ' justification,' really made man capable of good works or merits. For the sake of practical morality the idea of merits was brought back into the Christian religion ; only, no merit was possible apart from the first gift of grace. Grace being the ' radix merendi,' as the technical term ran, merit ceased to be presumptuous, it grew from a root of grace. Luther wrote on the margin of one of Tauler's sermons a couplet supposed to have been coined by Albertus Magnus, which sums up the theory :

Quicquid habes meriti, praeventrix gratia donat,
Nil deus in nobis praeter sua dona coronat.

16

The aim of the view was to root grace in the moral world, and the one means of securing this was ' merit ' thus defined.   As the rabbinic view believed the Law to be a merciful provision granted in order that by obedience to its ritual and moral enactments Israel might please God the more, and so acquire saving merit, the Latin theology after Augustine took grace as a creative ' virtus,' which infused love into the regenerate life, equipping man with moral power to gain merit before God and thus by means of due satisfaction to earn His mercy. Unlike the Eastern Church, which emphasized the vital fellowship of the believer with Christ through the Spirit, regarding truth and immortality as the supreme boons, the Latins operated with the conceptions of law and merit or satisfaction.   This accounts for the definition of hope by Peter the Lombard (*Sentent.* iii. 26), which Dante repeats in a prosaic canto of the Paradiso (xxv. 67–69) : ' Hope is the sure expectation of future bliss, which is derived from God's grace and previous merits (meritis praecedentibus).'   No NT writer would have phrased it thus ; the very language of merit was instinctively shunned by the primitive Church.   Yet the thought is theirs.   Hopes of heaven do imply moral conditions, if they are not to be presumptuous.   Future bliss is the gift of God's grace, which for normal people involves a conduct answering to the demands of grace ; this was what the Schoolman intended his readers to understand by ' praecedentia merita '—the moral obedience and service of God inspired by His initial grace.   These had to precede any entrance into bliss, but they were preceded and rendered possible by grace divine in the human sphere.

The aim of the theory was excellent.   Still, what God hath put asunder, let not man join.   The history of the Christian religion proves that grace and merit were never meant to be married.   From the union of these two more evil than good has arisen.   It is safer to express in other terms the truth which, at its best, the re-introduction of merit into a grace-religion like Christianity was intended to conserve.

6

The small influential group of Pharisees held that, while strictly speaking salvation depended on the keeping of the Torah, the conscientious worshipper might reasonably count on God's mercy at the end, for any defects in his record.

Probably very few calmly assumed that because they belonged
to the People, they were safe. John indeed warned his hearers
at the revival not to presume to themselves, ' We have a
father in Abraham ' (and therefore need no repentance), and
these hearers included Pharisees and Sadducees. But, short
of this crude assurance, there was some ground of hope found
in the fact that at any rate those who were born Jews were less
immoral and guilty than pagans. The expectation voiced by
the Wisdom of Solomon (xv. 1 f.) is characteristic of this
hope, in its higher and lower strata.

> Our God, thou art gracious and true,
>   Longsuffering and ordering all things in mercy;
> for even though we sin, we are thine, knowing thy dominion;
>   but sin we shall not, knowing we are reckoned thine.
> For to know thee is perfect righteousness.

The knowledge of the divine revelation in the Torah was
supposed to carry with it an ethical superiority to other nations.
As indeed it often did. Yet while this involved a strict
morality, it also tended to produce the feeling that God being
merciful would not be unduly hard upon the offences of the
People, whatever might be the case with idolatrous and lax
pagans.

The normal temper of scribism may be inferred from the saying
quoted in the Makkot 23b : " it was because the Holy One wished
to give Israel an opportunity to acquire merit that he gave them so
much Torah and so many commandments." Or, as a modern writer
sums the system up—" Man has got the ability to acquire merits before
the Heavenly Father. However weak and frail man may be, physically
and morally, he is in a position to gather merits in the eyes of God." [1]

As we have already noted, Paul's interpretation of Christ
as the real Torah or embodiment of God's saving will carried
him beyond this religion of merit. His insistence upon grace
is on its negative side a repudiation of such views of merit,
particularly as a distrust of anything like self-righteousness.

[1] A. Marmorstein, *The Doctrine of Merits in Old Rabbinical Literature*, p. 10.

The warmth with which he exposes self-righteousness indicates that he must have been conscious of it as a real temptation in his Jewish faith.   But it is noticeable that his sense of pride as the real danger to the soul, which lies at the root of his warnings against self-satisfaction on the score of merits, is bound up with his estimate of sin as self-assertion.   Disobedience is one of his common terms for moral evil.   Against the will of God which, he assumes, is known to the conscience of any man, Jew or gentile, people set up their own wills ; there is a deliberate choice of their own way, for which they are personally responsible.   In a deep sense this disobedience is obedience or slavery to Sin.   Sin, he once argues, is no longer to be allowed to control you, for you live under grace, not under law, i.e. outside the deadly sphere of the Law where death follows the sin of disobedience.   But this submission to Sin is self-chosen, and as regards God it is rank disobedience. " When I sin, I place my own will in a position of supremacy. . . .   The position of sin lies in the assertion—or rather in the practical adoption—of the maxim that my motives need no other justification than the fact that they are my motives." [1] It is this wilful self-assertion which Paul, like a true Hebrew, detects in sin as the ultimate evil, which Luther exposed when he laid bare egoism in the form of ' concupiscentia ' as the radical foe of faith.   Yet the significant thing is that the apostle finds the same temper reappearing in a nobler and yet equally mischievous form later on.   For moral energy tempts to self-assertion.   The man may now be active for God, not against Him ; but if he permits himself to consider that what he does is supremely important, as though the centre of the new life lay in himself, in his achievements or attainments, this self-esteem signifies that he is again setting himself up against God.

Self-righteousness is a weed that grows only on the higher slopes of religious and moral life, but it assumes a rich variety of forms.   It may be the complacent spirit of those who regard

[1] J. M. McTaggart, *Studies in Hegelian Cosmology*, pp. 151, 158.

their very religious doubts as a mark of superior intelligence, or their shortcomings as after all a proof of reality in religion (the modern type of ' publican ' is prone to reflect, ' God, I thank thee that I am not as other men are, like these Pharisees of church folk '). But (*a*) Paul encountered it primarily as an expression of the religious system with which he had broken. As a Pharisee he knew the self-conscious pride that tempted men to think they could bring God something that deserved His favourable attention. This religious satisfaction he calls καύχησις. It is irreconcilable, he argues, with the spirit of grace. After explaining how God's free grace is offered, he asks, " Then what of ' boasting ' (καύχησις) ? It is ruled out. On what principle (for νόμος here means religious system or principle) ? On the principle of doing deeds (ἔργων) ? Not at all, it is ruled out on the principle of faith. . . . If Abraham was justified on the score of what he did (ἔργων), then he may have some reason to be proud (καύχημα, some title to honour), but not before God. For what says scripture ? *Abraham believed God and this* (i.e. his faith) *was counted to him as righteousness.* Now a worker (i.e. the man who is a doer, ' der mit Werken umgehet,' as Luther puts it) has his wage counted to him as a due (ὀφείλημα), not as a favour (χάρις) ; but a man who instead of ' working ' believes in Him who justifies the ungodly, has his faith counted as righteousness." The antithesis is between ' charis ' and ' due ' or debt. Only on the latter religious system can there be any question of self-satisfaction about the moral qualities and achievements which are supposed to earn their due recognition from God. No one who had grasped what grace meant could rest on any such basis of merit as he faced God. " The moment religion gives place to merit, it becomes moralistic, which is to say, the doing of things by rule, for some outside end ; and as such it utterly fails to be our direct, natural, and right relation to God." [1]

[1] Oman, *Grace and Personality*, p. 62

Wherever Paul came across this weed, he uprooted it with a sharp stroke of his grace-message.   Thus when gentile Christians gave themselves airs as they looked at unbelieving Israel, he reminded them that they owed their position to grace alone.   What right had they to be proud, as though they had been chosen on account of some superior qualities ?   Let them remember the basis of their religious privileges and be humble, instead of becoming complacent as they compared their faith with the unbelief of the Jews.   *You owe your position to your faith* in the gracious favour and choice of God.   *You should feel awed instead of being uplifted* and self-conceited (Rom. xi. 20).   It was the spirit of this that Macarius the Egyptian ascetic of the fourth century had caught when he answered his own question, " How do men ever fall from grace ? " by replying, " It is as a man begins to be uplifted, to be censorious, to say, ' thou art a sinner,' while he considers himself to be righteous " (Homil. vii. 4).

(*b*) It might be supposed that a gentile convert would be less apt to be self-righteous than a Jewish, from Paul's point of view.   The one might be tempted indeed to plead either his moral record as a title to God's favour in Christ or his membership of the chosen race ; it is conceivable that the other might rely upon his moral aspirations, but surely, we might assume, the privilege of salvation would be so astounding an experience for the average pagan convert that he would be unlikely to take credit to himself or to consider that the grace of God came to him as a natural boon from the Creator to his creatures.   Normally this seems to have been the case.   At least there is no trace of such an attitude in the Macedonian churches.   But elsewhere it was different.   Thus the Achaian Christians at Corinth and elsewhere, or some of them, apparently needed to be warned against complacency.   Paul has an object in reminding them that the majority of their number were neither cultured nor prominent nor of good birth ; he would have them remember that they all owed their faith to the pure goodness of God, not to any previous qualities of which they could be proud or to which, they might assume, God would naturally pay attention.

God has chosen what is foolish in the world
to shame the wise ;
God has chosen what is weak in the world
to shame what is strong ;
God has chosen what is mean and despised in the world—
things which are not, to put down things that are ;

that no person may boast in the sight of God. You can see, he means, from your own number how little God thinks of intellectual achievements or of money or of position ; His methods make it impossible for any Christian to give himself airs. Then, to emphasize the fact that their religious standing is due to God alone, he adds : *This is the God to whom you owe your being in Christ Jesus.* If you are σοφοί or δίκαιοι or ἅγιοι or ἀπολυτρωθέντες, it is because of what God has made Christ to be to you, *so that, as it is written, let him who boasts boast of the Lord.* It was not any difficulty about the Law that Paul had in mind. These Christians seem to have been untroubled by that controversy. But the temptation to complacency had a wider range than the sphere of the Law. Any gentile convert was liable to regard himself as saved because he had somehow attracted the notice of the Lord by his character. It is to deny such considerations that Paul is writing thus, in 1 Corinthians i. 27 f. Speculative philosophy or religious theosophy had failed, he reminds his readers. That so-called ' wisdom ' of the world had not saved men. God had to take the initiative, and He took it by a way which seemed absurd in the eyes of men ; only faith could see the wisdom of His method, and that very faith was evoked by Him ; the Lord who had been crucified and raised from the dead, was the Lord to whom under God they owed everything in their religious life. For *when the world with all its wisdom failed to know God in his wisdom, God resolved (εὐδόκησεν) to save believers (πιστεύοντας) by the ' sheer folly ' of the Christian message* of the cross. In this way the apostle seeks to cut at the root of the subtle tendency to be proud of oneself as an object of the divine purpose. For those who believe are, from another and a deeper point of view, those who are called (κλητοί) or chosen. Instead of attributing their position as Christians to some superior insight on their own part, of which they might be proud, they are bidden to recall how their new faith had come to them, as an attitude produced by the manifestation of God's saving will in Jesus Christ His Son. Let them not boast of any acuteness or moral pre-eminence which had led to their being singled out for membership in the Church of God !

The terminology of Paul differs here from that of the synoptic tradition. In the gospels the call of God is an invitation which may be refused or accepted ; in Paul's teaching it is an effectual call. In other words, those whom Paul describes as called (κλητοί) are described as chosen (ἐκλεκτοί) in the gospels. Matthew's saying, ' Many are called but few chosen ' (xxii. 14) echoes the belief of contemporary apocalypses like the Apocalypse of Baruch (xliv. 15) and Fourth Esdras (viii. 1 : This age the Most High has made for many, but the age to come for few ; viii. 3 : Many have been created, but few will be saved ; ix. 15 : There are more who perish than shall be saved). Yet the meaning corresponds to that of the apostle, for in the light of the parable to which the saying is appended it is clear that what Jesus intends is, " few prove themselves ἐκλεκτοί by showing readiness to fulfil the conditions of the Call." It reflects the serious facts of life ; not all are careful to accept the stringent conditions of God's offer humbly and heartily. Jesus knew that under the demands for repentance and renunciation few found the narrow way to life. His teaching sifted his hearers. Grace might be for all but not all were for grace, when it revealed itself as Aufgabe no less than Gabe.

(c) There was indeed a legitimate sphere for pride. Christians might well be proud, triumphantly proud, of the rich resources they enjoyed in grace, in the cross of Christ, in the saving goodness of God, in the hope of glory ahead (Gal. vi. 14, Phil. i. 26, Rom. v. 2 f., etc.). Also, Paul recognizes that Christians may sometimes be proud of one another, as they mark the success of grace in shaping or inspiring character (see 2 Cor. i. 14, v. 12, ix. 3, 1 Cor. xv. 31, etc.).

One particularly interesting example of this occurs in a defence of his own apostolic methods (1 Cor. ix. 15 f.), as he explains the practice of Christian ministers being supported by the Church, and his own reasons for refusing to avail himself of this right. Exception had been taken to his refusal. Opponents had sneered, " You are afraid to claim the right, because your authority as an apostle is too insecure." He repudiates the charge passionately and declines to give up his cherished principle of working for his own living instead of receiving maintenance from the Church. *I would die sooner than let anyone deprive me of this, my source of pride* (τὸ καύχημα). *What I am proud of is not the mere preaching of the gospel.* (It is significant here that χάρις is a variant for καύχημα in some early texts.) *That I am constrained to do* (it's my ἀνάγκη). *Woe to me if I do not preach the gospel! I get a reward* indeed *if I do it of my own accord* (one is rewarded for voluntary service), *whereas to do it otherwise* (ἄκων, i.e. as I do) *is no more than for a steward to discharge his trust* (the thought of Luke xvii. 9, 10). *And my reward ? If reward is thus ruled out of my life as a service of God, what of the pride I spoke of ? What is left for me ? This, that I can preach the gospel free of charge, that I can refrain from insisting on my rights as a preacher of the gospel.* He is using freely the popular language about reward for work in the very effort to disclaim any thought of reward except in the work itself, in being able to do it free of charge. My ἀνάγκη he observes, with a touch of grave pleasantry, is the obligation to preach the gospel, but I do it gratis, and that's my pay, to do it without pay. His μισθός or pride is to spend himself on people without requiring them to spend anything upon himself.

On a broader scale he frequently writes as though it were no breach of the principles of humble faith in grace, for him to feel a legitimate pride in his work. *In Christ Jesus I can be proud of my work for God.* It is the work he has been able to do in the great gentile mission throughout Europe and Asia. With characteristic modesty he explains this achievement as *what Christ has accomplished by me in securing the obedience of the gentiles* to the gospel. But he recognized the place of a healthy satisfaction in work well done, done from the right motives and done with all one's powers. He told his

dear Macedonian churches how proud he was of them, and
how proud he expected to be of them when the End came and
the Lord returned to take account of how his servants had
acted during his absence ; *hold fast the word of life, so that I
can be proud of you on the Day of Christ, because I have not run or
worked for nothing* (Rom. xv. 17 f., 1 Thess. ii. 19, 2 Thess. i. 4,
Phil. ii. 16).   Such considerations help to explain the significance of the judgment in his outlook upon serious religion.

7

One of the most exhilarating experiences of the new faith
was its consciousness of freedom.   Paul represents this as
one side of the status into which God's grace had introduced
the Christian ; sonship and freedom were notes of the order
of the Spirit.   But it is not too much to say that in working
out his exposition of grace he found himself obliged to vindicate what may be called the freedom of God.   This was due
to the implications of his contrast between grace and merit as
principles of salvation.   For if men had any claim on God,
if they could accumulate merit sufficient to establish a case
for His attention to their needs, Paul felt that the pure goodness of God was infringed.   In his view God, to be gracious,
must be absolutely free to choose the method of His giving
and the objects of His boon.   The one determining motive
must be in Himself.   It was an unflinching inference from
his experience of grace and of what grace truly meant, that
God's favour could not be considered a matter of course in
any sense of the word.   He distrusted any moral claims of
man that appeared to lessen the pure favour of God in the
matter of salvation.   Hence the religious interests and intuitions which led him to speak of predestination.   Positively,
all in our position as Christians goes back to the will of God ;
that is the one guarantee of life here and hereafter.   Negatively, this rules out any independence on the part of man,
as though the vital thing were his choice, not God's, his will,

not the Lord's. Predestination, leading out into election, means that the good man must ever remember that no good actions of his will avail to save him, apart from the Will of God. It is a statement of the content of the grace-experience. As Christians we exist, not because we are created beings, but because God's saving will has created us anew ; life also has an end and object for each, with eternal values ; and finally, this involves a vocation for the individual. All this is due to grace. The explanation of man's present position in the order of grace must be sought, not in himself, but in the Will of God. Man is in enjoyment of freedom and fellowship, because God has been free to act.

But in Romans ix.–xi. this opens up into a special problem of providence, hitherto unnoticed. How is this divine freedom compatible with God's obligations to the Chosen People ? Stated abstractly, the line of argument in these chapters is this : God can do as He pleases (ix.), it is Israel's own fault if they are outside grace (x.), but Israel will eventually be saved (xi.). Only the second of these seems tenable ; the other two appear at first sight to reflect no more than a determinism and a patriotism on the part of the apostle which deflect rather than reflect his religious philosophy of " All by grace, and grace for all."

In Romans i.–viii. " all is of grace " is defended against the double objection (a) that grace is not necessary, since the Law of God avails for fellowship, and (b) that it is not adequate, since it leads to ethical carelessness about the will of God, as any teaching does that ignores the Law. In Romans ix.–xi. " grace is for all " is explained, as against the criticism that this does no justice to the privileged position of the People of God, which is attested by Scripture and history. No doubt each of these points raises the other ; " grace for all " comes into i.–viii., just as " all is of grace " enters into ix.–xi. But the predominance is as I have indicated.

(a) Hitherto Paul has urged the comfortable truth of election in order to reassure all Christians of their safe standing in God's purpose. Sometimes it had a special reference, as when he tells the Roman Christians that they were safe and free, instead of being enslaved as they had been under the Law ; the Law here as in Galatians is regarded as part and parcel of the cosmic system of Elemental Powers, *the angels*, *principalities and powers of the Height and the Depth*, which, he protests, will never be able to *separate* them now *from God's love in Christ* since He has taken a decisive, personal interest in those whom He called. Προέγνω . . . προώρισε . . . ἐκάλεσε. The experience of grace for all Christians goes back to God's will of love, which is more than any force or sway of sub-celestial fatalism. What determines our lot is not the planet under which we were born, much less the fact that we were born either inside or outside the Law, but the unconditioned goodwill of the living God. This must have been a true relief to many in that superstitious age.[1] But there was one particular appeal in election for gentile Christians. It freed them from the fear that they had not a sure place in God's People. When they were taunted by Jews or even by super-cilious Jewish Christians, " You are not the elect People, and therefore you have no right to God's promises, however you may rely upon the gospel of this renegade Paul," the apostle's teaching furnished them with reassurance. But as time went on, Paul found that another problem was raised by election in the sphere of grace, owing to the very success of the gen-tile mission. Sonship, predestination ? But were not these traditional privileges of another race ? What of the People who still claimed to be the chosen People, of God, ὃν προέγνω (Rom. ix. 4, xi. 2) ?

The normal view, for which the authority of Jesus is claimed in the synoptic tradition (Mark xii. 1 f., Matt. viii. 11 f.), is either that gentiles who believe join the patriarchs, whilst the Jews are left out, or that the privileges of the Jews have

[1] See Liechtenhan's *Die göttliche Vorherbestimmung bei Paulus und in der Poseidonianischen Philosophie*, pp. 33–39, on Rom. viii. 29 f.

ceased, owing to their rejection of Christ. God's purpose and calling have now passed to others, hitherto beyond the pale. Paul commonly shared this opinion. He had written to the Thessalonians a word of sympathy, which expressed his judgment on the situation. *You have suffered from the Jews who killed the Lord Jesus and the prophets, who harassed ourselves, who offend God and oppose all men by hindering us from speaking words of salvation to the gentiles. So they would fill up the measure of their sins to the last drop! But the Wrath is on them to the bitter end.* But in Romans ix.–xi. he has, for the time being, adopted another point of view. In this deep, difficult passage, it must be noted at the outset, the apostle is not arguing *ad hoc.* He is thinking aloud, putting doubts and difficulties which had assailed his own mind during his recent mission. In one sense, we may say, he is arguing against himself, that is against insurgent ideas forced upon him by the facts of life ; now that he had finished his missions to Asia Minor, Macedonia, and Achaia, he could look back upon the net result ; what he saw was that the majority of his converts had come from outside the chosen People and that Israel as a whole was recalcitrant. But while this is true, it is also true that the objector against whom he argues in this diatribe is not simply himself, torn by patriotic yearnings and by a lingering traditional belief in the election of Israel, but the average gentile Christian. He puts himself into the position of the gentiles as Christians, in whom, as he knew from experience, there was apt to be an air of superiority towards the Jewish people. His very gospel of freedom from the Law encouraged some to disparage the ethical and religious value of the Law, and also to plume themselves on the fact that they were now the People of God or at least the majority of the chosen Church. All through Romans this double interest runs, a protest against discarding the law, and a protest against the danger of self-righteousness. The latter was not confined to Jews, Paul was well aware. It was a temptation besetting those who accepted the gospel of freedom from the law ; they might and they did assume airs, not so much as they looked up to God but as they looked around at the Jews, who seemed beneath them now.

In vi.–viii. Paul had been exhibiting ' the law of the Spirit,' the moral obligations of the faith, with special regard to those who were prone to rest on their spiritual position as though it did not involve a very careful attention to conduct.   In ix.–xi. he faces the problem from another point of view.   In xii. f. he recurs to the argument of vi.–viii., but meantime he handles the situation in the light of a question raised by the argument of i.–v.   If Jew and gentile are alike sinful before God, and if gentiles are accepting the gospel more numerously than Jews, what becomes of the traditional privileges of Israel ?   These he had frankly recognized in passing, even in the sweep of his earlier argument (iii. 1 f.), where he seems to brush them aside in his eagerness to state a promise open to all and above the Law.   Yet historically the gospel was ' for the Jew first.'   The Jew might be and was as liable to God's judgment as the gentile, despite his privileges ; the latter counted for nothing as saving assets.   But that did not, in Paul's view, imply that the ancient People, the first recipients of God's favour, were now displaced from the purpose of God, much less that gentile Christians were to ignore and despise what God had been and would yet be to Israel.

We might infer that here he is crushing down a persistent doubt in his own mind.   ' If God can do as He pleases, why is man held responsible ?   What moral right has God to blame a stubborn sinner ? '   He must have felt repeatedly in the course of his mission the impulse to criticize the ways of providence, and what he says to the Roman Christians he must have said already to himself.   ' All men have not faith.'   But why ?   One may feel behind Paul's argument the same mental anguish as in the nineteenth canto of the Paradiso.   The damnation of good pagans haunted the Italian poet's mind.   He too questioned the wisdom and justice of God in condemning such clean souls simply because they lacked baptism and faith in Christ. " On the banks of Indus a man is born, where there is none to tell him of Christ, where none has read or written of Him ; all the man's desires and acts are good so far as human reason sees, and his life is free from taint of sin. He dies unbaptized, without knowledge of the faith ; say, is it just to condemn him ? Is it his fault, if he doth not believe ? " Dante's answer is, who are you to sit in judgment on the ways of Providence ? He shuts down the doubt by appealing to Scripture, just as Paul does. Besides, the creed of the mediaeval Church had decided the matter ; it was God's will, and God's will must be good, though human reason cannot always see this. Yet it is impossible to read Dante without realizing that this difficulty haunted his mind. It is no mere academic problem for him. Neither is it for the apostle Paul. But, unlike the Italian poet, he was not thinking about the personal salvation of individuals. What troubled Paul was the fate and future of Israel in the divine purpose. Normally he might have consoled himself, in view of human recalcitrance, with the reflection :

> These are the chosen few,
>   The remnant fruit of largely-scattered grace.
> God sows in waste, to reap whom He foreknew
>   Of man's cold race,
> Counting on wills perverse, in His clear view
>   Of boundless time and space.

But not when he came to Israel ! The argument of Romans ix.–xi. ends in a cry of ecstasy, but it begins with a cry of anguish, and of anguish over his own people. " I could wish myself accursed from Christ for my kinsmen . . . I have great heaviness and continual sorrow in my heart " over them.

Unless we shake off the notions of modern individualism, we misread Paul's words. The spiritual pride which he exposes so severely is not the pride of the elect individual who looks down or around upon the non-elect with detestable complacency, as if to say, " I am chosen, they are not. How noble I must have been, to win God's attention and be thus selected ! " In the primitive Church there is no trace of such an ugly spirit. We sometimes think that we overhear it in a passage like Romans xi. 18 f. : " Boast not . . . be not highminded, but fear." But this warning is addressed to a speaker or representative of gentile Christianity. Paul is dramatizing in his dialogue an opponent who stands for gentile Christians complacently pluming themselves upon their faith as against the unbelief of Israel. No doubt, theirs was an un-Christian attitude, but it was collective rather than individual ; it was the false feeling of superiority on the part of one section in the Church towards another. This is the one place in Paul's letters where ἐκλογή is used of races or nations (xi. 7) as an abstract term.

(*b*) In distress over the refusal of the Jews as a whole to accept God's gospel, he asks if God's ancient word of promise and purpose had failed. No, it is fulfilled, even though only some Jews believe, for ' Israel ' is not equivalent to born Jews. Just as God of old preferred Isaac to Ishmael, and Jacob to Esau, so to-day His Promise must not be regarded as bound up with the entire nation. There is from the first a selective action. This is scripture truth, the apostle declares. As God's Word is a word of promise, He has always reserved the right to choose its recipients, and history shows that the line of promise, that is, of grace, depends on something other than what men do after they are born. The divine purpose of election depends upon the call of God, not on anything man does (6–13). " But that is arbitrary and unjust." No, the apostle replies, and the form of his reply is significant. As usual he is preoccupied with the loving purpose of God, and his main interest is to prove that God is quite free to carry out that purpose of goodwill. *Are we to infer that there is injustice in God ? Never ! God says to Moses,*

> *I will have mercy on whom I choose to have mercy,*
> *I will have compassion on whom I choose to have compassion.*

You see, it is not a question of human will or effort but of the divine mercy.

Had Paul referred to the context of this word to Moses, in which goodness is the manifestation of the divine glory, had he even mentioned that the object of the selection was to make the People carry forward His purpose of blessing all nations, it would have been more clear that his conception of God is not autocratic. What embarrasses a modern is that Paul does not seem to be embarrassed by the difficulty that moral self-determination fades out before such an assertion of the unlimited will of God in determining human life. Even as it is, however, the emphasis upon the merciful goodness of God in His freedom should be enough to show that his argument is intended to suppose a God of grace. It is not as though God were a Setebos, exercising His will as He pleases.

> Such shows nor right nor wrong in Him,
> Nor kind nor cruel, He is strong and Lord.
> Am strong myself, compared to yonder crabs,
> That march now from the mountain to the sea ;
> Let twenty pass and stone the twenty-first,
> Loving not, hating not, just choosing so.

The apostle's argument deals not with individuals but with groups or collective masses of men, selected to fulfil a special function in the divine purpose throughout history. From the first, this divine purpose has met opposition. How this originated, Paul never explains. The origin of Sin is left a mystery. Only its effects in the shape of disobedience are noted, and these are viewed as in a sense within the divine mind and will.

It is the same idea as in the passage from Isaiah quoted by the synoptic tradition (Mark iv. 10 f., etc.) in order to explain why the parables of Jesus failed to convince many of his hearers. On the Hebrew view, if men disobey and defy God, they are responsible for their own actions, but the untoward result is also read as a consequence of the divine purpose. Nothing can happen apart from the will of God. So profoundly was this felt, that what we call secondary causes were ignored, and the issue of man's refusal to believe is viewed as the divine intention.

17

One effect of God's truth being preached is always that some pass while others pause, some are deaf and blind to Him whilst others respond. Such are the facts of life, and the Hebrew sought to explain them as ultimately due to the divine will. It was not merely that obstinacy was punished, that failure to use opportunities led to an increasing lack of sensitiveness, but that the very obtuseness was part of the providential order.

This explains the next illustration from the story of Exodus about Pharaoh. Paul is thinking primarily of the divine collective purpose of grace, and explaining how even contrary movements in human life are overruled by God. He brought Pharaoh on the scene, in order to exhibit his powers of favour to the People. The great Egyptian autocrat, who imagined he could defy and defeat God's purpose ! What was he but a puppet in the hands of providence ? This is why Paul uses some words from the Exodus-story. He is not thinking of the personal salvation of Pharaoh but of the part he played in the triumph of the divine aim on earth ; where we would speak of the providential result, he speaks of the whole crisis as designed by God. It is the theistic principle again which accounts for the language and the idea. The God who makes even the wrath of men to praise Him, is actually represented as bringing about that wrath or stubborn attitude towards Himself. Hence (this is the point of verses 19 f.) God has sovereign power, He is absolutely free to assign one life a favourable place and function in His order of being and to make use of others in order to forward His gracious design. Who can oppose His will, you ask ? There cannot be any question of resisting Him ! No, there is not any possibility of thwarting Him, but that is no excuse for blaming Him.

What underlies the argument is the twofold assumption of the Hebrew faith, (a) that all is of God, He can do as He pleases, and (b) that the consequences of human action, viewed from the theistic standpoint, may be conceived as purposed by God. As for the former, the thesis is undoubtedly pushed to an extreme, until Paul's logic seems to leave

God as an arbitrary ruler of the world. *God has mercy on anyone just as he pleases, and he makes anyone stubborn* (like the Pharaoh of the Exodus) *just as he pleases.* Here (*a*) and (*b*) are combined, in a staggering assertion. And the next words are still more staggering, for, anticipating a critic of this procedure, Paul would deny the right of any creature to question the justice of such action on God's part. *Who are you, my man, to speak back to God ? Is something a man has moulded to ask him who has moulded it, ' Why did you make me thus ? ' What ! has the potter no right over the clay ? Has he no right to make out of the same lump one vessel for a noble purpose and another for a menial ?* It is one thing to deny that man is free to act independently of God, but, in asserting against this anarchic view the absoluteness of divine will, the apostle goes beyond the mark. The objector will still protest, " Well, but if God is responsible for the most opposite moral results of human life, why does He go on finding fault ? Man is not responsible, and therefore he cannot be blamed for stubbornness. The divine Potter has himself to blame for bad pots." On paper Paul has no answer to this criticism. " A man is not a thing, and if the whole explanation of his destiny is to be sought in the bare will of God, he *will* say, Why didst Thou make me thus ? and not even the authority of Paul will silence him." [1] He will be apt to reply to Paul's question, ' Who art thou, O man, who repliest against God ? ', by saying, ' I am a man, and as a man I am not accounted for by an absolutist theory of God.'

One can understand an indignant critic [2] declaring that these verses (18–21) probably have added more to human misery than any other utterances made by man. But, although Paul is partly responsible for the misunderstanding, a misunderstanding it remains. For such assertions of the apostle are not to be isolated. He has two supremely religious interests in maintaining the authority of God ; one is to check anything like human independence and self-righteousness, and the other is to show that in bestowing favour God is perfectly free. His real concern in this argument for God as

[1] Denney, *Expositor's Greek Testament*, on Rom. ix. 20.
[2] J. Cotter Morison, *The Service of Man*, pp. 27 f.

absolutely unbound is to magnify His grace.   When we take
the whole argument together, this comes out.   Instead of
dwelling on the darker side of reprobation, for example, the
apostle turns over and again to the gracious aspect and aim
of God in providence.   Thus the next paragraph (verses 22 f.)
asks, what if it is all to exhibit God's great patience and mercy ?
He let the Pharaoh defy His anger for a time, only to display
His saving power on behalf of the People.   So to-day He has
a providential purpose even in permitting the disobedience
of Israel.   Look at the happy result, for yourselves.   You
owe your salvation to this providence, you gentile believers.
What if God means (in all this mysterious refusal of Israel to
believe) *to show the wealth that lies in his glory for the objects
of his mercy whom he has made ready beforehand to receive glory
—that is, for us whom he has called from among the gentiles as
well as the Jews ?*   And Israel, what of poor Israel ?   It is
indeed blind and insensible to grace.   But some at any rate
have believed ?   Also, he repeats, by a blessed mystery of
providence the disbelief of the majority in Israel has turned
to the benefit of the gentiles.   And lastly, will the unbelief
last for ever ?   No, it is merely temporary.   He speculates
for once on the future like a prophet ;   God has not spoken
His final word to Israel, all Israel will be saved before the
world ends.   That is, Paul views the rejection of Israel as a
strange means to the large, blissful end of exhibiting the full
sweep of merciful grace which is God's true object in the
world.   *For God has consigned all men to disobedience, that he
may have mercy upon all.*   On this hopeful note he ends the
discussion.   The impression of vindictiveness and irrespons-
ibility in God which some sentences do make is seen to be
the result of an impetuous emphasis upon the freedom of God
in providence ;   the total impression is of God desiring mercy
and acting in pure grace.   The rabbinic categories which
the apostle employs are not always helpful to a modern reader.
The optimistic view of the future of Judaism does not seem

to have survived the sharp experiences of the following year at Jerusalem. But through pleas and proofs which are not quite translucent one can detect a conception of God which, so far from being despotic, is in line with the earlier and the later teaching about free grace.

(c) The thesis of ix. 22 f. is that God, the God we know, is no celestial Potter, but amazingly patient with evil-doers, forbearing to visit His wrath on them, since He designs a gracious purpose and destiny for His chosen. *What if God, though desirous to display his anger and show his might* (as upholding the moral order), *has tolerated* (ἐν πολλῇ μακροθυμίᾳ=ἐν τῇ ἀνοχῇ, iii. 25) *most patiently the objects of his anger* (i.e. sinners who by their disobedience are) *ripe and ready to be destroyed ? What if he means* (by this restraint of just wrath, by the kindness that is intended to make for repentance, as in ii. 4) *to show the wealth that lies in his glory for the objects of his mercy* (belonging to the class of ' objects of his anger '), *whom he has made ready beforehand to receive glory—that is, for us whom he has called.* Unbelief and disobedience are drawn out, in the history of the race, yet the clue to this mysterious phase of providence does not lie in any weakness of God, much less in any toleration of evil, but in His deep, gracious design ; for God is both strong and just and gracious, and the ends of His grace are supreme. Men by their disobedience become *objects of his anger* ; Paul does not hesitate to speak of them as in one sense, i.e. from the standpoint of divine determination, appointed to that. But the heart of God lies in creating *objects of mercy* out of these sinners ; there is a selective providence which has already shown itself to us in the choice of (25–26) gentiles and (27) a minority of Jews as fit to receive ' righteousness ' or the right relationship of God and man (ver. 30 f.). Israel's freedom of choice is recognized. Looking round upon the unbelieving majority of Jews, Paul sees that they have failed to reach true religion as presented by God in Jesus Christ, because they preferred to rely upon law-obedience, not upon faith, the one real exercise of faith now being belief in Jesus Christ. They are wilful and wayward, *a disobedient and contrary people*. Instead of taking God's way, they have been so exasperated at His revelation of the real foundation of religion in Christ, that *they have essayed to set up* a religion of their own. That is, the appearance of Christ in God's order has precipitated their collapse. Yet they are to blame, Paul holds, since they have deliberately determined to ignore the great opportunity offered them by God. In the stubborn adherence of contemporary Israel to the Torah, Paul sees a misdirected zeal or religious purpose, due to their own efforts. They had made the Law their Christ, and God intended Christ to be the Law.

Their rejection is therefore their own fault. This is the argument down to the end of the tenth chapter. But in the eleventh there is a new development. Hitherto Paul has so emphasized the free grace of God that he has left out of account any susceptibility and quest on the part of gentiles or others who have accepted the gospel. All is referred to God's gracious will. *It is not a question of human will or effort* ultimately.; *gentiles who never aimed at righteousness have attained righteousness ; I have been found* (Paul quotes the divine saying) *by those who never sought me. Once you disobeyed God, and now you enjoy his mercy.* Now, he opens up a new prospect. He compares God's Church or People to a Plant, rooted by God in the soil of history, an Olive, which God has prepared. Some branches have been broken off, and replaced by shoots from a wild olive. That is, ' you gentile Christians owe your privileged position to the sheer goodness of God ; you have no cause to boast. Don't presume on your position, for if you do, self-conceit will lead to carelessness, and that draws down the severity of God. If you prove unworthy, you too will be cut off in turn.' *Supposing some of the branches have been broken off, while you have been grafted in like a shoot of wild olive to share the rich growth of the olive-stem, do not pride yourself at the expense of these branches. Remember, in your pride, the stem supports you, not you the stem* ('thou bearest not the root, but the root thee'). *You will say, 'But branches were broken off, to let me be grafted in.' Granted. They were broken off—for their lack of faith. And you owe your position to your faith* ('thou standest by faith'). *You should feel awed instead of being uplifted* (i.e. the profound reverence stirred in any religious nature by God's grace meeting not merit but faith, the awe that accompanies humility and gratitude in those who acknowledge that they do not deserve the high favour of His choice). *For if God did not spare the natural branches, he will not spare you either. Consider both the kindness and the severity of God; those who fall* (i.e. losing their position through unbelief) *come under his severity, but you come under the divine kindness, provided you adhere to that kindness* (i.e. indebted to it alone and loyal to its claims). *Otherwise, you will be cut away too.* The truth of personal responsibility which seemed to be ignored earlier is here brought forward. Men are free to choose and to determine their religious position. If they fail to maintain their faith, it is their own fault and they suffer for it, in the moral order of the world.

But alongside of this warning to gentile Christians goes a hope for Israel. God's gracious mercy has still as in the days of old preserved a remnant of them, a saving remnant. How deeply Paul realized the gracious character of God in the OT may be seen from his use of the story about Elijah and the prophets of Baal. Jesus had rebuked the vindictive spirit of Elijah in his disciples, but what interests the apostle is the reference to the remnant (Rom. xi. 2 f.). Did not Elijah receive from the Lord, in the hour of his despair over the national apostasy, the assurance, *I have left myself seven thousand men who have not knelt to Baal?* The inference is, *Well, at the present day there is also a remnant in Israel, selected by grace.* It is this gracious providence on which Paul fixes in the story ; he is ever on the outlook for proofs of God's saving goodness and purpose. It sounds a staggering argument, to compare the contemporary unbelief of Jews in Jesus Christ to the belief of Israelites in Baal, but the consoling reflection is that even when things seem at their worst there is hope. Not all are insensible to the true, living God. And, more than that, the very loyalty of this minority is referred to God's gracious election. The genuine remnant in every age owe their position to Him, not to themselves ; it is neither due to their unaided efforts nor to any inherited qualities or privileges.

The recourse to the remnant-idea is a fresh proof that Paul is not thinking of personal salvation but of the collective functions of those selected by God to carry on His purpose ; for the notion of a remnant in Hebrew thought was that of a small group preserving and transmitting divine truth. The end of the remnant was to regenerate the inert mass, if possible, in course of time. They were elect, as those who were chosen to spread the pure faith and thereby further the cause of the living God on earth. This is what the apostle has in mind as he adopts the category of ' the remnant ' in order to illustrate the gracious mystery of God's ways within the world of men.

(d) So far he has been arguing on the lines of his characteristic view of grace, but he now advances to a position which is the real difficulty in the whole argument, viz. that the mere fact of even a remnant being chosen within Israel indicates that God has still a future for the whole nation in the course of providence. This exceptional deliverance comes in xi. 11 f., where Paul reverts to his original question (verse 1 : Is the lapse of Israel from God hopeless ? Is there no future at all for Israel in the working out of the divine purpose ?) He falls back upon a new and naïve explanation. The lapse of the large majority cannot be final. Why ? Because, he ingeniously explains, Israel will become jealous of the gentiles enjoying what was once their favoured position ! In fact, he ascribes this to a providential purpose.

In admitting gentiles, God meant to provoke the unbelieving Jews to a godly jealousy or envy. ' Think of the gentiles sharing our sacred Book and promises and worshipping our God ! We must reassert our claim to them.' Furthermore, the apostle declares that his hope in the gentile mission had been to evoke this fresh zeal for God in the synagogue. To this pathetic but unconvincing argument he adds another (verse 16 f.), based on the idea of racial solidarity. The mere fact that there is already a minority of Jews who do believe the gospel proves that the good work will has only begun. It is an ἀπαρχή. God has only made a beginning with Israel ; as the root of the nation (patriarchs like Abraham) is holy, i.e. consecrated or in sure connexion with God, the branches of the Plant will follow. They are *beloved for the fathers' sake* (xi. 28, see ix. 5). One day God is sure to replace the Jews in their old position, since He *never goes back upon his gifts and call. All Israel will be saved* in the long run. It is a μυστήριον, Paul admits, but he infers it from the changeless purpose of God towards His ancient People.

To say that ' the gifts and calling of God are without repentance ' is a strong way of saying, ' once elect, elect for ever.' As applied to individual Christians it is intelligible, on the apostle's principles, but when it is thus applied to a nation like Israel it appears to run counter to what he has just been arguing, viz. that all is of grace. Elsewhere he frankly recognizes that ' in Christ ' there is neither Jew nor Greek, that the Church is made up of believers and is above any national or racial distinctions. Such is his normal position, based on God's grace. But at this point, owing to intense belief in the divine purpose which had taken historical shape within Israel, he modifies his view. Whatever may happen to the other nations of the world, out of which gentiles are chosen, there is one nation which has a function in the future on account of its function in the past, and that is Israel. Jesus had said, facing the unbelief of the People, *I would . . . and ye would not*, without entering into the mysteries of divine predestination and the contingent factor in human life. Jesus had not conceived a national future for

Israel in the kingdom.   Paul for once does.   The merits of the Jewish martyrs he never stresses, as do the writers of Second and Fourth Maccabees.   But he does come near to a conception like that of the merits of the fathers, in this argument that somehow the devout remnant in the past is a guarantee of the entire nation coming right in the future. There is a pathetic quality in his belief that the world-wide success of the gospel, which stirs his hopes, is bound up with some special endowment of religious value, attested by the past position of Israel in the course of revelation.   That this will be revoked, he cannot bring himself to believe.

The close of the whole passage is as impressive as the poignant opening.   In xi. 32 f. he anticipates the blissful end for which God thus works through the interaction of Jew and gentile during the brief period before the climax. Without discussing how Sin originated, the Sin which is responsible for all opposition to God, without explaining how Israel as a whole would come to believe in Christ, and without dwelling on the pains and penalties of disobedience, he is so sure of the ultimate triumph of God's saving will that he forecasts the happy consummation.   Philo once dwells on the deep truth of Jacob's word in Genesis xxxiii. 11, ' God hath dealt graciously with me, and I have enough.'   He quotes it from the Greek version, ἠλέησέν με ὁ θεὸς καὶ ἔστι μοι πάντα, adding that it expresses the rule of life, "for all things are anchored on the graciousness of God" (ἐν γὰρ τῷ τοῦ θεοῦ ἐλέῳ τὰ πάντα ὁρμεῖ).[1]   In a similar way Paul here concludes his survey of human history and destiny by referring everything to the gracious mercy of God.   But for him the dominating thought is of God's initiative ; it is not simply that the ways of God in the course of life are inscrutable ultimately, but that they are determined by Himself.   Again the apostle recurs to his fundamental conception that the one reasonable ground of hope in the mercy of God rests on the confession that it must be utterly undeserved by man.

[1] *De Sacrif. Abelis*, ix.

All His dealings with the human race are in accordance somehow with His final purpose of gracious mercy, and this excludes any claim or merit on the part of human beings. *God has consigned all men to disobedience, that he may have mercy* (ἐλεήσῃ) *upon all. What a fathomless wealth lies in the wisdom and knowledge of God ! How inscrutable his judgments ! How mysterious His methods !*

> *Whoever understood the thoughts of the Lord ?*
> *Who has ever been his counsellor ?*

Who has first given to him and has to be repaid ? All comes from him, all lives by him, all ends in him. Glory to him for ever ! The indignant question, *Who has first given to him and has to be repaid ?* gives the clue to Paul's dislike of speculation about the mysteries of election. He suspected in such objections to God's authority a desire to advance claims on the Almighty, as though men felt entitled to something from the Lord ; this, he felt, was utterly out of keeping with the religious sense of absolute indebtedness to grace divine.

> God whom I praise, how could I praise,
> If such as I might understand,
> Make out and reckon on His ways,
> And bargain for His love, and stand
> Paying a price, at His right hand ?

No, to praise Him aright one must be lost in wonder at the rich treasures of His gracious love and at the infinite resources of His own nature. It would be out of keeping for any race or individual to put forward some claim, instead of confessing that human life owes everything to His free grace. We are indebted to God, the apostle means. No devout soul, facing the deep realities of life, is disposed to think that God is indebted to man.

The responsibilities of a Creator to His creatures have been noted from the Alexandrian Philo to Rousseau's Savoyard Vicar. That God as creator should care for what He had made, with fatherly concern, was felt by Philo to be one reason why the Genesis story of creation was written (Opific. ii., see lxi) ; " it stands to reason that the Father and Maker should care for what has been brought into being," and this is the meaning of providence. Philo's stress on the divine Causality explains this emphasis. The Frenchman only echoed the same feeling in *Émile*. " Dieu, dit-on, ne doit rien à ses créatures. Je crois qu'il leur doit tout ce qu'il leur promit en leur donnant l'être. Or c'est leur promettre un bien que de leur en donner l'idée et de leur en faire sentir de besoin." Now Paul was not interested in divine Causality, and whilst for him the justice and goodness of God were axiomatic, it was in the new creation rather than in the creation that he found the deepest revelation of God. ' We are his workmanship, created in Christ Jesus.' As in the prophetic consciousness, God was the creator of the People as He was their redeemer, calling them into existence. at the Exodus, or as He upheld the moral order (see Isa. xli. 20, xliii. 1, xlv. 8), so for the apostle God really created the Church when He made it through the resurrection of Christ (see above, pp. 220–224). It is possible that this idea is behind even Peter's reference to the ' faithful Creator ' (1 Peter iv. 19, see ii. 10, Rom. ix. 25, 26). At any rate, the gospel of Paul includes far more than such a natural religion as Rousseau put forward. The divine instincts in man, the impulse to ' seek the Lord, who is not far from any one of us,' the feeling for goodness and duty—these were more than met, according to the apostle, by the God who had implanted them in human nature. But the deeply religious man is not apt to dwell on what God owes to him ; it is what he owes to his God that preoccupies or ought to preoccupy the mind. Rousseau was this or that, he sometimes looked at religion and wrote about it, but he was not a religious man.

The closing cry about the rich mystery of God's dealings with men is very different from the sigh of an exhausted thinker who, after exploring the problems of life and destiny, takes refuge in a confession that they are beyond his finite intellect. There is no sigh in the apostle's language. It is an ecstasy, elicited by his conviction that God's determining will abounds in goodness. In his hymn on Intellectual Beauty Shelley wrote :

> The awful shadow of some unseen Power
> Floats tho' unseen amongst us . . .
> Like clouds in starlight widely spread,
> Like memory of music fled—
> Like aught that for its grace may be
> Dear and yet dearer for its mystery.

Such is the temper of the apostle's closing cry. "Mercy upon all" is indeed a mystery, but it is a real mystery, that stirs the soul to exclaim, "O the depth of the riches both of the wisdom and knowledge of God ! How unsearchable are His judgments !" He had a much deeper notion of grace than Shelley had, but the unsearchable purpose of God working out mercy for all was 'dearer for its mystery' to his mortal mind.

V

THE LATER LETTERS

AS we have already grouped Philippians with the Macedonian letters, the later letters are Colossians and ' Ephesians.' For our present purpose the latter goes with Colossians ; even though it be held to have been written by a Paulinist, it is so near to Colossians that its grace-teaching may be reckoned as Pauline, in a sense in which we cannot speak of the Pastoral epistles, for example. There are four features of the Pauline teaching on grace in these later letters. The third sums up, with special vigour, a thought already present in the previous letters ; the other three are more distinctive.

I

A practical theosophy had appeared at Colossae. It was a Phrygian syncretistic movement which taught that while Christ had died and died a redeeming death, yet the world was still dominated by Elemental spirits of matter, who determined destiny, and that man had still to do something in order to complete the emancipating work ; more than faith and hope were needed, for final bliss. Evidently these ' gnostics ' considered that the faith of the Church was a position which required to be supplemented by some higher life or ritualistic philosophy, involving a *cult of angels*. The human soul must come to terms with the aeons or angelic powers through whom creation had been carried out and by whom in some way life was determined. One of the achievements of these aeons was the Old Testament. Consequently not only was reverence due to them as agents or embodiments of providence, but the dualism thus implied led to ascetic practices, to food taboos, for example, and even to circumcision. These retained their value in Christianity. When the apostle writes, scornfully, *Beware of anyone getting hold of you by means of a theosophy (φιλοσοφία) which is specious make-believe on the lines of human tradition (κατὰ τὴν παράδοσιν τῶν ἀνθρώπων)*, he means the claims of this ascetic movement, for παράδοσις here is a technical term for the tenets or rites of magical mysticism as committed by the deity or deities to their ' prophets ' (as in the Hermetic religion) and transmitted by them to the initiates. Against this amalgam of a theosophy it is argued that the divine revelation is completely made in Christ ; the Fulness of the divine nature was embodied in him, and no aeon in creation or in providence shared this. Therefore the representation of God in Christ was efficient, apart from any angelic power. *It is in him that you reach your full life*, the apostle insists. God's fulness is not expressed through any hierarchy of angels but through the unshared glory of the Son. It is Christ's prerogative. And this is the real grace of the gospel. *From our beloved Epaphras you learned to know what God's grace really is (ἐν ἀληθείᾳ i. 6).* It is not the truth about grace, Paul implies, to suggest that God's saving goodness comes through anyone except Christ, or that it is received by anything except faith ; ascetic discipline may sound and seem very humble, but it is an arbitrary method of religion quite out of keeping with the faith and baptism which are the genuine condition of the gospel. Paul is here repudiating once more the religious principle which he had refuted in Galatians and Romans, though it reappeared in a more subtle form as these Phrygian gnostics propounded it. The really new feature was the idea that Christ's power had to be supplemented ; the corresponding claim that faith must be completed by means of ascetic practices, based on OT regulations, was also new, but it simply meant in principle that salvation had to be earned by conduct. And to both inferences Paul offers strenuous opposition. Whether the theosophists used the term ' grace ' or not, we cannot tell. Probably they did not, if we may judge from the fact that the apostle does not refer to it in his

refutation.   But he is sure that such ' higher life ' teaching
is not *what God's grace really is*.

The Colossian Christians had learned the meaning of grace by practical experience, for he leads up to this allusion by reminding them
that as converts from paganism they owed their position to grace alone.
The universal sense of the term is again implied, when he speaks of
*that gospel which has reached you as it spreads over the world with fruit
and increase* till you too *learned to know what God's grace really is.*
The errorists had evidently tried to show that the gospel brought by
Epaphras on his mission was a local and provincial message, which
needed improvement.   Paul's assertion was that it is catholic, meant
for all and also capable, as results show, of reaching men everywhere.
Whereas this pseudo-philosophy of religion is local and, he adds, its
ritual asceticism is *of no value* ethically.   Let the Colossians recollect
gratefully that though once they had been pagans, living an immoral
life that deserved God's anger, they had been lifted out of their hopeless
plight, like other gentile converts all the world over, by the sheer favour
of God.   That is grace, real grace, he remarks ; and who know it
better than you do or should do ?   Any such idealistic theosophy as
these Phrygian religionists propounded was a travesty of the true gospel
of grace.   Its very attempt to revive ritual regulations of the Law,
as though these were meritorious in themselves, was a retrograde movement, which those who had experienced grace must know instinctively
to be superfluous and irrelevant.   Pelagius observes, " he knows God's
grace in truth who does not by evil deeds render God's benefits void."
Yes, but the apostle rather has the further thought in mind, that a
genuine experience of God's grace will not seek to supplement it with
any *rules and regulations* (δόγματα, ii. 14, 20) of human devising, since
such supplements really supplant it.

2

He had already noted that the moral order of the world
had not been destroyed by the outburst of sin and evil.   The
clue to this he had found in the grace of God (Rom. i.–iii.) ;
human nature had gone astray in discord and corruption,
but death had yielded to life when God's Grace intervened
at the coming of His Son into the world (Rom. v. 12 f.).   In

Ephesians he develops the thought on ampler lines. In the Middle letters he had had occasion to speak of the religious experience generated by grace as the outcome of an action of God which has metaphysical implications. That the coming of grace bears upon the world no less than upon the individual, is the truth underlying his use of the enigmatic term ' flesh ' in describing the deliverance brought by Christ. But now in these later letters the cosmic context of grace is prominent, and prominent through what may be called Paul's approach to a Logos-christology.

This speculation is due to his essentially religious conviction (*a*) that Christ is for the human race, and not simply to be understood in terms of messianic hopes with their suggestion of national privilege, and (*b*) that redemption is no more to be confined to release from the material any more than to emancipation from handicaps to righteousness incurred under the Torah. The range of Christ's work, in these later letters, is cosmic. The religious position guaranteed by grace is declared to involve an eternal value for God, which he expresses by the thought of pre-existence. He had always held this view of Christ in germ (see 1 Cor. viii. 6), but now it is worked out in the light of new demands. The real evils to be overcome in the world, he argues, go back to a situation which is cosmic or metaphysical, and they can only be met by a God Who is above creation, and Whose will or gracious purpose is prior alike to nature or to human nature. The very associations of the term Lord (*Κύριος*), in the LXX and Philo, with ' Ruler of the world,' made it the more easy for the apostle to express this faith as he does in 1 Corinthians viii. 6, Philippians ii. 6–11, etc. Of the two senses of ' Lord,' that of ' Lord ' in personal relationship to worshippers, which prevailed in the cults, did not suggest the other. Yet it is the other that Paul embraces—one proof more that he was strongly influenced here by Hebrew rather than by Hellenistic thought.

In both Colossians and Ephesians the pre-existence of Christ is assumed. As it is through him that the world is created, his position is central for faith, requiring no recognition of angels or aeons. All life is mediated for nature and

18

human nature through him. The rabbinic claim was that the Torah had been created before the world and that it was indeed the medium of creation. This fantasy was ignored by Paul ; he could not have taken seriously its corollary, if he knew it, that the Torah had been offered to all the world, rejected by gentiles and accepted only by Israel. But the Jewish habit of expressing the supreme value or ultimate character of anything by ascribing to it pre-existence lies behind the apostle's language, in the opening sentences of Ephesians, where the grace-relationship is traced back definitely to the eternal loving will of God. 'Blessed be the God and Father of our Lord Jesus Christ who in Christ has blessed us with every spiritual blessing in the heavenly sphere, choosing us in him, ere ever the world was founded, to be consecrated and unblemished [i.e. morally blameless] in His sight, destining us in love to be His sons through Jesus Christ—such being the purpose of His will—and all to the praise of His glorious grace [i.e. to bring out the glory of His generous goodness] bestowed upon us [literally, wherewith He has graced us, ἐχαρίτωσεν] in the Beloved, in whom we enjoy our redemption [or, deliverance], even the forgiveness of our trespasses, by the blood he shed—such was the wealth of His grace.' Thus deeply and surely is the position of Christians based upon a Will more firm than their own, a Will too which is essentially gracious. The good life is not only revealed as an ideal but to be realized by the reality of the good God. Calvin's comment is scholastically expressed, but it is accurate ; " the efficient cause is the will of God, the material cause is Christ, the final cause is the praise of His grace,' all three forming a unity of divine purpose. The repeated stress on the third thought is significant. For the writer it is impossible to think of God's eternal purpose without thinking of gracious love, just as His gracious love calls up before the mind His purposive action. What we have or enjoy (ἔχομεν) in the present, our marvellous experience of reconciliation to God, is not an after-thought on His part, much less a position which depends upon our merits and insight and efforts ; it is a destiny for which He has designed us from the very first. What we have is given to us. It is something for which God is to be blessed. In order to prevent self-sufficiency, as though Christians could pride themselves upon this as due to some privilege of birth or as an achievement of their own moral energy, as well as to prevent anxious fears lest it might not last, the apostle shows how present experience is the outcome of God's eternal goodwill in Jesus Christ.

Such is the theme of the first part of this long sentence, i.e. from verse 3 to verse 8. But it is followed up with a still wider sweep of thought in verses 8 to 14. As we have already seen, the inclusion of gentile Christians in the People of God led Paul to a new outlook upon the purpose of God in history. He now proceeds to explain how the experience of grace is not simply an assurance of forgiveness and sonship but a fresh insight into the world-wide purpose of God which embraces the Community and the cosmos, affording a revelation of what are the mysterious ends of God in the universe.

' Such was the wealth of His grace,' he continues, ' which He has lavished upon us with [the further blessing of] complete insight and understanding, by making known to us the secret (μυστήριον) of His will, the inner purpose of His own design being so to order it (εἰς οἰκονομίαν) in the fulness of the ages that all things in heaven and on earth alike should be gathered up (ἀνακεφαλαιώσασθαι) in Christ—in Christ in whom we [Jewish Christians] have had our heritage allotted us (as destined in the design of Him who works out everything in terms of the counsel of His will), that we should redound to the praise of His glory by being the first to set our hope in Christ, in the Christ in whom you [gentile Christians] also believed, when you heard the message of the truth, the gospel of your salvation, and so were stamped with the seal of the long-promised holy Spirit which is the pledge and instalment of our heritage [both ours and yours] that we may secure our divine possession—and all to the praise of His glory.'

This is the second theme of the lyrical outburst upon the wonder of grace divine. In the first theme the new feature is the association of God's choice of Christians with Christ as the eternal Son of God, before creation. In the second the writer is careful to show that Jewish as well as gentile Christians owe their position in the Church to grace, but he suggests that grace as the clue to God's loving purpose for the human race reveals a further marvel in the divine counsel. It is one conviction of this letter that by grace men are not simply reconciled to God but to one another, that the racial barrier between Jew and pagan, which had hitherto divided men, was now abolished in the light of a vast cosmic purpose, and that the reconciliation which had taken place in the Church was the initial phase of a world-wide reconciliation to be worked out through God's grace in Jesus Christ. This, the apostle argues, has been in the mind of God from all eternity, and it must be counted a further mark of His gracious goodness that Christians are now enabled to understand this. In other words, the relation of grace to knowledge is brought forward in a special fashion. But the object of this deeper knowledge is not to gratify curiosity. It is indeed light thrown upon the meaning of the world, but the aim of such higher revelations is to bring out the rich significance of grace in the Christian experience. It is insight due to revelation, and as such it ought to deepen the sense of the range and reality of fellowship with Him through Christ. There is an implicit warning against any tendency to isolate redemption from creation, as though reconciliation to God were no more than a gnostic or mystical extrication of the individual worshipper from material conditions. But the dominant conceptions are these : (a) gentile Christians in particular should appreciate the fact that their choice or election, so

far from being casual, is a vital part of God's eternal movement towards His ends in history, and (*b*) all Christians
should realize that their relationship to God through His
grace in Jesus Christ is absolutely secure, since it is fixed
in His original design for the human race. Throughout
the letter the writer urges the need and helpfulness of reflecting on experience. It is not a novel thought, of course, for
in the earlier letters the revelation of God's saving truth in
grace is frequently discussed. But in Ephesians this theme
is raised to a higher level. Nowhere else is grace so explicitly
connected with insight into the divine purpose.

Though the divine choice of Christians is thus referred to a pre-
temporal origin, Paul does not connect grace with creation ; grace
still is that expression of the divine love which appears in the coming
of Christ to deal with human sin and estrangement. Neither is there
any claim that the world was created for the sake of the Church or
People. Rabbi Akiba afterwards held, " Beloved are Israel who are
called sons of God (literally, the Place) ; but it was greater love to
let them know that they were called sons of God " (Pirke Aboth. iii.
20). This resembles the teaching of Ephes. i. 17 f., iii. 8 f., that the
grace consists not only in bestowing divine favour but in granting a
rich insight into its scope and meaning. Yet the content of the truth
of which Christians thus become conscious is much broader than that
claimed by the rabbi.

As the fact of experience which revealed this world-wide
range of God's grace was the choice of gentile Christians to
share in the sonship and fellowship of God, Paul emphasizes
the special grace of God to himself in commissioning him to
proclaim such a truth and hope. *You* gentile Christians, he
writes, *have surely heard how the grace of God which was vouchsafed to me in your interests has ordered it, how the divine secret
was disclosed to me by a revelation . . . that secret of Christ
which was not disclosed to the sons of men in other generations
as it has now been revealed to his sacred apostles by the Spirit.
namely, that in Christ Jesus the gentiles are co-heirs, companions,*

*and co-partners in the Promise.   Such is the gospel which I was
called to serve by the endowment of God's grace vouchsafed to me,
by the energy of his power ; less than the least of all saints as I
am, this grace was vouchsafed to me, that I should bring the gentiles
the gospel of the fathomless wealth of Christ . . . through whom,
as we have faith in him, we* (i.e. all Christians) *enjoy our confidence of free access* (προσαγωγήν).   It is the final expression
of a conviction which pervades Paul's teaching upon grace,
viz. that it was not simply by grace that he himself had been
saved, but that it was a special grace and favour to himself
that he had been privileged to bear the good news of this
grace for all to the pagan world.

3

Chrysostom calls attention to the fact that instead of the
ordinary Greek word for ' approach ' (προσόδον), our access
to God is described as προσαγωγήν, " which implies that God
brings us to Himself, for we cannot come of ourselves, it
was He who brought us."   A still more remarkable expression of this truth occurs at the end of the strong passage
upon grace and faith (ii. 4–10) ; *God has made us what we
are, creating us in Christ Jesus for the good deeds which are
prepared beforehand* (προητοίμασεν) *by God as our sphere of action.*
What a Jew called his Halacha is replaced in Christianity
by a Way of life and duty corresponding to the Will of God.
Instead of being *sons of disobedience*, gentile and Jewish
Christians alike are by their experience of grace committed
to a sphere of duty predestined for them by God.

The apostle is putting in his own way what a modern would express
by saying that in the true sense of the term we cannot choose our duties.
We may choose to evade them or to accept them, but they are there
for us in the moral order.   Nowhere else in the NT is there such a
sharp statement as this.   But it follows from what precedes.   " As
salvation is not the outcome of what you have done, neither is the saved
life left to itself to plan or to carry out its tasks.   All is under the deter-

mining providence of God." What elsewhere is generally called a privilege is here described as the object of election. That is, to ' know the things that are freely given to us by God ' is, in another aspect, to do the good deeds which He has prepared beforehand as our sphere of life. When the Christian wakens to find himself ' in Christ,' he discovers that he is not to revel in the expectation of future bliss, as if that were all. But he also finds that he has not to look around for the sphere of moral duties ; they are awaiting him as part of God's provision for his life, though, as Paul always pointed out, it requires reflection and sympathy as well as prayer to discern them.

The closest anticipation of this idea is to be found in a passage like 1 Corinthians ii. 2–9, where he insists that the gospel of " Jesus Christ the crucified Lord of glory " is not silliness ($\mu\omega\varrho i\alpha$), as Greeks imagined, but the divine wisdom—a mystery undreamt of, he admits, but nevertheless what God has prepared ($\dot{\eta}\tau o i\mu\alpha\sigma\epsilon\nu$) for those who love Him, and not merely prepared but revealed by the Spirit. This ' wisdom ' is the gospel of Christ who was crucified. And, he adds, ' we have received the Spirit which is of God that we might understand what God has bestowed ($\chi\alpha\varrho\iota\sigma\theta\dot{\epsilon}\nu\tau\alpha$) upon us.' The wisdom, he has already said, relates to the Lord of glory and has been meant from all eternity for our glory ; that is, the crucifixion, so far from being a shameful affair, was designed by God in His inscrutable purpose to result in final glory for us as well as for the Lord with whom our future is bound up. But the content of the ' wisdom ' is neither eschatological nor esoteric ; it is the present experience of God's promises and revelations which Christians have graciously received from Him. In other words, $\delta\sigma\alpha$ $\dot{\eta}\tau o i\mu\alpha\sigma\epsilon\nu$ $\dot{o}$ $\theta\epsilon\dot{o}\varsigma$ and $\tau\dot{\alpha}$ $\dot{v}\pi\dot{o}$ $\tauo\tilde{v}$ $\theta\epsilono\tilde{v}$ $\chi\alpha\varrho\iota\sigma\theta\dot{\epsilon}\nu\tau\alpha$ $\dot{\eta}\mu\tilde{\iota}\nu$ are the same ; the revelation or gift of this to Christians implies no doubt a future climax in glory, but only as the outcome of what is no longer a mere future hope. ' That we may understand ' them is not a prospect held out for the far-off end. Here and now there is a relationship to God, alive with duty, a gracious destiny into which the faithful may enter.

So eager is he to exclude any idea of man having a right to expect anything from God that he does not hesitate to stretch the truth of God's absolute freedom almost to the breaking point. Man is utterly indebted to God for his salvation. There would have been no hope for him, had not God in pure pity and grace intervened. We were as bad as you gentiles, he says, in the tremendous passage of Ephes. ii. 3 f. ; we Jews were in the same desperate plight as you were, thanks to our sinful disobedience. *We were by nature* (φύσει, i.e. in ourselves) *objects of God's anger, like the rest of men.* The only outlook for us was His wrath. If God had merely acted as our situation deserved, His wrath would have come upon us all and to the uttermost. ' But God '—there was another side to the situation ! ' But God, who is rich in mercy,' raised us from death to life, by His amazing grace. Under these words there is a passionate, grateful conviction that God acts towards sinners in a way other than their situation gives them any title to expect. *It is by grace you have been saved, as you had faith ; it is not your doing but God's gift, not the outcome of what you have done—lest anyone should pride himself on that ; God has made us what we are.* It is against religious complacency and to encourage the healthy pulse of humility that Paul thus maintains, ' All is of grace.'

His religious instinct led him to see that a humble soul must never presume on God's goodness, much less assert the right to it. When he preached to pagans, he brought out the truth that their moral instincts ought to incline them to the living God, Who had made them for Himself and had revealed Himself in nature as well as in human nature. This we may infer from the first chapters of Romans as well as from the speech at Athens which certainly reflect one appeal of his preaching to pagan audiences. Besides, there was the favour of their inclusion within the chosen People. Paul also believed, as we have seen, that God was under certain responsibilities to Israel ; His promises had to be fulfilled. Israel are *beloved for their fathers' sake. For God never goes back upon his gifts and call.* Yet the apostle's concentration of grace upon the redeeming work in Jesus Christ prevented him from dwelling on the relationship of God to man as His creature. It was not natural for him to plead with the psalmist,

Thy mercy, O Lord, endureth for ever ;
Forsake not the works of thine own hands.

When we read his letters it looks as though he was deeply conscious of God making Himself responsible for those who accepted the gospel offer, but hardly alive to any idea of God being responsible for making that offer. Yet in Ephesians he recognizes this. He tells gentile Christians frankly that once, in their pagan days, they were *outside Christ, aliens to the commonwealth of Israel, and strangers to the covenants of the Promise, devoid of hope and God* (ἄθεοι) *within the world.* But all the time, he adds, there was a secret purpose in the heart of God which included them. They might be indifferent to God (this is the real sense of ἄθεοι) but He was not indifferent to them. As yet undisclosed there was the eternal mystery or secret purpose that *in Christ Jesus the gentiles* were to be heirs, companions, and partners along with the chosen People in the Promise.

4

There is another aspect of the grace-teaching, under which some data from the earlier letters may be grouped.

(*a*) The call to worship in the Book of Common Prayer, " when we assemble and meet together to render thanks for the great benefits that we have received at His hand, to set forth His most holy praise, to hear His most holy Word, and to ask those things which are requisite and necessary, as well for the body as for the soul," is an echo of the counsel in Colossians iv. 2 : *maintain your zest for prayer by thanksgiving* (τῇ προσευχῇ προσκαρτερεῖτε, γρηγοροῦντες ἐν αὐτῇ ἐν εὐχαριστίᾳ). The Greek verb γρηγορεῖν, as used in the Psalter and in contemporary cults like Hermetism, denotes a reaction not simply against sleep but against the drowsiness of a worldly life which makes prayer languid. It is not a counsel to be on the outlook for an answer to prayer, nor is it merely eschatological ; the deeper thought is that by gratefully calling up before the mind all that God has done and been to faith, the humble confidence in Him which is the nerve of prayer is quickened. It is the same in Philippians iv. 5–6, though here the sense of the end is marked.   No need for panic or apprehension ! *The Lord is at hand. Never be anxious,* however, though trials befall you, *but always make your requests known to God in prayer and supplication with thanksgiving.* The consciousness of His grace and goodness is the atmosphere for quiet prayer, which prevents it from being taken as a means of putting pressure on one who is reluctant or aloof.   To thank God for something already received from His hand is the best way to learn the spirit of prayer to Him in any fresh emergency.

The more general function of thanksgiving is mentioned in connexion with faith exposed to misconceptions of Christ, who is the sole sufficient source of grace, *lead your life in Jesus the Lord, fixed and founded in him, confirmed in the faith as you have been taught it, and overflowing with thankfulness to God* (Col. ii. 7).   Here the apostle suggests that as they keep before their minds the true Christ, through whom alone all comes to them, they will not be so likely to attribute anything to intermediate powers or angelic aeons ; and again, thanksgiving is urged, since it calls up the evidence for that grace of God in experience.   Paul had indeed just touched the same note in another key, by praying that they might be ' strengthened with all might, according to his glorious power, unto all patience and longsuffering with joyfulness (no Stoic endurance !), giving thanks unto the Father who has qualified us to share the lot of the Saints in the Light ' (i. 11, 12). The lot may involve strain ; there may be trying experiences to temper and patience, but, it is implied, He who has graciously given them this privilege will not abandon them. Grateful confidence is the watchword for the struggle ; it nerves the Christian for anything, by reminding him of the God Who has taken him in hand.

Again, thanksgiving is closely related to the worship of the community.   After speaking of the need for harmony (in Col. iii. 14 f.), the apostle adds, *And you must be thankful—*

καὶ εὐχάριστοι γίνεσθε. It happens to be the only place where
he uses this adjective, but the context indicates that he does
so in the sense of ' grateful,' not in the other Hellenistic
sense of ' amiable ' or ' pleasant.' It is their relationship
to God, not to one another, which is fundamental. The
phrase might indeed sum up what precedes ; be peaceable
and friendly, you must be agreeable and pleasant to one
another. But more probably it denotes the thankfulness of
which he is about to speak in the next sentences.

Pelagius has this comment. " In nonnullis exemplaribus habet
' gratia estote ' : hoc est, nolite legi similare, quae vicem reddit, sed
gratiae quae ignoscit etiam inimicis et pro eis dominum deprecatur."
This apparently points to some reading like καὶ χάρις γίνεσθε underlying a Latin version. But " to the best of my knowledge, no other
authority for ' gratia ' has turned up " (Souter in *Cambridge Texts and
Studies*, ix. 121).

The apostle continues ' Let the word (ὁ λόγος, the inspiration) of Christ dwell in you (i.e. in your fellowship) with
all the wealth of wisdom (real wisdom for understanding and
undertaking life, such as the Spirit of Christ supplies, needing
no supplementary rules such as your local theosophy offers),
inspiring you to teach and train one another with the music
of psalms, with hymns, and songs of the spiritual life (i.e.,
real ' spirituals,' not profane ditties) ; praise God with thankful hearts.' The last five words render ἐν χάριτι ᾄδοντες ἐν
ταῖς καρδίαις ὑμῶν τῷ θεῷ. Some take ἐν χάριτι with what
precedes, in the sense of ' within or relating to the grace
of God.' But the context points to ' thanks ' as its meaning.
Indeed if the article is read (ἐν τῇ χάριτι) it might mean ' the
thanks ' just mentioned. For the sentence is a sequel to
Be thankful ; Paul first mentions worship as the opportunity
for showing thanks to God, and then (in the next verse) proceeds to the more general sphere. The addition of ἐν ταῖς
καρδίαις ὑμῶν does not imply an inner or silent act of praise

as opposed to outward expression, but simply that in such spontaneous outbursts thanksgiving should be uppermost. To sing praise to God with thankful hearts is parallel to εὐχαριστοῦντες in the next verse ('do all in the name of the Lord Jesus, giving thanks to God and the Father by him'). Indeed the idea of the passage is the same as that of the simpler statement in Eph. v. 19–20, where Christians are bidden to 'hold fellowship with the music of psalms, with hymns, and with songs of the spiritual life ; praise the Lord heartily (ᾄδοντες ἐν τῇ καρδίᾳ ὑμῶν τῷ Κυρίῳ) with words and music, and render thanks (εὐχαριστοῦντες) always,' etc.

The Greek implies musical accompaniments to some of the songs of praise, but ἐν χάριτι cannot signify ' with taste or charm.' The aesthetic sense is too weak for the argument. In the Colossians passage Paul may be using it with a slight suggestion of its positive meaning, as though ' grace ' were the subject and sphere of the praise, as is implied in the words about *teaching and training*. It may be asked how hymns of praise enter into this function. The answer is that primitive credal expressions often took rhythmical form, as in 1 Tim. iii. 16. The original words of such confessions of faith about Grace or the Gospel were probably sung, long before the Te Deum showed that praise could form one of the best channels for instructing congregations on their beliefs. Besides, as any thanksgiving calls up the character of God the Giver, it touches motives in His purpose and dealings which enter into grateful trust and intelligent obedience. What inspires Christian praise, whether it takes the form of repeating traditional psalms and songs or of improvising new songs to the Lord, as the Spirit sometimes prompted the early Christians, is ὁ λόγος τοῦ Χριστοῦ, the Gospel revelation made by Christ. The praise which is rendered to the Lord is inspired by the Lord through His manifestation of the divine goodness, which like the Torah is called ὁ λόγος as it denotes the active power and wisdom of God in the life of His people. " The truths taught or learned are to blossom, as it were, into hymns " (Cheyne, *Encyclopaedia Biblica* 2138). For all this there was some precedent in the synagogue but none in the mystery-cults. Christians accustomed to such pagan piety had to learn new methods of worship and fellowship ;

the hymn or psalm and the address or sermon, especially the former, was a creation of the joyful faith of the Church.

Already in the Middle letters Paul had used 'charis' in a special sense, corresponding to what we call 'grace' over meals, as appears in the statement (1 Cor. x. 30) on behalf of the liberal or strong Christian who is being hampered by petty scruples about what one might or might not eat and drink. The sound principle of freedom is put forward in the words, *If one partakes of any food after saying a blessing over it* (χάριτι), *why should one be denounced for eating what one has given thanks* (εὐχαριστῶ) *to God for?* The term χάριτι here cannot well mean, ' by depending on God ' ; it denotes ' with thanksgiving.' To *eat to the Lord*, in the analogous passage (Rom. xiv. 6), is to thank God for the food the man takes ; if he is sincerely able to do that, then no one has any right to fetter his freedom with scruples or taboos. So here. Possibly a grace like the first words of the twenty-fourth psalm was used. ' The earth is the Lord's and the fulness thereof.' In any case the argument of Paul is that by saying a blessing over food, by giving thanks to God for it, a Christian is right in the eyes of God and ought not to be criticized by other Christians. This application of ' charis,' however, is developed in the Pastoral epistles (see below), not in Paul's Later letters. On the other hand, while *thanks* (χάρις) *be to God* is not used instead of the verb, as in the Middle letters (e.g. Rom. vi. 17, 1 Cor. xv. 57, 2 Cor. ii. 14, viii. 16, ix. 15 ; in Rom. vii. 25 the verb is a well-supported variant), the noun εὐχαριστία is happily introduced in Ephesians v. 3, 4, with a slight play on ' charis ' as charm ; *no indecent, silly, or scurrilous talk—all that is improper ! Rather, voice your thanks to God.* That is, let your lips be full of what is anything but ' dis-graceful ' or ugly. This suggestion would at once be caught by anyone familiar with the nuances of ' charis ' in Hellenistic Greek (see above, p. 22).

Some confine the term here to gracious, refined speech, " der Ton feiner Bildung " (Odo Casel in *Biblische Zeitschrift*, xviii. 85), which was certainly the opinion of Origen in his commentary (*Journal of Theological Studies*, iii. 559). According to Jerome (see Harnack in *Texte und Untersuchungen*, xlii. 4. 163), he read not εὐχαριστία but εὐχαριτία, in order to bring out the fact that the apostle was not thinking of gratefulness but of graceful attractive speech on the part of Christians (εὐχάριτον δὲ καὶ χαρίεντα).

Thanksgiving or the praise of God was for Paul a natural expression of the joy and certainty with which God's grace had enriched life. In outlining the degeneration of men he instinctively notes, for example, how any recognition of God had passed out of their existence (*though they knew God, they have not glorified him as God nor have they given thanks to him*, Rom. i. 21), very much as the devout Jew Philo had observed in his treatise *De Opificio* (60) : " When evil began to overpower the virtues, the perennial springs of God's favours (χαρίτων) were closed, lest they should supply the unworthy. If the human race had had to suffer their due penalty, they would have been blotted out for their ingratitude to God (ἀχαριστίαν) their benefactor and saviour (εὐεργέτην καὶ σωτῆρα). But being merciful (ἵλεως) by nature, he took pity upon them and mitigated their punishment." For Paul one sure proof that Christians had a heartfelt sense of the utter goodness of God was to be found in their thankfulness and praise. It is significant that he attaches such importance to this practical proof, in letters full of arguments about the reasons for faith in grace. He seems to feel that the instinctive appreciation of God's saving goodness should voice itself, not as a substitute for intelligent faith but as the expression of that receptive spirit which is the atmosphere of the Gospel.

It is the same in his personal service, as he had already explained. The outcome of any efforts which he makes in the service of the Gospel is a fresh sense of God on the part of those who are helped, as they are

moved to thank Him for what is thereby conveyed to them through
the apostle's ministry. I am active, he says, I suffer and speak, but
it is all in your interests, so that the more grace abounds, the more thanks-
giving may rise and redound to the glory of God (2 Cor. iv. 15), not of
myself. The more richly the grace of God, i.e. His active power of
love, is realized in the ministry of the Church, the more heartily ought
men to be thankful to God Himself. Or, as he puts it elsewhere, the
supreme result inspired by any human service to others is thanksgiving
to God for having wrought such an unselfish deed. *Your generosity,*
of which I am the agent, he tells the Corinthian Christians (2 Cor.
ix. 11), *will make men* (throughout the Church, especially the recipients
of your liberality) *give thanks to God.* It is Paul echoing the word
of Jesus about men glorifying God as they see the good deeds of Christian
men ; the best thing in all this generous gift of yours, he means, is
that it moves others to praise God with thankful hearts as they realize
afresh how strong and gracious is His spirit prompting human nature
to be liberal and unselfish. In all this it is assumed that help is given
in the right spirit, for there are ungracious ways of being kind. To
be grudging or patronizing takes the bloom from any service of others.
Hence Paul, in speaking of the grace of Jesus Christ as the inspiration
of Christian helpfulness, had in mind the generous methods of his
mission ; his aid was never dealt out in anything but a gracious spirit,
whether it touched the souls or the bodies of men. So was it to be in
his fellowship. Any taint of display, for example, would prevent the
recipient from recognizing a divine spirit in the gift.

This pervading and overwhelming sense of God's grace
as giving and forgiving love explains the central position of
thanksgiving and gratitude in Paul's conception of Christianity. The very word reveals this nexus. *Εὐχαριστία* is
man's response to *χάρις*. God bestows His ' grace ' and man
in turn offers his thanksgiving to the Lord ; such is the
rhythm of the Christian experience, for Paul. The ancients
(see above, pp. 22 ff.) loved to play upon the double sense of
' charis ' as boon and thanks ; *χάρις χάριν γάρ ἐστιν ἡ τίκτουσ'*
ἀεί, Sophocles sings in the *Ajax* (522), ' a favour ever begets
gratitude.' Paul in his own way shares the same spirit, as

he repeatedly reminds his churches about the duty and habit of thanksgiving.

This was due in part to the tradition of worship in Jewish piety ; there gratitude prevailed, and the deeper implications of the Christian faith led to an unvaried stress on thanksgiving in worship. Thus it is quite in accordance with Paul's practice that when the author of the Pastorals gives counsel to the churches on worship, he mentions that *supplications, prayers, intercessions* or petitions *and thanksgiving* should be *offered for all men* (1 Tim. ii. 1). ' Thanksgiving for all men ' sounds strange, but in reality the writer had been trained to link thanksgiving and prayer so closely that in speaking of intercession for all men he had at once to add thanksgiving, although it is less applicable to ' all men ' than prayer.

The primitive form of eucharistic worship which Paul transmits (1 Cor. xi. 23 f.) has εὐχαριστήσας over the bread where Mark and Matthew have εὐλογήσας. There is indeed no difference between the two terms, which are used inter-changeably in the gospel of Mark for the same Aramaic word ; ' having given thanks ' is no more and no less than ' having said the blessing.' But Paul prefers εὐχαριστεῖν to εὐλογεῖν, and here he makes εὐχαριστήσας cover both the bread and the wine, which is all the more curious as he evidently knew that a blessing was said over the cup—*the cup of blessing, which we bless* (x. 16). No effort is made to interpret the eucharist in terms of ' grace,' however, any more than the sacrament of baptism. Indeed it is not till later, in Ignatius and the Didachê, that εὐχαριστία is used for the Eucharist. The notion of the sacraments as means of grace had not yet been conceived ; it might have been expected that the sacramental truth would have been expressed sometimes by means of grace-words, but all we have is εὐχαριστήσας.

The same term had been also used to describe ordinary worship (1 Cor. xiv. 15 f.), when the outpouring of the soul in gratitude to

God is supposed to do good to others as well as to oneself. If you Corinthians in your meetings are *blessing* (εὐλογῇς) *God in the Spirit* (i.e. with some ecstatic cry like ' Praise God ! ' in a foreign tongue or swept off by a rapture into some incoherent shout of praise), *how is the outsider* who wanders into your company, attracted by your fellowship and half-anxious to join you—*how is he to say ' Amen ' at the end of your thanksgiving* (εὐχαριστίᾳ)? Inarticulate praise is no help to others in the congregation, the apostle argues. It is implied once more that public thanksgiving is helpful to all concerned, and that even outsiders may learn from it no less than from sermons and addresses.

To conclude. The connexion of thanksgiving with prayer, which we noted at the beginning of this section, runs through all the apostle's letters. *Rejoice at all times, never give up prayer, thank God for everything*—these are counsels linked together in his very first letter (1 Thess. v. 16–18). This heroic temper of faith which dares to praise God, whatever happens, however unwelcome it may be to our natural feelings, is an uncommon virtue, which counsellors since Paul inside the Church have often pressed as a commonplace duty on the conscience. Thus, William Law writes that " to thank God only for such things as you like, is no more a proper act of piety than to believe only what you see is an act of faith." But it is a joy to read the witness of an outsider like Epictetus : " Had we understanding, what else ought we to do than in public and private to hymn and bless the Deity, telling of his favours (χάριτας)? Lame and old as I am, what else can I do but hymn the Deity? Were I a nightingale, I would act like a nightingale ; were I a swan, like a swan. But I am an intelligent man ; I ought to hymn God. This is my business, I do it, and I will not desert this post of mine, so long as I am allowed to hold it ; and I exhort you to do the same " (i. 16).

(*b*) Speech, however, is wider than song, and the apostle recognizes that grace applies to this larger sphere. " Let your speech or talk always be ἐν χάριτι, ἅλατι ἠρτυμένος."

19

In talking about their religion to outsiders, Christians are not only to be honest and faithful but to exhibit a gracious courtesy. *Learn*, the apostle adds, *how to answer any question put to you* by pagans, but part of this equipment consists in learning how to speak as well as what to say. More than intelligence is required. He is using a familiar metaphor, for ' salt ' meant wit in contemporary usage, and was associated with ' charis ' in the sense of charm. We may therefore render the Greek words *Let your talk always have a saving salt of grace about it.* Naturally the apostle plays on the double sense of ' charis ' ; he is trying to say two things at once, to discourage anything like insipid talk and also to urge the duty of discussing the Christian religion or grace with interested enquirers in the outside world, the point of ' salt ' being that it suggested an idea of saving or preserving from corruption, which was implicit in the Pauline idea of ' charis.' Hence the term *saving* in our rendering of the Greek, to include not simply freedom from insipidity or secular interests but also the religious aim of such talk on grace. " Don't let your talk be tasteless," he implies—" and by tasteless I do not mean insipid merely, in the current sense of the word, but devoid of religious power and saving per-suasion." The whole paragraph is devoted to contact with the pagan world, and the word about talk comes in the wake of an urgent warning that there is not much time left to bring pagans over. *Let Christian wisdom rule your behaviour to the outside world ; make the most of your time,* in the brief interval before the end ; *let your talk always have a saving salt of grace about it, and learn how to answer any question put to you* (Col. iv. 5–6). In other words, let your talk on religion especially be pointed, uplifting, and attractive. Good people may be dull or prosy or unattractive even in their efforts to commend the faith, as Paul well knew.

This metaphor of salt is common in Latin as well as in Greek. Petronius mentions together ' dicta, sales, lusus, sermonis gratia,' where salt means wit and 'gratia sermonum' pleasant talk (*Petronius*, Loeb edition, p. 352). Plutarch in his essay *De Garrulitate* (23) compares good talk to salt ; it gives a flavour to human intercourse. " Men talk either on their own behalf, if they want something, or else to benefit those who hear them " (the point made in Ephesians iv. 29), " or to give pleasure to one another (χάριν τινὰ παρασκευάζοντες). They season everyday life and work with speech, as one seasons food with salt. But why talk, if your words are no use to yourself, and unnecessary to the hearer, or void of pleasure or charm (χάρις) ? " The close tie between ' charis ' and words is evident in this passage, as it is in the same writer's description of Antony's language, " the witching charm (ἡ τῶν λόγων σειρὴν καὶ χάρις) of what he said " (Life of Marius, xliv).

The suggestion of pleasure or charm in language is certainly present to the writer's mind as he tells Christians elsewhere to make their conversation clean and profitable. *Let no bad word* (σάπρος here is quite general, not an equivalent for scurrilous or dirty) *pass your lips, but only such speech as is good for edification, as occasion may require* (τῆς χρείας)—a hint to well-meaning people, not to be irrelevant or talkative, which recalls the counsel of Epictetus (*Enchirid.*, 33), " Silence as a general rule ; say only what is needful (τὰ ἀναγκαῖα), and that in few words. Talk seldom, only when occasion calls for it, and never about athletics or food and drink—the usual topics—never specially about blaming or praising or comparing men. If you can, lead the conversation of the company over to what is becoming (τὸ προσῆκον)." Paul, however, adds ἵνα δῷ χάριν τοῖς ἀκούουσιν (Eph. iv. 29). This is more than ' to give pleasure to the hearers,' and yet such associations of the word linger in the phrase. We may render the play on the double sense of the term thus : *words that are gracious and a means of grace to the hearers*. It is a warning against the gossip and the low innuendoes characteristic of Oriental talk, and the counsel becomes positive by using the colloquial term ' charis.' " That it may minister grace " (AV) is closer to Paul's meaning than " that it may be agreeable or pleasant," but the latter nuance of the word has to be retained somehow. Our English adjective ' gracious ' may still serve in this connexion, unless it be associated with a certain air of condescension in some people's minds. The obtrusive person who insists on dragging in religion or on improving the occasion is ruled out by ' gracious,' equally with the person whose talk is coarse or commonplace.

The Greek use of διδόναι χάριν in connexion with human activity, as " to do a favour " or " to indulge " (one's appetites or passions), is absent from the NT. Indeed apart from this passage, the phrase is always used of God (see above, p. 34).

PART E
AFTER PAUL

THE NT Canon contains a group of eleven letters, homilies and pastorals, from the general literature of the early Church after Paul; if the Apocalypse of John, which is in epistolary form, be added, there are a dozen. Apart from this, the two gospels of Mark and Matthew, with Luke's historical work in two parts (Luke–Acts), throw further light upon the period preceding Paul no less than upon contemporary situations in the Church during at least half a century after the apostle's death.

How deeply Paul's teaching on grace had passed into the consciousness of the Church as a whole, whatever hesitations were felt about this argument or that, may be gathered at the very outset by a glance at the forms employed for opening and closing letters or documents in letter-form. What the apostle had stamped was retained, and retained not purely as a traditional form ; writer after writer modifies it freely, in order to make the wording suit a purpose of his own, but nearly all of them feel that grace ought to be the first word and the last in their compositions. It is the exception to find grace omitted, and even when it is left out there is some equivalent devised for the truth of grace, so profoundly was it realized that Christianity was above all things a religion of grace.

AFTER PAUL

I

(*a*) So far as the epistolary form at the beginning went, Paul's formulas were treated with a certain freedom.

(i) 'Grace and peace' were retained, with some slight alteration in the wording.

> *Grace and peace*
> *from God the Father*
> *and Christ Jesus our Saviour*

is the opening phrase in Titus, where, as Titus alone is addressed, *to you* (ὑμῖν) is omitted. The two Petrine epistles have

> *Grace and peace be multiplied to you,*

which in Clement of Rome is expanded into

> *Grace and peace to you*
> *be multiplied from God Almighty*
> *through Jesus Christ.*

The Apocalypse expands the same formula on independent lines :

> *Grace and peace to you*
> *from* HE WHO IS AND WAS AND IS COMING,
> *and from the seven Spirits before his throne,*
> *and from Jesus Christ, the faithful witness,* etc.

But the most independent wording is in Barnabas, who writes, *Hail* (χαίρετε), *sons and daughters, in the name of the Lord who loved us, in peace*. This recurrence to the older χαίρειν in a personal form does not mean any inadequate appreciation of grace on the part of Barnabas, however. He proceeds at once to rejoice over " the great and rich decisive actions (δικαιωμάτων) of God " on behalf of his friends, and over the

" grace of the spiritual gift implanted in their nature," just as at the end he closes with a grace-salutation which follows an allusion to peace in " May you be saved, O children of love and peace ! "

For the Petrine variant there is a precedent in the royal edicts of Daniel iv. 1, vi. 25 (peace to you be multiplied) ; πληθυνθείη is simply an archaic, richer form of εἴη.

For an admirer of Paul, Ignatius shows remarkable freedom. He begins generally with πλεῖστα χαίρειν (common in the papyri from the first century B.C. onwards), never with ' grace.' Once (Ephesians) χαίρειν is preceded by ἐν χαρᾷ. His salutations, which are unusually ample, contain not only the ideas of grace, however, but even the word itself (Magnesians, Romans). Like Barnabas he assumes that Christianity is grace-religion.

(ii) Between grace and peace sometimes mercy is inserted. This triple formula is used twice by the author of the Pastorals (First and Second Timotheus) :

> *Grace, mercy, peace,*
> *from God the Father*
> *and Christ Jesus our Lord*

which is expanded for special reasons by John the Presbyter (in Second John) into

> *Grace, mercy, peace will be with us*
> *from God the Father*
> *and from Jesus Christ the Son of the Father,*
> *in truth and love.*

Here not only is the indicative used in what Bengel calls a ' votum cum affirmatione,' but the writer associates himself with the group he is addressing and combines a Johannine phrase with a semi-Pauline salutation, the phrase (*truth and love*, i.e. true belief in the incarnate Son of God, and the spirit of love which it generates) defining the range of the salutation.

(iii) Otherwise it is, as in Judas,

> *Mercy, peace, and love be multiplied to you,*

or, as echoed in the Letter of the Smyrniote church on the Martyrdom of Polykarp,

> Mercy, peace and love
> from (or, of) God the Father
> and our Lord Jesus Christ
> be multiplied.

Polykarp makes the formula dual (Philippians) :

> Mercy and peace to you be multiplied
> from God Almighty
> and Jesus Christ our Saviour.

In the Pastorals the addition of ἔλεος is connected with the emphasis on Saviour (God our Saviour, 1 Tim. i. 1, etc.) ; the Sure Saying of Titus iii. 4–7 affirms that when *God our Saviour saved us*, it was done *from his own pity (κατὰ τὸ αὐτοῦ ἔλεος) that we might be justified by his grace.* Thus, two aspects of the divine favour, which Paul commonly embraces under the single term ' grace,' are set forth by two terms in the Pastorals. But this usage is not dominant.

Generally ' mercy ' was added in order to expand, with its rich LXX associations, the underlying thought of grace. This was the more easy as already ' mercy and peace ' had been linked together not only in the opening of a letter (e.g. Syriac Baruch lxxviii. 2) but elsewhere (e.g. Tobit vii. 12 in the text preserved by Codex Sinaiticus), whilst ' grace and mercy ' had become a familiar phrase, as in Wisdom iii. 9 and iv. 15, where it is associated with a word that denotes the personal attention and protective blessing of God—

> Grace and mercy are for His elect,
> And graciously He visits (ἐπισκοπή) His saints.

(*b*) Paul's lead was closely followed in the concluding words of a homily or letter. *Grace be with you* (First and Second Timotheus) or *with you all* (Hebrews, Titus) is indeed expanded into *the grace of the Lord Jesus Christ be with you all* in the Apocalypse, but grace is the common term of them all. Even when the closing words are a doxology, as became common in the post-Pauline letters (e.g. Judas, Second Peter, Second Clement, the Smyrniote letter, Diognetus xii., and

Rom. xvi. 25–27), the idea of 'grace' is present, and once indeed the term, i.e. in Clement of Rome (lxv.) : 'The grace of our Lord Jesus Christ be with you and with all everywhere who have been called by God through Him, to whom be glory, honour, power and greatness, eternal sovereignty, from eternity to eternity.   Amen.'   The simple *Peace to you* is retained only in First Peter and Third John.

A glance at the epistolary literature of the early Church after Paul reveals the significant fact that even later writers who finished off their letters differently liked now and then to sound the note of 'grace' towards the end.   Thus Ignatius who usually employed the pagan ἔρρωσθε with a Christian addition, once concludes 'Farewell in the grace of God' (Smyrn. xiii), and once declares that 'grace will be with' an unknown envoy (Polykarp viii).   The epistle of Barnabas ends, 'The Lord of glory and of all grace be with your spirit' (xxi).   And the letter of the Smyrniote Church on The Martyrdom of Polykarp practically concludes with 'Grace be with you all' (xxii).   By this time a grace-prayer had probably become the liturgical close for a service of worship.

II

THE PASTORAL EPISTLES

THESE documents from the primitive Church are more or less consciously indebted to Paul's lead upon grace. In several there is an independent treatment of the idea. This was but natural, as the acute controversy raised over the relation between the Gospel and the Jewish Law began to wane or to assume other forms. In others, the fundamental truths of ' All is of grace ' and ' Grace is for all ' were taken for granted rather than argued ; or, if either had to be argued against fresh developments in belief or in practice, the expression was rarely in terms of grace.

Of these documents in the wake of Paul one group demands notice at the outset, as it reflects the application of ' grace ' to a new situation by a writer who desired to interpret the mind of Paul for an age which, in his judgment, was tempted to deny or to misconceive the principles of the apostle's message to the Church. The three homilies called the Pastoral Epistles were composed by a disciple who wrote in Paul's name, with special reference to the moral discipline of the faith. He rightly felt that his master's teaching was against some forms of contemporary laxity. He insisted on the body of religious truth which the Church possessed and was bound to preserve, if the faith was not to be compromised by irregular innovations. In reiterating this, he alters the emphasis of the apostle here and there, yet in dealing with grace, which forms one of his categories, he reveals not only the new context required for the truth but some consciousness of what Paul originally intended by grace as a determining religious element in the gospel. In other words the Pastorals, i.e. the letters to Timotheus and Titus, show how a devoted Paulinist, with a mind of his own, was stimulated to transmit the apostle's message upon grace as upon other aspects of the Christian faith, and how in the course of transmission it was modified and altered, even by one who believed himself to be faithful to his master's genius.

Spiritualist or mystical theosophies brought risks to the truth of grace which were as insidious as any prompted by legalism of a Jewish kind. (*a*) The ascetic tendency fostered by dualism led to the notion of conserving the spirit by severity to the flesh, in the shape of taboos and prohibitions of food, as well as of fasting. The aim was either to weaken the flesh in the interests of the spirit or to please God by self-imposed restrictions. Evidently in the theosophy at Colossae such efforts were made. Paul finds it needful to restate the message of grace as it really was. But the movement assumed wider ramifications, as among the Encratites who advocated celibacy, or among circles influenced by the Neo-Pythagoreans in Italy, who for religious reasons advocated vegetarianism, on the ground that the propagation of the race was evil. (*b*) On the other hand, the libertine inference called for strenuous protests from the Church. One early gospel contained a special version of Matthew vii. 23, warning against the notion that the elect could sit loose to the moral commands of the faith : " Even if you are gathered with me in my bosom," said the Lord, " and do not my commands, I will cast you out " (quoted in 2 Clem. iv.). Both of these risks are reflected in the outlook of the Pastorals, especially the former. As Paul had already marked the danger of ascetic scruples in Romans, so the author of the Pastorals denounces a broader propaganda on the same lines, alleging that even when it professed to supply a more ethical discipline than the apostle's doctrine had demanded, it infringed the truth of grace.

(*a*) The writer does happen to use one phrase about ' charis ' which Paul avoided ; χάριν ἔχω is not a Pauline way of saying *I render thanks to God* (1 Tim. i. 12, 2 Tim. i. 3). As a matter of fact, it occurs only once in the whole of the NT (see below, p. 351). But apart from this our author has adhered closely upon the whole to the apostle's style and thought in speaking about ' charis.' Thus the allusions to grace as power for service are not uncharacteristic of Paul himself. They show

how this idea had stamped itself on the mind of his disciple, so that even a passage like 1 Tim. i. 12, after the opening words, does sound like what Paul might himself have written : *I render thanks to Christ Jesus my Lord, who has made me able for this* (ἐνδυναμώσαντι). So with 2 Tim. ii. 1 : *Be strong* (ἐνδυναμοῦ) *in the grace of* (literally, that is in) *Christ Jesus,* strong to bear the hard discipline of service for the Cause.

Equally characteristic is the turn of thought in 1 Tim. i. 13–14 where the verb from ἔλεος is used along with 'charis.' Blasphemer and persecutor as I was, the apostle is made to confess, *I obtained mercy* (ἠλεήθην) *because in my unbelief I had acted out of ignorance ; and the grace of our Lord flooded* (ὑπερεπλεόνασεν) *my life along with the faith and love that* (literally, are in) *Christ Jesus inspires.* The divine Mercy thus means Grace Abounding. It is the incommensurable quantity of grace that the verb rendered *flooded* is intended to convey to the mind. And the writer is careful again to make this the immediate source of a life possessed by Christian *faith and love.* The use of ἔλεος is all his own, and so is the plea of ignorance, but he is true to Paul's thought in maintaining that the gospel of grace is a saving power, not a vain speculation, and that in the train of grace the graces of faith and love follow.

(*b*) The ethical nexus of grace reappears in a broader sense, not as an autobiographical touch but as a general principle. At one point in the eucharistic service of the Eastern Church [1] the choir chant Ἐπεφάνη ἡ χάρις τοῦ θεοῦ ἡ σωτήριος πᾶσιν ἀνθρώποις. So there has entered into worship a grace-sentence from the Pastorals (from Titus ii. 11) : *the grace of God has appeared to save all men.* The writer adds, *and it schools us* (παιδεύουσα) *to renounce irreligion and worldly passions and* (the positive side) *to live a life of self-mastery,* etc. *All* is emphatic. It is specially used to explain that the scope of salvation is not confined to the class of which the writer has

[1] F. E. Brightman, *Liturgies Eastern and Western,* i. 393 (the liturgy of St. Chrysostom).

just been speaking, viz. the slave-class. ' I am speaking now not of one class but of us all.' Like 1 Peter ii. 19 this is a grace-sentence arising out of the special problems started by the position of Christian slaves within the Empire. Slaves had no rights before the law ; they were not considered as personalities. But the gospel came into their lives with the same royal demand as into the lives of any, with the honour of a hope which meant strict self-discipline. The latter idea, of grace as educative, is a Hellenistic conception, which tallies with the prevalent emphasis of the Pastorals upon the ethical implications of the faith. The saving quality of grace is still urged as the start and source of religion. But it is noticeable how the writer chooses ordinary phrases of the vernacular about the moral life in order to state what elsewhere is called faith and love, giving new expression, in terms of contemporary religious thought, to the vital nexus between grace and a good life. Grace opens up not into a new obedience or into a law of the Spirit (for in the Pastorals the Pauline conception of the Spirit is not prominent), but into a moral discipline of character.

The personification of Grace is accentuated by the use here as in Titus iii. 4 of a verb belonging to a noun (ἐπιφάνεια) which denoted in current phraseology the advent of a ' praesens deus,' the manifestation on earth of some deity hitherto unknown, who made his appearance in order to heal or help. The noun in the Pastorals (except in 2 Tim. i. 10) denoted the second Advent of the Lord, as in the one use of it made by Paul (2 Thess. ii. 8), but the verb is employed to describe the incarnation. Readers of the Pastorals would be familiar with the term as employed in contemporary references to the Emperor in the imperial cultus. By this extension of language the writer is able to convey, in terms less technical and more popular than Paul had used, the ideas of authority and of free favour which were implicit in Grace.

(c) It is quite in Paul's style that the writer handles the problem of a morbid asceticism, which was becoming already a menace to religion as well as to morals (1 Tim. iv. 1–5).

Paul is represented as predicting by divine inspiration the dangerous errors which were assailing the Church, particularly the devilish teaching of *men who prohibit marriage and insist upon abstinence from foods which God created for believing men, who understand the Truth, to partake of with thanksgiving* (μετὰ εὐχαριστίας). These last words are the pivot of the argument. *For,* he adds, *anything God has created is good, and nothing is to be tabooed, provided it is* taken (λαμβανόμενον) and *eaten with thanksgiving* (μετὰ εὐχαριστίας), *for then it is consecrated* (becomes holy) *by the prayer said over it* (literally ' by the word of God and prayer,' but the above rendering is accurate, for the ' word of God ' means the scriptural words used in saying a grace or blessing over food). The writer is opposing a prevalent tendency towards vegetarianism and abstinence from wine upon religious grounds. His language is strong, but his point is sane and timely ; Christianity or as he calls it *The Truth* lifts men above all such prohibitions and taboos, whether of Jewish or Oriental origin. Nothing is common or unclean upon the table, if a believing man is able to say grace over it sincerely, that is, to bless God for it and so to take it as a gift provided by Him. This is an approach to the connexion between ' charis ' and creation, the nearest in the NT ; εὐχαριστία (see above, pp. 286 ff.) is employed with a sense of what ' charis ' denoted, i.e. in the broad sweep of the term, God's goodness in all healthful food provided through His universe. Since Paul had argued about such scruples, a gnostic form of asceticism had arisen which, like Hindu asceticism ancient and modern, was based on a false philosophy of the universe, and the writer properly feels it his duty in Paul's name to warn the Church against its tenets and rules.

In writing οὐδὲν ἀπόβλητον the writer, as has been suggested, may have had in mind a Homeric phrase about the gifts of the gods—

In no wise are the glorious gifts of the gods to be tabooed (οὐκ ἀπόβλητ' ἐστί), Given by their goodwill.

This may have been proverbial, once the unedifying context of the saying (Iliad iii. 65 f.) was forgotten. Voltaire recalls the Homeric word in order to launch a naughty stroke at the theological disputants of his day, by reminding them that after all Homer had been before them in mentioning " la grâce efficace et gratuite." [1]

(*d*) It is an advance, however, when the writer brings grace into line with the sacrament of baptism. Here indeed he was only following a traditional belief, for although Paul never spoke directly of grace and baptism together, and though even in First Peter (iii. 21) the two ideas are not linked together, yet in Titus iii. 4–7 we have a so-called 'faithful saying' quoted, one of the Sure Sayings already current in the Church, which associated grace with this sacrament. The writer is contrasting life before Christ with life after faith in him ; the former spelled moral ruin, the latter is safety due to him alone, with moral energy flowing from it. All is of grace, and grace regenerates life. " After the kindness (or goodness) and love (φιλανθρωπία, affection) of God our Saviour appeared (ἐπέφανη), he saved us, not for any good deeds of ours but out of his own pity for us (κατὰ τὸ αὐτοῦ ἔλεος) by the water that means regeneration and renewal under (literally 'of,' i.e. effected by) the holy Spirit which he poured upon us richly through Jesus Christ our Saviour, that being justified by his grace we should become heirs (κληρονόμοι) to the hope of life eternal." The writer or rather the Saying which he cites has readers in mind who would understand incorporation into the Family of God through the medium of a lustral rite better than any other interpretation of the sacrament. The truth that the Christian life begins in an act of free favour on the part of God had been conveyed by the metaphor of adop-

---

[1] The phrase is Christian, but the practice of saying thanks over food was taken over by the primitive Church from the devotional tradition of Judaism. A contemporary apocalyptist, probably a Jew, takes this habit as a primary note of genuine religion. " Blessed among men shall they be who on earth have showed love to the Great God by blessing Him before they eat and drink " (Sibylline Oracles, iv. 26 f.).

tion, but a closer and more popular expression lay in the religious idea made familiar by cults of the day. None of these had anything so decisive as Christian baptism, but several, in their solemn rites of initiation, enjoined a sort of immersion into the fellowship of a ' saviour ' deity, with some assurance of life eternal. This high privilege of incorporation into the life of the deity, often represented in crude forms of ritualism but generally through sprinkling or ablution of the body, was graciously provided for worshippers, who, bathed, sometimes more than once, and thereby admitted to a new life, looked forward to salvation after death. It is in terms of this prevalent religious practice that the Sure Saying is expressed ; it unites the older Pauline view of justification by grace with the popular idea of rebirth and renewal through baptism as the saving process.

From the tone of Paul's argument in Romans vi. 2 f. it is plain that his teaching about baptism did not always carry with it a due ethical impact upon the moral conscience. Our author therefore prefers another interpretation which had become current in the Church ; while loyal to the central truth of justification by the grace of God as his great master had taught (though, if Paul had written the sentence, he would surely have put in a word about faith), he finds it needful to make this intelligible to ordinary Christians by having recourse to the popular ideas of re-birth or regeneration and renewal through baptism as the saving process. Again, the independence of the writer becomes clear. Just as he declined to accept the pseudo-asceticism that would impose religious taboos on food and drink—for in the primitive Church responsible teachers were not disposed to idealize the East indiscriminately nor to be uncritical in deferring to Oriental mysticism—so here he feels himself free to modify a Pauline interpretation in favour of one more suited to the moral issues of the faith in an environment of Asiatic paganism.

The Saying also shows once more the collocation of ' mercy ' with grace, as practically equivalent ; the words about being ' justified by His grace ' are a Pauline expression for the less

20

technical *saved not for any good deeds of ours but out of his own pity.* Μηδὲ διαφέρει τὸ ἔλεος τῆς χάριτος, is the comment of Theodore of Mopsuestia upon Galatians vi. 15. As for the closing reference to *heirs of life eternal*, it clinches the fundamental thought of undeserved favour. Not only is the initial act of the Christian experience due to God's pure favour, but even those who are renewed and thus committed to a career of moral obedience receive bliss at the end as a gift of God, not as the result of their own achievements. As in Paul and elsewhere, so here, the idea of ' inheritance ' is bound up with that of grace. To become heirs or to ' inherit ' was an early Christian way of declaring that one expected eternal life as a gracious bequest from God. " Inheritance is the enjoyment by a rightful title of that which is not the fruit of personal exertions," [1] and the very right to the title is conferred by God, on members of His Family, or Household.

(*e*) The weight falls on the truly Pauline idea of grace in the similar phrase of 2 Timothy i. 9–10, where the writer speaks of *the God who has saved us and called us to a life of consecration —not for anything we have done but because he chose to do it himself, by the grace* (κατ᾽ ἰδίαν πρόθεσιν καὶ χάριν) *which he gave us ages ago* (πρὸ χρόνων αἰωνίων) *in Christ Jesus and has now revealed in the appearance* (ἐπιφανείας) *of our Saviour Jesus Christ, who has put down death and brought life and immortality to light by the gospel.* The former part of the sentence is Pauline in thought and even in expression, although the gracious purpose of God, i.e. the great favour of His Predestination, is put in terms which commonly apply to actual experience. Paul normally says that God gives His grace to men when they receive the effects of it, as Calvin points out. Whereas here the Gift is pre-temporal. That is, we have the thought of Ephesians i. 3 f., but it is stated differently, though the aim is identical, viz. to emphasize the Gift as utterly undeserved. In the second part of the sentence, with

[1] Westcott, *Hebrews*, p. 168.

its allusion to the incarnation as an 'epiphany' or royal Advent, there is another reflection of the Hellenistic tendency to make 'knowledge' or revelation, with immortality as its supreme content, the dominant interest of the religious quest. This is woven into the strand of the older 'grace-theology.'

Both strands are also combined in a later writing which avowedly takes account of the Pauline letters. In the homily known as the Second Epistle of Peter, the author ends as he begins with a word on grace. Philo had rebuked profane lecturers of his day who dared to believe that the powers of the human mind were self-evolved. This, he protests, is the very spirit of Cain, to claim that " thought and perception and speech are the gift (δωρεάν) of their own souls." The godly know better ; the spirit of Seth, that good man, ascribes them to grace divine (χάρισι ταῖς θείαις, Post. Caini 4). So the author of Second Peter starts from the divine grace of ' knowledge ' and instantly connects it with moral purity. He prays, *May grace and peace be multiplied to you by the knowledge of our Lord, explaining that the Lord's power divine has bestowed on us every requisite for life and piety by the knowledge (ἐπίγνωσις) of him who has called us to his own glory and excellence, bestowing on us thereby promises precious and supreme, that by means of them you may escape the corruption produced in the world by lust, and participate in the divine nature* (i. 2–4). The language is saturated with Hellenistic thought, but the Christian ideas are not evaporated. Neither are they obliterated in the closing admonition, *Grow in the grace and knowledge (γνῶσις) of our Lord and Saviour Jesus Christ* (iii. 18). Grace here is not to be flattened into ' gift ' (" in donis," Erasmus) ; it retains its specific meaning. Two Greek words for knowledge are used, but there is no distinction between them. The argument is that everything in the religious life of Christians from start to finish is the gift of God, that this Gift involves moral passion on the part of those who are privileged to receive it, and specifically that ' knowledge ' (γνῶσις), the vaunted aim and proffer of so many contemporary cults, was satisfied in Christianity as a religion of grace ; or rather, as we might say, since the writer makes no use of grace elsewhere, the traditional term ' grace ' is reset by being interpreted in the light of such ' knowledge.' But it is ' knowledge ' of the Lord ; the OT sense of enjoying an inner fellowship with God as revealed has

not been lost.   There is indeed a trace of the tendency to interpret
Christianity as a revelation which consists essentially in immortality,
as in the eucharistic prayers of the Didachê, but we are still far away
from the later tendency to resolve grace into illumination or the enlightenment of susceptible natures.   Before the second century ran out,
this tendency had gone so far in certain circles that the original meaning
of ‘ Jesus receiveth sinners ’ was almost forgotten.[1]   The author of
this homily believes that the divine grace works through the knowledge
of our Lord for participation in the divine nature by escape from the
moral corruptions of the world.   But this hope of immortal life is
vitally connected with adherence to the Lord as deliverer within the
moral sphere.   As *the grace* of Jesus Christ implies forgiveness and
moral renewal, *the knowledge* which is collocated with it is not mere
speculative insight into truth or an ecstatic grasp of mystical aeons.
Nor is it reserved for a coterie of cultured souls.   The author in his
own way is true to the apostolic faith which he claims to represent,
when he implies that grace is for all, not only as a privilege but as a
moral demand which obliges Christians without exception to take sin
and evil seriously.   As Christian ‘ knowledge ’ has two sides, the author
of the Pastorals was able to put this truth effectively in 2 Timothy ii.
19 ; ‘ the foundation of God standeth sure, having this inscription, *The
Lord knoweth them that are his,* and, Let everyone that nameth the
name of the Lord depart from iniquity.’

The significance of the Pastorals is therefore twofold.
They witness to a steady maintenance in some circles, not
only of the original language but of some essential ideas of
Paul about grace as the saving action of God in Jesus Christ.
At the same time they mark the main lines of the later development ; all these characteristics of the Pastorals, the collocation
of ‘ mercy ’ with grace, the connexion of grace with baptism,

---

[1] Harnack, *Dogmengeschichte*[5], i. 190.   But there were evangelical voices.
In the rhapsody of Clement (Cohort. xii.), for example, Jesus in heaven is
represented as calling to men, “ Come unto me, I desire, I do desire, to impart
to you this gracious boon (χάριτος), supplying you with the full favour of
incorruption ; I bestow on you (χαρίζομαι) the Logos, the perfect knowledge
(γνῶσις) of God, my very self.”

the careful mention of moral goodness as the outcome and test
of grace, and the new outlook upon knowledge and immortality, are in varying degrees to be encountered as we
survey the other literature of the period, i.e. between the
death of Paul and the opening of the second century.

III

GRACE IN THE EPISTLE OF JAMES

THE concern about Christian morals which is reflected in
the references to grace within the Pastorals reappears
in a writing which verbally differs from Paul's traditional
teaching upon faith.   The epistle of James is a homily by
some teacher of the Church who from the Wisdom literature
in which he was trained selects a reference to grace.   It is the
only OT allusion to grace which is found in the NT, and for
that reason as well as for the use he makes of it the argument of
James is notable.   Three of his cardinal terms are faith,
trial ($\pi\varepsilon\iota\varrho\alpha\sigma\mu\delta\varsigma$), and wisdom ($\sigma o\varphi\iota\alpha$), but he never discusses
faith and grace, nor does he use ' grace ' in heartening his
readers under the strain of faith in life, as contemporaries like
the writers of Hebrews and First Peter do.   He has more to
say about $\chi\alpha\varrho\dot\alpha$ than about $\chi\dot\alpha\varrho\iota\varsigma$; instead of using the *grace
and peace* formula, he even retains the archaic $\chi\alpha\dot\iota\varrho\varepsilon\iota\nu$ in the
introduction to his homily.   His affinities to the Wisdom
teaching, where grace is by no means a central idea, helped to
determine his choice of other terms for his Christian message.
In point of fact, there is only one passage in the Book of Proverbs where ' grace ' has a truly religious significance, and
James' solitary and almost incidental allusion to grace is linked
to that verse.

In iv. 1–6 he cites this couplet from Proverbs iii. 34, either
(*a*) to explain how prayer succeeds or (*b*) in order to illustrate
an argument based upon a somewhat obscure interpretation of
another ' scripture,' whose exact origin no man knoweth unto
this day.   On the latter view (*b*), the writer is pleading for a
whole-hearted devotion to God (in ver. 4–5).   ' Whosoever
will be a friend of the world is the enemy of God.   Do you
think that the scripture saith in vain, " For the spirit that

He made to dwell in us He longs jealously ? " (Or, " the Spirit that He made to dwell in us longs, yearns for us even unto jealous envy.") No, (ver. 6) that divine word is not an idle word ; He gives (He does give) more (and more) grace.' Then the writer adds : *thus* (or therefore) *it is said* (in scripture),

> *God opposes the haughty,*
> *but to the humble he gives grace.*

Or, if envy be taken not in the good sense of the divine ' jealousy ' of love, either in the past of an indwelling Spirit which will tolerate no rival in the affections of Christians or as directed to the inward spirit of Christians, but in the lower sense of human envy, then ' the spirit that dwelleth in us ' might be said to be grasping and envious, devoted selfishly to secular interests, as in the AV (' lusteth to envy '), in which case the following words of ver. 6 would describe the divine response to the humble or the devout who, setting their hearts on God alone, receive His grace or favour ; He is the gracious friend of those who have no inner spirit of envious greed or worldly craving.

On the former view (*a*), the words of 4–5 are best taken as a parenthesis or as an aside, and in ver. 6 the writer is picking up the argument of ver. 3. *You* do *ask* God for what you want, you do pray, but *you do not get it* (i.e. something quite legitimate, such as money or health). Why ? *Because you ask* amiss, i.e. *with the wicked intention of spending it on your pleasures* (on self-gratification). Then, after (4–5) a protest that God cannot bear such divided allegiance, which implies that He withholds an answer to such selfish prayers, the writer proceeds to say that God does answer real prayers offered in the right spirit, in the proper attitude of humble faith whereby men rely solely upon Him and seek His favour for His own ends. Thus ver. 6 picks up the thought of ver. 3. *Yet*, though wrong prayers are not answered, *He gives grace more and more*, never grudging His friendship and favour to the humble and the penitent who want above all things His grace ; *thus it is said,*

> *God opposes the haughty,*
> *but to the humble he gives grace.*

Haughty people who pray, if they pray at all, for some private and personal end, which is sought irrespective of others or even at their expense, such self-engrossed persons are outside the sphere in which God answers prayer. In that sphere, whatever God may withhold, He never withholds grace from the whole-hearted, who seek Him and His kingdom first and foremost in this world. The blessing of grace is not for the self-satisfied or the self-engrossed ; it is for those who have no wrong ends in prayer, and it is unlimited. He gives more and more grace.

James has the cardinal idea of grace, i.e. the general belief in God as the source and standard of the good life, but he prefers to express it usually in other terms. The life of moral energy which he stresses is God's endowment, not a means of reaching Him. All comes from God, the great Giver. *Let a man* in need *ask God who gives to all men without question or reproach, and the gift will be his.* . . . *All we are given is good, and all our endowments are faultless, descending from above* (i. 5, 17) ; the Christian life is a regeneration due to *His own will* ; it is His *Word* that *roots itself inwardly with power to save the soul* (i. 18, 21) ; the inspiring spirit of life, with its moral imperatives for faith, is a wisdom *which comes down from above* (iii. 15). Such statements reproduce the essential idea of grace ; God is the giver of all, the first Cause of the religious life, the source of everything that constitutes Christian belief. All that is wanting here is the terminology of grace.

As we have seen, except for a single incidental allusion, the writer never employs the ordinary expressions, and indeed when he does so he uses an archaic phrase (διδόναι χάριν) which was avoided by other NT writers, as it colloquially meant ' to confer a favour,' or in Hellenistic usage ' to gratify.' Χάριν διδόναι is only used by NT writers in quoting Proverbs iii. 34, except in Eph. iv. 29, where (see above, p. 295) it has quite a different meaning (speech between man and man). Grace could be spoken of as ' given,' of course, but the active verb in the LXX phrase does not occur in the NT.

The precise meaning of ' more grace ' depends on the view taken of the context. ' He gives grace ' was in the writer's mind, from the OT citation which he was about to make ; he adds *more* in order to suggest that this grace continued to supply the just needs of the pious.   Hence, e.g. he adds, lower down, a promise for the future :

> *Humble yourselves before the Lord,*
> *and then he will raise you up.*

The words *He gives grace more and more* would then denote an assurance that answers to the humble faith that voices itself in true prayer would extend themselves throughout life. This corresponds to the interpretation already offered.   On the other hand, if the citation from Proverbs be taken in its original sense, grace would mean acceptance with God ; the lowly and humble who prefer God's friendship to that of worldly scoffers are rewarded by having a better, a more worthy, acceptance than the world can give.   *More* in this connexion would contrast the favour enjoyed among the proud with the better favour experienced by those who make God their chief aim and hope.   Or, if the words *He giveth more grace* be connected with what immediately precedes, i.e. with the rendering ' God longs intensely for your spirit,' the argument would be that as He thus makes a high demand upon men so He provides more grace wherewith to meet these requirements for whole-hearted devotion.   This seems more adequate than to adhere to the original sense of the quotation. Probably the writer used the maxim from Proverbs without reflecting on its original sense, simply applying it to the needs of his day quite freely.   *Grace* does not mean here what Paul meant generally by the word ; there is no special reference to the forgiveness of sins, for example.   On the other hand, it does mean more than mere ' acceptance.'   At the same time, whether the words *He gives more grace* are taken with what immediately precedes or with ver. 3, the general sense is that entire devotion to God, exhibited in faith and prayer or in the larger submission of our wills to His, leads to a rich and ever richer supply of His gracious blessing.

'God's grace does not slip into an impure soul, i.e. into a soul rich in lusts and travailing with many a worldly passion.' This remark of Clement of Alexandria (*Quis Dives Salvetur*, xvi.) corresponds to the thought of James. So does the argument of the earlier Clement of Rome (xxx.), who cites the text from Proverbs against people who give way to lustful passion and pride, adding, 'Then let us join those to whom grace from God is given.' Augustine took grace here in the narrower sense of pity ; at the opening of the *De Civitate Dei* he quotes the text from Proverbs to prove that it is God's prerogative to lower pride and to exhibit mercy to mankind, whereas human arrogance affects to exercise this function with its imperial claim ' parcere subjectis et debellare superbos.'

The proud whom James attacks are therefore not self-righteous persons who plume themselves upon their own merits and moral attainments ; theirs is the pride which is self-centred, arrogant, and unbrotherly, and James implies that such a lack of consideration for others, however it may clothe itself in religious forms and even have recourse to prayer, excludes men from the reality of the divine nature which, as Jesus has shown, is merciful love, and which therefore can only impart itself to the spirit of humility and unselfishness. It is not unimportant that James mentions grace as he encourages lowliness of heart and inveighs against pride. This is an indirect corroboration of the truth that the instructed Christian conscience tends to regard pride as the sin of sins. But pride is manifold. Paul met one type of pride by the retort, ' What hast thou that thou didst not receive ? ' James is not thinking of people who took credit to themselves for a good life or who relied on religious privilege ; he is rather indignant at those who actually dared to expect the help of God in order to further their inconsistent aims and plans.

> Yet so much bounty is in God, such grace,
> That who advance His glory, not their own,
> Them He himself to glory will advance.

When Milton wrote these lines, in the third book of *Paradise Lost*, he said something like what James intended by the words, ' He giveth more grace . . . giveth grace to the humble.' For the new and difficult virtue of humility which Jesus had revealed is here and elsewhere in the NT the spirit of those who are conscious that they owe everything to God, and who, with Him as their one hope and end, are therefore disinclined to make selfish demands upon their fellows.

IV

FIRST PETER AN EPISTLE OF GRACE

THE same verse from Proverbs is cited by another homilist, whose mode of thought is rich in grace. Bishop Leighton's first words in his commentary upon the First Epistle of St. Peter are, " The grace of God in the heart of man is a tender plant in a strange unkindly soil " ; he sees the apostle in this homily tending the growth of the plant. The writing known to us as the First Epistle of Peter has indeed several distinct usages of ' grace,' and the majority refer to the unkindly situation of the readers, who, as in the case of Hebrews and James, are passing through rough waters. The trouble, however, is entirely outward. No danger of wrong views is present to the writer's mind, and in this respect the homily differs from Hebrews. On the other hand, he thinks about grace not only as a power and privilege in the present but in connexion with the end ; this eschatological outlook is one of the two characteristic features in his treatment of grace.

Considering the size of the homily, ' grace ' is not infrequent. In fact Bede, who noticed that Peter began with grace and ended with grace and that he ' sprinkled the middle part of his epistle with grace,' naïvely concluded that this was intentional—" ut errorem Pelagianum omni locutionis suae parte damnaret " ! In reality Peter has no doctrinal aim in what he says about grace. It is the practical need of Christians in a period of persecution which moves him to mention grace in his interpretation of the faith, and in particular the need of hope and courage.

(*a*) He speaks of this in a fresh way. When Burke called chivalry " the unbought grace of life," he meant that the chivalrous spirit adorned human life with an ennobling grace. But Peter did not mean this when he observed almost casually (in iii. 7) that the Christian life or hope (for hope is the dominant note of the homily), i.e. all that Christian experience expects, is *the grace of Life*. This is not even, as Erasmus thought, a periphrasis for ' living grace.' ' The grace of Life ' means that Life is a grace. The apostle is urging husbands to honour their wives as also *heirs of the grace of Life*, that is, as accounted worthy by God of life eternal. ' Life ' here is eschatological, and one feature of Peter's mind is that he is the first Christian thinker who extends ' grace ' to include the eschatological blessings of God. It is also significant, though less significant, that he develops the idea in connexion with the trials through which men must pass before they enjoy this final boon. He proceeds to quote a psalm beginning, ' He who would love Life,' in order to show not only that this supreme blessing is an inheritance for God's people, assigned to them as a gracious possession, but that it also involves a moral course corresponding with God's requirements. *The grace* or boon *of Life* (here in its pregnant sense) is indeed a free gift, but it is enjoyed only upon certain conditions. Peter has his own way of stating what Paul said about grace opening up into a life of devotion and obedience, but the thought is identical. He is specially concerned with the suffering to which his churches were exposed, for example, and this leads him to assure them that their loyalty will be rewarded. *Once you have suffered for a little while, the God of all grace who has called you to his eternal glory in Christ Jesus, he will repair and recruit and strengthen you* (v. 10). The sure aim of God's grace, i.e. the final glory of his Life, will not be frustrated by any passing persecution on earth. Those who look for this triumph and for rallying experiences on the road to it need not shrink from the suffering involved in upholding the faith ; indeed they must not, if their hope is to be valid.

It is such considerations which make the apostle close by saying that he had written his short pastoral letter, *these few lines of encourage-*

ment, to testify that this is what the true grace of God means (v. 12)·
Unlike Paul, Peter has no heresy to meet.   When he says ' the true
grace of God,' he has in mind doubts about its genuineness which
might be started by painful experience of what it cost to be a Christian.
It is the practical aspect with which he is concerned.   The Christian
hope is not a bright illusion, but a real revelation of God's sure eternal
purpose which no hardship can upset ; this is the conviction which he
has set himself to *testify*, enlisting a strong term ($\dot{\epsilon}\pi\iota\mu\alpha\varrho\tau\nu\varrho\tilde{\omega}\nu$) which
no other NT writer uses.   ' Such, such as I have attested and described,
is the real grace of God.   *Stand* fast *in that grace*.'   For the present
faith and fellowship of Christians, to which they have been called by
God through Christ, is the sure standing ground for confidence and
loyalty during the rough, brief interval before the End.   Paul had been
obliged to warn the Colossians against the dangerous tendencies of a
local heresy, which threatened to make them forget *what God's grace
really is* ($\tau\dot{\eta}\nu$ $\chi\acute{\alpha}\varrho\iota\nu$ $\tau o\tilde{\nu}$ $\theta\epsilon o\tilde{\nu}$ $\dot{\epsilon}\nu$ $\dot{\alpha}\lambda\eta\theta\epsilon\acute{\iota}\alpha$).   But when Peter speaks
of $\dot{\alpha}\lambda\eta\theta\tilde{\eta}$ $\chi\acute{\alpha}\varrho\iota\nu$ $\tau o\tilde{\nu}$ $\theta\epsilon o\tilde{\nu}$, he has no speculative theory about grace in
his mind.   It is possible that *Stand in that grace* is an echo of Paul's
description of the Christian position as *this grace where we have our
standing*, but there is no contrast between this and any alternative theory
of acceptance with God.   His affinity with Paul rests not on anything
like what preceded Romans v. 2 but on the words that follow—*and we
triumph in the hope of his glory.   Not only so but we triumph even in
our troubles.*

   (*b*) Peter, however, expresses this by the thought that it
is the divine Call which lends security to life.   It is the motive
for good behaviour (i. 15), the inspiration of right living (' who
called you out of darkness into his marvellous light,' ii. 9),
the summons even to endure hardship (ii. 21, iii. 9) on the
way to bliss, and above all the guarantee of ultimate victory
(v. 10).   Such a Call is the Predestination of God entering
human experience, graciously creating a church which is the
object of the grace divine.   It issues from *the God of all grace*,
i.e. the God who is fully able and willing to equip his loyalists
from first to last.   Peter does not speculate about the origin
of this grace or salvation in eternity, however.   The new

feature in his treatment of the subject is that he describes it as a subject of intense interest to the OT prophets. The thought indeed is not new, but the expression is. 'Prophets themselves searched and made enquiry about that salvation of your souls, prophets who prophesied about the grace that was meant for you ' (i. 10). This is said in order specially to reassure such readers as were non-Jews by birth ; they may be certain that the religious hope to which they cling is not an upstart notion, but rooted in the sacred Bible ; the favour of gentiles receiving salvation had been part and parcel of God's purpose from of old. 'Grace' here again has the super-national range which we have already noted. How favoured the readers should think themselves that even inspired men of old had been deeply fascinated by their coming privilege of membership in God's chosen People ! More than that. This *grace* to which they had been called by God is bound up with 'the sufferings of Christ and his afterglory' (ver. 11), and it is a deep thought of the epistle that the sufferings of Christ which ended in glory had not merely been, as Monnier puts it, 'le fait decisif qui ouvre une ére nouvelle ' ; they were to be shared by all who bore his name and hoped for his salvation or grace at the end. Again, this is a thought akin to Paul, but it is put in a fresh form ; the experience is stated in terms coined or selected often by Peter himself, terms which are in their own way simple and effective.

(*c*) This hope of grace or final salvation, which rests on the resurrection of the Lord and is to be realized at his return, or as Peter prefers to call it, 'at his revelation' (ἐν ἀποκαλύψει), is held out as the saving encouragement for Christians during the sharp, short interval before the end. *Put your hope for good and all* (τελείως, 'trust perfectly,' as Tyndale renders it) *in the grace that is coming to you* (φερομένην) *at the revelation of Jesus Christ* (i. 13). Peter uses a common Greek idiomatic phrase, instead of the usual 'given' or bestowed, as we might speak of a boon to be conferred or of a blessing that is 'coming' to us. The objective and inclusive sense of *grace* is obvious here. It means more than power to endure and overcome present difficulties in this connexion ; so deeply does Peter identify ' grace ' with ' salvation ' in its full sense that he employs the term at this point to express what he has already spoken of as ' the inheritance reserved in heaven for you who are kept by the power of God unto salvation ready to be revealed at (or, in) the last time,' or as the salvation which at the end proves to be the outcome of loyal faith (i. 3–9). Φερομένην is a unique method of laying emphasis upon the undeserved character of the final grace, but he makes this practical point even as he bids Christians deserve it by resolute loyalty and obedience. Luther is right in explaining that this prized boon ' wird uns fur die Thür bracht und in die Schooss gelegt ohne unser Zuthun oder Verdienst.' Still, the outlook is eschatological, and φερομένην means not ' quae offertur ' (as in the Vulgate) but ' offerendam,' as the AV saw (' the grace that is to be brought unto you '), the first of the English versions to do so.

Instead of understanding the present participle in a future sense, some have taken it to mean that ' the grace is ever being brought, and brought in fresh forms, in virtue of the continuing and progressing unveiling of Jesus Christ ' (Hort). But while this is a true thought, it is not the truth which Peter has in mind. Here as in i. 7 ἐν ἀποκαλύψει Ἰησοῦ Χριστοῦ must refer to the final crisis, a crisis which for loyal Christians will prove no crisis but a vindication and a fulfilment of their best hopes and of God's saving purpose.

(*d*) It is almost paradoxical that Peter who thus emphasizes the unmerited nature of this grace should once use the term as a popular equivalent for ' merit.' But this Lucan sense does recur in the heroic argument of ii. 19, 20 : *it is* indeed *a merit* (χάρις) *when from a sense of God* (i.e. as being conscious of God, conscious that this rough experience is His will and that He is present in it to help us through) *one bears the pain of unjust suffering*. The emphatic word is ' unjust ' or wrong-

ful. *Where is the credit (κλέος) in standing punishment for
having done wrong ?   No, but if you stand suffering for having
done* what is *right, that is what God counts a merit*—τοῦτο χάρις
παρὰ θεῷ, that indeed calls for recognition at the hands of God,
it counts with Him as a favour, it wins thanks from Him as a
proof that you are true to your divine calling.   There is no
attempt to offer any philosophy of this, any more than of
Christ's pain.   The patient endurance of suffering which is
undeserved is part of the Christian duty of following the
example of the Lord, the apostle is content to urge, in a
practical manner, and without fear of being misunderstood
he ranks it as creditable or meritorious.   The very use of
κλέος in its common Hellenistic sense of praise or credit determines the sense of χάρις here.   The latter term means more
than a mark of grace ; it is an action or an attitude which,
though no doubt inspired by grace, is considered as deservedly
winning God's favour, ' Idem valet nomen gratiae quod
laudis,' as Calvin tersely put it.   Such a fine spirit as is exhibited in bearing wrongful punishment or smarting under
some flagrant injustice without resentment or bitterness is
described quite naturally as pleasing to God.   It is only a
slight extension of the same thought when Clement of Alexandria in the *Cohortatio* (xi.) tells Christians that by practising
sound moral self-control they can present themselves to God,
' so as to be not only His work but His delight ' (χάρις).

  ' Charis ' as royal favour or requital for services rendered was not
unknown in Hellenistic Greek.   Thus in the rescript of Darius I to
Gadatas, a provincial governor in Asia Minor, διὰ ταῦτα κείσεται
μεγάλη χάρις ἐμ βασιλέως οἴκωι.[1]   Similarly ἐξαίρετος χάρις is a
common Philonic phrase for God's particular favour to those who are
morally earnest (e.g. De Mut. Nomin. v), and the pious eunuch or
childless man in Wisdom iii. 14 is promised a choice favour, in the
shape of bliss within the heavenly sanctuary, for having lived a faithful
life (τῆς πίστεως χάρις ἐκλεκτή) ;   God recognizes his merits.   When

[1] Kern, *Inschriften von Magnesia* (1900), 102 f.

Paul once alluded to this idea of recompense, he avoided χάρις, however (see above, p. 247 f.).

(e) The usual variants for grace, such as election and inheritance, are employed freely. The homily is addressed to those *whom God the Father has predestined and chosen, by whose mercy they have been born anew,* and *born to an inheritance* reserved for them in heaven. Peter applies to them the language of the prophet ; they are *the elect race, the consecrated nation, the People who belong to Him,* their *faithful Creator.* But when he comes to speak of the service required within the community or church, he needs ' grace ' and no other word for his counsels. It is to reinforce the plea for a humble spirit among Christian ministers as essential to pastoral influence and authority, that he warns them (in v. 5–6) against an overbearing temper by citing the verse from Proverbs (see above, p. 315 f.).

> ' The haughty God opposes,
> but to the humble he gives grace.'

It is true that this is at once widened into a general word on submissiveness to God as the one safe attitude in a period of persecution, but Christian service within the Church is the original thought in mind ; only those who *put on the apron of humility to serve one another,* i.e. who refrain from pride towards their fellow-Christians as well as towards God, only they receive the favour of His aid. What this aid is, he has already indicated in iv. 10–11. ' As every man has received a gift or talent (χάρισμα), so you must serve one another with it, thus proving yourselves efficient (this is what ' good ' means, as a rendering of καλοί) stewards of God's manifold grace.' Gifts or faculties of service are as much due to God as the Christian life itself. Such is the underlying thought of the passage. Any tinge of domineering or even of the ' superior person,' he means, is fatal to Christian service ; it is only in the humble consciousness of dependence upon God that effective help is rendered within the Church. *If anyone renders some service* to the community, *it must be* not in virtue of his own achievements or with any desire to show off his powers, but *as one who is supplied by God with power* (note the connexion of ' grace ' and power again), *so that in everything God* (not the gifted man himself) *may be glorified through Jesus Christ.* The opposite of ' grace ' is self-display, just as in the other passage it is self-assertion. This conception of grace and χάρισμα is thoroughly Pauline, as we have already seen, though Peter does not use χάρισμα with reference to any ecstatic gifts. But the words about being *stewards of God's manifold* (ποικίλης) *grace* are by themselves. They bring out the double idea of a Christian dispensing what his Lord has provided, i.e. depending on Another for what he says in preaching or what he may have to impart otherwise, and also of distributing God's grace or bountiful revelation for the good of others and not for anything like self-praise.

The term for *manifold* was used here intentionally. Peter had already applied it to the trials and temptations of life (i. 6) ; he suggests that there is a rich variety also in what counteracts these trials. But the Greek term in classical usage carried associations of something intricate or subtle or, as we say, cunning ; and this may have been present to the writer's mind when he wrote i. 6. Some early texts (ℵ A) and versions insert ποικίλης in iii. 7, as though Peter wrote ' the manifold grace of Life,' but this is a homiletical echo of iv. 10.

What he means by ' the grace of Life ' corresponds to χάρισμα in the *Acta Justini* v. (πᾶσιν τοῖς ὀρθῶς βιώσασιν παραμένει τὸ θεῖον χάρισμα μέχρι τῆς ἐκπυρήσεως τοῦ παντὸς κόσμου), and the conception of χάρισμα as the preaching of the gospel reappears in the Letter from the churches of Lyons and Vienne (Euseb. H.E. v. 1) where the Phrygian Alexander is οὐκ ἄμοιρος ἀποστολικοῦ χαρίσματος).

(*f*) Peter thus exhibits an independent conception of grace at two points. On the one hand (*a*) he regards grace as the subject of the OT prophets, and on the other (*b*) he looks forward to grace as an eschatological blessing. The latter point of view is formally quite different from that of Paul, who looks forward to the end as the completion of sonship or salvation but never of grace ; grace for Paul is so completely manifested in the death and resurrection of Jesus Christ, so fully experienced here and now in the life of the Church and of individual Christians, that he does not make it an object of hope.   According to Paul, believing men have their standing in grace and ' rejoice in hope of the glory of God.'   Peter also holds that Christians have their standing in grace and that glory awaits them as they are loyal to their position (v. 10, 12), but grace is for him not so exclusively identified with the redemptive relationship of God and man, and therefore its wider connotation of divine blessing bestowed on life through the revelation of Jesus Christ enables him to speak of it in connexion with the final manifestation of the Lord as well as with his redeeming action upon earth.

The *grace* or favour of Life (iii. 7, 10) is a boon to be bestowed at the end, when Christ arrives (i. 13) ; in its fulness it is eschatological. The thought is common, but Peter, apart from the Didachê (x. 6), is the one authority for the use of ' grace ' to express it.   Others prefer ἔλεος (Judas 21, Hermas : *Sim.* iv. 2) or some other equivalent, and one pious soul reflects that the final bliss is beyond thought or speech. " What are the things prepared for those who await Him ?   The Creator and Father of the ages alone knows how great and fair they are ! " (Clem. Rom. xxxv. 3).

As for the former (*a*) aspect, it reflects no more than the conviction that the purpose of the gospel has been from the beginning.   Paul also believed that his message of redemption was attested by the law and the prophets, but he carefully avoids mentioning grace until he comes to the historical revelation of Christ.   Whereas Peter, believing that the OT is substantially a Christian book, puts this in the form of a statement that the prophets under the influence of the Spirit ' prophesied of the grace ' that was coming to the Christian Church.   Again we notice that while ' grace ' is being widened to include the content of the Christian religion, the vital truth is still retained, viz. that God gives and comes to man through Jesus Christ alone, although Peter never speaks of *the grace of the Lord Jesus Christ*, and connects grace as favour or saving aid with God pre-eminently.

V

ANOTHER VIEW OF GRACE AND THE END

THE belief in election, especially in its more apocalyptic setting, raised one problem, which was answered by a vivid hope. It was the problem of what may be termed Grace and Time. This arose partly out of the philosophy of history which the thought of grace involved. The Christian looked ahead as well as behind. He saw the grace of God in the far past, even in the eternal purpose which preceded history. But the future confronted him, especially in relation to two issues : the development of God's purpose in the world as a mission of grace, and the situation of the faithful exposed to cruel persecution. Would there be time for the former, and if so, how much ? Or again, could not the end be hastened in the interests of the latter ?

(*a*) In Justin's First Apology (xxviii.) he argues that if the punishment of Satan and his followers seems to be deferred, " this is for the sake of the human race, since God knows that some, some even yet unborn, are still to repent and so be saved." This was a century after Paul wrote. By that time the early Church was perplexed by the apparent delay in the fulfilment of primitive promises about the second Advent, but Justin seeks to interpret this in the light of God's dominant interest in repentance and salvation. The elect, he assumes, have not yet all come upon the scene. Till that happens, no final crisis of the world can take place. The long delay is really due to God's purpose of saving grace. Paul himself at one point uses a similar conception (Rom. xi. 25, 26), when he argues that some time must elapse before the full number of the elect gentiles enters the Church. But apart from this eschatological outlook, which is here adopted for a special purpose, the apostle emphasizes the fact that repentance as the condition of salvation is the end of God's kindly favour. Instead of a man presuming on this, he ought to turn it to moral profit, mindful of the divine object in such dealings. He apostrophizes a complacent Jew, who is content to think of God's doom as falling on ' sinners of gentiles ' for their misdeeds beyond the pale, and who at the same time is careless about the very same vices in his own life. *Do you imagine you will escape God's doom ? . . . Or are you slighting all his wealth of kindness* (χρηστότητος), *forbearance, and patience ? Do you not know his kindness is meant to make you repent* (Rom. ii. 4)? It is the thought which Bonaventura lifted to a higher level when he wrote,

> Tu amans paenitentiam
> Corda trahens per gratiam.

This teaching of the apostle upon the divine forbearance made a deep impression on the later church. One proof lies in the homily known as Second Peter. The anonymous author bids men *consider that the longsuffering of the Lord means salvation ; as indeed our beloved brother Paul has written to you out of the wisdom vouchsafed to him, speaking of this as he has done in all his letters.* The writer found in these letters, as he says, *some knotty points*, but there was no difficulty about understanding Paul's message about the grace of repentance. Some things might be hard to be understood, but not this, and it was a timely message still, he was convinced.

It was applied even to the repentance of Christians under persecution. Thus at Lyons and Vienne some recanted, but ' God desiring not the death of a sinner deals kindly with men for repentance (ἐπὶ τὴν μετάνοιαν χρηστευομένου),' and so gave them the opportunity of recanting their recantation, like Cranmer, and dying bravely for their faith.

(*b*) The original thought of Romans ii. 4 is like that of Epist. Arist. 188 where the king is advised to imitate " the universal gentleness of God by practising forbearance (μακροθυμία) and treating offenders more mildly than they deserve, thereby turning them from wrongdoing and leading them to repent " (εἰς μετάνοιαν ἄξεις). Whether or not Paul had in mind a passage like Wisdom xi. 24, it reflects the same truth :

> Thou art merciful to all, for over all Thou hast power,
> And thou overlookest (παρορᾷς) the sins of men that they may repent.

A similar view reappears in the interpretation of the delay in the second Advent offered by the writer of 2 Peter (iii. 9), when he invites his impatient readers to think of this as a mark of God's strong and patient grace, not as a proof that He had grown careless of their interests. Paul's teaching on the divine forbearance is extended to the future. The writer argues that *the Lord is not slow with what he promises . . . he is longsuffering* (μακροθυμεῖ) *for your sake, he does not wish any to perish but all to betake them to repentance.* In dwelling on the consideration of God the writer thus connects it with a generous desire for man's repentance ; the reason why the end is not imminent is explained to be this, that God who overrules time for the sake of men has graciously prolonged the interval prior to the end, in order that as many as possible may be included by repentance in the coming salvation. It is interesting to compare this with the exact opposite, in a saying attributed to Jesus, according to which God shortens the interval of waiting out of consideration for people who otherwise could not stand the strain of the pre-messianic persecution. Since the calamities which, on the apocalyptic view, preceded the messianic climax were not simply to be witnessed but also to be borne by the faithful, the encouragement held out to them is twofold ; they are assured that the delay has been foreseen by God and that He has actually shortened the period of exposure to hardship for their sakes. *Those days shall be days of misery, the like of which has never been, from the beginning of God's creation until now—no and never shall be. Had not the Lord cut short those days, not a soul would be saved alive ; but he has cut them short for the sake of the elect whom he has chosen* (Mark xiii. 19–20, Matt. xxiv. 21–22).

This apocalyptic saying about the elect is omitted in Luke, but he preserves a similar word in xviii. 9, 10 : *Will not God see justice done to his elect who cry to him by day and night ? Will he be tolerant (μακροθυμεῖ) to their opponents ? I tell you, he will quickly (ἐν τάχει) see justice done to his elect.* Nowhere else does Luke refer to Christians as the elect, either in the gospels or in Acts. But as elsewhere he pleads that what seems to be delayed fulfilment is a gracious act of God, who seeks to give men every possible chance of repenting, so here he suggests that the faithful must not lose faith in the divine justice as they are cruelly tried. The word reflects the same acute crisis as is implied in the Apocalypse of John.

In post-Christian Judaism the rabbis sometimes raised a similar problem. Thus in Joma 86a, 86b, Sanhedrin 97b, etc., we find a debate on the question whether the coming of messiah depended on the repentance of Israel. When one rabbi argued that the period of redemption depended entirely upon repentance and good works, and when another thought that " if Israel repented for a single day, messiah would come," a third more cautiously said, " messiah will come at his appointed time, whether Israel repents or not, but if they repented completely, God would send him even before his time."

The notion that prayer might hasten the end was not unknown even to the ancient Greeks ; Æschylus in a chorus (Choephor. 464, 465) remarks,

> Allotted fate remains fixed from of old,
> Yet for prayer it might the sooner come.

This happens to be the only passage in the synoptic tradition in which anything is said to be done for the sake of the elect. That God controlled time in the interests of His People was indeed a familiar belief within most circles of contemporary Jewish apocalyptic ; the specific note of this allusion to it lies in the reason given. An Enoch-prediction is cited by Barnabas (iv. 3) to the effect that ' the Lord has cut short the times and days in order that his Beloved would make haste and come to his inheritance.' Here the Beloved is messiah, but in the synoptic tradition it is for the sake of the elect that God thus acts. It is not quite obvious what is meant by the fear that none would be saved, were it not for such a merciful shortening of their trial.   Either it refers to their risks of life or to the danger of apostasy, the deadly sin.   In any case the point is that God orders time in the interests of faith.   This is a distinct note of grace, whether the ordering takes the form of shortening the sharp interval of pressure or of prolonging the period for the sake of repentance.

The Petrine epistle represents a less acute situation than is behind the synoptic saying or such a position of eager hope as is voiced in the Apocalypse of John where the cry of anguish is, ' How long ? ' and the welcome reassurance is that *there shall be no more delay* (as e.g. in x. 6, χϱόνος οὐϰέτι ἔσται).   But both interpretations of history rest upon a conviction that with God the interest in man's repentance and salvation is supreme, so supreme that He will (it is assumed that He can) alter the course of time and either extend or reduce the length of the decisive period.   Such an act of His will is regarded as due to His gracious consideration for man, a consideration so dominant in His mind that it determines the course of history.   Milton in his magnificent lines upon Time anticipates the day when

> Long Eternity shall greet our bliss
> With an individual kiss,
> And Joy shall overtake us as a flood,

when the just, their mortal course over, shall sit

> Triumphing over Death and Chance and thee, O Time.

The apocalyptic hope in the first century had the same outlook, though in a fore-shortened vision.   Religious faith, especially in the circles of apocalyptic piety, took time seriously but not too seriously ; it took nothing so seriously as the will of a gracious God, and naïvely believed that He would shorten or lengthen time in the interests of His people. The passages which have been just under review indicate a conviction that the saving will of God would never permit time-periods any more than Nature (this is one of the interests of the belief in miracle) to interfere with the needs of the soul.   When it was a question of faith or of loyalty, the gracious God could and would dispose of time as of anything else that hindered His creatures.

VI

GRACE AND GNOSTICISM

THE problem of grace and the good life was raised in a subtle form when gnostic mysticism began to move within the gentile churches upon an evangelical basis. Already we have distinguished three lines of criticism levelled against Paul's teaching of grace. (*a*) Some suspected it as dangerous to morals. By thus ignoring the Law, did not the apostle expose his converts to the perils of lax living ? Was it safe to set aside the Law, which, as the experience of the Jewish mission to proselytes had shown, was one of the surest methods of safeguarding the soul against pagan deterioration ? Such was the argument of the conservative Jewish Christians at their best ; these Chassidim of the Church felt a conscientious concern for the ethical health of gentile Christians. (*b*) Then there were the radicals of the Spirit, whom Paul evidently met in the Galatian and the Corinthian churches ; their criticism was that Paul did not go far enough, that the inner light of the Spirit was sufficient by itself, and that any place given to the Law or to an ethical interpretation of the Law was inconsistent with the real gospel. Perhaps affected by some mystical tendencies in contemporary Hellenism, they objected to any preaching of grace which insisted on moral duties and discipline instead of trusting wholly to the freedom of the Spirit in the believing life.

(*c*) While these two criticisms were tabled by some inside the Church, outsiders like the Jews argued that Christians who accepted Paul's teaching on grace might as well say, " Why should we not go on sinning that good may come of it ? If God pardons sin freely by His grace, there is no harm in breaking the Law. On the contrary, such offences will only serve to show His grace on a still greater scale." This

was resented by the apostle as a calumny. Whether he had
in mind not only a Jewish slander but also some expression of
(*a*) or of (*b*), it is difficult to say. The likelihood is that, on
the latter hypothesis, it formed a special development of (*b*).
But the antinomian interpretation did not become really
dangerous until it was based on a dualistic view of flesh and
spirit, such as is reflected later in the Pastorals and the epistle
of Judas. There is no clear evidence that in this developed
form it was present to the mind of Paul. From the tone of
his argument in Romans (iii. 8, vi. 1, 15) it may be inferred
that he was simply dealing with a current objection to his
gospel on the score that it endangered or ignored morals.

But speculative mysticism made this line of attack more
dangerous. Ultra-spiritual persons might and did allege
that the free man, saved by grace, could do as he pleased, since
any moral restrictions were part and parcel of the legal system
from which God had rescued the saints. When creation was
viewed as somehow the work of an inferior Spirit, then the
inference was drawn that the senses and the flesh need not
be regarded as vital to the truly spiritual life. A speculative
basis was thus afforded for a dualism which affected morals
seriously. It was against a phase of this antinomian movement
that Judas wrote his indignant tract. He seems to have met
teachers belonging to an incipient phase of the gnostic movement, who evidently held that moral distinctions were the
work of lower angels and subordinate powers within the
universe, and that perfection belonged to the spirit of the
elect, irrespective of anything that they did in the flesh. The
prophet denounces them as *impious creatures, who pervert the
grace of our God into immorality* (ἀσέλγειαν) *and disown our sole
liege* (δεσπότην) *and Lord Jesus Christ* (probably by some
docetic view about him which infringed belief in his true
humanity on earth). He deliberately uses the term ' grace '
here, as it denoted that freedom of the Christian from the Law
which forgiveness brought in its train. The Pauline stamp

of the word is unmistakeable in this protest. The teachers whom Judas attacks claimed that true freedom of the spirit, bestowed by God's grace, exempted a saint from any ethical regulations and restrictions upon bodily passions or impulses, since these belonged to the sphere of the flesh which was not only inferior but morally indifferent. Apparently some had acted on the theory that fleshly instincts and impulses could be indulged freely, without any effect on the free forgiven spirit. This ethical perversion went back to the same dualism which led them to shrink from associating the Lord Jesus with the material flesh directly. It is probable that these ultra-spiritualists shared a view like that attributed to Cerinthus, which removed the divine aeon Christ from Jesus before his death just as it refused to identify the divine endowment with him until after his birth. Such spiritual honour paid to the Lord is denounced by Judas as a denial of his true nature. The details of the heresy are obscure, but it is plain that to Judas grace and the full divine nature of the Lord Jesus are inseparable, and also that they are vital to the faith or *common salvation*. This is *the faith once for all committed to the saints*—by which the writer does not mean that there was a complete statement of Christianity, never to be altered, but that the truths of grace and of the Lord's divine nature were essential to the apostolic faith.

It was not exactly this spirit which Newman attacked when he charged the liberals of his day with attempting to ' halve the gospel of God's grace.' What angered Newman in his opponents was their indifference to the moral authority and severe discipline of the Church, not any carelessness in personal life but an aversion to the austere element in the Church's teaching.

> Ye marked it spoke of peace, chastised desires,
> Goodwill and mercy—and ye heard no more ;
> But, as for zeal and quick-eyed sanctity
> And the dread depths of grace, ye passed them by.

But Judas regarded these spiritualists as halving the gospel of grace in such a way as to lose it altogether, by acting upon a super-moral theory of the Christian life. The reference to ' grace ' is all the more significant as he elsewhere in his tract prefers ἔλεος ; he employs a term ' liege ' (δεσπότης) for the Lord which, though (as we know from Philo and Josephus) it was used of God in the Greek synagogues, was avoided by Paul. Yet the movement he is attacking is inexplicable apart from a perversion of Paul's teaching on grace. It has been thought that Judas himself was criticizing the apostle's interpretation of grace as antinomian in its effects. Renan [1] actually suggested that the tract was written as a covert manifesto of the apostle Judas, issued after the dispute at Antioch, one of " ces lettres haineuses " from the conservative party in the Jerusalem church against the heretic Paul, who had dared to bring a railing accusation against St. Peter, and who by his preaching of a free gospel was really making men immoral. The truth in this mistaken estimate lies in the fact that when Judas speaks of grace, he is referring to what Paul meant by the term, but to an antinomian exaggeration of it by some ultra-spiritualists who turned the cry of ' No Law in the Gospel ' into a risky plea for religious freedom from all moral discipline. If any locus is to be sought for the homily, it is probably in Syria, where the Simonian movement employed Paul's language about grace for its own ends.

What we have in this reference to ' grace ' is the earliest indication of a tendency which developed into one form of gnosticism. There was a profound interest in redemption, which appropriated the teaching upon grace, especially as it had been stated by Paul, but it was redemption from the body not of the body. This produced a mystical asceticism, which in turn assumed unmoral or even anti-moral forms. Union with the Deity was conceived by some sects in terms of marriage rather than of re-birth, and the same result followed which is to be traced in cults of the age that were bound up with mystical interpretations of

[1] *L'Apôtre Paul*, pp. 361 f.

the reproductive processes of nature. In the gnostic circles described by Hippolytus, the only theologian produced by the early Roman Church, we come across a full-blown expression of what Judas denounced in his tract. The *Philosophoumena* reveal a piety haunted by sexual images. " On dirait que l'image des relations et même des organes sexuels obséde leur pensée." [1] The danger of this symbolism was that in practice it became more than imaginative. When a gnostic like Valentinus employed marriage symbolism, it was in a high and pure form, but the popular usage dragged it down.

[1] De Faye, *Gnostiques et Gnosticisme*, p. 193.

VII

GRACE IN THE APOCALYPSE OF JOHN

IN the Apocalypse of John, though there are only the two verbal allusions to grace in the opening and closing salutations, the truth of the term is conveyed otherwise. In the prediction of *the holy City descending from God out of heaven* (xxi. 2), Augustine declared there was a vision of grace, ' quoniam caelestis est gratia qua Deus eam fecit' (Civitate Dei xx. 17) ; he marked here in his own way what Sir John Seeley marked at the famous close of his *Ecce Homo*, an expression of the divine creative power. All was of grace, in the prospects and preparing of the divine order. What the prophet expects and what he holds out as an encouragement to tried Christians is the realization of God's full presence with men, not as their achievement but ultimately as His provision for their needs and as the reward prepared for their fidelity. The Apocalypse is a tract for a bad time, and the same truth is expressed in the description of the faithful martyrs who overcame *by the blood of the Lamb and by the word of their testimony* (xii. 11). They had to prove faithful by confessing their faith bravely ; indeed *they had to die for it.* But, the prophet explains, the inspiring source of their triumph lay in the consciousness of redemption, which enabled them to tread pain underfoot and to bear the consequences of their witness. It was through the power as well as the example of Christ's martyr-death that they triumphed. As John had said in the doxology at the beginning of his manifesto, the Church owed everything to Christ : *To him who loves us and loosed us from our sins by shedding his blood to him be glory* (i. 5, 6) ! It is in this passionate devotion to the Lord for his redeeming love, that loyalty as well as inward peace and freedom lie. Faithfulness, in other words, depends upon faith in what the Lord

is and in what, being what he is, he has done in gracious
devotion to his own. Similarly the prophet in imaginative
phrase depicts his churches, for all their forlorn position in
the Empire, as cressets burning because the heavenly Lord
attends to them (i. 20) ; the explanation of their life in this
world is to be found in heaven, in their relationship to Christ
who moves with authority and watchful care over his communities. Such are some of the characteristic ways in which
the grace-idea is embodied by the prophet.

The one passage in which grace is connected with the
Spirit or with angels, i.e. beings, is in the epistolary opening to
the Apocalypse :

grace be to you and peace
from HE WHO IS AND WAS AND IS COMING,
and from the seven Spirits before his throne,
and from Jesus Christ the faithful witness (μάρτυς), *the firstborn from the dead,*
    and the prince over the kings of the earth.

The stately periphrasis for God (who is never the Father of
Christians in the Apocalypse) is at once followed by the
semi-poetic phrase about the seven Spirits, because they stood
next to the deity in the traditional mise-en-scène of apocalyptic
fantasy ; the author puts Jesus Christ last, as he means to
enlarge upon his functions and personality and to address the
final doxology to him. The nearest approach to this order
is in 1 Peter i. 2, but there *grace and peace* are not explicitly
derived from the three as here. The picturesque description
of *the seven Spirits before God's throne* is an archaic touch
borrowed from the symbolism of Zechariah and subsequent
apocalyptic. As the writer's usage shows (iv. 5, v. 6) these
Seven express the divine power active in the world of men on
behalf of faith. They do not correspond to the Spirit, for
the Spirit in the Apocalypse is prophetic. But, as the writer
inserts them in order to suggest the majestic God in action,
it was not inappropriate to indicate that the blessings of grace
and peace flowed from their ministry as part of the divine inter-

22

vention ; in point of fact, they do operate under Christ within the churches (iii. 1), as vital powers of the risen Lord (v. 6). It is prosaic therefore to identify them either with the seven angels of the Presence, known in Jewish speculation, or with the sevenfold Spirit of the later Church, much more to omit them as incongruous. The writer is here putting in a touch of original imaginative power, to fill out his conception of God as the creative source of religious life and as the absolute authority over the universe of men.

Were one to infer anything special about grace in such a unique context, it would be on the lines of associating it with the high power of the divine Spirit. Herrick once wrote :

> God's said to dwell there, wheresoever He
> Puts down some prints of His high majesty ;
> And when to man He comes, and then doth place
> His Holy Spirit or doth plant His grace.

But the Spirit was connected with grace at an early period in the Church. Thus Augustine at one point [1] was so perplexed by the absence of any reference to the Holy Spirit in the opening of Paul's epistles that he felt obliged to assume that ' grace and peace ' was an equivalent for the Spirit. " Gratia et pax quid aliud est quam donum Dei," i.e. the Spirit, since " the supreme Gift of God is the Spirit, which is therefore called ' gratia ' (boon)." When the endowment of divine power was not merely viewed as issuing from the Spirit but also as a semi-equivalent for the Spirit, and when one NT writer (see below) had even spoken of ' the Spirit of Grace, it was not long before grace and the Spirit were co-ordinated in the conception of the divine working upon human nature.

The Apocalypse is full of angels, but the prophet deprecates any worship of angels (xxii. 8 f.). Indeed there are no ' angels and ministers of grace ' in the NT. The saving aid of God is wholly transmitted through Jesus Christ. In the seventh book of Paradise Lost Milton was free to write that

---

[1] *In Rom. incoh. expos.* 11–14. The passages are gathered and discussed by F. Cavallera in *Recherches de Théologie ancienne et médiævale* (1930), pp. 369 f.

> God will deign
> To visit oft the dwellings of just men
> Delighted, and with frequent intercourse
> Thither will send His winged messengers
> On errands of supernal grace.

But Paul was too absorbed in the complete revelation of God through Jesus Christ to entertain any such idea. As a matter of fact, he found belief in angels opposed to belief in grace, from two different sides. One of his counts against the Law was that its origin had been connected with such secondary powers as angels ; unlike the Promise which was given directly by God, the Law had to be *transmitted by means of angels*. He thus reverses the Jewish tradition of the haggada ; instead of the collaboration of angels adding to the prestige of the Law, he considers that it denotes inferiority on the scale of revelation. Again, at a later period, he had to refute a theosophy which was insidiously deflecting some of the Colossian Christians by positing angels or aeons as a needful supplement to the relations between heaven and the soul of man. It was supposed that in creation and providence some angelic beings were active under God, and that they ought to be honoured as such. These *Elemental spirits*, as they are called, may have had something to do with the Law ; if so, this would account for one or two of Paul's allusions. But in any case there was a *cult of angels*, who were believed to be connected with an ascetic discipline by means of which man helped to emancipate his soul from bondage to the material. All this seemed to the apostle to infringe upon the full saving function of Jesus Christ. Consequently, in Colossians as in Galatians, the references to angels are disparaging. Even when such angels were beneficent, the author of Hebrews who, like the prophet John, allowed more to the ministry of angels, is careful to point out how Christ the Son of God is far more than any angel could ever be to the soul of man. He leaves a place for them as *spirits in the divine service, com-*

missioned for the benefit of those who are to inherit salvation, but Paul's sharp repudiation of angels is not thereby modified. Neither writer, not even the author of Hebrews, dreamt of anything like the intercession of angels.

Nor as yet was there recourse to another means of grace. When Maximus was being tortured to death at Ephesus during the Decian persecution for refusing to sacrifice to Artemis, he declared that he did not feel the pain of being scourged, mangled, and burned, ' because the grace of Christ remains within me, and will save me for eternity along with the prayers of all the saints,' i.e. of the martyrs in heaven who pray for him as they look down upon his ordeal.[1] This collocation of grace with the intercession of saints is not common, however.

[1] *Acta Maximi*, ii.

VIII

THE EPISTLE TO THE HEBREWS

THE author of Hebrews shows more originality in treating grace than any other writer of the NT after Paul. As we have found, the urgent problem of grace and the moral life was not always handled in terms of grace. The writer of James discusses the question of faith formal and real (i.-iii.) without any reference to grace. Peter simply warns his churches against abusing their Christian freedom, by telling them, with practical good sense, " Do not make your spiritual freedom a pretext for misconduct, live like servants of God " ; none of his motives (e.g. in i. 13–ii. 17) for a good life is directly linked to grace as grace. Even more striking is the procedure of the teacher who wrote Second Peter. In reproducing the bulk of the tract of Judas, he omits the one reference to grace, although he was dealing with a similar situation. No doubt he introduces grace elsewhere in his homily, but he takes other means of meeting the phenomenon of antinomian laxity in the second century. Clement of Rome does strike out a paradox by reminding Christians that they have ' come under the yoke of grace ' (xvi.) by their adhesion to the Lord Jesus Christ. But it is in writings like the Pastorals and Hebrews pre-eminently that ' grace ' comes to the front in presenting the faith as a moral incentive and security for the forgiven, and the author of Hebrews is the more independent thinker. This so-called epistle ' to the Hebrews,' which is in reality addressed to some group of Christians during the last quarter of the first century in order to reassure them that the Christian faith is the final form of religion, shows originality in its seven references to grace as well as to peace and faith. Two characteristics are noticeable. (*a*) The truth of grace is conveyed often in other terms, and (*b*) the few specific allusions to grace are generally stamped with idiosyncrasies of their own.

(*a*) As the LXX is the religious bible of the writer and his readers, and as he is tinged with Alexandrian philosophy, it is not surprising that the argument or interpretation turns upon the conception of ' covenant.' The line taken is not Paul's. Neither does the writer make any reference to the saying about the new covenant which was embodied in the Eucharist, although the burden of his argument is the same. Nevertheless, in elaborating the continuity as well as the contrast between the two great dispensations of revealed religion in history, he naturally fixes upon this as the most apt category for his thought. ' All is of grace ' is expressed in terms of this, for the implication of ' covenant ' is promises and purposes of God aiming at man's destiny. *Many were the forms and fashions in which God spoke of old to our fathers by the prophets, but in these days at the end he has spoken to us by a Son.* The revelation has always been of grace, and the Son is the final and full embodiment of that grace. In the beginning was the Word of God, and at the end it is God's Word which is everything. But the language chosen by this early Christian thinker is neither Pauline nor Johannine ; the cardinal expression for Christianity as the religion of grace is the new or the eternal covenant (διαθήκη), i.e. a relationship between God and man, a religious order or constitution, founded by God, and inaugurated by some historic act. A covenant means the saving purpose of God entering the history of mankind, whereby God and men live a common life. The rubric is the divine word, ' I will be to them a God and they shall be to me a People.' The first thing in a covenant is the divine ' I will.' On that gracious initiative all rests, the imparting of His grace to men and their service of Him and access to His presence. The essential idea of διαθήκη is grace, for although there are obligations and responsibilities attaching to it, duties binding on men in this Bond of Life, the existence of such a religious order depends on God ultimately. Men do not propose to make a διαθήκη with God, or to negotiate with Him as to its terms. It is always God who makes the covenant. It is His proposal, out of loving favour to men, desiring to have them in fellowship with Himself and to bestow on them the fulness of blessing which means their true life. These are the religious assumptions of ' Hebrews.' There had been in Israel, the author recognizes, a διαθήκη which was true but inadequate. ' The Law made nothing perfect,' i.e. the older covenant failed to realize the religious ideal, and God had to make a new or better διαθήκη, which He did by sending His Son. This is effective and therefore lasting ; it forms the absolute religious relationship of God and men, since it provides for the access of men to God by dealing with past sin (ix. 13–15) and guaranteeing through the sacrifice and intercession of Christ the full communion for which the soul craves. Christ *mediates a new covenant for this reason, that those who have been called* (οἱ κεκλημένοι) *may obtain the eternal inheritance which they have been promised, now that a Death has occurred which redeems them from the transgressions involved in the first covenant.*

Little use is made of election. Ἐκλεκτός is never used. Only those *called* by God receive His promised boon (x. 15) and Christians are once addressed as *partakers of the heavenly calling* (κλήσεως μέταχοι ἐπουρανίου, iii. 1), but there is no problem of Jews and Gentiles before the writer's mind ; his dominant thought is of the Church as the People of God, and it never occurs to him to discuss its relation to the unbelieving world.

In discussing God's promise to Abram (Gen. xvii. 2), " I will make my covenant between thee and me," Philo remarks that " covenants are drawn up for the benefit of those who deserve the free gift " (i.e. what God promises to give in the covenant), " so that a covenant is a symbol of grace, which God sets between Himself as the Bestower and man as the receiver." But, he explains, I shall not enter into further details, as I have already written two treatises on the whole subject, περὶ διαθηκῶν (Mutat. Nomin. vi.). Had these books been preserved among the voluminous tracts of Philo which the Christian Church treasured, it is possible that some anticipations of the covenant-argument in Hebrews might have been found within the speculations of the great Alexandrian. Yet, to judge from the scanty references to the subject in Philo, we hardly feel that the writer of Hebrews owed him much at this point. Our author is too engrossed with the Christian interpretation of sacrifice. As a covenant was inaugurated or enacted by sacrifice, he is really expressing the cardinal idea of grace as it was held by Paul, viz. that grace was manifested in the death of the Lord Jesus for sin and that it meant a living order of fellowship which rested on the divine favour. He does not put grace and the Law into an antithesis, as Paul did. But in his own way he reaches the same end by arguing that the final διαθήκη, by fulfilling all the hopes and promises of the earlier, leaves no place for any relationship to God except on the basis of Christ's gracious ministry. As he looks behind him and around him, he sees God always taking the initiative by His gracious will in history. He is writing to Christians who felt deeply the need of forgiveness if they were to have fellowship with God, and wherever the sense of sin is present there is little need of stressing indebtedness to God as the opposite of moral complacency or of religious self-righteousness. The danger present to his mind is rather that if they do not appreciate fully the decisive covenant of God in His Son, they may (i) either fall away from the faith under the trying ordeal of insults and pagan interference, or (ii) seek to supplement it with irrelevant aids.

It is in the light of these risks that his (b) specific allusions to grace are best understood, particularly in the light of the former (i). The need of encouraging and also of warning his readers as they bent under the strain of opposition, threw up most of the grace-words in Hebrews, beginning with the very first, in ii. 9, where we can overhear an echo of the older interpretation, which Paul had impressed upon the Church, in the passing remark that Jesus tasted death *for everyone by the grace of God.* The writer does not work with the Pauline conception of grace, but here he employs the term to express the divine goodwill and loving favour which lay at the heart of the Christian religion, and it is important to notice that he takes occasion to do so when he is treating the death of the Lord. Suffering, with all, the temptations which it started, was apt to instil into the mind doubts about the saving purpose of God. These the writer seeks to remove by assuring his readers that Jesus, the pioneer of their salvation, had also suffered, had been obliged indeed to suffer, in order to realize the divine purpose. But behind and below all that had happened to the Lord, God's grace had been working ; it had enabled Him to open up the way to God for them, and to identify Himself with those who suffered as they trod the same hard path of faith and obedience. Also, the extension of God's favour to *everyone* is another note of the grace here mentioned. In a word, the extra-national range of grace and its connexion with the death of Jesus, the divine Son, are the two aspects of God's goodwill which the writer seeks to combine.

There is an early and widely supported variant χωρίς instead of χάριτι, which is deeply interesting. But ' apart from God,' on any natural interpretation, does not fit in readily with the text of the passage. Further, it is not forced to connect ' grace ' here with what follows. The writer proceeds, ' For it became (ἔπρεπεν) ' God to make the great Pioneer of salvation ' perfect through suffering '—the suffering of death. It is a daring use of the word ἔπρεπεν. But the writer says that it was befitting or becoming for God to act thus, using a Greek word which in its adjectival form corresponded to the Latin ' decorum.' That is, it carried a suggestion which χάρις conveys, as though the author pled, " But it was a beautiful, a characteristic thing of God to do," to bring men to their true end through the suffering of His Son.

Χάρις was a word with so many facets that, even when it is used by a Christian writer in the deepest of all senses, it sometimes conveys a glimpse of one of its other meanings which is not inappropriate.   This is a case in point.

When the author wrote that Jesus *tasted death for everyone by the grace of God*, he meant more than that the Lord suffered by the kindly permission of God, or simply by favour of God. The whole action was of God, within the course of His eternal grace ; *by the grace of God* covers the divine motive, the mission of the Son, the very methods of suffering, and the wide object in mind.   Some [1] interpret the saying to mean that it was " a grace or signal favour on the part of God " towards His Son to appoint Him to have the honour of dying for all ; " whilst it is a humiliation to die, it is glorious to taste death for others, and by dying to abolish death and bring life and immortality to light."   On this view God was specially gracious to Jesus in giving Him this opportunity and privilege, and the writer's aim would be to show how there was an inner bright side to the outward indignities of the Passion.   But the words are wider, and they ought not to be read apart from the general thought that the suffering of Christ, so far from being accidental or arbitrary, was in keeping with the gracious will of God for men's salvation.   The practical inference is that Christians who have to suffer in their own way should remember that their Lord, in saving them, trod the same path of pain, and therefore has sympathy with them ; furthermore, that as they are called upon to face the shame and loss of trial for His sake, they have access to God's grace in time of need.

(ii) The heroic side of this may be seen in a reference to ' charis ' not as divine aid but as human thankfulness to God. It occurs in a passage which illustrates the writer's habit of regarding fellowship with God as worship.   This he puts in liturgical metaphors, sometimes with a quasi-philosophical turn to them.   The religious interest is to bring out the

[1] See, e.g., A. B. Bruce, *The Humiliation of Christ*, pp. 39 f.

gracious initiative of God, for worship is inconceivable apart
from sacrifice, fellowship is on the basis of forgiveness, and
therefore no one can draw near to God on his own terms. For
the writer it is axiomatic that men cannot on their own initiative, as they please, claim fellowship with the Lord ; He
has provided the means of their approach to Himself. But
once in His presence, they may well take heart, whatever happens in the material order of things. Whatever may be
shaken in the cosmic order, *let us render thanks* (ἔχωμεν χάριν)
that we get (are put in possession of) *an unshaken realm, and in
this way* (by showing our gratitude to the Giver) *let us worship
God acceptably* (xii. 28), for praise offered to God is one of the
two standing sacrifices that in Christianity are *acceptable* to
Him (xiii. 15, 16).

It is the one allusion in this homily to the primitive ' realm ' or
kingdom idea, but the fundamental thought is that of Jesus in the
saying, ' Fear not, it is your Father's good pleasure to give you the
kingdom.' The supreme reason for thankfulness lies in this gift of the
Realm. Since the writer imaginatively conceives the religious life as
worship or access to the presence of the living God, sacrifice forms one
essential feature of this approach, and here it is the thank-offering which
is stressed. It is to be offered in a spirit of reverent awe, but a grateful
appreciation of the privilege and position in which God has set Christians
will relieve them from panic and apprehension as all around them
outside the saving order is shaken and ready to collapse. Thank God,
in the fellowship of the διαθήκη which He has founded, there is a
kingdom which cannot be shaken !

(iii) Elsewhere the grace of God is the Christian religion—
as in xii. 14 f., where it is specially viewed as a calling to
consecration, i.e. to a life which shares the divine life of
holiness. *See to it that no one misses the grace of God* by his
graceless conduct. It is a warning to those already inside
the fellowship, not to outsiders, as if pagans or unbelieving
Jews were being urged not to miss the gospel call. The
writer naturally employs terms like ' holiness ' and ' holy ' in

developing his argument, but it is significant how frequently
he turns to the term ' grace ' in order to stamp some of his
most telling phrases on the mind.   Thus *the throne of grace*
is quite an original phrase (iv. 16) for the presence of the Lord
who is now crowned with glory and honour, heaven being
regarded, as was usual in apocalyptic and rabbinic piety, as a
royal court no less than a temple.   ' Let us therefore approach
the throne (not of might nor of majesty but) of grace with
confidence, that we (suppliants) may receive mercy (ἔλεος)
and find grace to help us in time of need.'   The throne is one
not of judgment but of grace.   Through Jesus Christ we find
favour, the writer means, sympathy with our weakness and
frailty in living the life of God within a world of temptation.
This gracious goodwill shows itself as a timely gift or provision
of mercy and grace.   The two terms are synonymous or
complementary.   ' Mercy ' is the gracious Lord showing
himself ready to welcome suppliants who fear to feel that they
may be left to themselves in temptation or severely judged for
their failures, whilst ' grace ' is the same sympathy shown in
practical aid.   One may make such a distinction as this, and
yet it is too sharply drawn.   By *the throne of grace* the writer
means all that God is to Christians in His realm.   Then, in
speaking of what this God does for His people in their straits,
as they find themselves tempted to apostatize, he expands the
word rhetorically by employing a LXX equivalent and then
taking ' grace ' in its specific sense of powerful help.   Those
who are devoted to His will can count upon His pity and
power, or rather on the power of His pity, as they meet the
onset of temptation.   This is the significance of ' grace ' here.

In the text (A) of the LXX which he used, the writer found Prov.
viii. 17 not as in the Hebrew ' they who seek me shall find me ' but
as ' they who seek me shall find grace,' that is favour.   As he turns
his sentence, λάβωμεν ἔλεος καὶ χάριν εὕρωμεν is a single thought,
and both sides of it touch εἰς ευκαιρον βοήθειαν.   He is not suggesting
that mercy (i.e. forgiveness) is followed by grace as a heavenly aid for

the forgiven who try to do better. Delitzsch caught the true meaning of the phrase when he remarked that *the throne of grace* is further explained as ' mercy,' i.e. divine goodwill laying to heart man's unhappy situation and by sympathy making it His own, whilst ' grace,' from a slightly different angle, is the goodwill which " of its own accord turns to one who has no claim upon its regard and devotes itself to befriending him."

The author of Hebrews in a phrase like this conserves the truth of God's majesty and lovingkindness better than the writer of the Pastorals (see 1 Tim. i. 17, vi. 15). By *the throne of grace* he means to represent the same God as the royal Father in whom Jesus taught his followers to believe with trust and awe. It is the accent of genuine reverence that belongs to all the deeper utterances of belief in grace, as for example in the moving stanzas of the Dies Irae :

> Rex tremendae maiestatis,
> qui salvandos salvas gratis,
> salva me, fons pietatis ;
>
> recordare, Jesu pie,
> quod sum causa tuae viae ;
> ne me perdas illa die.

What ' pietas ' and ' pius ' mean here is the divine affection. We have no English term for this noun or adjective. ' Pity ' and ' pitiful ' are too restricted. In the dedication to his translation of the Aeneid, Dryden explains that the Latin pietas " is more full than it can possibly be expressed in any modern language," and this difficulty of translation is intensified by the passage of the word into Christianity as applied to the Lord. ' Gracious ' would almost do in this connexion, especially as the companion note of awe is struck in the first line. Just as Paul, unlike Philo, speaks of ' grace ' and ' the Lord ' together, though he never happens to speak of the ' kingdom of grace,' so the writer of Hebrews touches the chord of deep reverence in his most trustful words. To appreciate the full force of *the throne of grace*, the word *throne* has to be emphasized no less than the word *grace*.

The first line of John Huss's eucharistic hymn, ' Jesus Christus nostra salus ' becomes in Luther's version ' Jesus Christus unser Heiland,' but the Scots Church rendered it ' Our Saviour Christ, King of grace,' for ' King of grace ' was a favourite phrase in Scots religion, as e.g. in their version of the Nunc Dimittis, ' Christ Jesus, King of grace.' The inseparable character of the divine majesty and grace was firmly held by the Scots Church. One of their vernacular hymns sang,

> O glorious God, whose might is infinite,
> Grant me Thy grace whom sin doth hold in thrall,
> To fight against my flesh.

Perhaps this is not far from the meaning of some enigmatic lines in the Agamemnon (183 f.) : δαιμόνων δέ που χάρις βίαιος σέλμα σεμνὸν ἡμένων. They come at the end of a stanza in the chorus where Æschylus is teaching the truth that suffering often leads to wisdom, even in spite of men.

> The heart in time of sleep renews
> Aching remembrance of her bruise,
> And chastening wisdom enters wills that most refuse,

as Walter Headlam rendered the words which end with παρ' ἄκοντας ἦλθε σωφρονεῖν. What follows seems to mean, ' maybe this (i.e. suffering, πάθος) is a kind gift forced on men by the august enthroned divinities," i.e. God has to make men accept a gift like this, almost against their wills. Even if the manuscript reading βιαίως be accepted, the sense might remain the same ; the divinities who rule by constraint (i.e. not allowing men to follow their own ways) are really kind or gracious, as they thus inflict suffering. The author of Hebrews teaches that the divine throne is a throne of grace in another sense indeed ; yet he too associates the tribunal or throne of divine majesty with ' charis,' and elsewhere shows that there are lessons to be learned by suffering under the hand of God just as Paul (see above, p. 164 f) declares in another way that suffering for the Christian may be a real privilege from God.

(iv) But it is not only in encouraging those inclined to waver or falter that the writer coins a fresh phrase about grace. In a sombre warning against apostasy (x. 28 f.) he goes further than in xii. 14 f. Instead of repeating the common phrase ' the grace of God,' he strikes out a new phrase, *the Spirit of grace*. If a man who wilfully rejected *the law of Moses* had to suffer the penalty of death, how much more severely will he be punished *who has spurned the Son of God, who has insulted the Spirit of grace*. Grace here is indeed the Christian religion, and as divine favour it is opposed to the Mosaic law. Also the writer has spoken of Christians as those who at baptism ' tasted the heavenly Gift, and were made partakers of the Holy Spirit, and tasted the good word of God.' But how did he come by the phrase *the Spirit of grace* ? Probably because an OT word occurred to his mind. In this paragraph he seems to be recalling one or two phrases from a prophetic section much read in the early Church on account of its messianic predictions ; I mean, Zech. xii. There the writer would read in his Greek text a promise that God in the last days was to pour out on His people πνεῦμα χάριτος καὶ οἰκτιρμοῦ. It is just possible that this formed the germ of his phrase.

If so, it was not what the prophet had meant, for the original promise is of a human disposition or spirit, which will make the people sue humbly for favour. He anticipates in the softened heart of Israel a tender spirit, penitent, beseeching, and in quest of divine grace. Whereas the writer of Hebrews means the divine Spirit which bestows grace on men. Still, the LXX translators may have taken the Hebrew to mean this, and there is equal uncertainty about the messianic promise in Test. Judah xxiv. 3 : ' he will pour out a spirit of grace upon you.' When Clement of Rome (xlvi) echoed the phrase, he used the OT verb ; ' Have we not one God, one Christ, and one Spirit of grace poured out upon us ? '

This is the last allusion to grace in view of the needs and dangers of Christianity as exposed to outward hardship, this solemn threat against the wilful apostate *who has spurned* (with flagrant contempt) *the Son of God, who has profaned the covenant-blood with which he was sanctified* (i.e. the sacrifice of Jesus which had admitted him to the divine fellowship), *who has insulted the Spirit of grace* (i.e. the Spirit whereby he had been regenerated). Like Peter he does not speak of the grace of the Lord Jesus Christ. Even the closing greeting is simply ' grace be with you all.' Usually he speaks of God and grace together, even though he links grace more directly than Peter does to the sacrifice of Christ. This makes it all the more remarkable that he alone uses the phrase about *the Spirit of grace*.

(v) But grace appears in another antithesis, not as against a religious system in past history but as against a contemporary movement or tendency. ' It is best ' (as Wyclif and the Rheims version after him translate), ' that the heart be established (strengthened, sustained in vigour) with grace, not with meats ' (xiii. 9). *The heart* means the inner life or character. And *grace* here denotes the inward revelation of God's gracious power, as the homily has already indicated. So far there is no difficulty. What is difficult is to understand *meats* (βρώμ-ατα. It is a much debated point, but the context shows that they are sacrificial, and that the contrast is between ' grace ' and some stress on sacrificial food as the alleged means of grace. *The right thing is to have one's heart strengthened by grace, not by the eating of food—that has never been any use to those who have had recourse to it. Our altar is one of which the worshippers have no right to eat :* ' Eat ' is the emphatic word ; the Christian altar provides no βρώματα, no sacrificial meal such as, for example, some of the mystery-cults may have offered, at which the votary partook of consecrated elements and thereby expected to be strengthened or divinized in soul. The words may be a protest against participation in such pagan sacraments. This interpretation is adequate to the language. But there is probably a further protest on the part of this mystical author against some novel doctrine of the

eucharist as an eating of the Lord's body.   He may well have
had in mind a contemporary realistic interpretation of the
eucharist which to him, as a spiritual idealist, was incompatible
with Christianity.   Our altar, he protests, is one of which the
worshippers do not eat.   The Christian sacrifice upon the
Altar in the heavenly temple or higher world, on which everything depends, has no connexion with a meal ; what we have
is the Sacrifice of the Lord, by whose grace our life is upheld,
and this excludes anything like a ritual meal.

IX

THE LUCAN USAGE

IN style and diction the affinities of Hebrews are with a Hellenistic writer like Luke rather than with any other NT author, and Luke also displays remarkable flexibility in handling ' grace.'

Not only does Luke use the term in the second volume of his work but in the Gospel he employs it also. This latter was a new departure, and though scanty it is significant, for it marks a free use of the word in its Old Testament sense and also the wider culture of Luke himself.

Even the non-religious sense of the noun appears (in Acts xxiv. 27, xxv. 3 and 9), of a favour done by one man to another, along with the corresponding verb χαρίζεσθαι (in iii. 14, xxv. 11 and 16) ; ' thanks ' is the ordinary meaning in Luke xvii. 9, and the Aramaic question of Jesus in the Sermon on the Mount, which Matthew renders by an equivalent like *What reward do you get ?*, becomes in Luke, ' What credit or merit is that ? ' (ποία ὑμῖν χάρις ἐστίν, vi. 32, 33, 34).

(*a*) The Old Testament sense of favour, either with God or man, explains allusions or OT reminiscences like those in Luke i. 30, Acts ii. 47, vii. 10 and 46, as well as the words in Luke ii. 52 describing how the boy Jesus *increased in wisdom and stature and in favour with God and man.* But a deeper note is struck in phrases like *He was filled with wisdom, and the favour of God was on him* (Luke ii. 40) and *Great grace was upon them all* (Acts iv. 33), describing the childhood of Jesus and of the Jerusalem church. ' Charis ' may be rendered *favour* in the former passage (where it amplifies ' wisdom,' the archaic expression for the divine element), as it recurs in this sense lower down, though Luke meant by it to convey the idea of God's blessing ; like the young Samuel Jesus was marked out from the first for a religious vocation. But this will not quite cover (*b*) the Acts-passage (where ver. 33 originally followed ver. 31). There is a tense situation at Jerusalem. The group of disciples as they pray feel themselves shaken and stirred by the Spirit ; they proceed fearlessly to preach the gospel, in defiance of the Jewish authorities ; *the apostles gave their testimony to the resurrection of the Lord Jesus with great power, and great grace was upon them all* (i.e. on the whole group, including the apostles). This obviously is the dynamic sense of *grace* which we have already traced, though it is fair to note that, although the fearless courage and the effectiveness thus enjoyed are an answer to the prayer *that Thy servants may be perfectly fearless in speaking Thy word when Thy hand is stretched out to heal and to perform miracles* (29–30), it is not said that such miracles accompanied the testimony at this point (as later in xiv. 3).

In the tragic and heroic episodes of martyrdom ' grace ' retained this meaning. When Polykarp of Smyrna was on his trial, defying the authorities, as he spoke, " he was filled with courage and joy and his face was full of grace," so much so that not only did he himself meet threats stoutly but the proconsul was astounded (*Martyrdom of Polykarp*, xii). So the Smyrniote church testified. Not long afterwards the churches of Lyons and Vienne also bore witness that in their persecution " the Grace of God acted as our general against the devil " by inspiring courage in those arrested for their faith (Eusebius, *H.E.*, v. 1.). Similarly Polykarp (op. cit., vii) asked permission to pray for an hour, when he was first arrested, but " being full of the grace of God he could not cease praying for two hours, so that his pagan hearers were astounded and many repented " of their action. But Luke ascribes more than this to grace. Thus *Stephen, who was full of grace and power, performed great wonders and miracles among the people* (Acts vi. 8). Hitherto in Luke's narrative only apostles had worked miracles. It is true that Stephen must have spoken powerfully as well as worked wonders, for the attack on him was due to the forcible arguments he employed against the colonial Jews (9–10). But deeds as well as words were the outcome of the power of grace or the endowment of the Spirit, which is in Acts the holy energy of God acting upon faith.

(*c*) The significance of the term in a passage like the description of the mission of Barnabas to Antioch is less obvious (xi. 22 f.). When he arrived, Luke observes, and had seen the *grace of God*, he *was glad*. There is a play on the word (χάριν, ἐχάρη), but more important is the use of *grace* here to denote the outward working of the gospel as might. The religious position of the group at Antioch seemed to Barnabas a direct effect of God's gracious power. And this involves further the ' catholic ' sense of the term, for the community had taken a new step by opening the church to non-Jews or Greeks, who were being admitted without having to accept circumcision and the Law. Instead of suspecting this forward movement Barnabas welcomed it, although it is evident that the Jerusalem church which had despatched him was not very sure about the new development. The full force of *grace* therefore in this passage answers to that which we have already seen in Paul's use of the term as a description of the non-national range of the gospel.

There is no hint that at Antioch any miraculous phenomena served to accredit the new movement. *The strong hand of the Lord was with them* is indeed given as the reason why so many non-Jews *believed and turned to the Lord*, but this archaic Semitism (see Luke i. 66) is used by the historian to describe the divine, decisive cause of what followed. Only a divine impetus could account for such wonderful results as ' grace among Greeks.'

The same meaning recurs later in the story of what happened at Pisidian Antioch (xiii. 14–49), where ' the grace of God ' becomes an equivalent for the Christian religion, or, as Paul and Barnabas would have said, ' the true faith of God's People,' implying forgiveness and fellowship with God realized by Jesus Christ for faith anywhere. Such grace is the doing of God (ver. 41) ; it means the raising of Jesus from the dead and the extension of the gospel to all nations, an Act of God so wonderful that it staggered Jews and also amazed gentiles.

These are the elements of ' grace ' in this passage. *After the synagogue broke up, a number of the Jews and the devout proselytes,* impressed by what they had heard, *followed* Paul and Barnabas who *talked to them and encouraged them to hold by the grace of God.* Luke uses here the same word for *hold by* as he does in xi. 23, where Barnabas exhorted the believers to *hold by the Lord ;* they were to adhere to the *Message of this salvation* which had been *sent* to them (ver. 26), i.e. to the saving power of God which had manifested itself in a religious relationship bound up with Jesus Christ the Lord and beyond any narrow national restrictions. It was almost unbelievable favour, yet they must hold to it. By Him, the apostles had proclaimed, by the risen Christ, *everyone who believes* (no matter what he had been by birth) *is absolved from all that the law of Moses never could absolve men from.* Luke employs the same language in narrating Peter's speech at the Jerusalem council (xv. 11). *It is by the grace of the Lord Jesus* alone, not by any imposition of the Law, *that we believe and are saved in the same way as they* (the non-Jews) *are.* This is as genuinely Pauline as the description of the Christians at Corinth—*those who by God's grace had believed* (xviii. 27). It is good and gracious of God to make faith open to all, or rather to make faith, a human quality, the sole condition of salvation.

The other Pauline sense of grace as equipment for mission-work recurs in a passage like xiv. 26, where Paul and Barnabas are said to have been *commended* by the church of Antioch *to the grace of God for the work* of the mission ; also in xv. 40 Paul and Silas are *commended by the brothers* at Antioch *to the grace of the Lord.* The commending was a solemn special commission regarded as a commission by the Spirit of power (xiii. 3, 4), which invested the emissaries with spiritual authority and force from God.

This idea is not, however, to be read into the language of xviii. 27, as though the Greek meant that Apollos ' proved of great service to those who had believed by the grace given to him,' i.e. by his gifts of learning and eloquence, although the latter meaning is possible. The omission of διὰ τῆς χάριτος from the ordinary text (ὑπεβάλετο πολὺ τοῖς πεπιστευκόσιν διὰ τῆς χάριτος) by some authorities under the influence of the Western text, really confirms the view that the words were taken with πεπιστευκόσιν, for they were left out as apparently redundant. If they are taken with ὑπεβάλετο, it must be assumed that they are put last in the sentence for the sake of emphasis, and this appears rather less natural.

Luke's originality in handling ' grace ' is at two points.

(i) There is no precise precedent, even in Paul, for his collocation of ' gospel ' and ' grace.' A phrase like that in xiv. 3 is indeed intelligible in the light of what has been already said ; the apostles are reported to have spent some time at Iconium, *speaking fearlessly about the Lord, who attested the word of his grace by allowing signs and wonders to be performed by them.* Those who preached his saving power had their witness corroborated by miraculous deeds, and the context indicates that again *grace* denotes the extra-national extent of the gospel, since at Iconium *a great body both of Jews and Greeks believed.* But it is a real extension of the term when Luke makes Paul speak of his *commission from the Lord Jesus to attest the gospel of the grace of God* (xx. 24), adding, *Now* (as I have to leave you) *I entrust you to God and the word of his grace ; he is able to upbuild you and give you your inheritance* (at the end) *among all the consecrated* (xx. 32). Paul very occasionally uses *gospel* with some explanatory genitive ; now and then he does speak of *the gospel of peace* or *the gospel of the glory of Christ* or *the gospel of your salvation* (Eph. vi. 15, 2 Cor. iv. 4, Eph. i. 13), but never of ' the gospel of God's grace,' although this would have been an apt formula for him. Luke, as we know, avoids the term *gospel* in his gospel, and this makes it all the more significant that the only two passages in which he employs it carry a distinct reference to the Christian mission as including non-Jews, for Paul's word about attesting *the gospel of the grace of God* follows the declaration that he had steadily borne *testimony, both to Jews and Greeks* (xx. 21).

This use of λόγος or Word is characteristic of Luke's style in Acts, where ' the Word (of the Lord or of God) ' suggests almost a personified power in the life of the Community. Even in his first volume Luke speaks of the Word as the Gospel Message or (as it may be rendered in Acts viii. 21, ' you have no share or lot in this religion '), ' the Religion,' but in Acts the vivid sense of the term is more marked. Just as Paul could speak of the Word speeding on and triumphing, so Luke tells of it spreading and prevailing mightily (vi. 7, xii. 24, xix. 20). Consequently a phrase like *God and the word of his grace* is naturally followed by a clause which may either mean *Who* or *which is able to upbuild you*; the collocation implies a sort of ' mystical independence ' of the Word, which is so charged with a divine or numinous power that the writer can speak of it side by side with God Himself, as in the difficult passage x. 36 f.

(ii) The same thought vibrates behind the reference in Luke iv. 22. When the congregation in the synagogue at Nazaret *marvelled at the gracious words that come from his lips*, the historian intends us to understand the winsome, attractive quality of what Jesus said. Luke is using the term in its aesthetic sense. But the context indicates that there is more in his mind. Bengel's comment, ' suavitas et gravitas,' is on the right line. Just as Milton meant more than charm when he spoke of Raphael's words to Adam as being " with grace imbu'd," so here it is the content as well as the expression which Luke suggests. Jesus had spoken of *the Lord's year of favour* as inaugurated ; he interpreted the prophecy as on the point of fulfilment by himself. The references to the widow of Zarephath and to Naaman are meant to bring out the inclusion of non-Jews within the range of the gospel-message, and Jesus implies that he is taking action on the lines of the prophecy. The preacher speaks in the spirit of his text, about a commission which requires power from on high. The connexion between the initial admiration and the

subsequent resentment on the part of the audience is not
clearly brought out, but the object of the historian is not
simply to lay emphasis on the fascinating effect of what Jesus
said but also to hint that his ' grace ' was wider than any
nationalist aid to Israel, and that he was prepared to do more
than talk of grace.   Hitherto Luke has only spoken of ' grace '
as applied to Jesus or as conferred on him in a general sense.
Now for the first time, indeed for the only time, he makes Jesus
speak in a way which recalls the word ' grace,' using the term
to signify not simply attractive but effective and universal.
It is ' grace for all,' a beautiful service of mankind which has
behind it power divine.

X

IN THE JOHANNINE LITERATURE

IN the ' Acta S. Acacii,' which describe the proceedings against a third-century confessor, the Roman Marcianus asks the prisoner in the course of the enquiry, " Who is the Son of God ? " Acacius replies, " The Word of truth and grace." " Is that his name ? " " You did not ask me about the name but about the Son's very power (de ipsa filii potestate)," Acacius answers. This cross-examination reveals a trace of the one passage in the Fourth gospel which alludes to grace, and at the same time indicates the meaning of grace in the passage, as the early Christians understood it. Whether ' potestas ' denotes power or authority or both, it means on the lips of this Christian writer that he considered ' grace and truth ' to be a description of divine, saving energy.

' Grace ' practically disappears from the vocabulary of the Johannine circle, as represented by the three letters and the Fourth gospel. As we have already noted, it does occur in the opening formula of the Second letter, where the Presbyter declares that *grace, mercy, peace, will be with us from God the Father and from Jesus Christ the Son of the Father.* But this is the only trace of the traditional language in the letters. The term never occurs in the homily called The First Epistle of John, and only once in the Fourth gospel. John preferred other terms, like ' righteousness ' and love in the Epistle, investing them with associations and ideas hitherto conveyed by grace. Like the previous writers of the gospel-narrative he never puts ' grace ' into the lips of Jesus, and in describing the gracious action of God he chooses specially ' give ' ($\delta i \delta \omega \mu \iota$). It may well be that this verb was used for the gracious attitude of God to men on account of a desire to avoid misconception or misunderstanding on the part of his readers. He may have

felt that ' grace ' would suggest to some a royal arbitrary fiat,
or that it might be interpreted in the sense of favouritism.
John might be " attempting to raise his readers above formal
notions about ' grace ' and ' reward ' into a high spiritual
sphere where God is regarded not only as the All-giver but
also as the Self-giver." [1]   This does not imply that the latter
thought had not been present to the mind of Paul, but merely
that John seeks to put it freshly and clearly for a new circle of
readers.   Furthermore, this view must not be pressed too far,
for, as it happens, in speaking of the Law John declares that
it was ' given,' whereas he does not use this expression for the
grace and truth of the Gospel (i. 14, 15, 16).   The passage in
the Prologue runs thus :

' So the Logos became flesh and dwelt (ἐσκήνωσεν) among
us (and we have seen his glory, glory such as an only son enjoys
from his father), seen it to be full of grace and reality. . . .
For we have all been receiving grace after grace from his
fulness ; while the Law was given (ἐδόθη) through Moses,
grace and reality came (or, are ours, ἐγένετο) through Jesus
Christ.'   And to explain how this came to be, he adds, ' No
man has ever seen God, but the divine One, the only Son (ὁ
μονογενὴς υἱός), who lies upon the Father's breast, he has
unfolded (ἐξηγήσατο) Him.'   Like 10–11, 14 is a five-line
stanza, in this grace-hymn of the early Church :

> Καὶ ὁ λόγος σάρξ ἐγένετο
> καὶ ἐσκήνωσεν ἐν ἡμῖν,
> καὶ ἐθεασάμεθα τὴν δόξαν αὐτοῦ,
> δόξαν ὡς μονογενοῦς παρὰ πατρός,
> πλήρης χάριτος καὶ ἀληθείας.

' Grace and reality ' thus sum up the revelation of God the
Father to men ; Jesus Christ is the full and the only medium
of the revelation, for it is not divided among Christ and other
heavenly powers or aeons, as some contemporary theosophies
alleged ; shimmering through the words and deeds of Jesus

[1] E. A. Abbott, *Johannine Grammar*, 2743.

and through his death and resurrection Christians had enjoyed a vision of the divine ' glory.'   On all these three truths the Gospel has much to say, but there is not another syllable about ' grace.'   As we read on, we see how from the divine Logos or Word embodied in a human personality there broke forth a moral splendour in which it could be said that receptive natures ' saw the Father.'   We see also why John chose a technical term of ancient Greek religion like ἐξηγήσατο, which was current in the sense of disclosing or interpreting divine mysteries by diviners or gifted seers, for in his Gospel it is the intimate union of the Son with the Father which unfolds and discloses the real truth of the divine nature ; the actions and expressions of the Son reveal the nature of God going forth to men and giving or imparting Himself to His own.   Thus, although there is indeed no actual word of ' grace ' in these pages, the idea is present.   When we read that ' God so loved the world that he gave his only Son that whosoever believeth in him should have eternal life,' or that ' God sent his Son that the world through him might be saved,' that ' the Son can do nothing of his own accord, but what he seeth the Father do,' and that ' this is life eternal, to know thee the only true God and Jesus Christ whom thou hast sent,' we realize that in the Son thus sent or given the divine purpose is revealed.   In other words, the reality of God's nature is gracious.   The divine love, as developed in the Johannine interpretation of the gospel, includes two of the ideas fundamental to the Pauline idea of grace, viz. that in life as it is really lived man is ever the receiver, and that God gives through Jesus Christ.

We have all been receiving grace after grace (χάριν ἀντὶ χάριτος) *from his fulness* is another way of saying ' by the grace of God I am what I am.'   John like Paul avoids the plural of ' grace,' but he comes close here to the wording of a writer like Philo, who remarks that instead of allowing men to become sated with his favours (χάριτας) God gives them gradually, bestowing 'ever new graces for older ones' (ἀεὶ νέας ἀντὶ παλαιοτέρων, De Post. Caini, xliii.). The phrase points to the rich and ripening succession of divine endowments for faith. 'Thou shalt see greater things than these,' 'he that believeth on me shall do greater works than the works that I do,' 'bring forth more fruit'—such words in the Gospel indicate what John has in mind.

Augustine was too restricted in identifying the first grace with faith or forgiveness and the second with immortality. Two other interpretations may be confidently set aside. (a) One is the view, first held by Origen and Chrysostom, that Christians receive the grace of Christ in exchange for the grace of the Law, God's earlier gift to the People. (b) The other is, that Christians receive their grace as the result of the divine grace bestowed on Christ. Thus Thomas Aquinas (Summa Theologiae, III. 76. i) argues that Christ's grace is the cause of our grace, since he in respect of his human nature received the firstfruits of grace from above ; our grace corresponds to this, as effect to cause. Melanchthon also (Loci Communes, s.v. 'de justificatione et fide ') read the sentence to mean that all the gracious promises enjoyed by Christians are the outcome of God's gracious favour to His Son, "qui nobis emeruit omnes promissiones misericordia patris, qui nobis conciliavit patrem." But this Latin interpretation is as unnatural as the Greek Church's view ; to read into grace for (or, after) grace the notion of "favorem erga nos, pro favore erga Christum," is a dogmatic application which, as Calvin said of Augustine's statement of it, is "pie quidem et scite dictum, sed ad praesentem locum minus apte." Neither is it natural to read the phrase as a reference to the further gift of the Spirit the Comforter, as D'Alés ingeniously suggests (Recherches de Science Religieuse, 1919, 384–386), meaning that the grace of the Comforter was bestowed in addition to the grace of the Incarnate Lord upon the experience of the Church. Indeed no effort to read any allusion (Bover in Biblica, vi. 454–460) to Christ's grace is successful.

The clue to this passage in the Prologue is to be found in realizing that 'grace and truth' (reality) is substantially a periphrasis for 'gracious Reality' or 'real Grace.' That is, in χάρις καὶ ἀλήθεια the καί is explicative, as it is in xiv. 6. The

Johannine view of truth as reality, i.e. the upper world or life of God which is the sole reality, determines the meaning of the phrase. Since 'truth' is the divine nature, or, as John also loves to call it, 'light,' it is ever imparting itself, and in order to make this clear he brackets it with 'grace.' Hence 'full of grace and truth' means 'full of self-communicating divine life,'[1] and the self-communication is not an emanation but God giving Himself through His Son in generous love to men. Such is the transcending privilege of Christianity, to experience this outgoing of God in gracious love for the sake of taking men into His own life. " While the Law was given through Moses (while of old the People lived on this divine gift, now) the gracious Reality of God is ours (ἐγένετο, has appeared upon the scene) through Jesus Christ." John does not connect 'grace' with pardon or forgiveness as Paul did, but in these words he is in line with the apostle's idea that grace was the vital action of God and Jesus Christ, and that it referred not to creation but to human nature in its deep need of the divine life.

It is possible that he chose 'grace' here on account of its traditional contrast with the Law. But he also had in mind the OT phrase about the divine 'grace and truth,' into which he pours his own meaning. No doubt in the LXX this was rendered ἔλεος καὶ ἀλήθεια, and it meant God's loving-kindness and faithfulness to His People, as in His love He was true to His word and to their interests. 'Truth' for John had a deeper range. But instead of using ἔλεος, a word which he avoids, he employs for once its broader equivalent, thanks in part to the Pauline tradition. How apposite the language was, may be gathered from the account of the giving of the Law in Exodus xxxiii. 17–xxxiv. 7, where the divine glory (δόξα) is the revelation of God as 'merciful and gracious (ἐλεήμων, slow to be angry, rich in love and loyalty (πολυέλεος καὶ ἀληθινός),' or from the words of the psalm (lxxxv. 9–10) about 'the divine glory (δόξα; the Great Presence) dwelling (κατασκηνῶσαι) in our land, as mercy and truth (ἔλεος καὶ

---

[1] Cheyne in *Encyclopaedia Biblica*, iv. 5218.

ἀλήθεια, His kindness and faithfulness) unite ' for the sake and saving of the People.

The motives of this reference to grace are more obvious than the background. It is clear that John has something in mind when he emphasizes ' receiving ' as the true human attitude to the revelation of grace. This may have been the need of meeting a contemporary tendency, even in the higher Stoicism, towards self-reliance. All the differences between primitive Christianity and the rising Stoic philosophy of practical religion, even the different estimates of faith and knowledge, of error and moral evil, go back to the ultimate antithesis that whereas man's reason was for the Stoics really the chief power in life, for Christianity the task was not to cultivate one's soul according to reason but to prepare oneself for a childlike relation to God. And this very preparation, as Max Pohlenz observes, " dieses Ziel nicht aus eigner Kraft sondern durch göttliche Gnade erreicht." [1] It is some such thin, confident phase of humanism rather than the particular self-righteousness opposed by Paul that John is controverting. On the other hand, ' truth ' for him is not precisely what it is for some of his contemporaries. That the soul was not left to itself in the universe, was widely believed. In the first section of his treatise *De Iside*, for example, the devout Plutarch observes that " man cannot receive aught greater, God cannot bestow (χαρίσασθαι) aught more august (σεμνότερον), than truth " (i.e. the knowledge of the divine nature) ; for all else that man needs God gives to him, but this He shares with him as His own possession. The spirit of this saying is akin to the Christian conception, but John does not mean by ' truth ' exactly this knowledge or intelligent perception of ' res sacrae.' His belief in the incarnation involves reality as well as knowledge in the content of ' truth.' A closer indication of what he is controverting would be either the

[1] *Gott. Gelehrte Anzeigen*, 1913, 649.

theosophy already met by Paul in Colossians, according to which the fulness of God was not wholly conveyed through Jesus as the Christ, or some other contemporary form of docetism. That only revelation can meet the need of man, that revelation is entirely summed up in Jesus Christ the divine Son, and that this is a personal favour on the part of a loving God, freely offered to men who are free to accept or to refuse—these are the elements of the truth which for once John expresses in terms of grace. His references to grace in the Prologue are, I believe, primarily determined by his sense of the relationship between the Christian faith and its earlier phase within Judaism. There were certainly gnostic thinkers already explaining that divine grace was confined to an élite who were born into this privileged position, and it is not unlikely that John had such in view when he argued that birth into the experience of grace was not due to *human blood* but to God alone ; he rules out any caste-predestination in the religious sphere. Some gnostics, the Simonians for example (Irenaeus, i. 23, 3), had actually compromised Paul's teaching by their view that one was justified by grace, not by righteous deeds, taking the latter to refer to morality as a product of the lower material world which mere angels had created. John's refusal to accept any distinction between God the creator and God the redeemer might therefore have contributed to his choice of other terminology than Paul's in order to state the Christian view. Nevertheless, on the issue of the gospel's relation to foregoing revelation, he writes as one to whom Paul's position was axiomatic. The son of Sirach had piously asked, ' Who hath seen Him, that he may unfold Him (ἐκδιηγήσεται) ? ' John knows the answer. He is confident that the Lord Jesus Christ, being full of the real divine grace, has unfolded God to men, and unfolded the divine life as a loving fellowship into which the right of access is graciously conferred by this Son of God, so graciously that believers of any nation have *the right of being children of God*, owing this birth of theirs to God, not to any inherited position or any eager impulse of the human spirit acting of itself.   Under the Law Israel had indeed the title to election as God's People, ἡ υἱοθεσία, the proud privilege of sonship.   But the deeper reality of this was now unfolded, John believes, in that relationship to the Father which Jesus the Son had opened up for all who chose to have faith in Him.   Whatever contemporary tendencies of religious thought may have been present to his mind, John's passing words about ' grace ' in this paragraph are not intelligible except in the light of what ' grace ' had already come to mean, in this connexion, to the apostle Paul.

When the OT revelation came to be depreciated by some gnostic groups, it was found needful to emphasize the truth that grace had been already working, though imperfectly, within the saints of the OT period.   " Never does God cease to benefit and enrich man, nor does man cease to receive His benefits and be enriched by God," Irenaeus argues (iv. 11) ;   " He who is one and the same Lord has indeed bestowed by means of his advent a richer endowment of grace on those who came later than was contained in the Old Testament," but this is all. It is a question of degree (see iv. 32. 3, 36. 4).   Clement of Alexandria frankly and ingeniously meets the difficulty raised in the minds of some Christians by the words of the Johannine prologue.   " The Law," he observes (*Paed.* i. 7. 60), " is ancient grace given through Moses by the Word."   Note, he adds, it is given " through (διά) not by (ὑπό) Moses, for it was given by the Word, through his servant Moses.   Hence it was only temporary, whereas ' the eternal grace and truth came by Jesus Christ.'   Mark the expressions of scripture ; it says ' was given ' of the Law, whereas truth being the grace (χάρις being either taken as a definition of ἀλήθεια or in the sense of ' gift ') of the Father is the everlasting work of the Word, and is not said to be given but to ' come ' (ἐγένετο) by Jesus, without whom nothing was."

XI

SUMMARY

THE literature which has been under survey reflects the main currents of early Christianity as it flowed through the half-century after Paul's death. The data indicate that ' grace ' had established itself as a characteristic term in the interpretation of the gospel, which was proving not only intelligible but highly serviceable, apart from the original antithesis between grace and Law. Some writers prefer other equivalents for the truth of grace ; some display considerable originality and independence in handling the term. But it was evidently in vogue and vital. Two further proofs of this may be given, from catholic and from gnostic usages at the opening of the second century.

I

When grace became a distinguishing feature of Christianity, that is, of the statement of the faith thanks to the propaganda of Paul, it eventually denoted the religion itself, especially when it was desired to differentiate it from Judaism. This, as we have seen, accounts for the allusion in the Prologue to the Fourth Gospel, and it explains why, in his remonstrance with Christians who were toying with the ritual and religious discipline of the older faith, Ignatius wrote, " if we live until now (i.e. after all this time, since our conversion) after Jewish rules, we confess that we have not received grace " (Magnes. viii.). The very prophets of the OT, he continues, pointed forward to Christ ; ' they lived in accordance with Christ Jesus ; that was why they were persecuted, being inspired by his grace.' Ignatius has his idiosyncrasies, but he does not hesitate to use grace-words such as Paul had coined ; the faith is a message and a means of grace.

24

Neither does the hymnist who wrote about the same time the Odes of Solomon. This Christian declares (xxiv. 10), for example,

> The Lord disclosed his Way,
> And spread abroad his Grace.

That is, Christianity is not only the Way but the Grace of the Lord. And this is by no means an isolated phrase. Indeed, this collection of hymns, from some mystical circle in the early part of the second century, affords glimpses of ' grace ' being used by a group whose cult-expression was otherwise nearer to the Johannine terminology than to the Pauline. Parallels to Paul are not infrequent. Thus the idea of Romans xi. 29 is echoed in iv. 11 f.,

> There is no repentance with Thee,
>   that Thou shouldest repent of any promise,
> for what Thou hast given Thou hast given graciously,
>   that Thou mayest not take it back.

But the usage is wider. ' Freely have I received Thy grace, I shall live thereby ' (v. 3), ' We live (or, rejoice) in the Lord by His grace ' (xli. 3), ' Be strong and be redeemed by His grace ' (ix. 5), ' Grace has been revealed for your salvation ' (xxxiv. 6), ' Grace belongs to the elect ' (xxiii. 2), ' For who shall put on Thy grace and be hurt ? ' i.e. by the evil One, iv. 7)—these indicate how grace had become a central term of the new religion especially within circles of Christians in touch with non-Jewish life. Some of these hymns certainly suit catechumens, if they are not intended for the newly baptized who thus confess the grounds of their faith. Often the truth of grace as the rescuing power of God is couched in terms that recall the Psalms, and sometimes in uncouth mystical metaphors. But a simpler passage like this reveals the central idea of grace alone as the basis of hope and experience (xxi. 1) :

> I raised my arms on high to the grace of the Lord ;
>   for my Helper had raised me up on high to His grace and His salvation.

Here the initiative is with the Lord, even though the primary reference may be to the baptized uplifting their arms, as was common in the Eastern Church after the ceremony. Again, the nexus of grace with the divine pity and the atonement underlies the lines in vii. 11–12, which imply that man as mortal is frail and sinful :

> He who created me when I was not,
>   knew what I should do when I came into being,
> wherefore he pitied me in His abundant grace,
>   and granted me to ask from Him and to receive of His sacrifice.

The Odes show that even where the Pauline terminology was not current, yet the distinctive ideas of grace could be held ; for although the writer never mentions the name of Jesus, he believes that all goes back to grace, that the gracious gifts of the Lord to the elect are pre-destined, and that grace is not only needed by the Christian throughout life but freely accessible through fellowship with the Lord who has died and risen in order to give gifts to men.[1]

In order to accentuate grace as that characteristic of the Christian faith which marks it off from Judaism, the author of the epistle of Barnabas actually inserts the term in the prophecy of Isaiah lxi. 1 2. He cites (xiv.) it thus : ' The Spirit of the Lord is upon me, because he anointed me to preach the gospel *of grace* to the humble.' Nothing could better prove the dominating impression of the term than this incidental touch. Besides, Barnabas offers a profound evangelical proof that the Cross was predicted in the OT, by recourse to the Oriental method of playing on numbers. He wishes to explain why Abraham circumcised " eighteen and three hundred men of his household " (Gen. xiv. 14). The spiritual significance of the scripture is this, Barnabas points out (ix. 7 f.). As Roman and Greek readers would understand, the number eighteen is composed of two letters, I (ten) and H (eight). " There you have Jesus," says Barnabas, since IH are in Greek the first two letters of ' Jesus ' ! " And because the Cross, signified by T, was also to have grace, three hundred is added—the Greek letter T being equivalent to three hundred. It is a quaint interpretation. But the close con-

---

[1] " The new note that is struck in the present Ode is that joy, grace, and love are predestined gifts, only for those who have ' put them on ' from the beginning, i.e. for the elect in the eternal counsels of God " (Bernard, *Texts and Studies*, Cambridge, viii. 3, p. 98).

nexion of Jesus and the Cross with grace, as distinctive of the gospel, is so important for Barnabas that twice over he brings in these novelties of interpretation for the purpose of making it clear and convincing to Christians who had been won over from the pagan world. He reads the OT as a book of grace in the Christian sense of the term ; the very prophets predicted the Lord as they ' had grace from Him ' (v. 6). Yet the full measure of grace divine could not come till Christ arrived, with the gift of the Spirit, and he starts by rejoicing over the privileged position of his readers in the order of grace : ' Such a rich gift of spiritual grace have you received into your nature ' (ἔμφυτον τῆς δωρεᾶς πνευματικῆς χάριν εἰλήφατε). ' I truly see in you the Spirit which the Lord so rich in love has poured out upon you.'

How naturally grace suggested power, especially in connexion with the Spirit (see above, p. 176), may be seen in Justin's reply to Trypho the Jew, who in a good-natured way had advised the Christian to give up his religious illusions about Christ ; ' be circumcised, as is enjoined, keep the sabbath and the feasts and the new moons of God, in fact all that is written in the Law, and then you may perhaps obtain mercy from God,' instead of risking your soul's welfare, as you Christians do, by ' listening to idle reports, and making a Christ for yourselves.' Justin's protest is : ' We do not confide in baseless fables (κενοῖς μύθοις) nor in irrational arguments (ἀναποδείκτοις) but in doctrines full of the divine Spirit, overflowing with power, and a-flower with grace (τεθηλόσι).' Similarly Origen argues (Cels. ii. 50), speaking of the Egyptian magicians who encountered Moses—' the power of the Egyptian magicians was unlike the supernatural grace of Moses,' for so we may render παραδόξῳ χάριτι. In the martyr-literature this is a frequent thought. Thus the Numidian martyrs in the third century are said to have been so full of ' the Spirit of vitality and grace (vivificationis et gratiae) ' that they could not rest content till they had inspired others to heroic deeds (Passio SS. Mariani et Jacobi iii.). Dasius the Roman soldier confesses that he is a Christian because " I have received from the heavenly King His free gift (δωρεάν), by His grace I live, and through His unspeakable kindness I am rich." Here δωρεά means the Holy Spirit.[1] There may be a Montanist tinge in the belief that a specially rich measure of grace was to be poured out upon the Church in the latter days,[2] but there is other evidence that this hope of grace as the Spirit not only of revelation but of power was shared by Catholics. When the hard times came and persecution had to be faced, it was natural that grace should be viewed as the divine power of Christ which alone enabled the faithful to endure pain and to hope for the happy end. Hence the doxology in the Martyrdom of Polykarp (xx.) is, " To him who is able to bring us all, by his grace and generous favour ($\chi \acute{\alpha} \varrho \iota \tau \iota$ $\varkappa \alpha i$ $\delta \omega \varrho \epsilon \tilde{\alpha}$), to his eternal realm by Jesus Christ his Only Son," just as in the later Martyrdom of Sabas (viii.).

2

As the great gnostic leaders drew upon Paul's teaching, it is not surprising (see above, p. 335) to find ' grace ' as a category of their systems. In the Valentinian theosophy which approached nearest to the Catholic faith, the Absolute is The Depth. This Reality was the absorbing idea of Valentinus, but, interpreting the universe in terms of love, he required to associate the Depth with other principles or aeons, which like Æschylus and Shelley he half-personified. Tertullian sarcastically observes that this epicurean deity of the Depth needed to be stirred up to think of production, and so he was furnished with a feminine aeon called variously Ennoia, Silence, or Charis. But Valentinus was probably offering a serious philosophy of religion in this imaginative setting. He teaches that from this union creation flows. On the Valentinian synthesis, therefore, Grace is cosmic rather than redemptive, but it is at the centre of the religious process. Grace was needed for the perfect life. Unfortunately our extant evidence for the actual opinions of Valentinus himself is too fragmentary to permit of any certainty as to whether he took the Absolute to be a great Monad or an aeon helped out

[1] See Cumont, ' Les Actes de s. Dasius ' in *Analecta Bollandiana* (1897), 11-15.

[2] *Passio SS. Perpetuae et Felicitatis* (i : exuperationem gratiae in ultima saeculi spatiam decretam).

by some other like Silence or Charis.   But there is no doubt whatever about the Ophites, for grace became a liturgical term in this circle.   As the soul passed through the various planetary spheres, flying upwards after death, the prayer addressed to each of the rulers ended with the words (ἡ χάρις συνέστω μοι, ναὶ πάτερ, συνέστω) :

> May grace be with me, father, grace be with me !

So at least Origen describes their faith (Cels. vi. 31).   They also believed that Jesus or the Messenger from heaven, the Christ, came down to rescue the spirit of man in his material plight on earth, and that the elect or spiritual minority needed to be born again in some sense.   Here, then, grace is recognized as the sole saving power of life, although it works on semi-magical lines.   For this element in their syncretistic system the Ophites were certainly indebted to the Church.

According to another view, in the Panarion (xxxi. 5–7) of Epiphanius, the Valentinian Charis is connected with redemption, as Sigê or Silence is with revelation.   The feminine Notion who is with or next to the Father or Absolute, is Charis ; this aeon bestows the treasures of the Absolute on those who are His within the mass of humanity.

Many gnostics, Simonians and Valentinians especially, were so absorbed in the thought of grace that they sought to appropriate it, or at least the supreme experience of it, to themselves, assigning a merely minor function of grace to Catholics. We, they alleged, have our grace direct from the aeons of the Absolute, and therefore as born spiritual beings are above any risk of falling from grace ; it is innate in us.   Whereas you poor churchfolk receive grace ἐν χρήσει, i.e. you have to use it in order to be pure and moral, and it is doubtful whether you all succeed.   This gnostic claim posits grace as the possession of a caste.   It is experienced φύσει, whereas Church believers need moral actions, if their grace is to be of any saving efficacy. It may have been against some incipient movement of this kind that the tract or epistle of Judas was launched (see above, pp. 336 f.). In any case, it indicates the strong religious appeal of ' grace ' to these semi-Christians, and the dangerous moral effects of their teaching. " Just as gold flung into mud retains its own quality instead of losing its beauty, since mud cannot injure gold, so they say," Irenaeus indignantly protests (i. 6, 4), " nothing can harm them, nothing can rob them of their spiritual substance, no matter what material action they take part in."

But no sect of gnostics made so vivid and outré a use of Grace as the Marcosians, who had even penetrated into the Church of Gaul under the eyes of Irenaeus (i. 13). Marcus was an adroit charlatan of the religious world, who blended mathematics and mysticism in a weird mixture, and who not only had ' Charis ' in his creed but in his liturgy. By prolonging the invocation over a eucharistic cup of white glass he managed to persuade the worshippers that thereby Charis, one of his upper aeons, distilled her own blood into the cup, whose colour deepened as the prayers continued. They were thus instructed that this Grace flowed into their lives (εἰς αὐτοὺς ἐπομβρήσῃ), as they partook of the wine-water ; by some conjuring trick Marcus contrived to produce the red colour in the liquid. The prayer for Charis ran : " May that Charis who is prior to all things, above thought and beyond words (ἡ ανεννόητος καὶ ἄῤῥητος), fill thine inner man and multiply in thee her knowledge, sowing the grain of mustard-seed in good soil." There was a special service for women. Marcus catered for them assiduously, promising them the gift of ecstatic prophecy as a spiritual gift. Irenaeus is indignant that anyone should dream of doing more than ask God for the grace of prophecy, but Marcus told the women worshippers impressively, "I would share my grace with thee, since the Father of all ever beholds thine angel before his face. . . . Receive first of all from me and through me grace. Adorn thyself like a bride expecting her bridegroom. . . .

Lo, Charis has come down to thee ; open thy mouth and prophesy." Whereupon, says Irenaeus, the deluded woman, believing that she was now a prophetess, made handsome presents to the presiding priest, and even gave herself to him, since the cup contained love-philtres. This ceremony seems to have dramatized the union of the soul to an angel or the Lord as Bridegroom and also the endowment of the human spirit with the gift of prophecy, all in connexion with Charis. Whatever truth there is in the tales of scandal, Marcus did make serious use of Grace in his performances. In connecting it with prophecy he was merely following the lead of Church fathers like Justin, for whom the Spirit of grace was pre-eminently the Spirit of prophecy. The idea of a heavenly marriage enacted or mediated by a prophet as inspired, is not uncommon ; [1] it probably lies behind the enigmatic allusion in Did. xi. 11 to realistic representations which savoured of impropriety, especially as it was now being used of individuals instead of the Church. Marcus evidently employed the feminine figure of Charis not only for this, however, but for his eucharistic teaching. Thereby he is unique in second-century circles of gnosticism.

That this practice of Marcus implies a connexion of grace with the eucharist in the Catholic Church, is not proved. Undoubtedly he employed the invocation or epiklêsis ; he actually pretended, his Christian critics said, to consecrate cups (ποτήρια οἴνῳ κεκραμένα προσποιούμενος εὐχαριστεῖν), as though they were the eucharistic cup. But neither Irenaeus nor Hippolytus suggests that this was a caricature of the Christian eucharist ; they refer his sleight of hand to magic, and believe that he was deluding his adherents by a common trick of magic. It is precarious to assume that the procedure of Marcus implies a popular form of the eucharist in the Church which already associated grace with some change in the elements.

Three small problems remain, raised by this very vogue of grace in the early Church.

[1] See Bousset's *Hauptprobleme der Gnosis*, pp. 315 f.

(i) It is unhistorical to assume that a nomism or moralism began to dominate the Church immediately after the Pauline or primitive period. The existence of such a tendency is plain, but it was not predominant. Had this been the case, the criticism of a sharp-eyed pagan like Celsus would have been pointless. What Celsus attacks is not a Christianity which was unduly moralistic but one which, to his mind, was insufficiently concerned about morals and too concerned about offering a free welcome on the part of God to sinners. The popular Christianity which he derides must have been far from a Judaistic piety which told men to be as good as they could and then God would be sure to forgive them. What Origen has to answer, in his reply to Celsus, is the reproach that the Church, as it preaches the gospel to all and sundry, does not begin by insisting upon ethical guarantees ; the very terms of the reproach prove that the Church was indeed daring at the risk of misconception to preach grace as Paul and the other apostles had understood it, that is, urging that whilst a good life was the supreme concern of faith, nevertheless the Lord could begin to deal with man on some other footing than moral worthiness.

Over and again the need of God's grace is found to underlie writings where careless or cowardly Christians are being disciplined and directed. Sometimes, as we have seen, the term ' grace ' is explicitly employed. According to ' Hebrews,' the inward life is strengthened by grace alone (xiii. 9) for the ethical requirements of the faith ; the burden of the whole epistle is that there is no way of avoiding apostasy or immorality except by a personal reliance upon what God is and does in His Son Jesus Christ. Again, is a church split by divisions and bad temper ? " I have faith in the grace of Jesus Christ," Ignatius replies bravely (Phil. viii. 1) : " He can free you from all this." Among ourselves, Clement of Rome declares (lv. 3), " many women have been strengthened by the grace of God to achieve manly exploits." He cites

Judith and Esther as OT examples of a courage which was plain in the local church, and refers such deeds of Christian women to grace. But, even apart from the actual use of 'grace,' the thought is everywhere, that the achievements of Christians, their moral impulses and activities, their powers and practices, whether active or passive, are the result of dependence on the goodness and aid of God. On this issue indeed the attitude of the early Church, as Titius [1] remarks, is much closer to that of Paul than at first appears. The Pauline language may be either dropped or used freely, as in Hebrews, the Pastorals and the epistle of Clement of Rome, but " one feels that fundamentally salvation is exclusively the gift of God and attained by faith. The works on which these writings lay such stress," are performed in dependence on God's grace, and they are works of faith, not substitutes for faith nor a supplement to faith but inspired by faith.

Take a single passage by way of illustration, from the Second Epistle of Clement, a homily of the second century (i. 7–iii. 4). Jesus Christ, he tells the Church, " had mercy on us and in his pity saved us, when He beheld all the error and ruin in our lives and our hopelessness of salvation apart from Himself. He called us when we were not, He willed that from nothing we should come into being." Then quoting the words, ' I came not to call the righteous but sinners,' the preacher explains their meaning. " This means that the perishing are to be saved. The supreme marvel is not to strengthen what is standing but to strengthen what is falling. This is what Christ has done ; He willed to save the perishing, and He saved many, coming and calling us who were already perishing. Since then He has shown such mercy towards us, so that we who are living no longer sacrifice to dead gods nor worship them, but through Him know the true Father, what is this knowledge (the real gnosis γνῶσις) ? " Not a theoretical idea or formal belief but—" this, that we do not deny Him through whom we have our knowledge of the Father. He himself has said, ' Whosoever confesses me before men, him will I confess before my Father.' This then is our reward (μισθός, i.e. that we are not denied but

[1] *Die Vulgäre Anschauung von der Seligkeit im Urchristenthum*, p. 144.

acknowledged), if we confess Him by whom we are saved. But (you ask) how are we to confess Him? By doing what He tells us and not refusing to obey His commands, by honouring Him not only with our lips but with all our heart and mind." The first part of this moving passage has surely everything but the term grace.

Admittedly the moral ideal of the age, i.e. conformity to law, affected the statement of Christianity as time went on. Thus awe did tend to become anxious, losing the full value of that confidence in God which accompanied it within the NT synthesis. Even in so beautiful a homily as Second Clement 'peace' is only mentioned once, and in the wake of an 'if.' The preacher argues, " If we are eager to do good, peace will follow after us. For peace cannot reach one who is subject to fear of men, putting pleasure in the present before the Promise that is to be " (x. 2). This is a wholesome argument against gnostics who were teaching that, instead of being fanatical, Christians should do their best to avoid suffering and martyrdom. It has the heroic note : God's gracious Promise of heavenly bliss ought to be man's chief end and hope, whatever these Laodicean liberals might say. Clement bids his church be faithful unto death, doing good, i.e. proving loyal and devoted to God. His word about peace is true, but it is not all the truth of the NT on this issue. Clearly there is a moralistic turn being given to the earlier teaching, as though God were no more than a God who remembers, reckons, and repays. In the same way, whilst Ignatius has a warm personal religion, which he frequently expresses in Pauline terms, he does not unite faith and love as the apostle does ; the nexus in 'faith working by love' is not the exact hinge of grace and the good life in the Bishop of Antioch's theology. But it would be one-sided to deduce from this a general failure to appreciate grace, as one-sided as to view the contemporary development of the ministry in terms of declension from a so-called ' charismatic ' ministry inspired by the Spirit to the level of an ecclesiastical organization.

(ii) In the Acts of Apollonius (xxxii.), when the Roman magistrate protests that he cannot understand what Christians mean by chattering about life and heaven, the martyr replies, " Well, I am sorry for you, sorry that you are so insensible to the beauties of grace (τὰ καλὰ τῆς χάριτος)." The Hellenistic associations of ' charis ' with moral aesthetic were so strong that it would not surprise us to find traces of this in the NT. But it was Augustine who first appreciated the beauty of ' grace.' [1] A man of his Platonic training found it natural to speak of God in terms of Beauty as well as of Truth and Goodness. In the NT itself the perception of this does not occur. Although there are stray allusions which imply that the aesthetic aspect of ' charis ' was present to the writer's mind (e.g. in Luke iv. 22, Eph. iv. 29, etc.), these are only on the fringe.

Now and then a Greek father would indeed read this traditional sense of ' charis ' into some of these allusions. In addition to the examples of this which we have already met, it may be noted how, in commenting upon περισσεία τῆς χάριτος in Romans v. 17, Chrysostom remarked that Paul uses this phrase deliberately instead of simply saying ' grace,' in order to show that " what we have received is no mere medicine, as an antidote to our wound, but health, comeliness (εὐμορφίαν), honour and glory." This is not simply the Greek instinct, leading Chrysostom to note the moral beauty of true religion, but a perception that as grace or salvation denotes life, there must be a bloom of health attaching to the full experience of God's grace. Hence εὐμορφία comes to his mind quite naturally, as soon as the positive wealth of saving grace is realized. Nevertheless, the interpretation is foreign to the text.

Two data are significant in this connexion. One is that in referring to the moral beauty of religion the New Testament writers do not employ ' charis,' although it was the natural expression for any Greek to use. Paul (Phil. iv. 8) like any noble Stoic commends to his readers *whatever is true, whatever*

[1] See Joseph Mausbach's *Die Ethik des heiligen Augustinus,* i. 63 f., 95 f., etc.

is worthy (σεμνά, conveying perhaps a touch of the ' august ' or
' noble '), *whatever is just, whatever is pure, whatever is attractive* (προσφιλῆ), *whatever is high-toned* (εὔφημα). Peter
recommends Christian ladies to adorn themselves not with
jewels and gay garb but with *the immortal beauty of a gentle and
modest spirit* (1 Pet. iii. 3, 4), and a later writer counsels
Christian slaves to adorn (κοσμεῖν) their religion by honesty,
submissiveness, and good service.   It is true that the last-
named appeal is linked to grace, for the writer instantly proceeds to add : *for the grace of God has appeared* with its exacting
ethical discipline.   But this is grace as God's power in the life
of faith, not as a principle of moral aesthetic (Titus ii. 9 f.,
see further above, on Heb. ii. 9, 10).   Also it is important
to notice that the noun for moral excellence, καλοκἀγαθία, plays
no rôle in early Christianity, though it was familiar to Jewish
Hellenism.   The word defies translation, like σωφροσύνη, but
it denotes goodness with a shining, rounded quality, and was
commonly used by Philo.   Thus he describes the earlier
oracles delivered by God through Moses as " evincing His
merciful and beneficent nature (ἵλεω καὶ εὐεργέτιδος) and
training men to moral goodness " (καλοκἀγαθίαν, Vit. Mosis ii.
23).   The author of Fourth Maccabees also employs it for
the moral beauty of virtue, which inspired the martyrs to die
(i. 10, etc.).   But it made no appeal to the early Christians
Apart from a solitary occurrence in Ignatius, for the perfect
flower of human character, the consummation of faith and
love in the Christian life (Eph. xiv.), καλοκἀγαθία dropped
out of the primitive Christian vocabulary, even among those
writers who were familiar with Jewish Hellenism.

So did the adjectival καλὸς καὶ ἀγαθός.   It had a slight footing in
Jewish Hellenism (e.g. Tobit vii. 7, ix. 6), where it was even applied
to highpriests (2 Macc. xv. 12, 4 Macc. iv. 1).   The Hellenistic Luke
actually uses it for the ' honest and good heart ' (viii. 15), but thereafter
it vanishes, except for a sarcastic allusion by Justin (Apol. ii. 2) to a
" perfect gentleman " of a pagan who ill-treated his Christian wife !

Of course τὸ καλόν means goodness (1 Thess. v. 2, 2 Cor. vii. 2 f.),
and it could be said, " Let our children learn how fair (καλός) and
great it is to revere God " (Clem. Rom. xxi. 8), but this is a secondary
use of the term.

In the second century the thought of a beauty in grace does
appear, however.   Once in English ' graceful' had the double
sense of handsome and religious ; Leonato could assure Prince
Florizel that he had " a holy father, a graceful gentleman."
The early Christians never had an adjective corresponding to
' grace-full,' but at three points they soon began to think of
' grace ' in its aesthetic sense as well as in its religious.

(a) As soon as the faith of the Church began to express itself
in symbolism or any artistic form, this aspect of grace becomes
visible.   In the catacombs, for example, where we possess the
earliest simple efforts of the Christian spirit to represent its
beliefs, it is significant that there are no tragic delineations of
the next world.   Heaven is a garden full of flowers and
fragrance.   Neither is there any sad picture of the crucifixion.
Outside of the Bible one of the most favourite symbols is
Orpheus [1] charming beasts by music ; indeed one of the
earliest of these representations in the second century shows
Christ as Orpheus surrounded by two sheep.   Or he is
pictured as a shepherd carrying a lamb on his shoulder.   It is
the strong gracious aspect of the Lord which is most frequently
depicted.   His accompaniments are song and sunshine.
When stories from the New Testament are depicted, it is
almost invariably the gracious acts of the Lord, his raising of
Lazarus, for example, or some miracle of healing.   The
incident of the woman in the city washing his feet is a specially
favourite subject.

How widely this interest was felt may be gathered from a sermon
by Asterius the Bishop of Amasea, a contemporary of Augustine.   It

[1] On Orpheus in early Christian Art, see V. Schultze in *Zeitschrift für
Neutestamentliche Wissenschaft*, xxiii. 173–183.

contains a curious side-light on society of the day. Preaching on the parable of the rich man and Lazarus, he addresses himself to wealthy Christians who wore on their robes religious pictures (ἀναλεξάμενοι τὴν εὐαγγελικὴν ἱστορίαν) of the gospel. The subjects were Jesus among his apostles, the wedding at Cana, the healing of the leper, the healing of the blind, the miracle of the loaves, the raising of Lazarus, and the story of the woman who was a sinner. Asterius speaks plainly about this custom. It is at any rate better, he admits, than the fashion of the pagan *nouveaux riches* who wore pictures of wild beasts. But, he adds, you would do better to sell these evangelic pictures and spend the money on helping blind and sick folk yourselves. Gracious deeds are better than pictures of grace, a better ornament for life. You think you are very pious as you wear such things—ἱμάτια κεχαρισμένα τῷ θεῷ! But the grace God prefers is in practical charity "Instead of depicting Christ, carry him about in your souls." [1]

(*b*) The application of 'grace' in the sense of beauty to the Lord was not made until the second century. It is first hinted by Barnabas (vii.), but Tertullian works it out in a passage at the close of his tract *Adversus Judaeos*, where he is contrasting the first and the second Advent. Quoting the fifty-third chapter of Isaiah, he notes how Christ when he came was, as the prophet had predicted, without attractiveness or grace of outward form, ' his mien without honour, defective as compared with men.' But at the second Advent he is to have a mien of honour and a grace not deficient as compared with men. Whereupon Tertullian boldly cites the forty-fifth Psalm as to be fulfilled in the Christ who comes to reign:

> Effusa est gratia in labiis tuis,
>   propterea benedixit te Deus in saeculis.
> Accingere ensem tuum circa femur tuum,
>   potens tempestativitate et pulchritudine tua—

a free translation from the LXX. What led to this development of thought was of course the prediction about the Suffering Servant of the Lord, that when men saw him there

[1] Migne *PG*, xl. 163 f.

was no beauty to make them desire him, no form nor comeliness
in his appearance.   Tertullian is really following the precedent
set by Irenaeus (*Haer*. iii. 19) who makes the Christ of the
second Advent, ' The Wonderful, the Counsellor, Fair to
behold.'   So the Alexandrians loved to insist that whilst the
Lord on earth had been indeed without outward comeliness,
he had inner beauty and grace.   Although τὴν ὄψιν αἰσχρός,
as Isaiah reports, yet who was nobler (ἀμείνων) than the Lord
Jesus, with his real beauty of soul and flesh, that is, of helpful
kindness (τὸ εὐεργετικόν) and of immortality from God
(Clement, *Paed*. iii. 1) ?   Such was the nearest approach to
what a modern poet calls the " loveliness of perfect deeds "
which marked the life of Jesus.

(*c*) Another aesthetic side of ' grace' appears in a quaint description of the apostle Paul's personal appearance which has
been preserved by the *Acts of Paul* (iii.).   He is represented as
" a man small of stature, bald, bandy-legged, strongly built, with
eyebrows joining, with a rather hooked nose, full of grace
(for sometimes he looked like a man and sometimes he had the
face of an angel)." [1]   Wherever the author got his picture,
from tradition or from his own fancy, he did not idealize the
apostle whom he admired.   What he had in mind in the last
words was probably the familiar sight of a plain countenance
occasionally lit up with some inward glow of goodness that
makes one forget the heavy features.   ' Grace ' here denotes
not friendliness but a supernatural charm, or at any rate what
Tennyson meant by saying that he used to see " the God
within him light " up Hallam's face as he talked.   It is grace
with the power of manifesting itself outwardly in the looks of
the Christian.

[1] L. Vouaux, *Les Actes de Paul*, p. 122.   The Armenian version adds
' curly hair ' and ' blue eyes,' and describes him as ' full of the grace and pity
of the Lord ' (' grace and mercy ' in the Syriac).   See Conybeare's *Monuments
of Early Christianity*, p. 62.

Sometimes the martyrs were described as having such a glow on their faces in the supreme hour of their ordeal At Lyons and Vienne it was noted that whilst the renegades looked sad and heavy, the loyalists walked from prison to torture and death cheerfully, ' with glory and much grace (δόξης καὶ χάριτος) blended on their faces ' (Euseb. H.E. v. 1.), so much so that ' their very bonds encircled them like a fair decoration.' Here δόξα καὶ χάρις denote the supernatural dignity and charm of moral heroism. The martyr as a happy warrior was ' attired with sudden brightness as a man inspired.' When the Carthaginian martyrs on March 7th, A.D. 203, left prison to meet their cruel doom in the amphitheatre, ' they walked as though to heaven, looking happy and radiant (hilares vultu decori), and if they shivered it was from joy, not from fear.'[1] So, when the venerable Polykarp was facing torture and death at Smyrna, ' he was filled with courage and joy, and his face was full of grace ' (Martyrdom of Polykarp, xii.), i.e. lit up with this inward glow. The physical effect remained even after death, in some cases. When the presbyter Pionius had been martyred at Smyrna during the Decian persecution, his friends found that the burned corpse looked like the body of a healthy, well-cared for athlete ; the martyr's face still shone radiant with a marvellous grace (ἐπέλαμπε τὸ πρόσωπον αὐτοῦ πάλιν χάρις θαυμαστή).[2]

(iii) In the *Epistle of the Apostles* (xliii.) the five wise virgins of Jesus's parable are allegorized into Faith, Love, Grace, Peace, and Hope. There is no such use of Grace in the NT. Nor is it employed as an hypostasis of the divine life ; the personifications of Grace in Paul, for example, fall short of the personification of Κράτος and Βία by Æschylus. On the other hand, there is some evidence that during the second century Christ was addressed as Grace. It was natural that such a usage should spring up in circles of worship first of all. Thus in the *Acts of John* (xciv.) the disciples hail the Lord,

> ' Glory to thee, Logos,
> Glory to thee, Grace '—

---

[1] *Martyr SS. Perpetuae et Felicitatis*, xviii.
[2] *Martyrium Pionii*, xxii.

where δόξα σοι, Χάρις, leave no doubt as to the meaning of the term.   This, however, was the practice of a sect on the circumference of the Church, and any evidence for a catholic usage is doubtful.   In the Odes of Solomon one hymn (xxxiii.) does begin by describing Grace as personal.   ' Grace again left (or hastened from) the Corrupter,' as Rendel Harris translates the Syriac, though Labourt and Batiffol prefer, " La grâce a revêtu la perdition'; in any case Christ is first personified as Grace and then as the divine Wisdom, who triumphs over Folly.   Another, though a less clear indication of the same tendency in worship, may be found in the Didachê (x. 6), where one of the outbursts at the eucharistic service, one of what Tertullian calls the ' vota suspirantia,' is ' Let Grace come and let the world pass away '('Ελθέτω Χάρις).   This, however, may be no more than what is meant, from another angle, by Ignatius when he bids Christians either fear the Wrath to come or love the Grace that has already come (Eph. xi.).   Christ is certainly called ' our Hope ' at an early period, and Tertullian seems almost to call him Salvation in the De Poenitentia (ii.) when he speaks of God promising men His grace if they repented, since the Holy Spirit enters the penitent heart ' cum caelestibus bonis.   Horum bonorum unus est titulus, Salus hominis.'   But the evidence for Grace as a title of the Lord is very precarious.

However this may be, there is nothing in the primitive Christian period which corresponds to the later use of Grace for God or Providence.   Shakespeare can say " by the grace of Grace," towards the close of Macbeth.   When Helena in All's Well that ends Well promises the king a speedy cure, if it be the will of God, she puts it thus, " The greatest Grace lending grace."   This English usage is no more than a relic from mediaeval custom.   And if in another quarter of the mediaeval Church Christ was personified similarly at an earlier period, it was owing to ignorance of Greek.   Thus " that by the grace of God he should taste death for every man " (Heb. ii. 9) became in Latin " ut gratia dei pro omnibus gustaret." But as " gratia " might be taken in the nominative case instead of the ablative by readers who neglected Greek, Primasius, the north African bishop in the sixth century, rendered the phrase " Gratia Dei Patris appellatus Filius, eo quod nobis a Deo Patre gratis sit datus et quod gratis pro nobis mortem sustinuit," while Thomas Aquinas, who was equally dependent on the Vulgate, cited the Glossa Augustini (" ipse Christus est gratia Dei ") in favour of this interpretation, which he regarded as possible. It is, of course, a pious error and nothing more.

The Didachê passage comes at the close of a description of eucharistic worship.

> " May grace come and this world pass away !
> Hosanna to the God of David !
> If anyone is holy, let him come,
>   if not, let him repent ;
> Maran Atha."

The first two phrases may be the opening lines of hymns to be sung, but more probably they are sudden cries that broke from the lips of the faithful in a tense eschatological mood stirred by the celebration of the eucharist. For ' grace ' the Coptic version does substitute ' Lord ' (see *Journal of Theological Studies*, 1924, 225 f.), but from this we need not infer that χάρις was taken as a personification of Jesus Christ and replaced by a less ambiguous and more direct term. The idea in the cry as in Ignatius seems more analogous to that of the closing sentences in Clement's Cohortatio (which in style recall the last words of the Phaedo). " It remains with you then to make the final choice which is the more profitable, judgment or grace ? For myself I hold that there is no comparison as to which of the two is the better. Nay, it were impious even to compare life with destruction."

CONCLUSION

THE language of the NT literature about grace bears the unbroken accent of men who are speaking out of a knowledge of the living God which they owe to Jesus Christ His Son, their Lord and Saviour.   They did not pick up this term or notion casually among items of religion scattered over the Mediterranean world of their day, dovetailing it into some fresh form of religious syncretism.   A throb of new life beats in every syllable about grace uttered in the first century. When uncompromising criticism deals with traditional misconceptions and modern vagaries alike, it indicates that, as Christianity began to take shape, one of its most distinctive truths was the truth of grace, in the rich sense in which we have been able to outline it.   This grace was in the environment but not of it.   Indeed few better services could be rendered to Christianity in these days than to retain and if possible to re-state the significance of grace as the NT writers sought to grasp it.   The discussions of this book may have seemed at times to be occupied with far-off words and phrases, but I hope they have not failed to make the reader sensible how deeply the Christianity of the NT was concerned with grace, and also to suggest that the conception which the various writers strove to express, sometimes in categories which have ceased to be real in our own day, remains a reality of religion still.   This holds its ground, whatever be shaken, this attitude towards God.   That is, unless we are prepared to discard the presuppositions of Christianity altogether. Now if ever there is need to maintain the vital truth that in the ultimate resort we must think of God's initiative, even although we have to confess that we cannot put our thoughts round it, of His free goodness coming to man, and coming not as a

cosmological right but as issuing from the heart and mind of
One whose relations to ourselves are higher than can be understood in the light of any interpretation which revolves around
the empirical study of man's tie to a social group in civilization
or to his place within the universe. Reflection upon the
latter aspect of life enters into any religion. Faith takes full
account, if it is real, of the activities and affinities that make
up man's relation to his immediate world of interests. Yet
there is more in faith than the consciousness of such an attitude. When the soul of man is not moved to cry aloud, " To
God be the glory ! " there may be religion indeed, but it is not
the Christian religion as founded by the Lord Jesus. And
while the history of the Christian Church contains many sad
revelations of how men have argued and acted with regard to
grace, it does prove that this glad cry is never silenced when
the truth of grace is understood and honoured.

The inner or mystical protest of the heart has its value
when Christianity becomes externalized in either assent to
doctrines of grace or belief in the historical expressions of
grace. " Nur das Metaphysische, keineswegs aber das
Historische, macht selig," said Fichte with reference to the
latter danger. " Das letztere macht nur verständig." It
was his reason for regarding the Fourth Gospel as supremely
valuable. But this protest may be so put as to involve a view
that runs counter to genuine grace. It is one quickening
fundamental of the Christian faith that the redemption of the
soul is not derived from any nobility or ability which is innate,
and that the emancipation of human life is something other
than the satisfaction of a metaphysical affinity between the
spirit of man and God, in virtue of which the divine spark or
germ comes to its rights. Whatever value may reside in such
efforts to do justice to human volitions and instincts, they do
not penetrate to the secret of the religious hope. One saving
merit of any presentation of Christianity which retains the
truth of grace, however crudely it may be expressed, is that it

prevents the faith from lapsing into a form of natural religion like this. ' Grace ' is an excellent touchstone for determining whether the mysticism which constantly claims a place within the sphere of Christianity is authentic or exotic. One may read pages of mystical verse and prose, often couched in biblical language, felicitous and graceful, without coming across the slightest reference to the words or even to the ideas of grace. The writers seem to be other-minded, they are unconscious of it altogether in their cosmotheism. This is remarkable and yet not so remarkable as at first sight appears, for the technical or pure mystic lives on the borderland of monism. By temperament he seeks unity and diversity ; he feels for the inward significance of the spiritual element in ordinary phenomena. No doubt, this is conceivably congenial to the theism of the Christian faith. When it approaches to what in his own way the scientist calls a sense of cosmic dependence, it may render life sensitive to a divine spirit not only breathing airs of Eden upon those who win their way to the inner world but actually making its way to them through the mystery and beauty of nature. The mystical soul thus become conscious of being reached, not simply of being rewarded.

> Think you, 'mid all this mighty sum
> Of things for ever speaking,
> That nothing of itself will come,
> But we must still be seeking ?

Such an attitude of openness to the spirit of nature is in line with the wise passiveness or dependence upon God which is always implied in grace, though it is not always present to consciousness. For certain natures of a mystical bent this forms an approach to the conception of a redeeming Grace that seeks out the soul. But the latter has its own conditions. The craving for unity or harmony frequently moves the mystic to think in terms of absorption or union with the divine essence, so that his aim is to be godded or goddified. It is a tendency which may be traced along various lines of devout speculation, from the Hellenistic religion of some cults in the first century to certain mediaeval forms of Christian mysticism. Whereas the genuinely Christian word is ' fellowship ' with God, which at once preserves the moral individuality of the soul and the truth of redemption through Jesus Christ, with more concern for sanctity than for sentiment. So sharply has this distinction been felt that an expert in comparative religion like Dr. E. Lehmann is bold to declare that the clover leaf of ecstasy, asceticism, and intuition cannot grow upon Christian soil. A hard saying, a very hard saying, but not unintelligible if one recollects what he means by intuition, for example, that is, the belief that by searching one can find out God, almost if not entirely unaided. He is thinking of the mysticism which assumes that we are saved by our inner spark or germ of divinity, by subtly setting to work some innate forces of contemplation or speculation, or by inducing through ascetic discipline a sense of the deity that becomes rapturous, as in the Hermetica or in Philo of old. When mysticism is taken as a direct and immediate consciousness of God, then indeed it becomes organic to the Christian faith ; but as that faith retains its native fibre of grace, it instinctively rejects any type of the mystical experience which, for all its use of Christian speech or symbols, is in reality a form of natural religion, the soul becoming ecstatically conscious of its own divinity. The faith elicited by grace includes contemplation as well as self-discipline, but not contemplation for its own sake ; it is rather a faith answering to the prophetic belief which renounces for the sake of fuller life and energy, at a touch of the living God within the realities of history, and which embraces the quietist mood as no more than a mood in the rhythm of experience. *I have been crucified with Christ, and it is no longer I who live, Christ lives in me.* So the great apostle once expressed his mystical absorption in the Lord. But, as it were, to guard against misconception, he at once added, *the life I now live in the flesh I live by faith in the Son of God who loved me and gave himself up for me.* It is this genuine faith-union with the Lord, drawing upon His grace, that distinguishes inner Christianity from such mystical ideals as subordinate fellowship with God to identification with the deity, union with the unconditioned, or absorption in the Absolute. " We are neither Brahmins nor Indian gymnosophists." This is true in a deeper sense than even Tertullian intended.

Also and still more decisively the truth of grace forms an acid test for all moralistic interpretations of the Christian religion. Between the pure moralist and the religious man there is mutual suspicion. The former distrusts talk about grace because it isolates man from his environment and ignores (so it is argued) the factors of human freedom and self-determination. One of the moralist's major counts against religious teaching about grace is that it renders man far too passive. He may even feel that a gospel of grace relieves man of moral responsibility or that, by encouraging self-abasement of a devotional or emotional kind, it discourages manly initiative and activity. In some cases his doubt is justified by extravagant statements of what grace involves, or by practical caricatures of its meaning. These have been notoriously one-sided and morbid. But in all fairness we must discriminate. Froude once protested vigorously against what he heard at an evangelical prayer-meeting, where the audience sang lustily,

> Doing is a deadly thing,
> Doing ends in death.

And so " to do our duty has become a deadly thing ! " It was not a fair criticism, for, however unhappily the thought was expressed, it was a truth. The hymn was right. It was trying to teach what Paul had taught about the error of trusting to one's own performances in order to win the favour of God.

' Agere sequitur esse,' as the mediaeval adage put it ; doing comes after being.   The truth of grace may have been often stated by the scholasticism of the Re-formed and of the Roman churches in such a way as to provoke remonstrance from any-one interested in ethical verve and health.   But from the very outset devotion, as men stepped into it, threw duty round them.   There was an eager assertion of the nexus between grace and the good life ; " God is able to make all grace abound toward you that ye may abound to every good work." No sooner did Christianity start than this effort was made variously and repeatedly, to show that in the experience of saving grace all the ethical motives were adequately provided, to deny that God cannot begin to deal with a human soul until it has by " doing " accumulated the requisite quota of respect-able conduct, and also to maintain that it is not proper for man at any stage of life to face God with no more than trust in his own personal resources and achievements.   Those who have not learned to train their faith upon the metrical version of the psalms may at least discover how grace orders life by catching the spirit of two lines like these from Psalm thirty-seven :

> Set thou thy trust upon the Lord,
> and be thou doing good.

All that the NT has to say about salvation or forgiveness implies a personal relationship to God, in which what we are determines what we do.

By insisting that ' grace and faith ' are the primary factor in the religious life, Christianity is not ignoring the moral consciousness but urging that unless the moral consciousness is to become feverish and futile, it must include a transcendent order, or rather, it must be in-cluded in such an order.   The moralistic emphasis upon the central importance of man's strivings and standards really corresponds to the old Ptolemaic astronomy, which made earth the axle of the universe, all heavenly bodies revolving around it in their courses.   So Comte assumed, for example ; humanity is our source and centre.   When

Christianity sounds the note of grace, it is upholding the new and true astronomy of religion : the world of human conduct moves within the sphere of the Sun, deriving from the Centre its light and impetus, and in that relationship is the final clue to what we know and what we do. At the core of the gospel this conviction lies, that to be thus humble, conscious of indebtedness to God, is to be strong. ' In the beginning God . . . Man shall live by every word that proceedeth out of the mouth of God . . . God was in Christ, reconciling the world to himself . . . God sent his Son that the world through him might be saved.' From such confidence in the God of grace, and not from the activism that scorns to think of man as receptive and responsive, real self-confidence arises, either in the shape of moral insight or of power to carry out the ends and demands of God which are thus revealed to faith. The moralist may speak of religious experience, but he does not mean by it exactly what the religious man means. For the latter, religious experience is the contact of mind or soul with an Object or Reality, other than itself. The desires and impulses of which man becomes conscious, his thoughts and emotions in this relationship, are ultimately elicited by this Reality, but while all such effects are interesting and while we become aware of them first in the order of being, they are not the sum total of the experience. It is the service of a truth like grace in Christianity that the recognition of it evokes at once a vivid sense of the powers and duties of life and a corresponding perception that in them we become aware of something or Someone other than ourselves ; this inwardness is fostered without becoming introspective, and moral energy is heightened without the risk of faith becoming no more than reliance on the quick, eager powers of personality. Any reading of life in terms of grace signifies that belief in a good Will at the heart of things is essential to an adequate sense of moral obligation, and vice-versa.

No one was more alive to this than the apostle Paul. It was part of his effective wisdom that the saving truth of grace was not exhausted by consideration of the guilty and depraved. He knew this power of God to deal with sinners at their worst, but he never imagined that the experience of grace was reserved for one particular temperament or class. On the contrary he was convinced that even in their best moments, when men are at some height of moral achievement, they become conscious, if they are really religious, that this good life is not good enough to bring them peace of conscience, as though they could face the verdict of God with calm assurance, simply on the record of what they had done or even intended to do. And this negative consciousness is accompanied by the positive sense that the very power of so living and acting is not their own ; all along, especially at certain sharp issues, they realize that they have been guided and guarded. If not at the time, then as they reflect on their experience, they are conscious of direction which has come to them, of a Power not their own enabling them to do as they have done, or, it may be, to leave undone what they were tempted to do. The better they become, the more sensitive they are on this point. There is nothing formal in their repetition of the deep word upon life, ' By the grace of God I am what I am.' Were it not for God's grace, they confess, where would we be ? This is by no means normal, it is true. To others the same truth has to come with shattering force, if they rely on self-conceit or self-respect, as sufficient to meet the needs of life. " Why not Grace ? " Attwater asks, in Stevenson's tale, *The Ebb-Tide*. " Why not the grace of your Maker and Redeemer, He who died for you, He who upholds you, He whom you daily crucify afresh ? There is nothing but God's grace. We walk upon it, we breathe it ; we live and die by it ; it makes the nails and axles of the universe ; and a puppy in pyjamas prefers self-conceit ! " But whether the truth of grace is realized by the moral experience which it generates or whether it has to be brought home to the stubborn mind by some sudden phase of life, Christianity is only reverting to type when in every age it persists in putting this message at the forefront of the gospel, either as a challenge to human pretensions which ruin life as they seek to exalt it, or as encouragement to poor souls who find it hard to believe in the sheer goodness of a redeeming God, not from any self-confidence but from lack of confidence and hope at all.   Certainly, in the latter case, this is to take a risk. But morality is always exposed to risk when it is transcended by religion.   Some forms of this risk are indeed gratuitous. Against them it is proper to protest.   The moral health of Christians has not seldom been spoiled by their very religious zeal, and it is always timely for the moralist to enter a caveat in such cases.   But there are risks which it is right and glorious to take.   This is particularly evident when religion has to deal with desperate cases.   To treat an offender graciously, to forgive sin without insisting first on any guarantees of better conduct, is at the very heart of Christian faith.   It involves belief in the offender, and although the belief acts as a moral force of regeneration and as a motive for recovering the better self, to the pure moralist this may seem and sound dangerous.   Indeed it is really inconceivable to him, since sin is not a term of morality at all.   Yet there is no gospel, no grace, unless a sinner who is not in a position to offer any guarantees can receive the benefits and promises of God.

Even short of religion, this principle of generous belief in man has been recognized as a moral reality.   " Fidelem si putaveris, facies," Seneca once told his readers.[1]   Believe in a man, and you make him better thereby, or at least you give him the chance of becoming better. ' Treat him as loyal, and you help to make him loyal.'   The moralist was rebuking the spirit of suspicion and reserve that makes an offender feel we do not trust him yet.   But it is a principle which goes beyond moral relations ;   and while the religious truth of free forgiveness covers a wider range, it includes this.   For the grace of God as pardon is no mere proclamation of an amnesty, leaving the offender now to do the best he can and to atone, as he may, for past misdeeds.   It is the reconciling Action of God that draws the sinner into life with God Himself, and dares to trust Him for the future.   Such is the risk taken by all love in personal relationships, no less in heaven than upon earth.   Were it not so, the moralizers would leave little hope for a ' poor sinner '

[1] Moral. Epist. i. 3.

in the shadows, who is perhaps more common still among the sons of men than limpid liberals imagine.

The sensitive saint (if we may apply the term to those who would not call themselves such) needs equally this objective truth of grace, for the sense of personal unworthiness may not only deter him from accepting some responsible position of service, or, as Paul would have said, from using the grace given to him, but also may foster a morbid introspection which endangers simple faith by overclouding the mind. Instead of looking to God and listening to God, as He meets the soul with grace, this disposition busies itself with self-analysis. It originates in a genuinely religious desire for reality, and yet we sometimes discover it passing unconsciously into a subtle form of moralism, which cannot be exorcised except by a deep sense of what grace means. Some penitently think that the message of God's loving favour is too good to be true for unworthy characters like themselves ; they find it hard at first to believe that God cares to have anything to do with the ungodly, as the gospel promises. But others upon a higher level have this difficulty ; their fine natures desire to be conscious that they deserve the good that comes to them from God or from their fellows. Now, so far as this forms a motive to better living, it is healthy. Those who are sensitive on this point are not likely to be ungrateful or selfish. Yet, if such a feeling be allowed to dominate the mind, it may produce a weakening effect on life, by rendering people self-conscious instead of allowing them to be natural, natural in the sense of being humble and content to be receptive. When we are treated in a way that is unexpectedly kind, even though we may be conscious that it is undeserved, the best thing is to thank God and take courage, not to examine ourselves anxiously as to whether we are really fit to receive the gifts of affection and trust that are lavished upon us. " I am more and more clear about this," Dr. Dale wrote in a wise letter,

" that we must be content to know the best things come to us both from God and man without our deserving them. We are under grace, not under law. Not until we have beaten down our pride and self-assertion, so as to be able to take everything from earth and heaven just as a child takes everything, without raising the question, Do I deserve this or not ? or rather with the habitual conviction that we deserve nothing and are content that it should be so, do we get into right relations with our Father in heaven or with the brothers and sisters about us. That principle is capable of a most fatal corruption, but in its truth it is one of the secrets of righteousness and joy. The craving to deserve can never be satisfied ; we have rather to try to be grateful for what we do not deserve." [1] It is indeed more blessed to give than to receive, but it is blessed to receive ; when others bless us with gifts of help, we do well to accept them in the spirit in which they are given, and in so doing to learn that this is the right attitude towards the unspeakable Gift of God. One side of what Paul taught, as Jesus had taught before him, was that we should not think of God keeping accounts with us, as though He were content to reckon with men on a debit and credit basis. It is not less important to avoid keeping a sort of inner reckoning in our own lives, even for the highest of reasons. Why should we dream that we cannot venture to enjoy what God bestows, without being certain that our credit balance with Him is secure ? It was not such a relationship that Paul meant when he wrote of " grace and peace."

. . . . .

The apostle Paul ! Our modern Alciphron must have realized, if he has followed us so far, that any deep argument upon the grace of God comes back before long to Paul, very much as any living issue in philosophy to-day calls up the name of Plato. Here is another illustration of this truth. We owe to the apostle Paul two sayings of the Lord, and I

[1] *The Life of R. W. Dale*, p. 541.

do not think it is fanciful to notice that both bear upon grace. One of these he recollected from oral tradition ; the other was spoken to himself. " Remember the words of the Lord Jesus, how he said, ' It is more blessed to give than to receive,' " and, " My grace is sufficient for thee."

The former saying, which is cited in order to commend charity to Christian folk, implies that such a generous spirit was in the Lord himself. From his own experience Jesus knew the happiness of which he was speaking. And the Paul who quotes this counsel of the Lord Jesus is the same Paul who could remind the Corinthians that they ought to be liberal with money, since behind all their life lay, as they knew, *the grace* (or, as Tyndale actually renders it here, the liberality) *of our Lord Jesus Christ*, who for their sakes had become poor. The rich religious life opened up for Christians by their Lord included a wealth of personal relationships as well as faith and hope. Jesus once told his followers that if they joined his fellowship and threw in their lot with him, whatever they might lose they would receive a hundredfold here and now in the shape of " brethren, sisters, mothers, and children." By his mission, undertaken at a great self-sacrifice on his own part, he had put Christians in the way of this wider tie with others. By purging them of self-interest he enabled them to gain a deeper vision of life and to enter into larger fellowship with others, a fellowship in which the spirit of giving brought unimagined bliss. The apostle's meaning is that " Christ gives us to possess not God only but men also as our riches, the unsearchable riches which we have in him. In doing so, he is devoting us to God and to men, in the fellowship of his self-sacrifice. He thus calls us to poverty, in calling us to the true riches." [1] The saying of the Lord which came to his mind corresponds to the same truth. A rich consciousness of God means a rich consciousness of our fellows, and the inspiration of the latter lies in the spirit with which the Lord

[1] J. McLeod Campbell, *The Nature of the Atonement*, p. 370.

Jesus put us into this relationship. It is the spirit of grace as deep giving, and money is but one illustration of such generosity, for after all, as the case of Jesus proves, the highest gift that can be given to men is life. The gifts of God are made to the active mind and will, and His gift of grace is no exception. It is intended to render men alive to the rich content of life as service and fellowship in which the Lord himself sought and found fulness of being. Only as it is so received, does it ever become a religious satisfaction and a moral reality.

The second saying strikes the note of power. " My grace is sufficient for thee," inspiring and sustaining a human creature in its endeavour to be loyal under some strain. Not only gracious consideration but moral stimulus is a deep need of life. After all the soul must receive from God if it is ever to give to others. And the gift of grace is often realized as a power making for effectiveness and constancy in a world where, as Paul well knew, Christians have a rough time in the flesh. The context shows that he was thinking of more than physical disability ; what had to be met was experiences of trouble, inward and outward, insults and adversities, the sort of things which dishearten man unless he can fall back on some inward power by means of which he is enabled to transcend them. Pain was pain to Paul as it was to Jesus, whether inward or outward. He never explains away his ' thorn in the flesh.' But he claims to possess in the experience of the Lord's grace a power more than equal to this or any other untoward happening of life. Such handicaps and hindrances may come in the providence of God to the most loyal ; their lives may be impoverished by other things than the lack of money. But it is the Christian conviction that the grace of the Lord is neither denied nor diminished thereby. Indeed it is brought out, for force in the moral as in the physical sphere is measured by the obstacles which it is found to overcome.

Round these two truths of grace, as Gift and Power, Paul's arguments really circle. He never calls God ' the Almighty.'

Only once,[1] in a quotation from the OT, does he ever use the adjective :

> ' I will be a Father to you.
> and ye shall be my sons and daughters,'
> saith the Lord Almighty.

For Paul, living in the new order of grace or the Spirit, it was God the Father, especially God as the Father of the Lord Jesus Christ, who guaranteed that life would not be left to itself, for in Jesus Christ as Lord the early Christians were conscious that the divine nature had come into play on earth. Already in the greater and later prophets of Israel the conception of God as Almighty had approached that of One who was free and able to realize His purpose for men, One whose desire, it might be truly said, was to make

> the whole world loyal
> Less by kingly power than grace.

From the first this had been the religious idea of God as all-powerful. The expression of it had been sometimes drawn from the nearest available analogy, the social pattern of the oriental monarch. But belief in the unlimited good will of God was so essential to the Hebrew mind that it acquired better forms of expression, such as that of the royal Father in the teaching of Jesus. ' Our Father who art in heaven, thy kingdom come, thy will be done on earth as it is in heaven.' This conception, in which the divine will is dominant because being love it is creative, is central to the truth of grace. Thus Paul sees in the world not a God who stands sternly aloof from the wrongdoing of His creatures but One who seeks to atone for their evil and enmity with the full power of His own being. This utterly selfless will of grace and mercy is for the apostle a revelation, and a revelation due to the Lord Jesus Christ, in whom God takes effective action on behalf of men. When the doubt arose, Has God power to carry out His purpose

[1] 2 Cor. vi. 18.

of goodwill ? Christians instantly recalled the resurrection of the Lord and the absolute self-sacrifice which this revealed. " All is of grace," in the light of the resurrection, was the other side of " God is able." For such divine love could command willing obedience, as no other power in heaven or earth could do, and Christians who in their own weakness knew that they were not always so willing or obedient as they should be, could count upon His grace to carry out the purpose which in grace alone He had begun.

They could rely upon this, as they listened to the quiet compelling voice of One who had done more than speak about the Will of grace. It has been observed that Paul happens to talk more commonly of Christians being " in Christ " or " in the Spirit " than of being " in God," but this is not nearly so important as the fact that he speaks of the grace of God and of the grace of the Lord Jesus Christ with equal emphasis. There is a difficult word in one hymn which the apostle quoted or composed ; Christ Jesus, we read,

> though divine by nature,
> snatched not at equality with God.

He snatched not, " he thought it not robbery." The Greek word is ἁρπαγμόν. What Oriental myth or cosmogony lies behind the symbolism of the hymn, we cannot tell ; neither is it clear what is meant by saying that Christ did not regard equality with God as treasure-trove, a prize to be seized and held. To remove the baffling allusion, some French critic—M. Salomon Reinach, I think—has proposed to read ἄπραγμον. This would mean, Christ did not take his position as a sinecure. He was no ' roi fainéant,' who thought the divine life an easy-going privilege, requiring no activity. It is a clever, irrelevant conjecture, but the idea is sound, for Christ, as Paul believed, acted on behalf of men. Instead of remaining alone and aloof in heaven, like some deity of the Epicureans, he took action. This was in one aspect his grace, in another, his obedience to the will of God for men in need, just as that will was grace divine.

It was this grace that Paul saw and taught others to see in the revelation of what he once called " the glory of God in the

face of Jesus Christ." There is no real parallel to it in the
first century. No god of a mystery-cult, no Son of Man in
Enoch, no Son of David in the Psalms of Solomon, provides
any suggestion of divine grace thus in action, manifesting a
character and quality so supreme. That God is glorious as He
is gracious, and that the light of this vision falls upon those
who look to Jesus Christ His Son, their Lord and Saviour,
was not discovered first by Paul, but it was he who first made
the Church fully conscious of this saving truth. It is not the
explanations of his Christian experience that matter ; it is
the experience itself, or rather the witness of that experience to
the creative Spirit of God in the personality of Jesus Christ as
' given ' to faith and effective for faith. After Paul it was not
possible for Christians who had in any sense grasped the
meaning of his gospel, to lose the figure of Jesus in vague
hellenism or messianism. Historically this is the real importance of Paul's teaching. Though ' John ' and others were
raised up after him to develop the truth as it was in Jesus, he
was the first to state some of its essential elements in terms of
grace. To praise an apostle is almost as ridiculous as to
patronize him, but we may at least be grateful that he so read
the mind of Christ, this pioneer of grace. In prospect of
visiting one church he hoped that he might impart to them
" some spiritual gift," some grace-gift. The effect of his
letters upon all churches who have had the grace to receive
such a gift, has been an impetus to understand that religious
experience for Christians is at bottom a saving experience of
God which is inseparable from devotion to the Lord Jesus.
Under all the varieties of our Christian religion there is an
identity in this high grace of God. From Paul to Pascal,
from Macarius to the Moravians, from Augustine to Luther
and Santa Teresa and Bunyan, you can mark its essential
features in natures far separated by opinion. As Saint-Beuve
protested, the state or experience of grace is one, " *un* au fond,
un par l'esprit et par les fruits . . . l'état intérieur, qui est,

avant tout, d'amour et d'humilité, de confiance infinie en Dieu, et de sévérité pour soi accompagnée de tendresse pour autrui." [1] It is known by these fruits. As Paul taught, one cannot hope to profit by the grace of the Lord unless one enters into his mind of selfless, thoughtful care for others ; devotion to him has no meaning apart from his spirit of self-sacrifice that prompts the soul to think more of giving than of receiving in the social order. Through forms of psychology and eschatology which are no longer ours, the apostle poured this supreme truth into Christendom. ' Adore and obey ' sums up his counsels for those who would enjoy the experience of the living God. The Lord is to be adored and therefore obeyed, adored for having brought such a good Will into the life of men. By ' grace ' he intends to represent not simply the fruits of unselfishness and consideration but the root. No adoration without obedience—and yet, obeying goes back to adoring ! For in the order of grace one soon discovers, more acutely perhaps than elsewhere, that man is an unsteady creature, unsteady because he slips so easily into the way of being proud or careless. He does not part from these vices by rising to the high level of grace. Even there he finds himself still apt to be self-satisfied or slack. More than that, he may fail in self-discipline. To be receptive is the condition of living under grace, but one may forget that to be receptive, in the truest sense of the term, requires not less force of character and strength of mind than to be acute and energetic. For these and other reasons the apostle Paul pressed grace upon the Christian conscience as the revelation of the Cross. There, he was convinced, grace was rooted and bore fruit. There, he knew, was the living growth of God that would kill off pride and moral laxity in human experience, if anything could. When he speaks of " grace and peace " or of " the grace of our God and of the Lord Jesus Christ," the dew of the morning lies on the words as it does on the last paragraph

[1] *Port-Royal*, i. 106.

of Plato's Republic or on the first sentence of Aristotle's Ethics, words which are dry only to the dull of heart. It is " God who is able to make all grace abound toward you, that ye may abound to every good work," and this grace or power of God which changes our nature into newness of life, dedicating us to obedience and good service, reaches us through Jesus Christ alone and him crucified. Paul's statements are sometimes couched in bygone modes of speech. They cannot be fitted into an exact programme or philosophy, for he availed himself of apocalyptic and mystical and juridical expressions quite freely in order to convey his message. The salient fact is that the message is a conviction of life, not abstract discussions about grace as an impersonal principle. He took this or that form of contemporary thought which lay to hand, in order to waken effective faith. What inspires his words on grace with the dew of youth is the assurance that in Christ God has done and is doing for men what they cannot do for themselves, and that the one way of enjoying His gift is by surrendering to this utterly gracious power of love which meets the soul in the sacrifice and spirit of Jesus the Lord.

In the letters of Paul there is strong, close thinking, but just because grace is a message and mission to all sorts and conditions of men we catch the thrill of adoring joy that grace evokes in those who receive it humbly and thoughtfully, as well as the echo of a serious fear that haunted him, the fear of men allowing such an experience to make them careless or complacent. It is one mark of continuity between his preaching and the teaching of Jesus that he had caught the urgent spirit of " Either . . . or " and " Now or never," with which Jesus faced men in the name of God. For Paul the offer of grace was critical and decisive. It was the supreme opportunity of life. A popular proverb in his day ran thus : " It is not for everyone to go to Corinth." But as his words have gone out into all the world, charged with a life and power that is not their own, some words of his to Christians at Corinth long ago still find the soul of man in any place or age. " I beseech you that you receive not the grace of God in vain. . . . Behold, now is the day of salvation." Now, now at last, now or never—now !

THE END